Ancient Egypt

ANCIENT EGYPT

A Cultural Topography

by

HERMANN KEES

Edited by
T. G. H. JAMES
Department of Egyptian Antiquities
British Museum

UNIVERSITY OF CHICAGO PRESS
Chicago Illinois

Originally published by Klotz Verlag
as DAS ALTE AEGYPTEN
First published in England in mcmlxi
by Faber and Faber Limited
24 Russell Square London W.C.1.
Printed in Great Britain by
Robert MacLehose & Co. Ltd Glasgow
All rights reserved
Published in the United States of America by
The University of Chicago Press
Chicago 37, Illinois

Translated from the German
by IAN F. D. MORROW

Dedicated with gratitude to all with whom I travelled in Egypt and to those who gave me hospitality there
1909–1954

Contents

Contents

LIST OF MAPS

Illustrations

Illustrations

Editor's Foreword

This book was planned as a kind of guide-book to Egypt in ancient times. Dr. Hermann Kees, who for many years was Professor of Egyptology at the University of Göttingen, had written many of the articles on Egyptian topics, particularly those on Egyptian places, for the great German classical dictionary, the *Real-Encyclopädie* of Pauly-Wissowa. In the years before the war he was pressed by friends to use the material he had collected in a lifetime of study and for these articles in particular, to write a historical geography of Ancient Egypt. Unfortunately the war came before he was able to make a start and after the war the loss of his notes compelled him to modify his plan. With the articles in the *Real-Encyclopädie* as the basis and with his memories of the Egyptian countryside refreshed by a visit to Egypt in 1951–52 at the invitation of the Ibrahim Pasha University of Cairo, Kees wrote the present book, not perhaps the great Baedeker to Ancient Egypt he had originally planned, but an account for a wider audience of how the unique natural characteristics of the land had formed and affected the nature of Ancient Egyptian civilization. A short general introductory section is followed by a long second part in which an overall picture of Ancient Egyptian life is presented viewed from a geographical standpoint. The third part of the book contains sketches of a number of the most important cities and regions which have been chosen to illustrate the theses of the second part and to give as wide a possible view of the differences found within what is in fact a remarkably homogeneous country.

In this English edition a number of additional maps has been added and the Egyptian proper names have been put into the forms currently used by Egyptologists who write in English.

T. G. H. James.

PART ONE

General Considerations

I

The Valley of the Nile and
its Settlement

The fertile valley of the Nile with a cultivated area of 13,300 square miles[1] and a population of about twenty millions (1947) to support, is one of the most densely populated agricultural areas in the world (average density of population 1,500 persons to the square mile). Consequently a traveller in Egypt today finds it difficult to believe that this oasis of civilization between deserts was not the cradle of the Egyptian race. It is possible that in the narrower sense it formed the Egyptian man known to history, but his origins nevertheless are to be sought outside its borders. In the Early Stone Age the Valley of the Nile, running northwards from Nubia, was an uninhabitable marshy country. Its bed, in Upper Egypt at least, lay at a much higher level than today (about 14 feet at Luxor) and its waters were dammed by the sandstone barrier of Gebel Silsilah south of Thebes, forming a lake which stretched as far as the Cataract.

The Delta which is that part of Egypt north of Cairo and which today contains about two-thirds of the total population of the country, was then for the most part covered by the Mediterranean. It gradually filled up with the deposits brought down by the Nile when the river deepened its bed in Upper Egypt — the so-called Sebile erosion.

The valley of the Nile south as far as Gebel Silsilah is from a geographical point of view really an oasis cut out of a limestone plateau. Judging from the flint tools and weapons which are the scanty remains of his civilization, palaeolithic man lived on the desert plateau which today stretches along both sides of the Nile

[1] From the Egyptian Government Statistical Yearbook 1949–50.

valley and which from the valley looks like rocky mountains rising up in steep cliffs (Pl. 1. *a*). The necessary precondition for such a civilization was that the desert, and particularly the Libyan or Sahara desert on the west of the Nile which today is completely barren apart from a few oases, must at that time have received enough rain to make it a savanna-like plain inhabited by animals similar to those found today on the plains of the Sudan and East Africa. Such animals were hunted by prehistoric huntsmen. Early palaeolithic strata yield bones which indicate the presence in these early times of hippopotami, buffalo, aurochs, wild asses, gazelles and ostriches which make up a typical mixture of large animals found in swamps and on plains. These strata are called Sebilian after Sebile, a place near Kom Ombo in Upper Egypt, where remains were first found corresponding to the European Capsian culture.

At the dawn of the Palaeolithic Age there occurred the decisive climatic changes which shaped the physical features of historical Egypt. The plains began to dry up; in the low-lying districts which received water from wells and from springs fed by deeply sunk watercourses leading from the marshy districts of the Upper Nile, many wells dried up with the result that men were forced to retreat into areas that still afforded them the means of livelihood. In the first place there were the Libyan oases which have survived to the present day; then the mountainous areas of primitive rock with springs in their gorges, such as, in the south, the Tibesti plateau and the Gebel Uwenat (6,232 feet high) which acts as the point of intersection for the frontiers of Egypt, Libya and the Sudan. Above all there was the valley which the Nile had cut out of the broad limestone region which stretched from the Theban area northwards, ending with the final spur of the Mokattam Hills on the north-east of Cairo and with the high ground of Abu Roash on the west. At first the valley was in the form of terraces and it was over these terraces and down the *wadis* which the rain of centuries had carved in the sides of the mountains that man climbed down to the Nile. This primitive inhospitable valley of the Nile was in character rather like the marshy districts found today on the upper White Nile and in the Bahr el-Ghazal in the Sudan. It formed a natural barrier between races which was far from being the case in later times when, with the beginning of navigation, the river tended

The Valley of the Nile and its Settlement

to become a connecting rather than a dividing factor in human life.

It is impossible and indeed, for the purpose of this book, immaterial to estimate the length of time taken for this development. The interval between the palaeolithic Sebilian culture and the Neolithic Age is calculated by geologists and archaeologists to have been as much as 8,000 to 9,000 years,[1] while the Palaeolithic Age stretches back beyond the boundaries of history or the study of civilization. The offerings found in the graves of the oldest cultures in the Nile valley provide good evidence for the last stage of the civilization of the Neolithic Age before the transition to the historical period in Egypt. This evidence can be supplemented by the rock drawings found especially in the *wadis* of the Eastern Desert (Pl. 3. *a*).[2] The animals found in these rock drawings are identical with those depicted as being hunted in the frontier regions of Egypt on the carved hippopotamus-ivory handles of flint knives and on the cosmetic palettes made of green schist from Upper Egypt. These knives and palettes date from the time of the unification of the two kingdoms of Upper and Lower Egypt about 3000 B.C.[3] We find the African elephant the existence of which is also attested by remains found in Neolithic strata on the northern shore of the Fayum, the kudu-antelope, the Gerenuk-gazelle, the wild-ass, the mysterious animal sacred to the god Seth, the baboon dwelling among rocks which was held sacred by the ancient religion of Upper Egypt and was known as 'the Great White One'. Occasionally we also find the rhinoceros the slaying of which on the plains of the Sudan Tuthmosis III boasted about in his temple at Hermonthis in later times. Vague representations of the rhinoceros are also to be found in the imaginative hunting-scenes of the Old Kingdom.[4] There are also the most unusual giant marsh-birds, the jabiru-stork, the mighty marabu and the shoe-bill.

Wild asses, wild cattle and, in particular, ostriches and lions were the animals of the plain that the Egyptian hunter sought

[1] S. Passarge, 'Die Urlandschaft Ägyptens' in *Nova Acta Leopoldina*, New Series, vol. 9, no. 58, p. 105.
[2] H. A. Winkler, *Rock-drawings of Southern Upper Egypt*, 2 vols.
[3] Cf. Kees, *Kulturgeschichte*, p. 53f.
[4] Winkler, *op. cit.*, I, pls. 20–1; Keimer, *Annales du Service*, vol. 48, p. 47f.

regularly right up to the time of the New Kingdom. On a commemorative scarab Amenophis III boasted that from the first to the tenth years of his reign (about 1413 to 1403 B.C.), he had killed 102 lions with his own hand; several of these were probably killed in hunting grounds outside Egypt proper, such as Upper Nubia. Ramesses III had a royal hunt after wild asses and cattle depicted on the Pylon of the temple of Medinet Habu.[1] The rest of the large animals found in these early records disappeared from the Nile valley at the outset of Egyptian history about 3000 B.C.; their principal refuge was in the plains in the interior of Africa, but at the beginning they probably also found a home in the marshy land of the Delta which had been formed by the flood-waters of the Nile.

The survival of large parts of the savanna country with afforestation infinitely richer than exists today was an essential prerequisite for the animals which continued to live in the *wadis* in historical times; there were giraffes, ostriches, antelopes, gazelles, ibexes and lions and traces of their remains are to be found even on the west of the Nile valley. The tiny rain-water oases in the Gebel Uwenat, the neighbouring Gebel Arkenu and in Gilf Kebir afforded pasturage for the herds belonging to the nomads of the Tibesti plateau up to quite recent times[2] in spite of diminishing afforestation. This is also particularly true of the *wadis* of the South-eastern Desert where the existence of rich forests, especially of acacias, was attested by nomads at the beginning of the nineteenth century.[3] Animal cemeteries are also found in places where today cattle-rearing is quite impossible.[4] It is therefore certain that the ravished countryside of the Eastern Desert is largely the result of the cutting down of trees to make charcoal and of the ruthless consumption of young shrubs and trees by the nomads' camels which first began to appear frequently on the frontier districts of Egypt after the beginning of the Ptolemaic Period. The remains of trees, especially acacias and sycomores, which are the principal species found in the desert borderlands, have also been found in areas which in late prehistoric times were used for cemeteries.[5] These areas clearly

---

[1] Kees, *op. cit.*, fig. 14.   [2] Almásy, *Unbekannte Sahara* (1939), p. 119f.
[3] Burckhardt, *Travels in Nubia* (London, 1819).
[4] Murray, *JEA*, 12, 248, cf. Säve-Söderbergh, *Ägypten und Nubien*, 25.
[5] R. Mond and O. Myres, *Cemeteries of Armant*, I, 7.

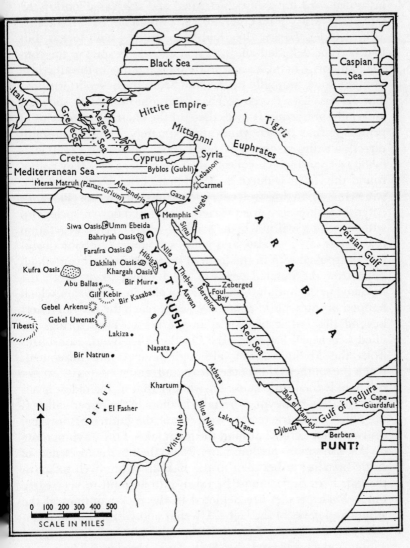

1. The Nile Valley and surrounding lands

lay outside the limits of the irrigated and cultivated land in the late prehistoric period otherwise they would not have been used as cemeteries. Earlier they had been covered with forests, but had become denuded and had remained so in spite of the continual increase in the area of cultivable land due to the alluvium brought down annually by the Nile floods since Neolithic times. The Eastern Desert also receives occasional thundery showers, especially in Spring. It owes these to the chain of mountains of primitive rock which runs approximately in a north-south direction rising to over 6,500 feet (Gebel Shayib, for example, is 6,888 feet) and which collects the rain clouds; thus they gather round the Gebel Dukhan or Mountain of Smoke of 5,248 feet, which in Roman times was called the Mons Porphyrites (Pl. 12. *b*). After these showers a great variety of coloured flowers springs up with surprising swiftness in the flooded *wadis* (Pl. 11. *b*). Vegetation is a matter of water also, and not of soil alone. Outlying downfalls of tropical rain in the form of severe thunderstorms which burst over the isolated peaks of the Uwenat (6,232 feet), the Arkenu (4,592) and the Gilf Kebir can also, in rainy years, which happen at intervals of about five years, reach the Libyan desert beyond the Tropic of Cancer in the north. Then springs are filled which will last for years. On the other hand, rainstorms from the Mediterranean, although much more infrequent, reach the southern side of the great sand sea.[1]

There is then little cause for wonder that in the oldest levels of civilization in Egypt, especially in those of the upper valley of the Nile, the characteristic weapons of the hunter or, in some districts such as those around the great lake of the Fayum, those of the fisherman predominate. Nevertheless the presence of cattle-breeding tribes akin to the Bakkara who dwell today in the Northern Sudan must be taken into account in very early times. Such peoples are depicted in the rock-paintings of the gorges and caves of the Gebel Uwenat and Gilf Kebir, and can undoubtedly be considered the predecessors of the negroid Tibbu and Gurân and the Arab cattle-breeders.[2] The cattle-breeding nomad is a specific type of African Hamite whose natural vigour and resolute character acquired through his struggle for existence equip him to become a nation-builder

[1] Cf. Almásy, *op. cit.*, p. 175f.
[2] Winkler, *op. cit.*, II, cf. the coloured plates in Almásy, p. 136.

ruling over racial groups of agriculturalists. This is the case with the Sudanese tribes of more recent times. The Libyan oases have always been zones of transit or rallying points for races drawn from all quarters. The Siwa oasis, the site of the oracle of Amun, which is on the border of Cyrenaica, and the Senussi oasis of Kufra in the heart of Libya afford good examples not only of this fact but also of the part played by oases in mingling the races chiefly through the traffic in women from the negroid south.

The inhabitants of the early prehistoric settlement at Merimdah on the western edge of the Delta certainly belonged to that class of semi-sedentary nomads who live in tents or huts, keep domestic animals and grow corn at least for the duration of their stay. Their place in the history of civilization is too isolated to allow us to classify them with any reliability. They have, however, with some probability, been assigned a place parallel to the oldest known Upper Egyptian cultures of Der Tasa and Badari.[1] Similar transitional types of semi-sedentary nomads are to be found at all times on the Libyan and Arabian sides of the Delta, and especially in the Fayum which is in reality a Libyan oasis. Here is demonstrated the undoubted power of the soil of Egypt to turn its inhabitants into peasants or, as they are known today, *felaheen*. The practice of house-burial which is found among the people of Merimdah is quite foreign to the true nomadic way of life. It is also not found among the prehistoric cultures of Upper Egypt, but has recently been brought to light in a cemetery at el-Omari near Helwan just south of Cairo.

We have already noted that in contrast to this type of culture, the early stages of the Neolithic cultures in Upper Egypt are characterized as a hunter's world. This fact is particularly true of early stages of the predynastic Naqada civilization which is called Amratian after a typical site excavated at el-Amrah south of Abydos. Amratian sites are found between Thebes and Asyut to the north with undoubted centres for settlement in the regions of Ballas and Naqada together with el-Khozam opposite on the east bank of the Nile and in the neighbourhood of Qau el-Kebir, the ancient Antaeopolis. In this latter area the levels

[1] H. Junker and O. Menghin, 'Vorberichte' in *Anz. Wien. Akad. phil.-hist. Kl.* (1929, 1930, 1932, 1933, 1940); E. Baumgartel, *Cultures of Prehistoric Egypt*, I, makes it parallel to the Naqada II culture.

to be assigned to the Tasian and Badarian cultures reveal even more primitive experiments in burial methods, household equipment and pottery in particular which clearly demonstrate the connection with the older Nubian-Hamitic civilization.[1] We do not know, however, why the earlier Naqada culture was confined to the Thebaid. Herodotus in his history (Book II, chapter 4) says that he was told by the Egyptian authorities that before the reign of Menes, the first king of Dynasty I, the whole of Upper Egypt was a marsh with the exception of the Theban nome, that is the area which corresponds to the later Theban theocracy, extending north to Middle Egypt. This story is probably unfounded and was invented to enhance the fame of the unifier of the two kingdoms, but it may contain an echo of a popular tradition that the decisive step for the regulation of the flood-water of the Nile was taken in Upper Egypt. For Herodotus subsequently talks (in chapter 99) about the construction of dykes south of Memphis at the time when this city was laid out at the start of Dynasty I, suggesting that it was the problem of life or death for Egypt which was then being dealt with.

The animal-world of the hunter appears again in the early Naqada culture on the ivory handles of flint hunting-knives, in the ornamentation of their sheaths and also in the shapes of the cosmetic palettes which were mostly made of schist; pottery too was decorated with representations of animals and birds and vases were shaped in animal forms. Dogs and weapons accompanied a man in his grave.[2] This world and its ruling spirits left marked traces in Egyptian religion. The strong beast of prey played a dominant role in the cult and the Egyptian kingship being the incorporation of divine power, chose its personification of protective power in this field. The creature which predominated in royal symbolism from the beginning of Egyptian history was the swift falcon, the desert hunter which slew the game. The king also wanted to be the wild bull which the huntsman had learned to fear as his most dangerous adversary on African soil. At the beginning of history the king called himself 'Scorpion',

[1] G. Brunton and Caton-Thompson, *Badarian Civilization*; Brunton, *Mostagedda and the Tasian Culture*.

[2] For a good survey see A. Scharff, *Grundzüge der ägyptischen Vorgeschichte* and in *Handbuch der Archäologie* (1938). More recently, J. Vandier, *Manuel d'Archéologie égyptienne*, I.

'cat-fish' or 'uraeus'. He had the power of the magical Seth-animal, that mysterious desert-animal which assumed a fabulous character at the threshold of historical times; it disappeared beyond the Egyptian's horizon just like the winged griffon of the hunter's imagination and that frightful creature with panther's head, snake neck and hippopotamus body which was sometimes depicted on monuments of the time of the unification of the two kingdoms.[1] The principal figure in Naqada art, the African elephant, is missing, however, from the royal symbolism of the early dynastic period; it reappears as the 'water-elephant' in certain hunting scenes in the Old Kingdom while in the tomb-paintings of the feudal lords of the Middle Kingdom who were devoted to hunting it is placed among the fabulous animals under its old name, as for example in the tombs of Beni Hasan.

The chief companion of the ancient Egyptian king was the swift greyhound, the Upper Egyptian jackal which the people of Asyut chose as their local god. In inscriptions of the New Kingdom the king was fond of comparing himself with the 'swift moving jackal who circles the land in the twinkling of an eye'. In royal mythology the greyhound used by the huntsman to track down game, to point and to kill was called 'the one with the sharp arrow who is more powerful than the gods', these victory-bringing arrows 'opened the way' and hence the jackal was called Wepwawet or 'Path-opener'; they made him the 'Guide of the Gods' in particular of the companion gods of the divine king, the protagonist of the unification of the two kingdoms 'who had victoriously conquered the two lands (i.e. Egypt)'.

There was also the female vulture Nekhbet, 'the one of el-Kab' and 'the White one of Nekhen' who became the Upper Egyptian tutelary deity and the mother of the king, who suckled and cared for him. Beside her cult there probably existed in early times in its native el-Kab another cult of the wild cow, which was later superseded.

The spirit of an aristocratic age lived on in the ancient legends of the gods. A hunter's tale tells of the divine huntsman Onuris who returned from the depths of the south-eastern desert with a wild lioness he had tamed. This legendary hero reminds us of the lion-taming hero who wears foreign clothes and has a beard

[1] E.g. Schäfer-Andrae[3], pp. 187, 189.

like an Asiatic beduin and who appears on the late predynastic knife-handle found at Gebel el-Arak, south of Abydos. He is even more like the huntsman in the paintings in the rock-tomb at Hieraconpolis which date from about the same time, that is to the period of the Naqada II culture.[1] In ancient myths we read of the struggle for mastery between the royal animals, the bull and the falcon, who tear themselves to pieces, the bull losing its testicles and the falcon his keen eye.[2] The sacrificial ritual also retained naturalistic features in its preference for wild animals of the desert.[3] The sacrificial ox must be captured with a lasso as if it were in its wild state. Likewise there was the white oryx antelope, 'the white beast' which was hunted by the royal falcon and slain by it as 'the enemy of the god' (i.e. of Horus), the ibex, the dorcas gazelle and other animals which the lords of the desert, above all the lion, devoured for food and whose blood they drank. The fact that in historical times these wild animals were replaced in sacrifices by domestic stall-fed animals was in the nature of an expedient adopted by an agricultural community; and this all the more so in that the ordinary man was permitted to make offerings of small animals such as goats and sheep.[4] The ritual texts nevertheless rigorously maintained the fiction of the earlier practices.

In the beginning untamed and hostile powers were everywhere. The art of the age when the two kingdoms were united still exhales the atmosphere of primitive savagery. It gives eloquent expression to the fact that a people had become rulers of the whole of Egypt who even in the time when they had been huntsmen and nomadic cattle-breeders had contained in themselves the instinctive capacity and power to create a state.[5] The king is the wild bull who destroys enemy towns and tramples their chiefs under his hoofs. Even official inscriptions of Dynasty XVIII (about 1568–1317 B.C.), put words such as these into the mouth of the god Amun when talking to Tuth-

---

[1] Both illustrated in Schäfer-Andrae[3], pp. 184–5, and Scharff, *Handbuch der Archäologie*, pl. 56. For the legend of Onuris, see Junker, 'Die Onurislegende' (*Abhandlung Wien. Akad.*, 59, 1–2).

[2] *Pyr.*, 418a; cf. Schott, *Mythe und Mythenbildung im alten Ägypten*, 70.

[3] Kees, 'Bemerkungen zur Tieropfer der Ägypter und seiner Symbolik.' (*Gött. Nachr. phil.-hist. Kl.*, 1942).

[4] See below, p. 37.

[5] Illustrated, Schäfer-Andrae[3], *loc. cit.*

mosis III: 'I cause them (the enemy) to see Your Majesty as a young bull with strong heart and pointed horns against whom it is impossible to fight.'[1] The king is also the lion who, on the so-called 'battlefield' palette mangles the bodies of the enemy; he is also the falcon who rips their towns to pieces and brings back their inhabitants in bonds while the vultures eviscerate the corpses of the fallen like carcasses after a hunt. At this period in Egypt there was created a particular type of lion-portraiture in which the beast was shown with wide-open jaws and bared fangs. It was abandoned with other memories of the savagery of primitive times as early as Dynasty I at the beginning of the Thinite Period when the wild beast was tamed as in the myth of the desert huntsman Onuris.[2] The evolution of lion-portraiture in Egypt followed therefore an exactly opposite course to that which it followed in Mesopotamian art in which the type of the angry beast became the rule.

Unfortunately Anthropology has up to now been unable to determine with any degree of certainty what race or national group brought this oldest civilization into the land of the Nile. During the Naqada period the valley of the Nile from Nubia to the frontier of Lower Egypt, just south of Cairo, was dominated by a rather small, finely boned race of men with short skulls, designated the 'Brown Mediterranean race'. At Tasa in Upper Egypt, however, in strata belonging to a culture precedent to the Naqada culture, beside this Mediterranean type there was also found a coarser-boned type with square skulls that physically resembles the so-called Giza race. To judge by the contents of graves and by actual representations of men this latter race was undoubtedly the creator and upholder of the Old Kingdom with its capital at Memphis (Pl. 32a and b); its presence as early as the First Dynasty burials at Saqqara and Helwan, in the middle of the Memphite domain, has lately been established.[3] Until it has been proved that the Giza race of the Old Kingdom had a possibly northern origin, that is an origin in the North African border lands, the supposition that it appears in the oldest stratum of culture in the Thebaid between 5000 and 4000

[1] *Urk.*, IV, 616.
[2] Kees, 'Die Befriedung des Raubtieres' in *ÄZ*, 67, 56f.
[3] Derry in Z. Y. Saad, *Royal Excavations at Saqqara and Helwan (1941–1945)*, 249f.

B.C. must remain doubtful. The leading authority on this subject, Dr. D. E. Derry, draws attention, nevertheless, to the fact
that the distinctive characteristics of this race are again found
in burials of the ruling class of Dynasty XXII which undoubtedly consisted of people of Libyan origin.[1]

It is clear that peoples of different races took part in the
settlement of the Nile valley. Thus the undoubted connection
between the finds in Tasian and Badarian strata on the one hand
and Nubian discoveries on the other, for example in pottery and
in certain funerary customs such as the wrapping of the body in
animal skins, proves no more than the possible preponderance
of an individual race. Moreover, the restriction of the Amratian
culture to the Thebaid and the lack of knowledge at present
about what happened in Middle Egypt before the first burials
in the Gerzean cemeteries of the Naqada II culture, present a
problem. If we knew more about Lower Egypt greater differences would certainly be revealed not only in the matter of race
but also in the character of settlements. The frontier districts of
the Delta like the Libyan oases, but unlike the valley of the Nile,
must have been clearly recognized transit and pasture zones for
the peoples on the frontiers, the Libyans on the north-west
coming by way of Lake Mareotis, and the Asiatic beduin on the
east, coming by way of the racial bridge north of Suez. At the
beginning of history the north-west part of the Delta up to and
beyond the Canopic branch of the Nile, which the Egyptians
called the Western River, and indeed beyond Sais in the east,
was inhabited by a predominantly Libyan population which
was of the same origin as the brown Mediterranean race of the
Nile valley. This territory corresponded in area to the three
Delta nomes, the 3rd (western), the 5th (Saite) and the 7th
(barbed harpoon), it also possibly included the 6th (desert bull)
and the 4th (the upper arrow nome). At all events the falcon
god of the west nome (No. 3) was called 'Horus from Libya with
the striking arm' and the Egyptians of the Old Kingdom
characterized the arrow goddess Neith, 'the terrible one' of Sais,
as 'Neith from Libya' as if she were the chieftainess of this neighbouring people with whom the inhabitants of the Nile valley
were at all times at war.[2] These struggles were the continuation

[1] *Annales du Service*, 39, 549f.
[2] On the problem of the Libyans, see Hölscher, *Libyer und Ägypter*.

of the warfare waged in primitive times for places of refuge from wasted or overpopulated districts. They finally resulted at the beginning of the first millenium B.C. during Dynasties XXII–XXIII in the invasion and conquest of Egypt by the Libyan hordes.

Small groups of Asiatics were certainly settled permanently on the eastern frontier of the Delta. Egyptian history contains frequent references to these intruders, for example at the end of Dynasty VI about 2250 B.C., then the Hyksos invasion about 1700 B.C. and later the story of the Israelites in the Land of Goshen. Even today Arab beduin can be seen with their tents and herds in the country north-east of Fakus and in the Wadi Tumilat. In some of the Pyramid Texts of the Old Kingdom the ancient epithets used for Andjti, the nome god of the 9th Delta nome (of Busiris) are 'chief of his nome' and 'the one at the head of the eastern nome'.[1] These epithets show that at the beginning of the historical period the Egyptian felt that the frontier between his country and 'abroad' lay well within his land. He transferred the centre of gravity of the eastern nomes remarkably far westwards and certainly beyond the Damietta branch of the Nile. Proof of this can be found in the legend of Osiris, King of Busiris, who was killed in the 'land of the gazelles', that is to say on desert soil; in this connection local legends point to the 11th Delta nome, that of the 'dismembered bull' which lay to the east of the Damietta branch of the Nile.[2] All this points to a defensive position against the eastern frontier regions of the Delta. Perhaps there is also a connection between this state of affairs and the slowness with which the eastern Delta was opened up from a cultural point of view; this delay being revealed in the noticeably small number of administrative districts in the area until after the Hyksos period and the subsequent necessity for radical changes in the administrative boundaries.

From a politico-economic point of view it should be remembered that the observations of experienced geographers like S. Passarge have shown that frontier districts composed of vast swamps and marshes afford good basic living conditions for cattle-breeding and especially for breeding oxen. This fact is proved by the case of the Nilotic tribes of the Southern Sudan. That the Delta was the home of cattle-breeding in Egypt in

---

[1] *Pyr.*, 183a, 220c, 1833d.   [2] Kees, *Götterglaube*, 258, 404.

historical times is proved both by pictorial representations and inscriptions from the time of the Old Kingdom and by the number and importance of the Delta cattle-cults;[1] cattle are the nome emblems of the 6th, 10th, 11th and 12th Lower Egyptian nomes — the ancient nomes of Xois, Athribis, Leontopolis and Sebennytus. It must be remembered, however, that in Egypt the pastures on which the herds graze are not meadows, which do not exist in the European sense, but uncultivated plain covered with rushes, isolated marshy clumps of bulrushes and papyrus and shrubs; country which the ancient Egyptian represented by the hieroglyph 𓈗. Heavy cattle clearly could not be kept on the poor salty land of the desert borders on which sheep and goats were quite content to graze (Pl. 5. *b*). In the autobiographical inscription of a nomarch of the Heracleopolitan period (about 2150 B.C.) the apparent possibility of alternative grazing is suggested in the words: 'I filled his land (of the 12th Upper Egyptian nome) along the river banks with oxen and his low-lying fields with small cattle.'[2] Here, however, we have only a makeshift in comparison with the more favourable conditions to be found in the 'papyrus land' of Lower Egypt round the great marshes and lagoons and including the flood lands that lay bare and dry during the brief period of low water. This 'papyrus land' is represented in the reliefs of the tombs at Saqqara dating from the Golden Age of the Old Kingdom. A typical marshland, the Elearchia of later antiquity, which lay near the lagoons to the east of the Rosetta mouth of the Nile, preserved the memory of the Bukoloi, the cattle herdsmen, in its emblem right down to times when the economic condition of Egypt, and particularly of Lower Egypt, had changed profoundly.[3]

It is impossible to discover from the assignment of the nome emblems whether or not these cattle herdsmen were descended from the ancient Libyans and were a surviving group of these Hamitic nomads. Their territory in the 10th to 12th nomes, called the Bull Kingdom by P. E. Newberry,[4] seems to have

---

[1] Kees, *Kulturgeschichte*, 18f.   [2] *Urk.*, I, 77.

[3] On the way of life, see Diodorus Siculus I, 43; for the risings of the Bukoloi in A.D. 172 and again under the early Arab régime, see Wiedemann, *Herodots zweites Buch*, 371f.

[4] P. E. Newberry, *Egypt as a Field for Anthropological Research*.

been in a part of the Delta east of the centre, around the Damietta branch of the Nile.[1] It is also questionable whether the nome signs of these nomes do not date from a prehistoric period; they are found for the first time during the Old Kingdom. Nevertheless a nomadic origin in the desert borderlands for these people is further indicated by the designation 'desert bull' given to the nome animal of the 6th nome (of Xois), a definitely marshy district, which was the centre of Elearchia.[2]

A local legend existed in the 3rd Lower Egyptian nome, which is to the west on the Libyan border, about a divine cow, Sekhet-Hor — 'who remembers Horus' — who suckled and reared the royal child.[3] It is a variant of the myth about the primitive god who grew up, hidden in a papyrus thicket from the pursuit of his enemies. This Horus Myth, from the manner of its presentation, must be an elaboration of historical times, though the cult itself is older; the Cow-goddess is presented as the mythical mother of her neighbour, the Horus of Libya, just as Isis is, at Sebennytus in the eastern Delta. In the Old Kingdom the figure of Sekhet-Hor became, as it were, a general Egyptian protectress of cattle. Under her auspices the counting of cattle by the king took place — one of the bases of the tax on property. Cow-worship existed at all times in the borderlands of Egypt to the west as far as Cyrenaica in Libya, either under the name of Hathor, the mother of Horus who was god of heaven, or subsequently under that of Isis. We should also mention the two best-known bull cults of Egypt, that of Apis at Memphis and that of Mnevis at Heliopolis.

In the present state of our knowledge it would be sheer supposition to compare the cattle-breeders of Libyan origin in the eastern Delta districts with shepherds of an Asiatic, Semitic type. Nevertheless from the religious point of view, the ancient cult of the ram at Mendes in the 16th Lower Egyptian nome may be cited in support of this supposition. An historical argument for the racial division of the Delta can be found in the fact that it was only the north-west Delta that offered real resistance to the Horus Kings of Upper Egypt at the time of the unification

[1] This mouth in antiquity was known as the Bucolic mouth as well as the more usual Phatnitic mouth, see Herodotus, II, 17.
[2] Sethe, *Urgeschichte und älteste Religion*, § 186.
[3] Kees, *Götterglaube*, 75f., 210.

of the two lands. Evidence of this resistance exists in the memorials of the victory which show that this part of the country was occupied by a powerful racial group. Their ultimate subjection could then, by an historical simplification, be represented as *the* victory over the Lower Egyptian half of the country (represented as the Red Crown of Sais or Buto). Moreover it must be assumed that the lagoon districts of the northern Delta were very thinly populated and remained on a cultural level similar to that found in the Neolithic strata on the northern shores of Lake Qarun in the Fayum. These people lived by fishing, capturing water-fowl, breeding domestic animals like sheep, goats and pigs and by cultivating small patches of barley and emmer.[1]

In cults also we find conditions existing in direct contrast to the 'useful' cattle cults. This state of affairs is reflected in the old nome signs: thus that for the 15th Lower Egyptian nome in the north-east Delta is the ibis; the neighbouring nome of Mendes has a fish-goddess, the 'first of the fish'; another nome, which apparently changed its name in later times, had during the Old Kingdom the crocodile as its emblem.[2] This latter sacred beast is depicted in one of the representations of the seasons in the Sun-temple of Niuserre in a hut-like shrine standing on an island in the Nile; in this case, however, it is transposed to the western half of the Delta, perhaps to the 7th Lower Egyptian nome.[3] The crocodile is also a royal creature with whose appearance out of the flood-waters the dead king compares himself in the Pyramid Texts and of whom an inscription at Karnak of Queen Hatshepsut of Dynasty XVIII says: 'I am the raging one who seizes powerfully, and if he seizes, there is no-one who can be freed from him.' A heron ruled over the legendary birthplace of the gods at Buto corresponding to the Horus falcon of Nekhen (Hieraconpolis) in Upper Egypt in the royal symbolism of unified Egypt. The harpoon used by the hippopotamus hunters and fishermen was the sign of the 7th Lower Egyptian nome in the north-west of the Delta while the arrow of the terrible goddess Neith of Sais was the emblem for the vast territory of the 4th and 5th Lower Egyptian nomes in the central Delta. Egyptian hunter's lore even in the Old Kingdom supposed that

[1] Caton-Thompson and Gardner, *The Desert Fayum*; see also below, p. 74.
[2] *Urk.*, I, 2, 6.   [3] Kees, *Götterglaube*, pl. VI, c.

1. *a.* Cliffs and Boats (near the Gebel Haridi in Middle Egypt).

1. *b.* Boats and a *sakiyah* near Old Cairo in 1909.

2. *a*. Landscape in the Cataract region south of Aswan.

2. *b*. The Second Cataract from Gebel Abusir.

the Delta was the last refuge of the red 'water-elephant' in the representation of which with a powerful tusk growing out of the lower jaw and in spite of the missing trunk, the idea of the African elephant clearly exercised a greater influence than that of the rhinoceros. The Delta and in particular its north-western part was the home of the tales of the divine harpooner who, in the guise of Horus, killed the mighty hippopotamus with the aid of Neith who was skilled in the use of weapons or of Isis who was learned in magic and who directed the harpoon. The dead hippopotamus was then divided up among the gods at a ceremonial banquet amid the jubilation of the people of Buto or Busiris, who were their subjects — an unmistakable recollection of the magnificence of the ancient royal hunts of the god-king. It is understandable, therefore, that King Usaphais of Dynasty I had himself represented as the hippopotamus — conqueror[1] and that in Dynasty XVIII Tuthmosis III had funerary scarabs cut on which he is represented as the successful harpooner of hippopotami.[2]

Myths tell the story how the crocodile was a helper at unfortunate events in the world of the gods; he pulled out of the river and brought to land both the severed hands of Horus according to the 113th chapter of the Book of the Dead, and also the body of the drowned Osiris. Myths also tell of the marshy hiding-place of the primeval god who grew up watched over by beneficent powers in a lonely unknown spot — 'one knows not where' — the very same papyrus marsh which the inhabitants of Buto claimed they possessed in the floating island of Chemmis of which Herodotus tells in Book II, chapter 156. Others made the same claim for the distant marshland north of Behbet el-Hagar, the town of Isis, where the most northerly town of Egypt was situated on Tell Balamun, the place known to later generations as the 'Island of Amun'.[3]

From the economic point of view the Delta was the great reserve of land for internal colonization. It was rendered access-

[1] Petrie, *Royal Tombs*, II, pl. 7, 5–6.

[2] Winlock, *The Treasure of the Three Princesses*, 35, pl. 19G (the number 30 refers not to the distance but belongs to the writing of the word for 'harpoon').

[3] Gardiner, *JEA*, 30, 35f. Tell Balamun lies in the area of the 17th Lower Egyptian nome which first occurs as an independent nome in the New Kingdom; previously it probably formed part of the 12th (Sebennytic) nome.

ible only after centuries of work on canals and dykes and far
into the late days of the New Kingdom it maintained great
herds of oxen for landowners of the Nile valley where pastures
failed in summer.[1] The marshes, lagoons and the branches of
the river with their papyrus thickets provided moreover the
favourite hunting grounds for the royal hunt; such could be
found on a similar scale in Upper Egypt only around Lake
Qarun in the Fayum.[2] According to Pliny (XXVIII, 121), the
best place for capturing hippopotami for the games at Rome in
imperial times was the Saite nome to which the animals had
withdrawn from more populous districts in search of food and
safety. According to Arab reports the last hippopotami to be
found north of the Cataract of Aswan, occurred on the Damietta
branch of the Nile.

A land with such an ethnically disparate population did not,
however, possess the strength necessary for the creation of a
state. The Egyptians always spoke of the 'two halves' of the
Delta and took them into account in their administrative
organization; and this was more than a simple geographical
division inasmuch as the 'central island' — the district lying
between the two chief arms of the Nile — was sometimes distinguished independently.

Lower Egypt nevertheless from the point of view of politics
and administration in ancient Egypt, is not simply identical
with the Delta. Not only were broad frontier districts reckoned
as part of Lower Egypt but also those transit zones round the
apex of the Delta where, not fortuitously, the modern political
and economic centre of gravity lies at Cairo. In this latter area
belonged also the ancient cities of Memphis and Heliopolis. It
included on the west the nomes of Memphis (Nr. 1) and Letopolis (Nr. 2) and on the east those of Heliopolis (Nr. 13) and
Bubastis (Nr. 18). It should be noted here that the nome of
Bubastis, the Upper-Royal-child-nome of the classical lists, is
absent from the list of nomes on the shrine of Sesostris I at
Karnak; so too are the 17th Lower Egyptian nome in the
northern Delta and the 19th and 20th nomes in the eastern
Delta. Possibly Bubastis was at one time included in the Heliopolitan nome. The 10th Lower Egyptian nome of Athribis, the
modern Benha, in spite of its island-like position at the apex of

[1] See below, p. 88.   [2] See below, p. 226.

the Delta, may also have been included among the transit zones.

South of this area of contrary forces begins the valley proper of the Nile; it starts near Cairo, not far from ancient Memphis, where still lies the port for the transshipment of goods from Upper Egypt.[1] At Saft el-Hennah whose local deity, Sopdu 'the sharp one', reveals in form and name the character of the place as frontier guard against Asia,[2] the natural route from Asia emerges from the Wadi Tumilat. Here on reaching the Nile the route divides into two, continuing westwards to Bubastis (modern Zagazig) and turning southwards to Heliopolis near the modern el-Matariyah, north-east of Cairo. This is the natural district for exchange and transit. It may be possible to define its borders politically, but culturally and racially they will remain fluid.

In the predynastic civilization of Upper Egypt a sharp cleavage can be observed between the cultures of the first and second Naqada civilizations. The later Naqada period, now mostly called Gerzean, is represented most clearly in cemeteries in Middle Egypt north of the entrance to the Fayum, an area not settled by the Amratians of the earlier period. In the remains of this later culture the mark of the hunter is less frequent than before; hounds and weapons are rarer as funerary offerings. Ship designs are noticeable in the decoration of pottery, akin to those found in rock-paintings executed in a similar style in the *wadis* of the eastern desert (Pl. 3.*a*), especially in the Wadi Hammamat and its side valleys. These Nile sailors were not, as has formerly been too readily assumed,[3] newcomers who at that time came from the east by way of the barren coast of the Red Sea. They found their way into the desert valleys like the men who in earlier times went there to hunt game; but they searched for the beautiful hard stones which are to be found in these valleys. The later Naqada period ushered in the golden age which lasted up to the time of Zoser in Dynasty III — the age of abundant brightly coloured stone vases shaped by craftsmen with stone drills in an exceptionally laborious fashion. The pottery of the period also imitated the stone vessels in shape and

---

[1] See below, p. 171.

[2] For Sopdu, 'Lord of the Foreign Lands', as an Asiatic Beduin, see Borchardt, *Das Grabdenkmal des Königs Saȝhure*, II, pl. 5, cf. *ÄZ*, 75, pl. 4a.

[3] See Kees, *Gött. gel. Anz.* (1939), p. 492f.

decorative motifs and was therefore a cheap substitute for them.

This period reveals through the emphasis laid on navigation that the means of livelihood had been enlarged to include transport and commerce. These were factors inseparable from the economic life of the dwellers in the valley of the Nile from that time onwards. They assured them the cultural and political predominance over the north which about 2980 B.C. resulted in the unification of the kingdoms by the Upper Egyptian kings from Hieraconpolis. Ships, hunting expeditions and tribal battles are the chief subjects in a painted rock-chamber of this period near Hieraconpolis and also on the carved knife-handle from Gebel el-Arak, the finest work of art produced before the commemorative slate mace-heads and palettes of the period of unification.[1] This later Naqada civilization imposed itself on the Amratian culture in the Thebaid and as a result there arose for the first time a civilization common to the whole of Egypt from the borders with Nubia up to Turah just south of Cairo and on the threshold of Lower Egypt. Judging by the small sculptures from Hieraconpolis, the reliefs and rock-paintings, the people who were in authority, including the victorious Upper Egyptian kings, still belonged to the mysterious delicately formed race with short skulls from which the Amratians developed.[2] The difference between the peoples of the two cultures was marked especially by an economic transformation; it was not the result of any racial movement from the east. The more firmly the population became settled in the valley of the Nile, the more did pasture give way to arable land. Cereal crops were grown no longer in the *wadis* as in the earliest times and perhaps still in the Badarian period, but on ground inundated by the Nile. Sailors and farmers were the leading men in the Nile valley and these settled people began to hate the desert from which their ancestors came. It was a foreign land and it was contrasted unfavourably as the 'red' with the 'black' fertile soil which gave Egypt its name *Kemet* ('the Black'). Similarly the free nomads of the desert profoundly despised the *fellaheen* tied to the soil. Everything that comes from the desert, everything that moves about in it is sinister to the peasant's eyes, even

---

[1] Schäfer-Andrae[3], pp. 184, 185.

[2] Good examples, Schäfer-Andrae[3], pp. 180-1.

if it is only so peaceful and harmless an animal as the dainty gazelle or the fleet hare. Out of the desert and especially the south-western desert come sand-storms and bad weather which are undoubtedly sent by Seth, Lord of the Libyan Desert; thence also comes Pakhet, the 'tearing' lioness, or her comrade lioness Sekhmet, 'the Mighty', whose home is 'up in the desert valley' near Memphis. They send the hot south and west winds in summer which bring 'the pestilence of the year' which kills people.[1] According to legend Sekhmet, by order of Re', King of the Gods, once destroyed nearly all the first race of men when they were beginning to make settlements, until the god saved the remainder by a stratagem. Nevertheless, in the temples of Egypt the gods had on feast days to be brought a blood-red drink as a sacrifice; then they would become drunk to the accompaniment of music and dancing and their anger would be stilled.

According to the ancient aristocratic belief only a beast at liberty and not a domesticated animal could serve as a sacrificial offering to the god.[2] The donkey which was the beast of burden of historical Egypt was brought into the country from the south during the Naqada period, but it was an object of abhorrence to the gods and was therefore as little suited to serve as a sacrificial food-offering as were the domesticated dog or pig, goat or sheep. When the Horus-kings of Upper Egypt conquered Lower Egypt and found that other ideas prevailed there in respect of swine, they forbade their use both for sacrifice and for consumption because swine 'are abhorrent to Horus'.[3] These beliefs of a non-peasant class who observed the characteristic Egyptian ritual, cut across peasant ideas according to which wild animals down to the water-fowl which the bird-catcher snared in marshy thickets were 'enemies of the gods' to be slain and destroyed; similarly men of the superior culture held river fish to be 'abhorrent' despite the fact that such a belief was wholly contrary to the notions of the common man.[4] Henceforth choice fat oxen from the stall and goats and sheep from the poor

---

[1] Kees, *Götterglaube*, 8.   [2] See above, p. 26.

[3] See below, p. 91. The inhabitants of the settlement at Merimdah were confirmed pig-eaters, see Menghin in Junker, 'Vorbericht Merimde' (1933) in *Anz. Wien. Akad.*, p. 88.

[4] Kees, *Kulturgeschichte*, 58f.; see also below, p. 92.

man, but always males, were brought for sacrifice to the god. In contrast to the religious and mythical beliefs of the Delta the surviving Upper Egyptian cattle cults permitted a wild animal to be discerned in the ritual. Even the well-known Hathor fetish, the sistrum, which the Egyptians called 'the female soul with its two faces', seems in its mingling of animal and human characteristics to have associated with it a more indomitable force than is evident in the cow-deities of Delta nomes, the kindly maternal animal in the form of Sekhet-Hathor or the cow who bore the divine calf of Sebennytus as the sun-god.[1] Perhaps for this very reason Hathor as Queen of Heaven is placed on the upper rim of the Narmer palette.[2]

In Upper Egypt apart from certain figures like the fertility god Min of Coptos, 'the Lord of the Herds,' the rational world of cattle-breeders accorded precedence to the ram-cult of the shepherds. In historical times this cult, mostly under the name of Khnum, extended from Elephantine in the south by way of Esna, Hur near Hermopolis in Middle Egypt, Heracleopolis (Arsaphes) and the 21st Upper Egyptian nome, then by Memphis and Letopolis (Kherti) down to the western border of the Delta on the Libyan frontier. In this cult we see the veneration of a fertile domestic animal, 'the tame ram,' which does not conform to the ancient aristocratic demand for equality of birth in sacrifice and worship. Only a few of the historic Khnum cults underwent a domesticating transformation from the worship of wild animals to that of tame animals; such was the cult of Khnum on the 'island of herbs' near Minia in Middle Egypt where an ibex had been worshipped.[3] The importance of the Khnum cults, however, clearly grew in historical times. They frequently take the place of another local or nome deity as in the 11th Upper Egyptian nome where the Khnum replaced the divine Seth animal at Shashotp (Hypselis), in the Heracleopolitan nome where the ram Arsaphes replaced a tree spirit (the nome emblem) and in the Delta where the ram of Mendes replaced the fish-goddess Hat-mehit.[4] At the height of the Old

---

[1] The sign of the 12th Lower Egyptian nome shows a cow and a calf. The name Sebennytus (Zabnuti) means 'the divine calf'.

[2] Schäfer-Andrae[3], 189 *et al.*

[3] Kees, *Götterglaube*, 80, after Jéquier, *Monument funéraire de Pepi II*, vol. II, pl. 33.   [4] See above, p. 32.

Kingdom Khnum was elevated to the dignity of a royal god: the king is called the 'son of Khnum' in the Pyramid Texts;[1] he is attended, just as was the case with the mighty bull, by the queen as 'the beloved of the ram'; he is the image made by that creator-god who after the fashion of the potter formed gods and men. Understandably, therefore, the great Cheops had as his full name Khnum-Khufu — 'Khnum — he defends me'. Nevertheless this veneration did not prevent certain local ram-cults such as that of Kherti of Letopolis and of 'the one before his wall' in Memphis, from subsequently sinking into virtual oblivion.

Towards the end of the Naqada period the representation of the gods in human form had already begun, as is revealed by Egypt's oldest figure of a god, the archaic statue from Coptos of the ithyphallic fertility god Min swinging a herdsman's whip.[2] As Schott has shown, this anthropomorphism was the prerequisite for the creation of the myths of the historical period.[3] The civilization of the huntsmen, fishermen and nomads began to retreat to remote places; or else their way of life became the privilege of a class of courtiers and this in itself was a limitation on its influence. A gulf which was not created by racial differences began to open between the existing inhabitants of the Nile valley and the bulk of that part of its population which remained static in an earlier stage of civilization because nature denied them the opportunity for evolution. Such were the Nubians, the Libyans and the nomads of the eastern desert. The ancient tribal emblems of these racial groups became in the days of Egypt's greatest civilization part of the professional outfit of soldiers and huntsmen,[4] or survived as symbols in cults. The penis-sheath of predynastic times continued in daily use by Libyans whereas in Egypt it became part of the ceremonial dress of the king together with the animal tail attached to his girdle or the emblems of primitive deities.[5] The ancient statues of Min of Coptos similarly show the slight side-whiskers of the Beduin. The Egyptians moreover saw nothing unusual in the fact that gods of their own borderlands in their functions as lords of foreign lands assumed

[1] *Pyr.*, 1298.   [2] Schäfer-Andrae[3], 179.
[3] *Mythe und Mythenbildung im alten Ägypten*, 93f.
[4] Kees, *Kulturgeschichte*, 58; Hölscher, *Libyer und Ägypter*, 27.
[5] E.g. in the case of Zoser in the 'offering dance', cf. Firth and Quibell, *The Step Pyramid*, II, pl. 15, 42.

Asiatic-beduin characteristics; so with Sopdu of Saft el-Hennah in the Old Kingdom[1] and later with Seth of Tanis. It had after all already happened with the ancient hunting hero on the knife-handle from Gebel el-Arak. The lawless beduin was nevertheless *the* enemy whose slaying for the sake of law and order was chief among the royal duties. The art of the Thinite period is dominated by pictorial representations of this theme.

At the time when the unifying Gerzeans ruled in Upper Egypt there existed near Ma'adi close to the historical frontier with Lower Egypt a densely populated colony of a peasant type.[2] A strong influx of eastern immigrants must at that time have reached Egypt by way of the racial bridge at Suez and the eastern districts of the Delta. These immigrants brought with them not only coveted raw materials such as obsidian, island-marble from the Aegean and Asiatic lapis-lazuli but also all kinds of innovations of technique and design by way of the trade routes from Syria and Palestine. Among these innovations were motifs from the Jemdet-Nasr culture which flourished in Mesopotamia around 3000 B.C., extending as far as Syria. These motifs were readily incorporated into the highly developed Upper Egyptian crafts of making cosmetic palettes out of schist and of carving in ivory. Such were heraldically arranged representations, for example the motif of the tamer of wild animals which could be used to illustrate the Egyptian huntsman's saga; also the decorative employment of figures of fabulous beasts elsewhere than in hunting scenes.[3]

The ornamentation of the ancient stone figures of Min of Coptos represented as Lord of the Eastern Desert and the forerunner of Pan Euodos of the Hellenistic age, with desert animals and Red Sea mussels, was in itself an acknowledgment of the intercourse with foreign lands. To account for the undoubted Asiatic influences which reached their highest peak towards the close of the later Naqada period, at the time of the Ma'adi settlement when preparations were in train for the unification

---

[1] See above, p. 35.

[2] Preliminary study of Mustapha Amer and Menghin, *Excavations of the Egyptian University in the Neolithic Site of Maadi* (1932, 1933); cf. Scharff in *OLZ* (1939), p. 730f. The necropolis belonging to this site has recently been discovered.

[3] Scharff, *Die Frühkulturen Ägyptens und Mesopotamiens.*

of the kingdoms, it is enough to assume the existence of regular commercial relations and, on the eastern frontier of Egypt, an infiltration of Asiatic tribes which never wholly ceased. It is, however, a matter of relative unimportance to assume a complete regrouping of the population in Egypt as the result of racial migrations from the east, whether they came from Arabia to Upper Egypt as Schweinfurth and Petrie held, or first entered the Delta over the narrow route by Suez which seems unlikely from what has up to now been revealed by excavation. The Egyptian world of the gods in historical times was in no need of foreign support, despite frequently voiced suggestions to the contrary[1] — whether the cult of the sun-god at Heliopolis or the beliefs of Osiris in Busiris or the idea of Isis the goddess of the throne. We must get used to the narrowness of the world known to primitive man. Furthermore we can perceive that beside the pseudo-historical strands which are chiefly responsible for these hypotheses (such a strand occurs in the great myth of Horus of Edfu who hunted Seth across the north-eastern frontier of Egypt into Asia), there are very many more recent notions formed for the first time in the New Kingdom after the war with the Hyksos or even later down to Persian times.[2]

Undoubtedly it is in the Egyptian language that we encounter Asiatic influences even more so than in the innovations in art and technique. The language of historical Egypt unquestionably contains Semitic elements added to an African foundation and these elements exercised a far-reaching influence. The real question, however, is to what extent this is due to an Egypto-semitic connection in predynastic times and how much to a secondary influence dating from the beginning of the historical period.

The connection with the Semitic languages is shown by the artificial triliteralism of verbal roots and the fact that changes in their meaning are effected by the addition of prefixes or by internal changes such as reduplication or gemination of parts of the root; such changes in form are called conjugations in Semitic languages. The connection is also revealed by the Egyptian per-

[1] Recent examples are S. A. Mercer, *Études sur les origines de la religion de l'Égypte* (London, 1929) and the article by H. Stock on the Eastern Delta in *Welt des Orients*, I, 3 (1948), 135f.

[2] Kees, 'Kultlegende und Urgeschichte' in *Gött. Nachr. phil.-hist. Kl.*, 1930.

sonal pronouns and by the construction of the majority of tenses with the help of unstressed suffix-pronouns. Most remarkable of all, however, is the resemblance of the Egyptian Pseudo-participles (as Erman called them at the time of his discovery) with the Semitic Perfect, particularly in the stage of development represented by the Akkadian Stative or Permansive.

The Pseudo-participle is considered by the classical school of thought established by Erman and Sethe as peculiarly ancient and as 'the sole surviving relic in Egyptian of the Semitic finite verb'.[1] The endeavour, however, that was made to indicate with this verbal form the pronunciation of the pronominal endings including the position of the vowel, (as was also the case with the later 'syllabic' writings of foreign words in Egyptian from the time of the Middle Kingdom), points to the fact that these forms were felt to be foreign. They were, therefore, as early as Old Egyptian subjected to a separate orthographic treatment which differs noticeably from the purely consonantal writing of the pronominal endings in the case of the ordinary suffix-conjugation.[2]

The question here, therefore, is not one of a primitive correspondence with Semitic but of an enrichment of comparatively recent date which preceded the stage of the language known as Old Egyptian by only a short time. We have therefore, the possibility of looking for a period of strong Semitic influence in the realm of language at the beginning of the historical period. At present it remains impossible to establish whether this was the time of the Jemdet-Nasr culture which was contemporaneous with the cultures of Ma'adi and the Gerzean period.

As a result of A. Scharff's theory that the Gerzean civilization of Middle Egypt was to be attributed to a progressive 'northern people', it has been suggested that the invention of hieroglyphic writing resulted from the knowledge of Babylonian writing. Analogies, however, are wanting.[3] The first Egyptian written characters appear on cosmetic palettes of schist as annotations

---

[1] Gardiner, *Egyptian Grammar* (3rd ed., 1957), § 309.

[2] The suggested solution offered by Erman, *Ägyptische Grammatik* (4th ed.), § 325, 'that the endings in Egyptian are extended' is impossible from the point of view of the history of language.

[3] For the history of the script, see Sethe, *Die Entstehung der Schrift* and Schott, *Hieroglyphen*.

to pictures. They belong to that turbulent period which preceded the unification of the kingdoms and which did not waste time on words. The great events of that time produced an historical sense and with it the desire to perpetuate the events with name, place and circumstance in addition to the picture. The oldest hieroglyphs, therefore, show the surroundings, tools, weapons and similar objects of this and its subsequent age at the time of the creation of the Egyptian state.[1] It seems improbable that a 'northern people' who at the most played a passive role in the creation of the state should have given in the matter of writing the decisive cultural stimulus. It was, moreover, a long journey by way of annotations, notes, names and titles before the ancient Egyptian learned to perpetuate connected sentences on monuments. It was not until the beginning of the Old Kingdom that these attempts finally met with success. The final predynastic period must indeed have been a time of great vitality and of swift development; but it should not be credited with more than lay within its power.

This reservation applies also to the attempt made by Sethe to deduce from dogmatic claims contained in royal funerary inscriptions of the Old Kingdom the existence of a unified kingdom with its capital at Heliopolis in predynastic times. It applies also to the attempt of Borchardt to couple the existence of this hypothetical unified kingdom with the introduction of the so-called Sothic calendar in 4236 B.C., which has been described by Eduard Meyer as 'the oldest definite date in world history'.[2] The Sothic calendar presumed a calculation for the year based on astronomical observations of the heliacal rising of the star Sothis. This method was used with all the implied consequences for the calendar first in the abortive reform of 237 B.C. (the Decree of Canopus) and then in the Julian Calendar. The ancient Egyptians, however, contented themselves with a characteristic compromise between their mutable civil year of 365 days (which was nevertheless by far the best achievement of the ancient world in regard to the calendar until Roman times) and the calendar of feasts composed of lunar months.[3] In spite of all the

---

[1] Scharff, 'Archäologische Beiträge zur Frage der Entstehung der Hieroglyphenschrift' in *Sb. bayer. Akad. phil.-hist. Kl.* (1942), 3.

[2] *Geschichte des Altertums*, I, 2, § 197.

[3] Kees, *Kulturgeschichte*, 300f., cf. below, p. 49.

authority with which such hypotheses are brought forward it cannot be denied ultimately that the knowledge and ability for theoretical reflection with which they credit the ancient Egyptians, lay beyond the capacity and conception of primitive men living in a world of magic.[1] The ground has recently been taken from beneath the grandiose structure erected by Eduard Meyer, Ludwig Borchardt and Kurt Sethe by the reduction of all the traditional dates of the ancient oriental civilizations following upon the revision of Mesopotamian chronology.

The national fate of Egypt was predominantly determined from the South. This was the case at the beginning of history at the time of the unification of the kingdoms; it was again the case when the Theban Menthuhotpes about 2040 B.C. restored the unity that had been lost; it was evident once more in the liberation of Egypt from the Hyksos domination when Medjay and Nubians fought at the side of the Theban kings, about 1580 B.C.; and finally, at the appearance of the Ethiopian kings in Egypt in the Eighth Century B.C. There were, indeed, exceptions, in particular the great rulers of the Memphite Old Kingdom, then in the New Kingdom the soldier dynasty of the Ramesses' from Lower Egypt to whom the heretic Amenophis IV had gambled away the Theban inheritance. On the other hand, the Saite kings of the Late Period and their successors from towns in the Delta are no true exceptions; their family and their followers were of Libyan origin; they stemmed from the western marcher area from the oldest conceivable race of rulers in the valley of the Nile which we are able to distinguish.

[1] O. Neugebauer in *Acta Orientalia*, 17 (1938), 175f. For a reaction against the possibility of predynastic observations of the rising of Sothis, see Parker, *The Calendars of Ancient Egypt*.

PART TWO

The Topographical Framework of Egyptian Civilization

II

The Countryside

A. THE NILE AND THE SEASONS

For Egypt the Nile is its source of life and its chief means of transport; from the point where it breaks through the barrier of granite at the Cataract of Aswan down to its mouths it has a length of about 750 miles. Egypt's whole economy depends on it; the Egyptian farmer cannot count on the rainfall. Only the Delta and principally only its northern part lies within reach of the winter rain of the Mediterranean. At the present day Alexandria enjoys annually about 25 to 30 days of rain with a rainfall of about 8 inches, while Cairo and its environs has on the average, mostly in January, $1\frac{1}{2}$ to 2 inches. In the upper Nile valley on the other hand for as far back as our knowledge reaches, rain has always been an exceptional phenomenon, the accompaniment of occasional storms and less a blessing than a catastrophe, associated in people's minds with the dangerous powers of the desert. Nevertheless rain in the desert that filled the springs for years to come could seem a beneficent miracle; so it did to the author of a hymn praising Min, the Lord of the Eastern Desert, as 'the one who sends the rain-clouds', which has been preserved in an inscription commemorating an expedition to the quarries of the Wadi Hammamat led by King Nebhepetrē' Menthuhotpe of Dynasty XI, about 2010 B.C.[1] But often rain never fell for years.

The water-supply of Egypt is regulated by a remarkable collaboration between the two streams of the Nile, the Blue Nile and the White Nile. The former flows down from the Abyssinian plateau (Lake Tana) through a deeply eroded channel, as also

[1] Couyat and Montet, *Inscriptions du Ouadi Hammâmât*, no. 110.

47

does the Atbara, the only tributary of the Nile which enters the main stream north of Khartum; the latter rises in the area of the African lakes. The Blue Nile and, to a lesser extent, the Atbara carry down the vast volume of the summer rains from June to September and thus bring the flood-water into Egypt. The White Nile, on the other hand, has its waters dammed back for a time by the flood-water of the Blue Nile at their junction above Khartum and it then contributes to bring about only a gradual lessening of the flood and in this way prevents the Nile from drying up in the dry season, as happens to the Atbara in its lowest reaches.

The Nile flood determines the farmer's seasons. The year begins with its rise and it is divided into three seasons, 'Inundation', 'Going down of the Inundation' (Cultivation) and 'Drought' (Harvest). Its varying height means either bumper crops or hunger. Consequently it is of vital importance to study this natural phenomenon and, if possible, to regulate it. Whoever solves this problem controls Egypt and its inhabitants.

According to Egyptian beliefs all water is connected with Nun, the primordial water that lies beneath the earth. The primordial hill, 'the oldest land,' rose up out of Nun at the time of the creation of the world and it is spoken of in such terms as: 'Nothing was heard of it since the time when this land which has risen out of Nun was given boundaries.'[1] One of the favourite themes of Egyptian myth is that on this hill lived the primeval god, also the sun-god. According to this legend the flood-waters rise out of caverns that are supposed to exist near the island of Bigah in the Cataract of Aswan,[2] and perhaps also near the whirlpools in the river at Gebel Silsilah, south of Thebes. Even for the Nile in Lower Egypt a special point of origin was sought, in the typically Egyptian way of thinking, at the point near modern Cairo where the important canal to Heliopolis branches off and where up to modern times at the height of the inundation the opening of the dams was begun in ceremonial fashion.[3] Nilometers enabled the height of the inundation to be measured, the best-known of these being at the 'House of the Inundation' near Old Cairo, in more modern times on the southern point of

[1] In the chapel of Hatshepsut at Karnak.
[2] See below, p. 310.   [3] See below, p. 54.

3. *a.* Predynastic boat in a rock painting in the Wadi Abad.

3. *b.* Grain boats on the Nile.

4. Field workers in the Tomb of Ti at Saqqara.

the Island of Roda. This Nilometer furnished the official readings for use by the government in Memphis and there was another on Elephantine Island at the end of the First Cataract. After the conquest of Nubia in the Middle Kingdom the observation posts were advanced to the narrows of the Second Cataract at Kummah and Semnah to enable a more timely watch to be kept on the approach of the flood. But even when the Egyptians of the New Kingdom advanced their observation posts to Napata at the beginning of the Fourth Cataract the old ideas about the origin of the Nile were not abandoned. In the Ramesside period sacrifices to the Nile certainly dating from primitive times were offered up anew at Gebel Silsilah, south of Thebes, in the third month of summer (on the 15th of the month Epiphi) before the beginning of the inundation and again two months later (on the 15th of the month Thoth) 'so that there should not be a lack of water'.

Egyptian astronomers of the Old Kingdom observed that when the star Sothis, after disappearing for 70 days, rose for the first time in the early morning *before* the sun had risen, it denoted the beginning of the season of inundation. Hence they associated the 'coming forth of Sothis' with New Year's Day and, assuming that their calculations were correct, they possessed the possibility of acquiring a sidereal year of $365\frac{1}{4}$ days which would have been more accurate than the civil year of 360 days (made up of 36 dekans in 12 months) plus 5 epagomenal or intercalary days, by which the Egyptians made their official calculations from the days of Dynasty V.[1] At the time of the unification of the two kingdoms about 3000 B.C. the 'coming forth of Sothis' fell on the 23rd June (by the Gregorian Calendar) when even on the Nilometer at Memphis a rise in the level of the river would already have made itself noticeable. It is, however, exceedingly doubtful whether the Sothic year, which has played such an important part in researches into the Egyptian calendar, ever achieved any practical importance beyond its use in the initial calculation and in the announcement of the seasonal festivals.[2] Nevertheless particular importance has recently been

---

[1] On the mythical origins of the epagomenal days as the birthdays of gods, see Kees, *Götterglaube*, 259f.

[2] Sethe, 'Die Zeitrechnung der alten Ägypter' in *Gött. Nachr. phil.-hist. Kl.* (1919), 311f.

attached to the observations of Sothis in respect of the determining of the start of the first of the lunar months of the year,
with the new moon following the 'coming forth of Sothis'.[1] Whatever the case, however, what was of greater importance for the
Egyptians was the observation of the rising of the inundation
and the noting down of the maximum levels registered by the
Nilometers. From the time of the unification of the two king-
domes royal annals recorded these measurements. In this concern for the inundation is to be found also the key to the administrative organization of the state. Admittedly these measurements, and particularly those made at the official gauge near
Old Cairo, were recorded at different periods according to
different standards of measurement. They could probably, however, be adjusted to standard.

In the annals from the Thinite Period up to Dynasty V,
between about 2950 B.C. and 2500 B.C. the rise of the Nile, probably measured in the neighbourhood of Old Cairo, was on an
average about 4 cubits (approximately 7 feet); therefore a
recorded High Nile of 8 cubits and 3 fingers caused in the following year 'flooding of all the western and eastern (?) nomes'
in the Delta.[2] Lists compiled in the reign of Sesostris I, about
1950 B.C., give the following, far higher, figures for the desirable
height of the flood-waters at various places on the Nile:
Elephantine, 21 cubits, 3⅓ palms, (approximately 39 feet); 'the
House of the Inundation' near Old Cairo, 12 cubits, 3 palms
and 3 fingers (about 21½ feet); for Diospolis or Tell Balamun, the
most northerly town of the Delta, 6 cubits, 3 palms, 3 fingers
(about 11 feet).[3] The many measurements recorded up to
Roman times reveal a further rise of about 20–30 per cent with
the result that the figure for Elephantine reaches 24 cubits, 4
palms (about 42 feet)[4] and, as an idealized figure, 28 cubits (i.e.
equal to 4×7)[5]; for the 'House of the Inundation' at Old Cairo

[1] Parker, *The Calendars of Ancient Egypt*.

[2] The Palermo Stone, *verso* l. 3, no. 4, according to Sethe's explanation.

[3] *JEA*, 30, 34, fig. 1.

[4] Inscription from Edfu: 24 cubits, 3 hand-breadths, 1 finger. Measurements on the Elephantine nilometer in the time of the Roman empire:
25–26 cubits (exceptions!), see Borchardt, *Nilmesser*, 54, 16f.

[5] The 'Famine Stela' of Zoser of Ptolemaic date, l. 6; similarly, Plutarch,
de Iside, 43 and Aristides, *Rhetor. Aigypt.*, II, 485 (Dindorf ed.).

The Countryside

the figure becomes 14–16 cubits,[1] while for the Northern Delta it remains unchanged at 6–7 cubits.[2] This increase can only partly be explained by the rise in the bed of the river which, according to Lyons, amounts to about 4 inches a century; in the course of the centuries separating the reign of Sesostris I from 150 B.C. the rise in the bed would amount to about 6 feet or 3 cubits 3 palms. The fact that ancient writers made use of theoretical and idealized figures is proved by a completely reliable statement by Strabo (Book XVII, 788) that when Petronius was Prefect 12 cubits, that is about 21 feet, of flood-water assured an abundant harvest. He adds that with only 8 cubits there was still no shortage whereas before his time apparently 14 cubits had to be attained before bountiful crops were assured. This measurement of 12 cubits corresponds almost exactly with the Memphite standard under Sesostris I about 2,000 years earlier. As a check on these figures it should be mentioned that in the Third Century B.C. for the purpose of constructing dykes at Memphis the figure of 12 cubits was taken as the highwater mark whereas the actually recorded heights attained by the flood-waters in the years 259 B.C. and 258 B.C. were respectively 10 cubits, 3 palms, $1\frac{1}{6}$ fingers and 10 cubits, 6 palms, $2\frac{2}{3}$ fingers.[3] An inundation that reached the height of 14 cubits at Memphis must therefore have overflowed the dykes.

The heights recorded in these figures were not apparently measured from low water, for its level on the monument of Sesostris I is taken to be almost the same throughout the whole length of the Nile with 4 cubits, 2 palms, $3\frac{1}{3}$ fingers for Upper Egypt and 4 cubits, 3 fingers for Lower Egypt. According to Borchardt, however, all the Nilometers in the country measured from a fixed zero at Roda with a theoretically assumed fall from Elephantine to Memphis. The big rise in the measured numbers, especially for Elephantine, cannot be accounted for by the fact that because of the narrowing of the river through the cataract

[1] 14 cubits (2 × 7), so Plutarch and Aristides, *loc. cit.*; Strabo, XVII, 788; Pliny, *Nat. Hist.*, V, 58, described as Nile of 'hilaritas'. 15–16 cubits, so Herodotus, II, 13. 16 cubits, so Pliny, *loc. cit.*, described as Nile of 'deliciae'. Cf. also the statuary groups of the Nile with 14 children (of the time of Vespasian).

[2] 6 cubits, Plutarch, *de Iside*, 44 (for Mendes and Xois). 7 cubits, the Famine Stela, l. 6, Aristides, *op. cit.*

[3] Wilcken, *Archiv f. Pap.*, 6, 398–9, on *P.S.I*, vol. V, 488.

the highwater mark at Elephantine is higher above low water than is the case at Memphis (Lyons estimates about 23 feet for the former and about 16 feet 6 inches for the latter), or in the Delta where the river broadens to an incomparable extent. The explanation must be sought in the predetermined zero on the gauge.

B. IRRIGATION AND SOIL

The control and utilization of the flood-waters of the Nile was effected in a number of ways: by the building of dykes to protect certain parts of the countryside from flooding, such as gardens and villages; by the construction of enclosed areas or 'basins' to hold the flood-waters which would be released at the right moment by the piercing of the dams; by the laying out of canals for distributing and conducting water from the 'basins' for irrigation purposes; and finally by sinking wells and using the *shâduf*, a water-raising appliance, for the irrigation of gardens. It was because these artificial constructions were more easily carried out in Upper Egypt than in the Delta that Schweinfurth placed the cradle of Egyptian civilization in Upper Egypt. In this he was thinking less of those rudimentary beginnings of artificial irrigation of land on the river-banks such as S. Passarge later had in mind.[1]

The 'basins' of the modern irrigation system, which has been steadily falling into disuse since the construction of the great dams in the valley of the Nile, varied in area from 2,000 to 40,000 *feddans* (2,500 to 50,000 acres). The smallest, therefore, covering at least 2,500 acres, was obviously far bigger in area than those of the Hellenistic Period,[2] which were already, at least in the Fayum, in part turned over to two-crop farming. The fertile Nile mud, which is nevertheless poor in nitrogen content, collected in these 'basins'. One of the oldest administrative titles in the nomes of Lower Egypt and one which was later to be held in high esteem as an historical survival, was that of 'canal-digger'. The official bearing this title was certainly empowered by virtue of his appointment to conscript temporary labour for such work. He is the predecessor of the historical

[1] *Die Urlandschaft Ägyptens*, 132f.
[2] Schnebel, *Landwirtschaft in hellenistischen Ägypten*, 52.

nomarch; while the *Strategos*, his descendant in Graeco-Roman times was far more occupied with irrigation works than with military affairs.[1]

To make as much land as possible accessible to the flood-waters was always regarded as the test of good administration. The princely rulers of the nomes in feudal days specially prided themselves on their achievements in irrigation in years when the flood-waters were low and particularly so if the neighbouring nomes suffered want.[2]

The fact that the spectre of years of famine was invoked precisely in times of internal dissension reveals how strongly the universal dependence upon control of the flood-waters promoted the impulse towards a unified state. Similarly today the greatest anxiety of Egypt is lest the incoming waters of the Nile come under foreign control.

The value of the land depended upon whether it was reached by the normal inundation, could be irrigated artificially, contained springs or lay beside a canal. In assessing annual taxes the State took into consideration the varying productivity of arable land and also the estimated yield of the harvest. Varying land values necessitated a complicated system of assessment and even exercised an influence upon land laws. Details however, largely await elucidation. Flood-water had to be kept away from riparian land and from village enclosures, but it could cover all the land between the boundaries of the villages and edge of the desert (Pl. 18. *a*). It was there that the retreating flood-waters remained the longest in pools.

In the days of basin-irrigation the *felaheen* distinguished between *rei*-fields which were covered by the flood and *sharaki*-land which required artificial irrigation. The ancient Egyptian division of land into what was called 'lowland'[3] and 'upland', apart from the 'islands' that were occasionally the subject of special mention,[4] did not correspond exactly to these two cate-

[1] Cf. possibly the inscriptions on the statue of a Ptolemaic *strategos* from Tanis (Cairo 687), see Kees, 'Tanis' in *Gött. Nachr. phil.-hist. Kl.* (1944), 174.

[2] Vandier, *La Famine dans l'Égypte ancienne.*

[3] In Egyptian *ḫrw*, see *Äg. Wb.*, III, 322; from the Amarna Period, *nḫb*, cf. *op. cit.*, II, 308.

[4] The decree of Sethos I for the temple of Osiris at Abydos distinguishes low land (*nḫb*), islands and upland and 'every formerly productive field', ll. 24–5.

gories. According to evidence from the time of the New Kingdom it is clear that the bulk of arable land was classed as 'upland' with the result that the Greeks translated the Egyptian word simply as 'mainland' or 'corn-bearing land' (*sitophoros*).[1] 'Upland' was therefore, not always *sharaki*-land even though inscriptions from the feudal period of the First Intermediate Period make it appear that to conduct Nile-water to the 'upland' was regarded as typical: 'I made upland into marsh, I let the Nile flood the fallow land' and 'I brought the Nile to the upland in your fields so that plots were watered that had never known water before'.[2] 'Upland' was, therefore, contrasted apparently with 'lowland'; it was such land as could be denied flooding when the inundation fell below normal, but which was normally productive, and consequently, taxable. Real *sharaki*-land was used for orchards and vegetable gardens.

Strabo (Book XVII, 789) says that the flood-waters of the Nile rise for 40 days, that the country then remains for 60 days under water and that afterwards the waters subside rapidly so that cultivation must be speedily carried out. These time limits do not wholly correspond with the normal course of events. The inundation customarily begins at Aswan as early as the end of May or the beginning of June and it attains its height during the first half of September. Further north the dates are somewhat later: at Memphis about 8 to 14 days. The Coptic calendar places *Lelet en-nukta*, 'the night of the drops,' on which, according to ancient myth, a tear-drop from the eye of Isis causes the Nile to rise, on the 18th of June (the Coptic 11th of Baûna). This date is quite near to that 23rd of June (in the Gregorian calendar) on which about 3000 B.C. the theoretical New Year of the Sothic calendar began. At the present day in the second half of August there is celebrated in Cairo at the place where the former canal to Heliopolis, the Fum el-Khalîg, branched off from the Nile, the festival of the piercing of the dam, when it is hoped that the water will rise to a height of 16 cubits (28 feet) on the Nilometer of Roda. In reality, however, the inundation at this point mostly does not reach its height before the middle or the end of September, or sometimes even the beginning of October.

[1] Gardiner, *Wilbour Papyrus*, II, 26–9.
[2] Griffith, *Inscriptions of Siut*, Tomb V, l. 7, Tomb VII, ll. 22–3.

Artificial constructions were able to control the flooding and, in particular, to slow down the rate of subsidence, in a manner similar to that in which it is controlled today by the dams. The lake called Moeris in the Fayum, the predecessor of the Birket Qarûn, was praised by classical authorities as the oldest work of this kind.[1]

The natural phenomenon of the inundation of the Nile had suggested even to the ancient Egyptians the establishment of a national labour service composed of peasants in order to utilise labour at a time when agricultural work was at a standstill. Under the term 'corvée' this service was still notorious at the time of the construction of the Suez Canal. The organization of many activities in the early periods of Egyptian history was clearly based on the three-monthly period of the inundation. This is clear when we remember that Herodotus (II, 124) was told of the three-month shift used for the workmen employed on the building of the pyramid of Cheops; it can be seen in the Pyramid cities of the Old Kingdom where the duties of the mortuary priests were divided into watches (*phyles*) using the ancient nautical terms taken from the transport system. Again, in temples the services were organized in hourly and monthly duties in such a way that 4 shifts regularly relieved each other each month; that is to say that each shift was liable to serve for three months annually.[2] This efficient organization can be traced back to the great kings who built the pyramids and whose reward has been to be regarded by tradition as slave-drivers — a tradition fostered no doubt more by the Greeks than by the Egyptians who would have regarded such actions as unavoidable and natural. From a technical point of view this organization of labour was the prerequisite for the construction of the colossal buildings of the Old Kingdom (Pl. 14. *b*).

The critical period for the farmer was that season called 'the coming-forth', which included the time when the inundation reached its height and the subsequent start of the sowing when the peasant confirmed 'the earth has made its appearance and it is ready for ploughing'. 'The quicker the drying-up, the speedier the ploughing and sowing', says Strabo. Hence it was in this season that the Egyptians celebrated the great festivals

[1] See below, p. 220f.
[2] Kees, 'Die Phylen . . . im Dienst der Tempel' in *Orientalia*, 17 (1948), 71f.

which for the most part had an agricultural background. From their nature these festivals could not, by conforming with the slightly incorrect civil year of 365 days, gradually advance through the seasons; they had their dates determined, or at least revised from time to time according to a fixed year calculated with the help of observations of Sothis.

The king, who was a god and the embodiment of the power of the land, inaugurated these festivals. The god of the land and the king always celebrated their festivals in common. The festival of Sokar, the god who dwelt in a cave on the edge of the desert,[1] began in Memphis on the 26th day of the fourth month of the inundation season, (known as the month of Choiak). At this festival the herds were driven round the walls of the city as if they were going round the threshing-floor in the threshing season. Their necks were hung with trusses of onions and they ploughed up the earth of the god who was himself called 'the Hacker'. The myth suggests that this cutting up of the earth was the preparation for the burial of Osiris which took place on the 30th day of the same month. At this time the *Djed*-pillar was set up as a symbol of renewal and continuity; for the next day, which began the new winter season (the 1st day of Tybi in the Theban calendar), was considered as another New Year's Day for the year and as the canonical coronation day for the king, who was Horus. The king thus regenerated himself at the time of the beginning of the cultivation after the manner in which Horus assumed dominion as the son of the god after the burial of his father, Osiris, the old king. The closeness of the tie between the Egyptians and the soil is revealed by the veneration accorded to the earth-god Geb to whom honour was paid by the hoeing of the ground and whom the myths of the Old Kingdom elevated to the first place in the world inasmuch as he was the spokesman of the gods and the heir of the ancient god Atum of Heliopolis.[2] Their hymns praise him and the unpersonified Nile as the preservers of life.

The State, or, more precisely, the king's commissioners, paid especial regard to agriculture as the core of Egyptian economy, which the peasant had carried as a heavy burden through the centuries. Water-rights, changes brought about by the action of the current especially on islands and riparian land, boundary

---

[1] See below, p. 148.   [2] Kees, *Götterglaube*, p. 227.

stones — all these matters had to be supervised. They were the business of the 'overseer of the fields' and of his assistant, the surveyor. According to a papyrus dating from the Middle Kingdom, from Haragah at the entrance to the Fayum, the measuring of cultivated land preceded the harvest and in that place would seem to have been carried out on the 15th day of the second month of the inundation-season.[1] At this period the calendrical seasons did not coincide with the natural seasons and this date corresponded in fact to about the 19th of January. The results of the survey furnished the material on which the harvest-tax was based. The State for its own convenience preferred to burden its tenants with a fixed tax on produce and in this way to throw upon their shoulders alone the risk of bad years. We know that Ptolemy Philadelphus acted in accordance with this principle and from the evidence of financial documents from the Ramesside Period it seems to have been in operation already at that time.[2] It is certainly not by chance that in the New Kingdom among the sins from which the judge in the other world must absolve the dead before they can gain salvation are (as the 125th chapter of the Book of the Dead enumerates): lessening of the arable area, falsifying the boundaries of the arable land, 'damming up the water in his time,' illegal damming up (of the 'basins') and the selfish infringement of water-rights and land-rights to the injury of a neighbour.

Planning, Production and Distribution are the chief tasks of the state-controlled natural economy. In Ancient Egypt the harvest was the result of the winter season to a far greater extent than today and had to be gathered in during the spring months of March and April; this meant storing up supplies for two seasons in the granary. The grain had to be sufficient for all engaged on public works from those employed on canal- and dyke-construction to the stone-masons in the quarries, the workmen engaged on building the pyramids, tombs and temples, and also the officials who, in theory and, in early times, literally, lived 'from the table of the ruler'.[3] In periods of fully developed private business every landowner, every government authority, each temple and each religious foundation had to calculate and

[1] Smither, *JEA*, 27, 76.
[2] Gardiner, *JEA*, 27, 62, on Turin Papyrus 1887.
[3] Kees, *Kulturgeschichte*, 196.

distribute the supplies, independently of what legal foundation their property rested upon. The test of the government of the day was whether it was successful in this task, as the nomarchs regularly maintained it was in their idealized biographies written for posterity — 'I was the computer for the consumption of Lower Egyptian grain (barley), one who dispensed water in broad daylight'[1] — or whether, notwithstanding the most exact assessments and harsh oppression of tenants, the result was only empty granaries and demonstrations by hungry workmen.[2] After the dissolution of the Old Kingdom the decentralized feudal state demonstrated frequently that, in spite of the flamboyant optimism of its rulers, local self-interest was the sole means of defence in the struggle for existence: 'When Upper Egypt was in a bad state' . . . 'I closed the frontiers' so that supplies and the harvest might suffice in the writer's nome. For at such times grain ships voyaged far into the country bearing corn-merchants who endeavoured to create a shortage.

Among precautionary measures clearly were the provision and distribution of seed-corn. We learn from feudal times that loans of seed-corn were made to be repaid at harvest time. An exemplary nomarch praises himself for having remitted payment of these loans in years of scarcity. Teams of oxen were also lent out for ploughing and threshing.[3]

The harvest months were the first two of the summer or 'harvest' season, Pachons and Payni in the Theban calendar; they correspond to the spring months of Northern Europe. In the month of Pachons, apparently on the eve of the new moon, the great festival of Amun-Min was celebrated in Thebes when the king cut the first sheaf of emmer as an offering to the god and a white bull was led along in the procession. This festival sprang perhaps from the ancient festival of the 'going-forth of Min' which was mentioned in the inscriptions in the tombs of the Old Kingdom in the Memphite Necropolis. At the same time, on the day of the new Moon at the beginning of the month Horus of Edfu began his annual journey to visit Hathor of Denderah in the course of which harvest rites were again performed, in this case the treading out of the corn. At this time also was held the festival of Termuthis, the 'nurse-snake' and

[1] *Op. cit.*, p. 40, after Griffith, *Siut*, V.
[2] See below, p. 277. [3] *Op. cit.*, p. 41.

protectress of the granaries, who lived in the fields. In Thebes during the New Kingdom on the 1st day of Pachons which was called 'the birthday of the corn (Nepre)', Termuthis was brought the first fruits of the harvest in her character as mother of the corn-god,[1] a custom which was allowed in later times by the landowners and nomarchs and is so today by the village headman. In the Fayum in the Hellenistic Period the festival of Isis-Termuthis was not celebrated until the 20th of Pachons,[2] in the middle of March, when the whole countryside took part and a tenth of the harvest was presented to the goddess. The harvest tax of which we have evidence from the time of the New Kingdom as being paid to the State, was probably derived from ancient royal prerogatives; apparently not even the temples were exempt from it.

Model letters used by students training for the civil service in the New Kingdom paint a graphic picture of how miserably the peasants fared when the harvest was poor and the royal scribe landed on the quay with his Nubian policemen to assess the harvest. A saying that was old in those days declared sarcastically of the peasant: 'His reckoning lasts until eternity.'[3] Myths grew up naturally around farm life. The corn that was trodden out on the threshing-floor, and this was done in Ancient Egypt by the hooves of animals driven round and round the circular threshing-floor, was Osiris who was 'struck', or it was the serpent-enemy who was impaled on the fork. And as the animals who were doing the threshing were driven on by blows this meant that they were being punished because they trod upon the god Osiris in the corn. For the god lived in the corn, he nourished man and beast with it, he sprouted anew out of the earth in which he was laid as a corpse and which 'was hoed' for him for his burial. Other myths declared that the god was drowned in the 'new water' of the inundation that spread over the land after the harvest and that he revealed himself in this way by his fertilising power.

The ancient Egyptian farmer like the modern *fellah* clung to

---

[1] Wreszinski, *Atlas*, I, pl. 188 (from the Tomb of Khaemhat, the Overseer of the Granaries of the time of Amenophis III).

[2] Vogliano, *Primo rapporto degli scavi . . . di Medînet Mâdi* (1936), p. 44; see below, p. 225.

[3] Erman, *Literatur der Ägypter*, pp. 103, 246f.

the soil notwithstanding all his worries. His realism and his hopes were reflected in two notions about eternity: he expected to do for the gods in the other world the same forced labour that he did on earth and against this he sought to protect himself after his own fashion. Among the popular funerary texts inscribed on coffins from the beginning of the Heracleopolitan period onwards are found, therefore, spells that guarantee a man reunion in the other world with his family, including his servants, by order of the gods[1] and 'freed from the enforced service to Seth, from the numbering of great Isis, from the side of Osiris, Lord of the West' or, more briefly, 'freed from every god, every goddess, all the dead, each one of the dead'. Others bear a label such as 'It is not allowed that one of the blessed should be required to work in the Underworld' or 'No work to be done in the other world'. For this reason the dead as a precaution had substitute-workmen, the well-known *ushabtis*, placed in the grave with them so that they could 'answer' in the dead man's name when the dead were summoned to work. The Egyptian word for 'answer' was *usheb*, hence the name *ushabti*. On the dykes, however, where in Egypt men were enrolled for compulsory 'hourly work', stood the 'condemned', 'to whose charge something had been laid in the Island of Fire,' particularly blasphemers against the gods.[2] The Egyptian conception of paradise was, nevertheless, largely of a peasant nature. In 'the Field of Reeds' under the 'Spirits of the East' the blessed tilled and harvested, admittedly in divine proportions; even in paradise the Egyptian could not wholly free himself from his earthly cares.

At the time when the structure of the State became many-sided complications arose out of the obligations of people towards the performance of public works and the servitude brought about by conscription by royal commissioners. From the time of Dynasty V we know of royal decrees of exemption for foundations, in particular for the Pyramid cities established in connection with the royal mortuary temples, then for temple lands and, at the close of the Old Kingdom, for pious foundations endowed by privileged private individuals, usually relations of the king; the decrees declared such establishments to be

[1] Kees, *Totenglauben*, 308f.
[2] De Buck, *Coffin Texts*, IV, Spell 317 (Transformation into the Nile).

'protected and free'. This dispensation, however, did not mean that the inhabitants of such places were to be freed from all secular work by reason of their priestly 'hourly service' — the Egyptians were too practical to expect that — but only from certain public taxes and specific menial duties which were usually enumerated in each case. Such people therefore, had their estates 'reserved' but they had to carry out all the work needed on them, as, for example, the cultivators of the *sharaki*-land attached to the Pyramid cities or the usufructuaries of pious endowments.[1] Such exemptions also served as if they were statutes of self-management and gave protection from interference by the all-powerful provincial authorities. Within the foundations, however, life undoubtedly went on in the manner in which it is ironically portrayed in a model letter dating from the Ramesside Period: 'The priest stands as a cultivator and the novice works on the canal . . . he is wet through in the river and he makes no distinction between winter or summer, whether the sky is windy or whether it is raining.'[2] It is interesting to find that we can illustrate this description with a scene from the tomb of Panehsy, a priest of Amun at Thebes at this time.[3] A *w'eb*-priest (novice) is here portrayed ploughing with a team of oxen while his wife scatters the seed. From this scene it would appear that even a priest of high rank, in this case a priest of Amun, might have to plough and to plough not just in the Field of Reeds of the other world but on temple land which the priest and his family cultivated just like the inhabitants of the ancient Pyramid cities.

C. PROPERTY AND USUFRUCT

The Egyptian monarchy was divine and in consequence the king was theoretically the sole owner of the land. He possessed the deeds of bestowal granted him as heir of the King of the Gods, 'the secret of both persons (Horus and Seth), the *meks,* which my father (Osiris) gave me in the presence of Geb'.[4] Here we can see an indication of the trust in the written word commonly held by Orientals who always demand the production of

---

[1] See below, p. 158.   [2] *Papyrus Sallier*, I, 7, 6.
[3] Foucart, *Tombeau de Panehesy* (*Mem. Inst. fr. or.*, 57, 2), fig. 23.
[4] See *ÄZ*, 52, 68 (from Edfu).

title-deeds when claims are made in respect of rights specified in them. Consequently the king carried them clearly in his hand in a case called the *meks* as, for example, on the jubilee of his accession, the *sed*-festival, when he ran round the field cere-monially four times; an action called 'traversing the earth' in ritual texts where it is elevated to the status of a divine action symbolizing taking possession anew of the land. The king was accompanied by the warlike jackal-god, Wepwawet of Asyut who represented Upper Egypt while the Lower Egyptian half of the realm was personified by the Apis bull of Memphis moving 'at a quick pace' as it was wont to do at the periodical 'running forth' of Apis to fertilize the herds.[1] Here again we can observe the contrast between the wild animal of Upper Egypt and the useful breeding animal of the Lower Egyptian farmer. Here clearly two different formative elements of the 'Two Lands' find unwitting expression in their two representatives.

The king, like a great lord who makes presents to his guests, could give away portions of the god's property as 'gifts' to gods, such as by assigning to them cattle specially counted for this purpose or estates together with their revenues and livestock. He could also give estates, cattle and servants to members of his family or to people whom he regarded as their equals because of their position in society. All such 'gifts' were, therefore, in principle royal prerogatives transferred to particular persons and at no time was the right of the king to take back his property contested no matter how harshly such an action might some-times affect a whole class of persons. A way was sought, how-ever, as was usually the case in Egypt, to make practice conform to altered circumstances so that a principle that threatened the security of private property should be deprived of its severity in application. In early times, and perhaps as late as Dynasty IV (when the government of the State was essentially confined in patriarchal fashion to members of the royal family who, as sharers in the godly power, were qualified to act in the king's name), the subsistence of the whole country could be assured by the produce of nature. The supply and distribution of this produce was entrusted to a royal Master of the Food, the 'Overseer of Gifts'. This system which was modelled on that of a large family, was no longer adequate when at the height of the

[1] Von Bissing and Kees, *Re-Heiligtum*, III, 7f.

The Countryside

Old Kingdom it became necessary to employ others to carry out the king's commands. The increasing number of those 'honoured before the great god' clamoured also for a greater security of possession and the right to personal disposal of property for the purpose of providing for their families.

From this situation arose two typically Egyptian principles for action. In the first place there was the attempt to secure hereditary tenure of office or at least the reversion of office by father to son together with all acquired property; secondly the desire to set up at the tomb a perpetual endowment for the cult of the deceased. These two aims were interdependent. The king himself set the example while the legend of Osiris and Horus idealized the person of the heir. The maintenance of the endowment for the cult of the deceased was added as an obligation to the right acquired by the eldest son in his role as 'master of all my possessions'. In accordance with the rules laid down for the endowment the eldest son, as heir and new head of the family, could call upon his brothers and sisters to share in the duties of the cult of the deceased in return for a share in the produce from the land belonging to the endowment.

Confronted with this opposition between the desire for hereditability and the royal prerogative the Egyptians were, from time to time, successful in discovering temporary means for overcoming a seemingly irreconcilable conflict of principles. Thus a favoured person could, with the king's approval, obtain for himself 'in turn', that is at second-hand, endowments for funerary offerings that had perhaps been assigned by a former king on behalf of his deceased mother.[1] At the same time, therefore, that the newly appointed mortuary priest entered into service he took over the control of the old foundation. In this way expenses were saved and the continued existence of the old endowment formally assured. Otherwise the time would have come when the king had nothing more to give away as endowments and then the claims of the living would become stronger than piety towards ancestors. There can be no doubt, therefore, that at those times when decisive changes took place in the structure of the State, such as the accession to power of a new dynasty, old endowments came to an end and their revenues

[1] So already in early Dynasty IV, *Urk.*, I, 4, cf. Kees, *Kulturgeschichte*, 246f., and Kunker, *Gîza*, III, 5f.

devolved upon new beneficiaries. In the New Kingdom and particularly during the Ramesside Period for which we possess extensive documentary records, it can easily be seen from tax-lists and priestly titles to what extent the funerary cults were kept alive or in practice ignored in the older mortuary temples, by observing whether or not they had their own priest assigned to them. During the Late Period pious rulers like the Saite kings of Dynasty XXVI certainly made an attempt to 'renew' (by which is meant 'provide for') the funerary endowments established for themselves by earlier kings with famous names, by making certain that some beneficiary took charge of them. Nobody, however, would have considered making new donations for this purpose.

The rights and privileges granted to anyone could, therefore, at any time be withdrawn in so far as this was not contrary either to the tradition that made the rewarding of services by the ruler a duty, or to the actual wording of an attested decree. In point of fact far-reaching regroupings of private property were brought about by changes of government. This possibility is well observed in the case of the petty kingdoms of the princely nomarchs which had sprung up in Upper Egypt during the feudal period that succeeded Dynasty V and had become virtually independent after the break-up of the Old Kingdom, these little principalities were mostly liquidated during the Middle Kingdom and the process was finally completed during the New Kingdom. A unified state with a centralized administration is naturally opposed to feudalism. It is doubtful whether the nomarchs, as they themselves maintained, were actually only reviving as lords of the manor claims dating from remote antiquity; unfortunately we know too little about the organization of the country in early times to judge in this matter; but it does seem that the pretensions of the nomarchs to establish petty kingdoms with divine origins which would make them the equals of the kings of Egypt in the matter of divine prerogatives, were suspiciously designed to serve a purpose. For as far as we can see with our present state of knowledge the historical petty princedoms of the nomarchs in feudal times were created by governors who had been appointed by the king and who had become firmly established in their provinces.[1]

[1] Kees, *Kulturgeschichte*, 201f.

The Countryside

Apart from the mortuary endowments and nomarchs' land two other categories of land-ownership were of importance: temple and other pious foundations for the service of the gods and private property given as gratuities to veterans together with the subsidiary category of soldiers' settlements.

Temple property rested upon the same legal basis as the endowments of the Pyramid cities and of the royal mortuary temples. Its continuance was also affected by historical changes and was closely dependent upon the fortunes of the kingdom. The very scanty information that we possess certainly points to the fact that up to the time of Dynasty IV, the time of the builders of the great pyramids, the amounts disbursed for the upkeep of the Pyramid cities and the royal mortuary service exceeded the expenditure on the temples of the gods. The king as the 'great god' was positively the centre of the world, and he was this in no vain sense. It did not imply any contempt for the gods or any insolent pride as the Greeks suggested on viewing the Great Pyramid at Giza. It accorded with the correctness of the world order as it was known to that age.

It was not until the accession of Dynasty V with the accompanying predominance of the Heliopolitan worship of the sun that gifts to temples became considerable. Preference was given to the tutelary gods of the state sanctuaries and then to Rē'-Harakhte and Hathor, the gods of the sun sanctuaries recently established by the kings.[1] The lands required for this purpose were for the most part provided by the Delta nomes. That the new buildings and endowments of the 'Son of Rē'' bore the character almost of purely family concerns is shown by the customary formula used in the deeds of gift: 'King X made this for his father Rē'.' In the New Kingdom the state temple of Amen-Rē' at Karnak was the recipient of such rich gifts that it was assured pre-eminence for all time. The case was not the same, however, with all temples. Tax records show that the temples of Lower Egypt with the exception of a few in Memphis and Heliopolis, even in the days of Dynasty XX (about 1150 B.C.), possessed no land in Middle Egypt between Minia and the Fayum; the temples of Upper Egypt as far south as Hermonthis on the contrary held large estates in this area.[2] In

[1] Palermo Stone, see *Urk.*, I, 240–9.
[2] Wilbour Papyrus of the time of Ramesses V, edited by A. H. Gardiner.

Upper Egypt proper the situation with regard to temple lands was even more one-sided. In contrast, however, the temple of Khnum at Elephantine in the extreme south of the land held property in the Delta.[1] In this respect the Delta still served as a district for colonization and it was only during the Saite Period (663–525 B.C.) that this situation altered for the benefit of the most venerated temples in that fertile lowland. Influenced by the immense size of the property figures in the Great Harris Papyrus, A. Erman assumed that they showed the whole extent of the property owned by the temples in the reign of Ramesses III (about 1160 B.C.).[2] But Schädel has shown that these figures referred only to the new endowments made by that king.[3] This misunderstanding happened through the omission of the ancient wealth of the temples of Amun at Karnak and Luxor and also of the famous provincial temples such as those of Khnum at Elephantine, of Horus at Edfu and of Hathor at Denderah, to mention only a few of the better-known names. The Theban section of the papyrus on the other hand enumerates the donations and gifts made to the mortuary temple of Ramesses III at Medinet Habu and also those to the sanctuary built by Ramesses III in the forecourt of the Temple of Karnak. Similar new foundations at Memphis, Heliopolis and Piramesse and at provincial temples complete the lists.

Ramesses III for his new foundations at Thebes expended 909 square miles of land containing 86,486 people, for those at Heliopolis 167 square miles and 12,364 people and for those at Memphis 11 square miles and 5,685 people. If it is assumed that the area of cultivable land in Egypt was no smaller at that time than it is today, then it means that Ramesses III up to his death in a time that was shaken by external and internal crises was able to assign to his own endowments in the land almost 10 per cent of the agricultural area of Egypt. This could not have been possible without encroaching on older endowments, in particular those made for the mortuary temples of his predecessors. Schädel puts the position as follows: 'The legal situation must have been of such a nature that the property of a funerary temple reverted to the Crown on the death of its builder and that the obligation of caring for the preservation of

---

[1] Gardiner, *JEA*, 27, on Turin Papyrus 1887.
[2] *Zur Erklärung des Papyrus Harris.* [3] *Die Listen des grossen Papyrus Harris.*

the cult rested upon the Crown. This obligation was associated with the practice by which the property of these buildings was secured for Amun by the endowment of a new mortuary temple and was probably enlarged in the majority of cases.'[1] The divine kingship thus regarded itself as autonomous in the matter of royal endowments and had only to respect the sacrosanctity of institutions set up for perpetuity. Their sacrosanctity, however, largely depended on the posthumous fame of the founder. Proscribed rulers like Hatshepsut and the kings of the Amarna period, half-forgotten rulers and, more especially, officials and courtiers who finished their careers in disgrace could not count on any consideration and their benefices were allowed to lapse. The matter was quite the opposite, however, with cults that gained in sanctity like that of Amenophis I and his mother Ahmes-Nefertari which flourished in the west side of Thebes in the Ramesside Period. The young Ramesses II gives us a very candid picture, naturally for the sake of his own fame, of how, after the death of his father Sethos I, things looked very black for his great endowments in Abydos.[2]

The inventories in the Great Harris Papyrus do not permit of any comparison with the statement of Diodorus (in Book I, 21. 73) that one-third of the land was owned by the temples. Our only source of knowledge of the total landed possessions of a temple is the inventory, compiled at a later date, of the lands possessed by the temple of Horus at Edfu, a provincial temple in the upper Thebaid situated in poor country.[3] According to this source, in the reign of the last Egyptian king, Nectanebos II, this temple owned 13,209 *arouras* of land, i.e. 8,806 acres, in the four nomes of the upper Thebaid, of which 5,660 *arouras* were of what was called 'new land', that is insular land, and 7,548 of irrigated land which was in reality 'upland'. The bulk of the land lay in the nome of Edfu while the high proportion of insular land is characteristic for the narrow valley of the Nile. It includes the land surrounded by canals in the area subject to the inundation.

A similar picture of the conditions of land-ownership in the district north of Hermopolis is contained in the tax lists preserved in the Wilbour Papyrus which was written 10 years after

---

[1] *Op. cit.*, p. 48. [2] See below, p. 248.
[3] W. Otto, *Priester und Tempel*, I, 263f. The lists in Brugsch, *Thesaurus*, 538f.

the death of Ramesses III. Even the land owned by the principal temple of the area was parcelled up into plots mostly of 5, 10 and 20 *arouras* ($3\frac{1}{4}$, $6\frac{1}{2}$, 13 acres) while plots of 40 *arouras* (26 acres) occur only very rarely.[1] These plots were interspersed between properties belonging to the Upper Egyptian temples, especially the domain of Amun and the royal mortuary temples. If it is remembered that climatic conditions in the Nile valley favour small holdings, it becomes obvious that a central administration or a uniform system of inspection of such widely scattered properties was impossible or, at least, uneconomic. Accordingly we observe a whole army of officials, overseers of cattle, clerks, superannuated military officials and numerous 'stewards' (193 are named alone) at work, who were rightly feared by the peasants for their harsh exactions.[2] We may well wonder how many usufructuaries without qualification may have been included in their number! Conditions on the *khato*-land which was cultivated for the Crown were better in so far as holdings were there mostly of 10 to 20 *arouras*, that is between $6\frac{1}{2}$ and 13 acres in size; while there were also holdings of over 100 *arouras* and even some of 200 to 340 *arouras*.[3]

Nevertheless, at this time there were large blocks of holdings being cultivated for the same person. First in this class of land-owners was Usimare'nakhte, the son of the powerful High Priest of Amun, Ramessesnakhte, and himself the chief official of Amun and at the same time, apparently, the chief assessor. Second to him was a standard-bearer of the Residence. The consideration which the State in its then relatively powerless condition was obliged to show towards these two men cannot have contributed much towards the national economy.

The inventory of the landed possessions of the temples reveals that these originated in donations from all quarters and not only from the kings. The more that private landed property was increased by royal gifts the greater was the effect of the royal example of gaining favour through gifts of land, cattle and bondsmen. Such gifts profited both the temples of the gods and the royal mortuary temples. An example of this practice in the New Kingdom is the endowment established in Memphis by an official of Amenophis III who had been greatly enriched by the

---

[1] Gardiner, *Wilbour Papyrus*, II, 72.
[2] See below, p. 73f.   [3] *Op. cit.*, p. 181.

King; it was for the chapel containing his King's statue which
was associated economically with the neighbouring temple of
Ptah.[1] Another case is that of a senior official who had been a
royal scribe and an architect of the mortuary temple of Ramesses III; he made a donation of a domain for Amun out of his
estate on the west bank of the Nile.[2] It is significant that in this
latter case the donation consisted of newly cultivated land in the
north-west Delta which had previously been marsh (*birket*). The
fact that the donation stela with its usual representation of the
presentation of the field to a divinity became more common in the
time of the theocratic state, especially during Dynasties XXII–
XXIII was no accident. In later times the officials and army
officers of the Saite kings created conspicuously large foundations and, for the first time, in Upper Egypt on behalf of temples
in the Delta. Such foundations could not have been considered
unless they had been preceded by expropriations from the leading classes of Upper Egypt.[3] Thus, for example, the royal Chief
Official and Overseer of the Treasury, Peftjaudineith made
under Amasis of Dynasty XXVI a donation of the estate of
Kerkeusiris which consisted of 1,000 *arouras* (about 670 acres) to
the temple of Osiris at Abydos.[4] Likewise, in the fourth year of
the reign of Apries (584 B.C.) the General Neshor transferred
1,600 *arouras* (about 1,070 acres) within the 10th Upper Egyptian
nome (Antaeopolis) to the famous temple of the ram at Mendes.[5]

The usual representation on the donation stelae proves that
such gifts were made in the king's name and probably the kings
ascribed to themselves these 'voluntary' gifts made by their subjects. In this respect we have only to recall the assertion of
Ramesses III in the Great Harris Papyrus. Naturally the wealth
that enabled such gifts to be made did ultimately come 'from
the favour of the king'. Moreover, while the temples certainly
gained from them they had in return to grant priestly sinecures
or administrative posts to approved government servants and
soldiers. From the time of the New Kingdom this system of

---

[1] Petrie, *Memphis*, V, pls. 79–80, with translation by Gardiner; cf. Kees,
Kulturgeschichte, 247.

[2] Gardiner, *JEA*, 34, 19f., on *Annales du Service*, 47, 15f.

[3] Kees, 'Zur Innenpolitik der Saïtendynastie' (*Gött. Nachr. phil.-hist. Kl.*,
1935).

[4] Louvre Stela A., 93.   [5] *ÄZ*, 72, 40f. (stela in Copenhagen).

benefits had come increasingly into use. Hence whatever came directly or indirectly to the temple by the royal hand was in this way again made to serve the interests of the State.

It is quite clear that because of this reshuffling all land could not be subject to the same law with regard to title, at least according to the law of usage. In the Old Kingdom it is noteworthy that both *sharaki*-land, which required artificial irrigation and therefore needed increased labour, and newly settled land — so-called 'settlements' or 'new villages' — were favoured when donations were made and invested with privileges, the purpose being clearly to promote internal colonization. Officials frequently held endowments for the cult of the dead which were known as 'the foundations of NN' (where NN stands for the names of the owners of the tombs), the endowment lands being in the districts where the officials carried out their duties. Such was the case with Metjen, a master of the hunt, as early as the beginning of Dynasty IV.[1] Hence the endowments held by the nobles in the Old Kingdom as new foundations or as royal gifts, inasmuch as they were not feudatory, lay in preference in the Delta nomes, like those of Ptahhotpe who was buried in the Residence and of his father Akhtihotpe who was vizir under Asosi.[2] Their estates reveal the same economic weakness of dispersion that is found in the temple properties of the New Kingdom were built up in the same way. One special class of inhabitants of the Pyramid cities of the Old Kingdom who cultivated land there as a royal funerary endowment, took their designation from a word meaning 'garden, terrace, upland'.[3] The royal decrees of protection were directed precisely towards the replenishment of the ranks of the cultivators by conscription. A decree of Pepi I on behalf of the two Pyramid cities of Snofru states: 'My Majesty has ordered that the tenant farmers of these two Pyramid cities be brought up to full strength and that all the children of the residents be numbered off so that they may be placed under the control of these two Pyramid cities.'[4] In this case it was for the most part a question of *sharaki*-land. The levies mostly consisting of landless persons

[1] *Urk.*, I, 4 for 12 settlements of Metjen in three Delta nomes.
[2] Davies, *Ptahhetep*, II, 25–7 and pl. 4, 15; see also below, p. 188.
[3] *ḥntiw-š*, mostly translated 'farmer'; opposed by Junker, *Gîza*, VI, 15f.
[4] *Urk.*, I, 212; on which see Kees, *Kulturgeschichte*, 43.

gained a better social standing in the new foundations. Henku the nomarch of the 'Cerastes-mountain' nome on the opposite bank of the Nile from Asyut illustrates the customary law with regard to reclaimed land in the words: 'I settled villages that lay waste in this nome with cattle and people from other nomes and those who had been slaves in these (other nomes) here I raised to be notables (with landed property).'[1] While in Upper Egypt *sharaki*-land and upland were used for such improvements, in the Delta flood-land and marsh were used. Ordinary arable land appears to have been excepted from these special forms of settlement and it is in such land that we must suppose lay the bulk of the royal land. It seems that survivals of these traditional customs continued to operate in the distinction between royal and temple land at a time when the temples had long since possessed enormous estates and herds. By chance we learn from a dispute over a priestly benefice in Teudjoi (modern el-Hibah) in the Saite Period that an overseer of land, acting as the representative of the Treasury, took possession of arable land on the island of Hibah which was cultivated by the priests of the temple of Amun at Hibah, on the grounds that a temple could own property only in the area of 'open land' and therefore beyond the limits of the inundation.[2] From the same time (the reign of Amasis, 568–526 B.C.) dates the endowment we have already mentioned of 1,000 *arouras* for a new foundation from open land in the Thinite nome for the service of the temple of Osiris at Abydos and which was principally cultivated for market gardens and vineyards. Again it was *sharaki*-land.

Nevertheless, restrictions of this kind were not always observed in practice. Just as arable land was available in the Old Kingdom for the small-holders of the royal Pyramid cities (the *ḥntiw-š*), so too could temples own similar land under some title or other. At the close of the Feudal Age the nomarch of el-Kab was accordingly confirmed by the king in the ownership of the 'God's Land' in the district of Agni north of el-Kab on the east bank of the Nile. It consisted of 200 *arouras* of low land and 1,200 *arouras* of upland, and in this case the best land was included in the temple estate.[3] Tuthmosis III in speaking of his great dona-

---

[1] *Urk.*, I, 78 (from the beginning of the Heracleopolitan Period).

[2] Griffith, *Catalogue of the Rylands Papyri*, III, 101; on 'open land' or plain, see above, p. 30.   [3] Tylor, *Tomb of Sebeknakht*; L. *D.* III, 13b.

tions in Upper and Lower Egypt to the temple of Amun mentions 'tillage', 'gardens' and 'hoed fields' that 'are to be subject to the tax on cultivated land and are to produce the proper produce [for the daily offerings to the God . . .]'.[1] In this case, however, it may only have been a question of the surrendering of the usufruct or of the heavy tithes from the land in favour of the temple.

Documents dating from the Ramesside Period and the succeeding transitional period show that a distinction was then drawn between the so-called *khato* land, which was cultivated on behalf of the Treasury, and the 'lands of the free' (the *nmḥi*), especially in the category of land classified as upland. In this respect lands belonging to temples were frequently called '*khato* land of Pharaoh' and in this way were made subject to the Crown.[2] We are unable to decide at present whether such land was derived originally from royal foundations and had remained burdened by specific limitations or whether the king for some special reason had encroached on the temple estates by virtue of his supreme right of ownership. The relations in respect of ownership between Crown property and temple property were at all events so fluid that in times of distress confiscations would certainly not have stopped short of temple property. For such autocratic action it was not necessary first to have a Cambyses!

The political testament of the Heracleopolitan King Merikarēʿ advised the heir to the throne as a matter of proved experience to reward the levies and in particular his personal entourage with pensions, lands and herds. Ancient tradition and the dictates of prudence demanded that such action should be taken. From the time of the New Kingdom small estates also frequently owed their origin to the rewarding of veterans with land and serfs as an expression of gratitude for services rendered to the king. Thus a famous veteran who had served Ahmose, the king who liberated Egypt from the Hyksos, acquired at el-Kab two gifts each of 5 *arouras* of land as a reward for repeated proofs of bravery.[3] Again, the estate of a certain Mose over which a protracted legal battle was fought between the heirs in the Ramesside Period originated in a reward given by Ahmose

---

[1] *Urk.*, IV, 746 (at Karnak).

[2] Gardiner, *Wilbour Papyrus*, II, 167f.; Gardiner translates ꜣḥt nmḥi as 'tenanted land'.   [3] *Urk.*, IV, 6.

to one of their ancestors.[1] A similar system of compensations and rewards probably existed already in the Old Kingdom for the 'peaceful Nubians' mentioned in the protection decrees who were in reality Nubian auxiliaries in the royal service.[2]

Economically, especially from the Ramesside Period onwards, the preponderance of royal foundations shifted from the temples of the gods to the royal mortuary temples, particularly to the Ramesseum and Medinet Habu.[3] This change, however, indicated in general a return to the custom of the Pyramid Age.

In the Ramesside Period another economic question, that of farm labourers, became urgent. We know from documents that in the New Kingdom the independent farmer had to change over to working the land with paid labourers and slaves.[4] The great Crown domains and temple estates overcame the difficulty by employing prisoners of war who were settled on the land in gangs and in the reign of Ramesses III a colony of convicts is known to have existed.[5] The origin of such convicts is revealed for example in the decree of Sethos I for the Temple of Osiris at Abydos: in line 73 the penalty for the theft of temple cattle is laid down as the cutting off of the nose and forced labour on temple lands. All these things show how difficult it was to satisfy the demand for labour on the land. Unreliable temporary workers and the increasing pressure from taxes and requisitions, especially in wartime, threatened a breakdown in the agricultural life of the country. Grave crises occurred in the late Ramesside Period from these causes. The letter of an official written in the reign of Merenptah of Dynasty XIX reports: 'Of the cultivators of the estate of Pharaoh which is under the authority of my lord, two have fled from the stable-master Neferhotpe as he beat them (probably when requisitioning). Now Look! The fields now lie abandoned and there is no-one there to till them.'[6] This passage throws light on the injuriousness of the requisitioning system against the misuse of which the regent Horemheb had already taken action.[7] We can see in this

[1] Gardiner, *Inscription of Mes*, 8.
[2] *Urk.*, I, 211 (Dynasty VI).   [3] See below, p. 274.
[4] A Dynasty XVIII contract, see Gardiner, *ÄZ*, 43, 27f.
[5] Papyrus Amiens 5, 3 = Gardiner, *Ramesside Administrative Documents*, 7.
[6] Papyrus Bologna, 1094, 2, 7f.
[7] For examples see below, pp. 78, 90, 103.

situation too symptoms of decline which resemble the flight of cultivators from the land in the late Roman Period in Egypt. In the Ramesside Period the Government sought to protect itself against this flight from the land by granting estates to men of all classes — priests, retired army officers, soldiers (including foreigners) or artisans — who had to cultivate the land at their own expense. This system also, however, seems to have failed completely, probably for the reason that preference in making grants of land was given to the members of those families which the impotent Crown had to placate because it was under an obligation to them. Despite a skilfully devised scheme of taxation and levies the final result was empty granaries in the capital, Thebes, hunger marches and sit-down strikes by workmen in the Necropolis. Such disturbances began as early as the reign of Ramesses III, the very ruler who, by his foundations, sought to become the greatest benefactor of the Egyptian gods.[1]

D. FARMING AND HORTICULTURE

It is from papyri of the Hellenistic Period that we acquire our earliest detailed information about methods of agriculture.[2] The three chief cereals were barley (*iot*), emmer (*boti*) and winter wheat, and of these it was the six-headed barley that was mostly grown in the Old and Middle Kingdoms; it was classified by variety into Upper Egyptian and Lower Egyptian barley. By the time of the New Kingdom, however, grain returns such as those contained in the Wilbour Papyrus of Dynasty XX date present emmer (*boti*=Greek ὄλυρα) in the first place. This position it continued to hold down to the Late Period when Herodotus (Book II, chapter 77) reported that it was the grain chiefly used in Egypt for κυλλῆστις-bread. The introduction of Hellenistic methods of cultivation raised the proportion of winter wheat in the winter grain crop to 65–99 per cent and wheat became in consequence Egypt's chief export as cotton is today. Excavation has shown that emmer (*triticum dicoccum*) and barley (*hordeum vulgare vel hexastichum*) were grown in the neolithic settlements on the north side of the Fayum;[3] and recent

[1] See pp. 66, 277.
[2] Schnebel, *Landwirtschaft im hellenistischen Ägypten*, 218f.
[3] Caton-Thompson and Gardner, *The Desert Fayum* 46f.; see above, p. 32.

The Countryside

Italian researches in the Saharan oases have revealed that the wild emmer (*triticum spelta var. Saharae*) that grows there is the prototype of the Egyptian varieties.[1] It is still not clear, however, to what extent the ancient Egyptian distinguished between the different varieties of emmer.

There were also other grains not yet identified which are mentioned in the offering lists or actually found in the model granaries placed in tombs. It is questionable whether durah (*sorghum vulgare*) or Indian corn, the favourite summer and autumn crop today, was grown in ancient times to any extent worth mentioning.

Agricultural records from the New Kingdom were unfortunately drawn up for people who understood them and the calculations they contain involve too many unknown factors for us to arrive at conclusions about the yields of the various crops. The lists of the Wilbour Papyrus (of about 1150 B.C.) seem to be based on the assumption that from the *khato* land of Pharaoh in Middle Egypt 5 measures of corn might be gained from one *aroura* ($\frac{2}{3}$ acre) when the land is average and 'upland'. In the case of a small number of farms made up of land of high quality the figures are 10 measures of corn to the *aroura*.[2] Other classes of land which, because of complicated ownership were assessed proportionately for the various owners (mostly small holdings of only a few *arouras*), were reckoned at the even lower figure of $1\frac{3}{4}$ sacks (?) per *aroura*. Since, however, the precise quantities of the measures involved are not known and, in so far as we do not know whether the figures in the lists are assessments of crop yields or assessments for taxation purposes, it is only with many reservations that it can be pointed out that the standard valuation of 5 measures to one *aroura* agrees with remarkable exactness with the modern average yields for wheat and barley: one *feddan* of land on an average produces 5 *ardebs*, the *feddan* being about the size of an acre and the *ardeb* about $5\frac{1}{2}$ bushels.[3]

Grain prices in Egypt, in spite of the state-controlled economy,

[1] R. Ciferri, 'I frumenti etiopici nelle oasi del Sahara' in *Quartaer*, IV (1942), 187f.   [2] Gardiner, *Wilbour Papyrus*, II, 29, 178f, 199f.

[3] Gardiner, *op. cit.*, 71. Wheat: Lower Egyptian average, 5 *ardebs* from 1 *feddan* with a maximum of 8 *ardebs* from 1 *feddan* of converted Basin land. For barley, according to the Official Almanac (1937), the average yield for the provinces of Middle Egypt was 6 *ardebs* to the *feddan* with a minimum of 2–3 *ardebs*.

at times fluctuated violently. In particular, at the end of Dynasty XX, the period of the Wilbour Papyrus, the price of grain, as a result of bad farming, rose by leaps and bounds on the market in Thebes.[1] This fact is all the more significant because about seventy-five years earlier Egypt under Merenptah was able to come to the aid of the famine-stricken land of the Hittites with supplies of grain. The breakdown of the economy must therefore have happened very suddenly in the Twelfth Century B.C. during which the reign of Ramesses III marks the turning point. We are not much better informed about the price of land because such figures as we have are derived chiefly from purchase contracts of Dynasty XXI or later, a period by no means distinguished by economic prosperity.[2] Prices ranged from 5 to 6 *kite* of silver (45·5–54·6 grammes) for one *aroura* ($\frac{2}{3}$ acre) of arable land beside a canal near Memphis to one *kite* (9·1 grammes) for 'upland' near Abydos, $\frac{1}{2}$ and $\frac{2}{5}$ *kite* for an *aroura* of 'clear common land' (i.e. not leasehold land overgrown with weeds) and $\frac{1}{5}$ or $\frac{1}{6}$ *kite* for an *aroura* of 'weed-infested, exhausted land' in an 'upland' district in the time of Dynasty XXII.[3] We do know that in Middle Egypt in the reign of Akhenaten a man exchanged with a herdsman 3 *arouras* of arable land for a cow of assumed value of $\frac{1}{2}$ *deben* of silver (i.e. 5 *kite* or 45·5 grammes);[4] but we cannot use this evidence to discover the price of land because the circumstances accompanying the exchange are unknown. Nevertheless the figures seem extremely low in comparison with those found in Egypt in modern times where in the prosperous days of 1927 one *feddan* (about one acre) of good land in Upper Egypt was worth about £300 and when rented brought in £12 to £15 (i.e. about 4–6 per cent of its value). One gains the impression that in the bad times following Dynasty XXI there was very little demand for leasehold land and that the fear of not finding a tenant was greater than the notorious land-hunger of the peasantry.

In addition to grain, oil-producing crops formed an important

[1] Černý, *Archiv Orientální*, 6 (1933), 173f.

[2] Munier in *Receuil Champollion* (1922), 361f. (Dynasty XXI date); Blackman, *JEA*, 27, pls. 10–12, l. 12 (Dynasty XXII); *ÄZ*, 35, 13–16 (Dynasty XXII), cf. Malinine and Pirenne, *Documents juridiques*, IIe serie, pp. 18, 24f.

[3] *3ḥt št3 tnl* 'fields with scrub and tired land' (Gardiner, *Wilbour Papyrus*, II, 29).

[4] Berlin Papyrus 9784, 16–17 (from Kahun); see Gardiner, *ÄZ*, 43, 31.

part of Egyptian agriculture. The oil produced was used by the Egyptians in large quantities in their food, for ointments and medicines, for toilet preparations and for their lamps.[1] Oil was customarily used as a payment in kind given to workmen employed by the State. The commonest oil (*kiki*) was obtained from the castor-oil plant, and, from the New Kingdom at least, sesame was also cultivated for its oil which, in the Hellenistic Period was the most highly valued in the oil monopoly. Saffron produced a red dye and also the well-known κνῆκος-oil. The harvesting of flax — a winter crop in Ancient Egypt as it is today — provided a favourite subject for the reliefs of the tombs of the Old Kingdom.[2] Flax was the foundation of the famous Egyptian linen industry and it also contributed to the supply of oil. In representations of gardens we see the lettuce which was thought by the Egyptians to be the aphrodisiac of the fertility god Min. Lettuces were grown in small beds shaped like small tanks that had to be watered laboriously with earthenware jars[3] in the days before the invention of water-lifting devices like the *shaduf* (a bucket suspended from a pole) or the *sakîye* (a wheel with water-pots attached). *Shadufs* can be seen in representations of gardens in tombs of the New Kingdom; the incomparably more efficient *sakîye* (Pl. 1. *b*) is known definitely to have been in use in Egypt only in the Ptolemaic Period.

Among vegetables onions and leeks served as food for the common people, as is the case today. The word for leek, *i̯ꜣḳt*, meant, 'revered' or 'holy', while at the Sokar festival (or more precisely on the eve of that festival, the 25th day of the month Choiak which was called the 'Day of Godliness' in the festival calendar) circlets of onions were worn round the throat in the procession.[4] Another medicinal herb was dill which was called *amsety*. It was elevated to become one of the four divinities of the Canopic Jars who protected the stomach and entrails of the

---

[1] Keimer, *Die Gartenpflanzen im alten Ägypten*, I (1924).

[2] L. Klebs, *Die Reliefs des alten Reiches*, 53f.; Griffith, *El Bersheh* II, pls. 8–9, dates the flax harvest in Middle Egypt to the 23 Khoiak (of the wandering year), which is equivalent to the 26th March (Gregorian) in 1940 B.C.

[3] Wreszinski, *Atlas*, III, pl. 59 (Dynasty VI), cf. *Beni Hasan*, I, pl. 29 (Dynasty XII).

[4] Calendar in the tomb of Neferhotpe (*Mem. Inst. fr. or.*, 5, 3–4, and pl. 3, l. 40f.; cf. the representation in *Oriental Institute of Chicago Communication*, 18, p. 81, fig. 35).

dead so that they should not suffer hunger or want. In this way it personified certain vital characteristics of men in divine form. There were also the leguminous plants as much loved today as they were in Ptolemaic Egypt, such as beans (a field of beans, known in Arabic as *fûl*, in flower in the Fayum can be seen on Pl. 7. *b*) and lentils. In ancient times they also had gourds and various members of the melon family (*cucumis melo, citrullus vulgaris*). Garden produce in common with all other property was threatened by confiscations and arbitrary requisitions to such an extent that the great edict of the military dictator Horemheb (about 1345 B.C.) dealt in detail with particular problems such as the seizure of saffron-flower oil in which the 'servants of the bed-chamber of Pharaoh' seem to have been officially involved and even the seizure of kitchen vegetables from small-holders and farmers.[1]

Early Egyptian potters of the Predynastic Amratian Period for the most part chose the shapes and patterns of flask-shaped gourds as models for their vessels. In later times, however, Egyptian artists showed less interest in the products of the common everyday crafts. What attracted them and what seemed to them valuable for the owners of tombs as far as gardens were concerned were the trees, in particular the fruit trees and the vine. Respect for trees is universal. In the almost treeless land the solitary old tree represents shade and protection. A deity was thought to dwell in trees. In late temples there are nome-lists which attribute to each nome one or more sacred trees, mostly sycomores such as are still to be seen sometimes on the edge of the desert, acacias or fruit trees like the *ished* tree, the Christ's-thorn tree (*Zizyphus spina Christi*, in Egyptian *nbs*) and the date palm.[2] These trees were to be planted in the cemeteries so that the tree-deity, which usually took the form of the goddess of heaven, could pour out cooling drinks for unfortunate dead. Such trees overhung wells (as on Pl. 9. *a*) and today in Egypt wherever one sees that characteristic Egyptian landmark, a grove of acacias, there will almost certainly be in its shade a *sakîye* or water-wheel, driven by animals. The ancient Egyptian went to astonishing trouble to lay out a garden with pools near the tomb, perhaps at the foot of the path leading up to it, so that

---

[1] Decree of Horemheb at Karnak, ll. 22f., 32f.

[2] Brugsch, *Dictionnaire géographique*, p. 1358f. (Edfu).

the soul of the deceased person might drink there.[1] In the hot
bay in the cliffs at Deir el-Bahari tree-bordered avenues led up
to the mortuary temples of Menthuhotpe and Hatshepsut. The
trees were planted in deep-dug pits filled with soil[2] and there
were also papyrus-pools and garden-like plots decorated with
statues. We also learn from the inscriptions in the tomb of
Hepdjefi of Asyut, of Dynasty XII, that there was a garden
below his tomb in which stood a statue of the deceased. The
gods too sought gladly the protection of trees.[3] Thus the crocodile of Suchos is often strangely represented beneath trees as if
it preferred the groves to the sun-drenched sand-banks of the
Nile.[4] Trees were supposed to grow around the borders of
heaven and under them sat the celestial gods, like shepherds
sitting at the edge of the pastures. At the very beginning of the
world the sacred *ished* tree in Heliopolis unfolded itself on the
appearance of the sun-god (*Book of the Dead*, chapter 17); on the
eastern edge of the world where the solar theology placed the
Field of Reeds of the Blessed stood 'the two sycomores from
Turkis between which Rē' goes forth, which have sprung up
from the seed sown by Shu at that eastern door out of which Rē'
goes forth' (*Book of the Dead*, chapter 109). Common too are
local deities with names such as 'he under his olive tree' in
Memphis where Hathor was also venerated as 'Mistress of the
Southern Sycomore'. At Heliopolis could be seen the *ished* tree,
the tree of life on the leaves of which the god set down the names
and years of the kings to serve as their annals. A specially
charming custom from the New Kingdom onwards was the
presentation of 'bouquets of life' generally tied to staves as
tokens of good wishes and carrying the blessing of the god of the
locality from which they came. Down to Ptolemaic times a victorious king was offered them on his return from a campaign[5]
and on coronation days and other great festivals the king received them from the hands of the priests. High officials were
similarly honoured. A particular fame attached to those coming
from the Temple of Amun at Karnak and also to those from
the funerary temple of Ahmes-Nefertari on the west bank of the
Nile at Thebes; similarly to a 'bouquet of life from the Lord of

---

[1] Kees, *Götterglaube*, pl. 3a.   [2] Cf. p. 112.
[3] On the shrines in gardens in Amarna, see below, p. 299.
[4] E.g. Kees, *Kulturgeschichte*, fig. 40.   [5] See below, p. 191.

the *ished* tree' in Heliopolis which was composed of sprigs from the sacred tree of Annals and which was handed to the recipient at the entrance to the temple by the High Priest on great festival days such as the last day of the month Mechir.[1] Envoys bearing bouquets of life from all the temples in the country actually accompanied Psammetichus II on his campaign against Syria about 590 B.C.[2]

The growing of trees in Egypt is today practically restricted to gardens with the exception of the date-palm groves which surround villages (see Pl. 16. *b*) and which attain their largest extent in the neighbourhood of Memphis. The date-palm is useful and its presence considerably increases the value of land. As early as the Old Kingdom the State took advantage of this usefulness and levied special taxes on irrigation works and fruit trees just as it does today on the date-palms around the villages and in the oases. A protective decree of Dynasty VI for the Pyramid cities stated accordingly: 'My Majesty has ordered that canals, ponds, wells, leather skins (possibly water-raising devices) and sycomores in the two Pyramid cities (of Snofru) are not to be taxed.'[3] The utilization and extension of horticulture depended as much on wells as canals. From a law-suit originating in the Oasis of Dakhlah in the time of Dynasty XXII we discover incidentally that there existed a legal distinction between the 'water of Pharaoh' which was Crown property and the 'water of private persons'.[4]

A kitchen-garden laid out on the west bank of the Nile at Thebes during Dynasty XVIII by the Overseer of Architects Enene contained mostly date-palms.[5] He also planted dôm-palms and sycomores (which today are only to be found from Thebes southwards), persea trees (*mimusops Schimperi*, in Arabic *lebach*), 'sweet-fruit' trees (*balanites aegyptiaca?*), tamarisks, Christ's thorn trees, pomegranates, willows, some other unidentified trees, and figs and vines. In the Old Kingdom there existed a special 'House of *ished*' which was charged with the administration of the revenues from orchards from which allocations were made for various purposes such as offerings to

---

[1] British Museum stela, 155 (in *Hieroglyphic Texts*, VIII, 39).
[2] Rylands Demotic Papyrus, IX.
[3] *Urk.*, I, 212.   [4] Gardiner, *JEA*, 19, 19f.
[5] *Urk.*, IV, 73; reproduced Wreszinski, *Atlas*, I, pl. 60a.

5. *a*. Cultivation in the Fayum near Hawara.

5. *b*. Flocks on the western edge of the cultivation near Bet Khallaf
in Middle Egypt.

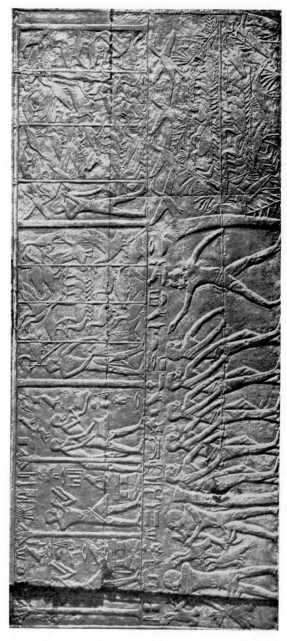

6. Bird catching and poultry rearing from the Tomb of Nefer-seshem-Ptah at Saqqara.

the dead.[1] When the fruit harvest was represented on the walls of tombs it was always the harvesting of figs that was chosen, not that of dates.

It is surprising that the olive which is so characteristic of the Mediterranean is not found. Although its cultivation was attempted often in the New Kingdom, as in the reign of Ramesses III, even in the time of Strabo (early First Century A.D.) it was only to be found in the nome of Arsinoe in the Fayum and in the gardens of Alexandria (Book XVII, 809). It was clearly best suited to the Libyan coastal region and this may be the reason for the ancient reputation of Libyan oil in the offering lists. Nevertheless olive oil had been imported from early times in large quantities from Palestine. In Egypt itself the place of the olive tree was taken by another oil-producing tree which botanists have conjectured to have been *moringa aptera*.[2]

In orchards vines were the object of special attention, a situation very different from that obtaining today in which Islam has restricted the growth of vines to areas inhabited predominantly by a Greek or Coptic population. The use of the hieroglyphic sign of vines in the writing of the words for 'orchard' and 'gardener' shows that the planting and care of vines was a gardener's most important task. Viticulture is most satisfactorily carried on in border districts. The best-known centres of cultivation in ancient times were the oases of Khargah and Dakhlah in the desert west of the Thinite nome. Another such district was the coastal area of the Delta, especially around Pelusium and Tanis in the north-east[3] and present-day Mareotis in the north-west where, according to ancient opinion, the best Egyptian wine was produced.[4] Wines from the estates 'on the western river', which meant the Canopic branch of the Nile, were also highly thought of and were to be found in the cellars of the palace of Amenophis III at Thebes and later at Amarna.[5] Offering lists of wines which played a great part in religious

[1] *Urk.*, I, 175-8.
[2] In Egyptian *b3k*; on its determination, see Keimer, *Gartenpflanzen im alten Ägypten*, I, 30.
[3] See below, p. 195.
[4] Kees, articles 'Marea', 'Mareotis', in Pauly-Wissowa, *Real-Encyclopädie*.
[5] Hayes, *JNES*, 10 (1951), figs. 4-6, nos. 10-11, 20, 46, 47, 57; *City of Akhenaten*, I, pls. 63, 64, III, pls. 81, 82, 85-90.

ceremonies as festival drinks, as opposed to the common barley-
brewed beer, mention the following as choice brands during
Dynasty XIX: Lower Egyptian wine, wine from Imet (a place
about nine miles south-east of Tanis), wine from Hamet (near
Mareotis?), wine from Pelusium, wine from the estate named
'Star of Horus on the height of heaven' (which came, according
to the ancient sealings on the stoppers of wine jars, from a royal
estate of Zoser, possibly in Khargah) and wine from Asia.[1] Viticulture was perhaps originally restricted to royal domains which
were also required to supply the royal tombs. From the sealings
on wine jars we learn about many of the royal domains and also
the names of the head gardeners or stewards. The educated
Egyptian took the greatest possible care of his wine. The stoppers
of wine jars in the New Kingdom such as those from the
Ramesseum at Thebes and those from the royal city of Amarna
bore not only the place of origin but often also the year and the
name of the head gardener. It is no surprise therefore that viticulture, being the superior form of horticulture, was frequently
and minutely represented in tombs, especially during the New
Kingdom. The gardens represented were, however, invariably
orchards containing assortments of fruit trees after the kind
described by Enene. The same fact emerges from the accounts
of the most famous vineyard of the New Kingdom, which was
situated in the royal domain of Ramesses II called 'The Upholder of Egypt' (*ka-en-keme*), somewhere probably in the
neighbourhood of his residence Piramesse in the Delta.[2] Some
514 vineyards and orchards are listed among the donations of
Ramesses III to temples.[3] The King boasted to Amun: 'I made
vineyards for you in the Southern Oasis (Khargah and Dakhlah) and again in the Northern Oasis (Bahriyah) without number and in Upper Egypt countless others. I multiplied them in
Lower Egypt into hundreds of thousands. I furnished them
with gardeners from among the foreign prisoners.'

The Egyptian's love of nature showed itself also in his attitude
towards flowers and decorative plants. Water- and marsh-
plants received greater prominence in ancient Egypt than elsewhere. The papyrus-marshes and open country bordering on

[1] Kees, *Kulturgeschichte*, fig. 49 (from the temple of Sethos I at Abydos).
[2] See below, p. 201.
[3] Harris Papyrus, I, 67, 15, and 7, 10 (Theban part).

the cultivated land occupied a place in the sentiment of the Egyptians somewhat like that held by woods and forests in our life. It was there that his pleasure lay in hunting birds and in fishing — amusement pure and simple, a mood that he sought to express in the garden of his house. Plants were used heraldically to represent the two parts of the country, the 'green' papyrus for Lower Egypt and for Upper Egypt a plant that has variously been called lily, nightshade or a kind of rush. Divine powers are also hidden in plants. A charming myth tells how at the creation of the world the primeval god arose out of the primeval waters in the form of a lotus which opened its bloom by day and proudly displayed itself on the surface of the water. The citizens of Memphis addressed this primeval god in the words: 'O Great One, which you are, who went forth out of the earth and loosed yourself from the primeval flood, you who went forth from Nut (the Sky), O Great Power, born of Geb (the Earth) . . . formed from the body of that holy field that is the body of the land of the Earth.'[1] They named him 'Wholly beautiful' (Nefertum) and made him the son of Ptah, their King of the Gods. Subsequently when the myth assimilated human elements it was said that the primeval god who was the youthful sun-god, rose from out the primeval waters seated upon a lotus bloom, which was itself a variation of the legend of the primeval hill that rose from out of the flood, or of the nest in the marshes where the primeval god emerged from an egg. The worship of Nefertum was held in such high regard in Memphis probably because he, being the lotus, was also Lord of Fragrance and the coronation unguent. From time immemorial the Egyptians had known how to press blossoms to gain perfume. It is known that in the Late Period oil of lilies was used for the ceremonial anointing in the king's presence of persons taking up office;[2] but in this connection it should be noted that the Egyptians were not very precise either in their botanical or in their zoological knowledge so that the same word was used for the lotus and the white lily (in Greek σοῦσον, in Egyptian *sšn*). The extraction of perfume was performed by means of a sack press such as was

---

[1] Kees, *ÄZ*, 57, 92f. = *Religionsgeschichtliches Lesebuch*, Pt. 10 (Egypt), p. 13.

[2] In the Rylands Demotic Papyrus, IX, cf. Kees, *Kulturgeschichte* p. 52. *sšn* as the label on an oil jar from Meroë of the time of Aspelta, see Reisner, *ÄZ*, 70, 37.

used for wine; its tutelary deity was Shesmu who was already well known at the time when the Pyramid Texts were composed (Dynasty V or earlier). According to the myths, however, he was less occupied with his useful work as Lord of ointment-cooking than as a bloodthirsty torturer in the Other World into whose hands it was disastrous to fall.

Flowers formed part of every Egyptian festival. Papyrus blooms plucked in the marshes were brought to the benign Hathor whom the court ladies of the Old Kingdom served as priestesses. The Egyptian goddesses following the example of Hathor, carried papyrus stalks as sceptres, especially the pacified lion goddess Sekhmet and her like companions. Garlands of flowers decorated wine jars at feasts and even the mummy at the time of burial as a symbol of the continuance of life. The pillars of the festival bower were decked with bundles of flowers and this pleasant custom inspired Egyptian art in the Old Kingdom to produce one of its most individual creations, the plant column based on a cluster of papyrus stems with the flower buds forming the capital, the papyrus-flower column (representing a single stem and bloom) with open capital and the palm-trunk column (see Pl. 17. *a*). We know, however, from the buildings constructed by Zoser at Saqqara that these columns were preceded by experimental forms embodying different plant motifs, fluted and ribbed pillars. The prototype for all these architectural innovations was the ancient wood and reed festival-hut covered with matting. It is typical of things Egyptian that we cannot put a name to the botanical original and say whether it belonged to the cypress family, was the horse's-tail plant or the *heracleum giganteum*. The same is the case when we try to identify the plants in the impressionistic paintings on the floors of the buildings of the Amarna Period. Their effect is surprisingly naturalistic but they are in no way true to nature.[1]

Egyptian ornamentation, which is so largely based on floral motifs, is dominated by the papyrus and the lotus, two species of the latter being used, *nymphaea caerulea* with pointed petals and *nymphaea lotus* with rounded petals. Next to Minoan art Egyptian art had the deepest creative understanding of nature and it enriched the decorative art of the world with motifs the influence

[1] See below, p. 299.

of which spread through Syrian, Assyrian and Persian art to Ionian art and the art of the Greek mainland. Here again it is true that the originals of many of the plant motifs employed are not known with certainty. From comparison with actual Egyptian wreaths and garlands it appears that the floral rosettes and pendants used in architecture are derived from the Egyptian corn-flower (*centurea depressa*) or the pomegranate flower; but to the Egyptian form and colour were of primary importance, fidelity to nature secondary. The same is the case with exotic plants. The Pharaohs and their successors, the Ptolemies, introduced many new varieties of foreign plants and flowers, especially from Asia. Tuthmosis III had a whole series of these foreign plants and flowers depicted in the festival temple at Karnak along with foreign animals; but this alleged booty from Syria of his year 25 does not meet with the botanist's approval.[1]

His garden was where the Egyptian sought and found relaxation. There he could enjoy the sweet breath of the north wind sitting in a pavilion beside a pool just as he hoped to do in the Other World. The garden is the scene for love-songs; the garden-maid, the dainty slave who poured wine for her master is, in the rococo manner, the invariable subject of New Kingdom poetry: 'The loveliest one is to go with the beloved into the field.' This expression was nevertheless less lascivious in meaning than it perhaps sounds to us. Out of respect for social conventions even the eroticism of the New Kingdom did not dare concern itself with the person of the mistress of the house. A roundabout way, therefore, was chosen; the lover poses in the servile guise of a birdcatcher, which was more appropriate for association with the garden-maid. Trees, flowers, music and love — these all belong together. Dancing-girls sing 'gay songs' to the accompaniment of the lute on the festival way; their songs and dances often being modelled on those used in the worship of Hathor. As Queen of Heaven Hathor was called 'the Golden One'; she was the wife of the 'Golden Horus' and became the tutelary deity of love, in which role she quite abandoned her originally wild characteristics. This explains the thanks given to Hathor in the love songs because it is she who sends the beloved.[2] The gardener's daughter sends the beloved

---

[1] *Urk.*, IV, 775–7; Wreszinski, *Atlas*, II, pls. 26–33.
[2] So Papyrus Chester Beatty, I, *verso*, col. 5ff. (ed. Gardiner).

'the little sycomore which she has planted with her own hand' together with a letter inviting him to a rendezvous in the garden and to a revel: 'Come, and spend the day in merriment, and tomorrow, and the day after — three whole days and sit in my shadow. . . .' 'But I am discreet and speak not of what I see.'[1]

E. DOMESTIC ANIMALS

Something has already been said in the introductory chapter about the beginnings of cattle-breeding in Egypt. Here, therefore, all that is needed is a few words about the part played by domesticated animals in the fully developed agricultural life of Egypt; for at all ages his cattle were the pride of the Egyptian landowner. The ox took first place and it is in this respect that conditions have fundamentally changed since ancient times. Today the water buffalo is seen everywhere in Egypt and it is of little value for breeding purposes. To see them makes one feel transported to primitive Africa. The blame for this state of affairs rests partly on Turkish maladministration but more so on epidemics that have rendered all attempts at improvement nugatory. Even the ancient Egyptians gave up such attempts as fruitless, as is confirmed by papyri from the reign of Ptolemy Philadelphus and, for earlier times, by pictorial representations of the import of cattle. During the New Kingdom cattle were imported from Asia, including humped cattle[2] of the kind seen today among the Shilluk in the Upper Nile, and even from Cyprus and Hittite Asia Minor. Such cattle could not have been in the nature of customary tribute such as the southern peoples brought from their country; they were, on the contrary, specially picked for breeding purposes.[3]

In the Old Kingdom there was a long-horned breed of cattle reminiscent of the Watussi cattle of the Masai plains in East Africa, and short-horned and hornless varieties which seem to have vanished in the New Kingdom. Similarly the ancient

[1] Erman, *Literatur der Ägypter*, 312–13, from a Turin papyrus.

[2] Pied, humped cattle imported from Syria are shown in Theban Tomb no. 162, cf. Davies, *JEA*, 33, pl. 8. For a humped cow with a figure of an Asiatic as a head ornament in a procession of offerings, see Kees, *Ägyptische Kunst*, fig. 42 (from Luxor).

[3] Milking cows from Kush and Phoenicia for the temple of Amun, *Urk.*, IV, 743 (time of Tuthmosis III).

domesticated sheep of Egypt with its horns characteristically twisted like those of a goat had already been replaced in the Middle Kingdom by the highly valued fat-tailed sheep (the ram of Amun).[1]

To be able correctly to estimate the economic importance of cattle-farming it would be desirable to see figures for the herds maintained throughout the country. In cases where such figures are available, inasmuch as they are 'ideally' and not 'actually' conceived, the same caution and critical treatment is necessary as for quantities of booty captured by military expeditions where large numbers certainly act as symbols of great victories. When a well-to-do mortuary priest of the Pyramid of Chephren boasts of his 1,055 cattle of various kinds, 2,235 goats and 974 sheep,[2] these figures seem modest beside others of the same kind; but they look exaggerated when placed beside the booty from Libya in the eleventh year of the reign of Ramesses III — one of the few credible enumerations of its kind: 3,609 cattle, 184 horses, 864 donkeys, 9,136 goats and 23,120 + 5,800 sheep.[3]

Another credible piece of information is that reported by Renni an early Dynasty XVIII nomarch of el-Kab, a region with little cultivated land (Pl. 21. a). He states that he mustered for the cattle levy 122 cattle, 100 sheep, 1,200 goats and 1,500 pigs, and that this achievement, when reported, earned him the King's praise.[4] The occasion was probably a levy on produce. Unfortunately we know nothing of the system of capital. We only know that the periodic numbering of property which in the Thinite Period was called the 'numbering of gold and of land' and took place every two years in general, was in the Old Kingdom called the 'numbering of oxen and all small cattle'. The importance of live-stock, therefore, appears to increase with the cultural expansion of the country so that the tax on animals (which was certainly a sort of poll-tax like the ἀπογραφὴ κτηνῶν of the Ptolemaic Period) became the most important item in the taxation system. The payment of the tax in the feudal period was organized by the nomarchs and their officials in the presence of an 'overseer of the herds of the king'.[5] Among the herds there were cattle belonging to the king which must prob-

---

[1] Kees, *Kulturgeschichte*, 20. [2] L. D., II, 9.
[3] H. H. Nelson, *Medinet Habu*, II, pl. 75. [4] *Urk.*, IV, 75.
[5] Newberry, *El Bersheh*, I, pl. 18 (Dynasty XII).

ably have been treated from the point of view of the tax just like private property. In the New Kingdom when administration was centralized, the overseer of cattle of Pharaoh collected the cattle tax throughout the country. Nevertheless private owners, especially the temples, had in addition their own overseers of cattle. Against the exaggerated figures of the older period can be set those found in the inscriptions of the Heracleopolitan Period which were composed in a style more personal than formerly. Allowing for the fact that this was a time of depression and that it is chiefly members of the middle class who speak, what we hear from them is genuinely more moderate: 'I got 28 donkeys', says an official from Upper Egypt; and in addition he acquired a ship, 3 male and 7 female servants through his father's kindness.[1] A priest of Denderah of about 2060 B.C. boasts: 'I got 3 heads (servants), 33 bulls, 13 donkeys, 100 goats', as well as 4 boats and 5 punts.[2] Another man lists 40 servants, 54 cattle, 36 donkeys, 260 goats and 3 boats and 7 punts.[3] In accordance with the true state of affairs it is the holding of donkeys that is given prominence in that donkeys were the principal working beasts.

Quantitative figures are unfortunately lacking for the great land-owners of the New Kingdom. Nevertheless it is known that favoured people like Enene, the chief architect under Tuthmosis I, who was also overseer of the granaries of Amun, kept herds of cattle in the Delta.[4] This conforms with the old practice with which even the Asiatic Hyksos rule in Lower Egypt did not dare to interfere: 'The finest of their fields are ploughed for us, our oxen are in the Delta. Emmer is sent for our pigs, our oxen are not taken away' — so did his counsellors try to calm King Kamose concerning the state of affairs.[5] Things remained unchanged in the Ramesside Period. Thus Ramesses III boasts that he has presented Amun in Karnak with five herds of cattle in the Delta (undoubtedly part of the animal booty of the Libyan wars); of these one was kept beside the 'great river' (the Canopic branch of the Nile) and another

---

[1] *Annales du Service*, 15, 207.   [2] Petrie, *Dendereh*, pl. 11 (Nakhte).

[3] Cairo J.45600. A Theban nomarch of this time on the other hand speaks of herds he has acquired, see Kees, *Kulturgeschichte*, 41.

[4] *Urk.*, IV, 72.

[5] The Carnarvon Tablet, see Erman, *Literatur der Ägypter*, 82.

beside the 'water of Rē'' (the Bubastite branch in the East Delta). To look after these herds 3,264 men were employed who were certainly also Libyan prisoners of war for the most part.[1] The office of overseer of the cattle of Amun was therefore an influential and much coveted post.

Live-stock prices are first met with in documents of the Ramesside Period. According to quality a bull fetched from 30 to 120 *deben* of copper, a *deben* being an Egyptian weight of about 91 grammes; a donkey fetched about 40 *deben* and a goat only 2.[2] In considering the trade in cattle we must remember that the temples needed a large number of sacrificial animals and that the bull was regarded as the best for slaughter. The endowment lists of the Sun Temple of Niuserrē' of Dynasty V record for a single festival the following sacrificial animals: 10 fat oxen, 1 (ordinary) ox, 1 oryx-antelope or 2 fat oxen, 100 oxen and 2 oryx-antelopes — a real hecatomb.[3] Such were the expenses entailed by ceremonial public festivals at which food had to be provided for more than 100,000 persons. From a document of Sheshonk I we learn that the modest-sounding donation of a single ox for the daily sacrifice in the temple of Arsaphes at Heracleopolis necessitated that the high priest, who was also the nomarch, should contribute two months' supply of sacrificial oxen (about 60 annually) and that every class right down to the shepherds, gardeners and stonemasons had to contribute according to their means.[4] In the light of this knowledge we can calculate the economic consequences of the colossal endowments that Ramesses III made for the Theban temples alone for their permanent possession — 421,362 head of oxen and small cattle and in addition as a special gift, perhaps for breeding purposes, 297 bulls. He further donated 45,544 head of cattle of various kinds to the Heliopolitan temples, 10,047 to those at Memphis and 13,433 to other temples.[5] Although the sacrifices ultimately served as the food for the priests and for the vast crowds attending the festivals, such a voluntary contribution in kind was, nevertheless, a very heavy burden on agriculture for the benefit of certain privileged classes.

Leather, the by-product of cattle-rearing, serves as another

[1] Papyrus Harris, I, 10, 7–11.   [2] Kees, *Kulturgeschichte*, 24.

[3] *Op. cit.*, 250; cf. below, p. 156.   [4] *Rec. de Trav.*, 31, 33f.

[5] Erman, *Zur Erklärung des Papyrus Harris*, 14.

good example of the extent to which the Egyptian State demanded tax on all raw materials and all commercial products,
a matter in which it served as the teacher of the Ptolemies. As in
the case of the output from the manufacture of linen, so part of
the production of hides was obviously liable to the tax; the
nomarch as chief priest had claims on the payment received for
the hides of sacrificial animals.[1] It was for this reason that protective ordinances in the Old Kingdom freed certain endowments or temple estates from the hide-tax.[2] We do not know
how this tax was regulated. In practice, however, in the East,
the need of the moment was the decisive factor and the strongest
need requiring constant fulfilment was for the indispensable
leather sandals of the army and the State labour corps. Here
again the ordinances of the dictator Horemheb afford an insight
into the practice in the land.[3] There were two divisions of troops
stationed respectively one in Upper Egypt and one in Lower
Egypt on the lands of shepherds; they were requisitioning
troops who confiscated by force and threat, even falsifying the
owners' brandmarks on hides. So when the time came for the
scheduled requisitioning at which the overseer of the cattle of
Pharaoh was present, the cry went up on all sides, 'They (the
soldiers) have seized them from us!' 'This is a shocking affair!'
said the Regent in reproof and went on to decree that whoever
in future was caught in any such action would receive 100 blows
and 5 bloody wounds while the leather he had confiscated
would be seized as stolen property. It was hoped in this way to
strengthen the authority of the State which, since the reign of
Tuthmosis III had been dissipated by upstarts of all kinds,
especially by former soldiers.

We have already seen that Upper Egypt possessed sufficient
pasturage on dry soil on the borders of the desert for small cattle,
sheep and goats (Pl. 5. *b*). This state of affairs obtained also for
Lower Egypt, especially in the Libyan frontier districts, the
Mareotis and the land to the west of it. Documents from the time
of the unification of the Two Lands already record vast booty in
cattle from these districts. In general the goat is the domesticated
animal of the small man and it is therefore a sign of provincial
poverty during the Heracleopolitan Period when we find a

[1] Sethe, *Lesestücke*, 74 (Munich Glyptothek stela no. 3).
[2] *Urk.*, I, 286, 12; 289, 10.   [3] Ll. 25–8.

scribe of the Theban nome claiming as a good deed: 'I gave a goat to him who had none.'[1] Although the ritual, which was based on aristocratic ideals, forbade the goat as an animal for sacrifice, it, or rather the he-goat, was nevertheless used as such by the middle classes.[2] Suggestions of this practice come to us from inscriptions, such as the statement of Hepdjefi the nomarch of Asyut under Sesostris I that for every goat sacrificed in the temple he received a basket of charcoal as a tax.[3] Officially the he-goat, like the pig, was in the symbolism of sacrifice proscribed as being the physical embodiment of Seth, the enemy of Horus.

Since they require a moist soil pigs have been kept in the Delta from time immemorial. In remote antiquity they were used there as food and were also certainly sacrificed to the gods.[4] When, however, that land was conquered by the Upper Egyptians the victors regarded these practices with horror; swine were unclean in their eyes. The prohibition which they proceeded to impose on swine was founded on a divine myth behind which it is still possible to discern the real reason for the suppression of a popular custom. According to this myth Seth in the guise of a black bear blinded Horus' eye, on account of which Rē', the King of the Gods ordered: 'Abhor the swine for Horus' sake.' 'And so there arose the hatred of the swine for Horus' sake.... But when Horus was a child his sacrificial offering still consisted of swine....' The knowledge of this myth should serve to reveal 'the reason why Buto (the ancient Predynastic capital of Lower Egypt) was given to Horus' (*Book of the Dead*, chapter 112). Consequently in historic times a swine-sacrifice together with one of a he-kid appears in the calendar of festival only in connection with the preliminary celebrations of the old Memphite festival of Sokaris (on the 24th of the month Choiak). Similarly Plutarch says that occasionally a pig is sacrificed at the full moon.[5] Theology explained this proscription of the pig

[1] *Urk.*, I, 151.

[2] Junker, *Miscellanea Gregoriana* (1941), 117; Kees, 'Bemerkungen zum Tieropfer der Ägypter und seiner Symbolik' in *Gött. Nachr. phil.-hist. Kl.* (1942), 71f.

[3] Griffith, *The Inscriptions of Siut*, I, 292.

[4] For Merimdah, see above, p. 37.

[5] H. H. Nelson, *Medinet Habu*, III, pl. 158; Plutarch, *de Iside*, 8, cf. Herodotus, II, 47 (offerings to Selene and Dionysus).

as a punishment inflicted on the enemy of the gods for his having injured the eye of heaven, but it could have been a popular custom reinterpreted to suit the times. The shepherd could attend the Thinite ritual of the king's *sed*-festival as a traditional figure;[1] but the swine-herd was excluded from all religious affairs, as Herodotus observed.

In fact, however, herds of pigs would not have been kept in Upper Egypt unless pork was eaten and it has been shown that they were kept even by the temple of Osiris at Abydos. That pork was eaten in the State's workman's village in the Theban Necropolis during the Ramesside Period can be deduced from the finds made there.[2] The prohibition therefore actually applied to the upper classes, particularly to the divine king, to the royal officials and to the priests. Fish from the Nile came under a similar prohibition. We know of primitive beliefs, some even in Upper Egypt, which held fish sacred. Place-names like Latonpolis (Esna), 'the City of the latus fish', Lepidotonpolis (Meshayîkh) in the Thinite nome and Oxyrhynchus in Middle Egypt testify to this reverence for fish, while in the Delta the deity of the nome of Mendes was called 'First of the Fish' (*Ḥat-meḥyt*). Officially, nevertheless, fish were an 'abomination' despite the fact that at the time of the unification of the Two Lands the royal power was personified by the powerful cat-fish.[3] The Egyptian word for 'abomination' was written already in the Old Kingdom with the determination of the hieroglyph of a fish. Anyone who ate fish was unclean and was forbidden from entering a funerary chapel. The original conflict of attitudes towards fish was never resolved. Thus there are myths that sanctify and vindicate the fish. The fish of Abydos appears as the helper of the sun-god in his journey across the heavens and even as the image of the dead who became transformed into Osiris (for Osiris was in fact drowned).[4] On the other hand, however, there was the command of the King as Horus. At the great city festival in Edfu fish were trampled on the ground in honour of Horus, symbolizing his enemies. The Ethiopian kings held with particular

[1] Von Bissing and Kees, *Re-Heiligtum*, II, pl. 11, 27.
[2] Keimer, *Bulletin de l'Institut d'Egypte*, 19 (1936–7), 149.
[3] Schäfer, *Von ägyptischer Kunst*[3], 149, fig. 112; cf. Emery, *Tomb of Hemaka*, pls. 17, 18.
[4] Kees, *Götterglaube*, 65f.

firmness to the orthodox views in this respect. Piankhi (about 730 B.C.) refused to receive the subject princelings of Egypt who were all of Libyan origin, with the exception of one, 'because they were uncircumcised and ate fish, which is an abomination to the Palace.'[1] Can an echo of this austere dogmatism be found perhaps in the ancient refusal of the nomadic tribes to accept the customs of a race of fishermen and peasants? Historically it would be all the more peculiar because the Ethiopian dynasty was itself probably descended from tribes of southern Libya.

Egypt is a land of water-birds. In the migration season the lagoons of the Delta, the reed-banks of the Fayum, the canals, ponds and flooded fields are crowded with thousands of water-birds, ibises, pelicans, cranes, cormorants, herons of all kinds, flamingoes, ducks and geese. All such served in their time as models for common hieroglyphic signs and there are many ancient representations of flocks of these birds. The ancient Egyptian was inclined to liken a crowd to 'a bird-pond at the time of the inundation'. Characteristically also we find on a stela of later times from Tell Far'un to the south-east of Tanis and not far from Lake Menzalah an address to tomb-visitors and festival-guests which expressly mentions 'those who come in the time of the inundation to look for birds'-nests'.[2] For the rest of the year ancient Egypt was empty of birds with the exception of birds of prey and the sociable white heron nowadays called Abu Gurdani, which in Egypt takes the place of the rook in northern Europe (see Pl. 5. a). Today the country is just as empty, as Bengt Berg tells us. Out of fourteen species of wild duck that are found there in the autumn and that were among the most frequently represented in ancient Egyptian art, only one now breeds there. Many of the birds whose nests the Egyptians thought it proper to put into scenes of papyrus thickets such as in the representation of the seasons in the Sun Temple of Niuserrē' and on the causeway leading to the mortuary temple of Unas, were figments of the imagination of the artists.[3]

---

[1] *Urk.*, III, 54.

[2] Cairo, J.85932; see Drioton, *Bulletin de l'Institut d'Egypte*, 25 (1942–1943).

[3] Schäfer in the text to Wreszinski, *Atlas*, III, pl. 106; cf. Bengt Berg, *Mit den Zugvögeln nach Afrika*, 64.

The Egyptian fowl-house (Pl. 6) was filled with a mass of birds that were caught in autumn and winter on the reed banks with a clap-net and then put into fattening pens. We see them passing in front of the owner when his livestock was paraded for his inspection; we see them again as they are carried into the temple as offerings, geese and all kinds of duck in the fore, then Nile geese (grey geese), bald geese, pintail ducks, ibises, cranes and herons, and sometimes quails from the fields. Roast goose was one of the greatest of delicacies and in the Old Kingdom stuffed crane was also highly esteemed. In the endowment lists of the Sun Temple of Niuserrē' the figures for a single feast-day include as many as 1,000 geese, while in the lists of offerings in Ramesses III's mortuary temple at Medinet Habu the birds of all kinds run to thousands. The special donations of Ramesses III are said to have totalled 426,395 water-fowl in the course of thirty-one years. These birds mostly went to his endowments for the Theban temples, but some went to temples at Heliopolis and elsewhere. The annual total on an average, therefore, came to 9,350 for Thebes and 1,200 for Heliopolis. The regular offerings for Amun and for the statue of the king in his mortuary temple alone required daily 2 Nile geese and 30 ordinary birds without reckoning the special requirements of the innumerable festivals.[1]

All these creatures were the victims of an exacting sacrificial symbolism which in the case of the harmless birds seems so grotesque to us: 'But birds, they are the souls (images) of enemies.'[2] None the less, the holders of temple benefices certainly ate them with pleasure 'after the god had been appeased with them'.

In order to meet such demands temples also kept fowl-houses. A clear picture of this arrangement is given in the endowment document of Sethos I for his temple of Osiris at Abydos: 'He has offered him water-fowl in his fields, their number being like the sands of the shore; so that his house was like the fields of Chemmis (near Buto) because of the chattering of the birds of passage and of the breeding fowl, of every bird of the marshes.'[3] There are many references to the construction of nesting houses for the

[1] H. H. Nelson, *Medinet Habu*, III, pl. 146, list 6.
[2] See above, p. 26.
[3] The Nauri Decree, l. 18f.; see Griffith, *JEA*, 13, 193f.

temples.[1] Moreover, foreign birds were imported as booty or tribute and 'they', as Tuthmosis III expressly says, 'lay an egg every day.'[2]

The provisioning of the Court with poultry in the days of the Old Kingdom was the business of men like Ti who possesses a famous and beautiful tomb at Saqqara. His titles included those of 'overseer of the bird-ponds' and 'overseer of the marshes'; he was also 'overseer of sacrificial-cattle' and 'overseer of the gifts in the House of Life', offices that made him the provider of food for the royal table with the honorary title 'Controller of the Palace'. This office was in effect a princely honorific because hunting birds with a throw-stick was a sport of the nobles. In reality bird-catching was the dirtiest occupation imaginable and it was left to professional fowlers from the lowest classes.[3] Nature-loving Akhenaten built himself an aviary in his northern palace at Amarna splendidly decorated with wall-paintings and provided with niches for nests and with drinking troughs.[4] Mythology also made use of the idea of a paradise of birds for its stories of the creation such as the one in which the primeval god was hatched from the egg of a water-fowl in a papyrus-marsh. Even in Egypt's most enlightened period during the New Kingdom, the cult of Amun returned to the popular idea of the god seen as a Nile goose.

It was strictly forbidden to fish or to catch birds on the sacred lake of the temple, a prohibition that was expressly reiterated for the Abaton, the sepulchral abode of Osiris.[5] Similarly Ramesses IV declared before Osiris in Abydos: 'I ate nothing I should not eat, I did not fish in the sacred lake, I did not hunt with the bird-net, I did not shoot a lion at the festival of Bastet.[6] Among the domestic fowl were counted the doves whose value for the fields was probably as much overestimated in Ancient Egypt as it is in modern Egypt where tower-like dove-houses can be seen everywhere in the villages (see Pl. 7. a). Accordingly the dove takes second place only to the wild-duck, the usual representative of water fowl, as the favourite motif in the decoration of ceilings in the New Kingdom.

---

[1] *Urk.*, IV, 745 (from Karnak); Ricke, *ÄZ*, 73, 124 (Karnak); Louvre Stela A.90 (Elephantine).

[2] *Urk.*, IV, 700, 14.   [3] Kees, *Kulturgeschichte*, 25 with fig.

[4] See below, p. 299.   [5] See below, p. 328.

[6] *Religionsgeschichtliches Lesebuch*, Part 10 (Egypt), 42 (stela in Cairo).

III

The Nile and Egyptian Civilization

A. THE NILE AS A MEANS OF TRANSPORT

Hardly any country in ancient or modern times has been so dependent on its waterways as Egypt. Only local traffic between villages and to and from the river banks makes use of land routes on either side of the river. Roads in the true sense scarcely exist and for the most part it is the dykes besides the canals that serve as the predetermined routes for man and beast. It is by ship that one travels and that goods are conveyed up and down the river. This Egyptian attitude towards movement is so natural that in Ancient Egyptian all words concerned with this aspect of life are determined by the idea of sailing: to travel south is 'to go up-stream', to travel north is 'to go down-stream' even when referring to travelling outside Egypt. Inasmuch as goods could be carried so easily, whether pots or corn or stone from quarries, a fusion of culture developed such as could never be achieved in countries like Greece with natural inland frontiers. This fusion was the compensation contributed by a unique means of communication and transport which also obliged the people of the country to cohere in the attempt to achieve a common control over water-supplies. Good organization was all that was necessary.

For such organization no costly preparations had to be made. Harbours were unnecessary on the river and their existence was in fact forbidden by the varying water-levels of the Nile. At all times throughout history, one landed, as one does today, on the sandy bank of the river, drove in the mooring peg and made fast the boat prow and stern (Pl. 9. *a*). On ceremonial occasions such as the arrival of the barque of a god or of the train of barges bringing Hatshepsut's two colossal obelisks for the temple

96

7. *a*. Pigeon houses on the West Bank of the Nile at Thebes.

7. *b*. Landscape in the Fayum with beans in flower.

8 Papyrus thicket from the tomb of Mereruka at Saqqara.

of Amun at Karnak, the rite of 'taking the foremost rope' took place, a solemn act performed by the king in person.[1] In navigation as in all other departments of life, the royal prerogative was supreme and a private person would participate only by concession.

A ferry service was operated even in the poorest localities where in fact it was a greater necessity for daily life than anything else. The ferryman was an important figure both for men and animals. His occupation was regarded as lucrative even though the mite due to him was actually paid in a handful of farm products. Even the royal dead would have fared badly in the Other World without a ferryman. Many spells therefore guarantee their crossing the waters of heaven in the event of a refusal by the ferryman of the Field of Reeds, or of the 'curved canal'.[2] The unwilling ferryman obviously represents a common type, otherwise funerary texts from the time of the royal Pyramid Texts would not have mentioned him so often. First he had to be wakened from his sleep, then he made his excuses — his boat was leaky, he had no rushes, no planks, no cords with which to repair it; furthermore he could not assemble even the most primitive type of vessel such as one meets today on canals in Upper Egypt made of pots tied together with planks laid on top, a kind of raft which the ancient Egyptian called a 'work of Khnum' (Khnum being the god of potters).[3] The person seeking to be ferried across had again and again to show his knowledge and to contrive magical assistance. 'One who looks behind him' was a favourite name for the ferryman because he moved the ferryboat forward with a pole like a punt, looking backwards himself; such a one could be as much a hindrance as a help.

The dead also, accompanied by whole funeral cortèges, had to be transported across the river on the way to the necropolis, or at least had to cross canals or travel along them; and at the time of the inundation boats and cargo-vessels sailed over the land right up to the edge of the hills.

Religion as early as the Old Kingdom laid on the well-to-do the obligation of ferrying across any who were without boats,

---

[1] Naville, *Deir el Bahari*, VI, pl. 154, cf. below, p. 245.

[2] Kees, *Totenglauben*, 110f.

[3] *Book of the Dead*, chapter 99, introduction, cf. Kees, *Miscellanea Academica Berolinensia* (1950), II, 2, p. 77f.

particularly the corpses of the poor, just as it was their duty to bury those who had no son to do it for them. A proverb runs: 'Do not make a ferry for yourself for hire across the river, nor endeavour to make money from it. Take money for ferrying only from those who have it and refuse to take from him who has it not.'[1] Similarly the idealized biography of a Middle Kingdom official boasts of its subject as follows: 'I never refused to ferry a man', by which a poor man was meant.[2] Likewise the eloquent peasant in the story presents as a typical example of the bad and selfish man 'the ferryman who transports only those with the price of the fare'. The real situation was, however, quite different and the State was the first to lay its hands on this tempting source of revenue. In the Ptolemaic Period there was a tax on ferries 'in the King's House', a sort of poll-tax. Ptolemy Philadelphus, who otherwise understood completely how to extract the utmost from every taxable object, remitted the tax on ferry dues in the nome of Mendes when it was pointed out to him that no such tax had ever hitherto been levied there.[3] Nevertheless this tax, like the transit duty[4] may be counted among the oldest basic rights which nomarchs exercised by a delegation of the royal prerogative. Moreover, until recent times there existed throughout Egypt a sort of local ferry monopoly over which the villagers exercised strict control.

In Egypt nature has placed limitations on river navigation. The broad bed of the river except at the time of the inundation is shallow and full of sand-banks the positions of which constantly alter (Pl. 21. *a*). Consequently navigation is confined to the daytime and even today there is scarcely a ship's captain who will sail his ship at night except as a matter of urgent necessity; which fact considerably lightens the task of supervising river traffic. The prevailing north wind — the cool wind beloved of the Egyptians — is the favourable wind by which the boats with their huge lateen sails move upstream; going downstream they float with the current or are rowed if the need requires haste. The river does not in all places flow from south to north. In the great bend between Nag' Hammadi and Qena, the region that contains the ancient city of Ḥu (known to the Greeks as Diospolis Parva) and Chenoboskion, ships are obliged

---

[1] *Amenemope*, 27, 2–5.   [2] Sethe, *Lesestücke*, 79 (Stela in New York).
[3] *Urk.*, II, 42–3.   [4] See below, pp. 105, 208, 321.

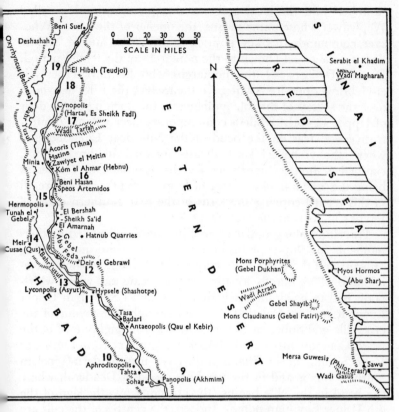

2. Middle Egypt and the Eastern Desert (North)

to sail from east to west or from west to east for a considerable distance and to do so they have to follow a zig-zag course by tacking which wastes a great deal of time; otherwise laborious rowing has to be employed. The Arabian desert in places drops abruptly down to the Nile (Pl. 1. *a*) as at the Gebel Abu Feda which acts as a wall on the east bank for a distance of 22 miles from just north of Asyut up to the plain of Amarna. An internal frontier is drawn there and one that is not there by chance; for here is the northern frontier of the Thebaid — 'ubi montes finiunt Thebaidem' rightly says Pliny in his *Natural History* (Book V, 61). Today there is still a noticeable difference in the people south of Asyut and also in the flora, the dôm-palm being the most common tree. The name Asyut signifies 'sentinel' or 'watcher' and the local god was the quarrelsome dog called Wepwawet whose name means 'the opener of the ways'. Whoever commands this key position controls the fate of Middle Egypt, a fact well known to the nomarchs of the feudal period. During Dynasty VI the nomarchs who lie buried at Deir el-Gebrawi opposite Asyut gave themselves the title 'he who is over the secrets of the sole audience at the opening of the door of Upper Egypt';[1] while a contemporary peer whose administrative seat was on the bend of the Nile near Chenoboskion where the Gebel el-Tarif thrusts forward its broad bluff, claimed a similar importance for the approach to Thebes as being the 'opening of the door of Upper Egypt'. They were all in this regard copying the lords of the real 'southern door' of Egypt which lay at the cataract at Aswan.[2]

Travelling along under steep cliffs always provided anxious moments for ship-captains because gusts of wind made sailing difficult and there were also eddies in the water. In such places and also where islands lay athwart the stream and where whirlpools had to be circumnavigated as at Gebel Silsilah in Upper Egypt it was natural that the sailors sought the favour of the crocodile god Sobek or Suchos who was the mighty lord of the river. Consequently cults of Sobek are found at Kôm Ombo, at Gebel Silsilah, at the 'Island in the river' near modern Gebelein south of Luxor and in the neighbourhood of Denderah where the bend in the Nile begins (the crocodile was the sign of the 6th Upper Egyptian nome). Indeed, the centres of the cult are scattered throughout the land up to the marshes of the Delta. The boatman who stands in the water pushing and heaving to refloat his boat stuck on a sand-bank knows well why he makes offerings to the dangerous lord of the Nile.[3] The precipitous cliffs on the Nile are particularly convenient for quarrying stone because the stone can be loaded straight into the cargo-boats (see Pl. 1. a).

Natural obstacles restrict navigation in the valley of the Nile. In the south the cataracts serve not only as the dividing points of races but also as barriers to through-traffic. The cataract at Aswan which forms a granite barrier six miles long from Elephantine in the north to el-Hesseh in the south (Pl. 2. a), is

---

[1] On this title, see Kees, *ÄZ*, 70, 83f.   [2] See below, p. 311.
[3] Kees, *Studien zur ägyptischen Provinzialkunst*, pl. 1 (from Hieraconpolis).

navigable by experienced sailors when there is a good depth of water. There is an inscription on a granite rock on the island of Sehel in the Cataract which is dated to the eighth year of Sesostris III (1870 B.C.), the time of the subjugation of Lower Nubia. It records the boast that a canal 150 cubits long, 20 cubits wide and 15 cubits deep had been constructed in the Cataract.[1] Another inscription on Sehel records that in the fiftieth year of Tuthmosis III (about 1454 B.C.) this ship-canal was found blocked with stones and excavated anew.[2] The course of the canal ran from the Great Cataract south of Sehel northwards passing to the west of that island.

If the First Cataract is only just navigable the Second at Wadi Halfa presented sailors with an insuperable obstacle. The bed of the river is here broken up by ridges of greywacke and granite into innumerable rapids and channels for a distance of more than sixty miles (Pl. 2. b). Vessels are pulled over these rapids only at great risk and with many losses. So great were the risks that they were taken only in time of war. On his return from the Nubian campaign in the nineteenth year of his reign Sesostris III noted in an inscription on the island of Uronarti (Malikarti), north of Semnah, that he had had ships dragged through the rapids and that 'it was anything but easy to get through by dragging the ships because of the time of the year'.[3] This statement can easily be believed because the inscription is dated to the second day of the fourth month of the season of inundation, according to our calendar the middle of March 1859 B.C. At this time began the period of low water. (The Egyptian date does not accurately reflect the time of the year for at this period that actual year and the calendrical year were out of step.) Scarcely better results were achieved in getting vessels over these rapids at the time of the campaign against the Mahdi in the Sudan. Traffic at this point has really no choice; it has to make a detour over the desert, especially since further obstacles barred the way upstream. On the other hand these natural obstacles did simplify the task of those charged with keeping watch on traffic, whose surveillance covered the country like a finely meshed net.

[1] De Morgan, *Catalogue des Monuments*, I, 86–7 = Sethe, *Lesestücke*, 85.
[2] De Morgan, *op. cit.*, I, 85, no. 18.
[3] *Bulletin of the Metropolitan Museum of Art*, 29 (1931), 66.

Topographical Framework of Egyptian Civilization

Within Egypt itself everything, both men and goods, moved by river. The king and his officials needed ships for travelling just as much as did the landowner for shipping grain, the temple official, the overseer of the quarries and the officer who had troops to move. The naïvely practical autobiographical inscriptions of middle-class Egyptians in the feudal period enumerate proudly the extent of the deceased person's property in ships as well as cattle, men and land.[1] The ownership of ships meant the difference between life and death in times of famine when grain had to be brought from a distance. But shipbuilding was equally important during the fat years that preceded the lean years as tomb-representations show. Important too in such times were fully-laden cargo vessels bringing the necessities of life from the estates of the funerary endowments. In the time when Egypt possessed a great empire the king and the temples could transport home by ship the wealth of the world in abundance. The tomb-representations of each period show its particular possessions.

It is not surprising when we consider the totalitarian demands of the divine kingship that the State should have enforced its prerogative also with regard to navigation and that its demands assumed at times very oppressive forms for its subjects. Among the basic rights of the king was the provision of arrangements for all royal journeys which were naturally for the most part by ship. For these journeys local authorities had to provide everything that was necessary and this service was extended to cover also the journeys of the king's messengers and other officials. In ancient times the fulfilment of these servile obligations was called 'the service (following) of Horus'[2] and as it invariably had to be performed at the time of the 'paying' of estate and commercial taxes the years were dated by it from the Thinite Period up to and including the reign of Zoser in Dynasty III. The decrees of exemption in the Old Kingdom show that the temporary presence of the Court or even only of a king's messenger was a very oppressive burden upon all who were obliged to provide the necessary maintenance. Pepi I, for example, decreed for the two Pyramid cities of Snofru at Dahshur: 'My Majesty has ordered that all engaged in business or farming in these two Pyramid cities shall be released from any

[1] See above, p. 88.   [2] Kees, *Kulturgeschichte*, 46.

obligation to provide for any messenger whatsoever travelling upstream or downstream either by water or on land.'[1] This king also freed the endowment for a statue of the Queen-mother Aput in Coptos from any form of service for 'any messenger who travels upstream on any mission whatsoever', and more expressly from any form of service 'under the Horus-service'.[2]

Under the vastly different conditions of the great empire Tuthmosis III made the Phoenician ports serve as the assembly area for his armies. His 'Instruction for the fitting-out of harbours' tested the organizational abilities of the technical branches of the Egyptian army;[3] for the success of the campaign into the interior of Syria really depended on their work. It is not astonishing therefore that the commanders and army scribes trained for such tasks should have showed themselves utterly ruthless in their own country in enforcing the commandeering of supplies, an operation carried out in the king's name with the help of the local mayors. The soldiery with their officers, scribes, grooms and a host of others, by their plundering earned for themselves during the war between the Thebans and the Heracleopolitans the opprobrious description 'the evil terror of the King's House'.[4] They were called this by the son of the nomarch of the Hermopolite nome. It is very significant that it was precisely the military dictator Horemheb who attempted by means of severe punishments to suppress all transgressions against farmers, peasants and sailors.[5] He himself had witnessed the demoralization of an army that had been maintained in the country for two generations without engaging in any serious fighting and whose privileges dated from the reign of the great Tuthmosis III. He had also witnessed the supplanting of the old governing class in all the spheres of administration and even in the service of the gods by generals, royal aides-de-camp and retired army scribes. An old ordinance still found inscribed in the tombs of the viziers of Dynasty XVIII, made the vizier the official chiefly responsible for the entire system of transport: 'It is he who provides ships for anyone for whom they must be provided.'[6] Horemheb placed the chief blame for the 'loss of

---

[1] *Urk.*, I, 210; cf. I, 286 for the temple of Min at Coptos.   [2] *Urk.*, I, 214.
[3] Erman, *Literatur der Ägypter*, 264–6, after Papyrus Anastasi, IV, 13, 8f.
[4] Anthes, *Hatnub Graffiti*, 23 and 34.
[5] Decree of Horemheb (Karnak), ll. 14–20.   [6] *Urk.*, IV, 1116.

authority in this land' on the excessive requisitioning of ships. By this arbitrary action the boatman was 'deprived of his property and lost the reward of his labour' especially if he had contracted himself for the performance of public works or works for the royal kitchens and offices, or if he had borrowed a boat to engage in hired transport. Anyone who in future engaged in such practices would be condemned to have his nose cut off and to be transported to Sile on the north-eastern frontier for forced labour.[1] Since, however, traditional rights and privileges were involved it was apparently impossible in this case to draw the line wisely; for we hear much the same complaints at much later periods. Thus Ptolemy Euergetes II in his great Amnesty Decree which was intended to put an end to party strife in Upper Egypt in 118 B.C., was compelled to forbid officials to confiscate vessels for their personal use.[2] Similarly Petronius Mamertinus the Roman proconsul in the time of Hadrian complained of the same evil in a decree: 'I have noticed that many soldiers travelling through the country demand boats, draught animals and labour, which they have no right to do. . . . The citizens through these practices suffer acts of violence and encroachments on their rights.'

A widespread symptom of corruption was the overcharging of travelling expenses. Horemheb again has something to say on this subject.[3] In the Amarna Period the overseers and table-scribes of the royal harîm seem to have led the way in this abuse by extorting from mayors under the authority of decrees dating from the reign of Tuthmosis III money for travelling expenses allegedly in arrears but manifestly never due. 'But see! Pharaoh travels to the Festival of Opet (to Thebes) every year without delay and everything must be made ready before the coming of Pharaoh'. The Dictator realistically emphasized that this objectionable procedure injured the lower classes from whose property the mayors could recoup themselves with impunity. The royal harîm with its innumerable inmates from Asiatic princely families must have displayed, particularly in the reign of Amenophis III and the 'middle-class' Queen Tiy, a refined luxury for the upkeep of which the demands were correspondingly great.

Navigation and commerce were regarded as royal preroga-

[1] See below, p. 194.   [2] *Tebtunis Papyri*, I, 5.   [3] *Loc. cit.*, l. 28f.

tives from which the king granted concessions that were to be used partly for the direct service of the State and partly for private benefit. This practice was similar to the granting of the post-monopoly by the German Emperor. Consequently, anyone who travelled or sent goods by river had to pay dues, especially on goods. In the first instance the collection of these dues was entrusted to nomarchs in the nome capitals and they in oriental fashion did not fail to line their own pockets. In the feudal period, however, these hereditary officials considered themselves to be territorial lords and, like the king, demanded transit dues for the stretch of river under their authority. This state of affairs is reflected in names like Asyut 'sentinel' or 'watchman'; here in later times was the Theban and Hermopolitan guard-post on the border of the Thebaid, 'a customs-post for goods coming down from the Thebaid', as Strabo says (XVII, 813). The same was the case with Shedia, the port on the Nile for Alexandria; and the practice is also illustrated by a passage in an inscription in the tomb of Djehuti-hotpe, the nomarch of Hermopolis in the middle of Dynasty XII: 'The Counts (nomarchs) who lived in former times, judges and canal-administrators who meted out justice in this town, appointed to supervise the weighing (of goods) on the river'.[1] The feudal lords, as usual, traced back these rights to primitive times. It is clear that at a time when the authority of the State was weakened by internal dissension such a system could degenerate into a form of trade warfare with its attendant extortions, the whole situation resembling that promoted by the robber barons of mediaeval times. Many fortifications like those set up by the Theban nomarchs under Dynasty XI on the eastern cliffs of the Nile at Gebelein above the 'Island in the river' and which dominated the southern approach to Thebes, were designed to control the river traffic and to act as a toll-gate for the collection of transit-dues.

At the beginning of the Late Period a powerful family in Heracleopolis in Middle Egypt owned a general concession as 'ship-masters' for the entire length of the river from Elephantine to the customs-post south of Memphis.[2] The Dodecaschoenus in

---

[1] Newberry, *El Bersheh*, I, pl. 14 = Sethe, *Lesestücke*, 77.

[2] Griffith, *Catalogue of the Demotic Papyri in the Rylands Library*, III, 71f., see below, p. 217.

Lower Nubia was not included in this privilege and was controlled by its own special regulations; similarly Lower Egypt over which the Saite kings enforced their rights by their own power. These ship-masters raised taxes in the king's name throughout the land and remitted them to the king and in this process they themselves became no poorer inasmuch as the manner and amount of the tax collected was left in oriental fashion to their own judgment. On the frontiers of Egypt royal officials stationed in border forts executed the king's prerogatives in regard to navigation and commerce.[1]

Privileges, concessions and special rights of all kinds in the course of time encroached more and more on the originally unequivocal fundamental laws and the result was permanent dissension and arbitrary actions.

B. SHIPBUILDING AND PORTS

The building of ships was largely governed by the question of raw materials, the suitability of a site for a ship-yard and the purpose for which the vessels were to be used. Apart from constructions of the most primitive kind such as those which the old spells for the dead describe as serving as the sun-boat and which continued a fanciful existence as almost incredible divine barques, the papyrus-boat was also a survival from primitive times.[2] The material for its construction was to be found everywhere in pools and canals and more especially in 'the land of the papyrus', the Delta. In addition ropes were needed to tie together the separate bundles of papyrus. These ropes were made partly of papyrus and partly perhaps of hemp or something similar. The result was a light boat suitable for gliding over shallow pools and through papyrus swamps and therefore useful to fishermen, hunters and bird-catchers. All down the ages this type of vessel continued to be used for sport and pleasure on the ponds and canals of country estates (Pl. 25. *a*). Similar boats of reeds are used today in the Sudan and in Abyssinia.

In building ships the Egyptian made use of the ancient art of 'fitting together'. Such construction depends for its success

---

[1] See below, p. 320.
[2] On types of ship, see Kees, *Kulturgeschichte*, 110f.

largely on the material available and Egypt lacked good timber for keels, ribs and masts. Of the trees native to the country only the sycomore at the very most provided suitable limbs and this tree was a fruit tree that could not be cut down at will, neither could shipwrights obtain it by the favourite method of confiscation. Permission to fell sycomores, by which was probably meant all fruit trees, was reserved by ancient decree for the vizir.[1] Hatshepsut on one occasion ordered the felling of sycomores 'throughout the whole country' because the timber in the neighbourhood of the First Cataract was not by itself sufficient for the building of the colossal barge to carry her two obelisks to Karnak.[2] The obelisks weighed about 323 tons and the barge was at least 269 feet long. This occasion was exceptional, however. In other cases a virtue had to be made of necessity; the skill was developed of putting together beams and planks shaped out of knotted and twisted acacia timber by means of pegs and joints. Nevertheless the ships so built of planks joined and bound together proved themselves sea-worthy, even on the high-seas. Schweinfurth saw in the Sudan similar vessels built of acacia wood and also on the coast of the Red Sea where Arab dhows are the result of a similar lack of good timber.[3] At all events there must have been repairs enough to be done on such vessels. The miserable picture of leaking boats beside the wharfs that is evoked by certain ferryman's sayings in the funerary texts (e.g. the *Book of the Dead*, chapter 99), may very possibly reflect an everyday sight.

Local reserves of timber, particularly those in the neighbourhood of the royal residence, were spared by felling timber elsewhere, in the places where it was most required. Thus the richer timber resources of the Nubian *wadis* were exploited for the building of the great barges that brought stone from the quarries at Aswan. Weni reports that King Merenrē' sent him to excavate five canals in Upper Egypt and to build three broad ships and four towed barges out of Nubian acacia wood which the headmen of the three Nubian districts and of the Medjay felled for him.[4] The loads carried by these boats were used in

[1] *Urk.*, IV, 1113.
[2] Naville, *Deir el Bahari*, VI, pls. 153–6; cf. Kees, *Kulturgeschichte*, 115.
[3] *Im Herzen von Afrika*, 24, cf. Newberry, *JEA.* 28, 64f.
[4] *Urk.*, I, 108–9.

the building of the royal mortuary monument at Saqqara. The same was the case with everything. On another occasion when Weni had to bring an offering table from the alabaster quarry of Hatnub in Middle Egypt he had the use of a barge 60 cubits long and 30 cubits broad, built in 17 days, again from the local acacia wood.

In the time of the Empire when Egyptian rule extended as far as the Fourth Cataract the timber reserves of Nubia were certainly called on to contribute largely to the Egyptian economy. Tuthmosis III expressly states that he laid on Nubia the duty of supplying ships and timber as tribute.[1] The wood brought from south of the Second Cataract was, however, mostly of the kinds highly valued for artistic and craft purposes, ebony and the like. Such wood was of no use for the building of the great Egyptian sea-going ships.

For this reason, from very early times, wood to fulfil this requirement was sought on the slopes of the Lebanon in the hinterland of the Phoenician coast where the best timber in the Near East grew. It is no exaggeration to say that their lack of timber brought the Egyptians to this coast and that the coniferous trees of the Lebanon, the *abies cilicica* and related species, exercised a decisive influence over the development of Egyptian navigation.[2] The knowledge that the Lebanon was rich in timber had reached Egypt in very early times, through the commercial enterprises of the First Naqada Period. The Thinite kings undoubtedly exploited the area for it would be difficult otherwise to understand the representations of ships on the tablets of Aha.[3] These boats are accompanied by the tag '*meru-wood*' which was one of the best known of the coniferous woods. The chief port of the Lebanon was Gubli (called Byblos by the Greeks) and there many Egyptian objects have been found, the oldest identified belonging to the reign of Khasekhemui of late Dynasty II. The first ships were probably built there on the spot to avoid the risk of sending large consignments of timber by sea. Traffic between the Lebanon and Egypt grew so rapidly that early in Dynasty IV Snofru could record the arrival of

[1] Gebel Barkal stela, see *ÄZ*, 69, 33–4.
[2] In Ancient Egyptian, '*š*, formerly, but incorrectly apparently, translated 'cedar', cf. *Ägyptische Wörterbuch*, I, 228.
[3] Petrie, *Royal Tombs*, II, pls. 10–11.

a convoy of 40 ships with so-called 'cedar wood' from the Lebanon.[1] Nature also lent a hand in the trade in that the prevailing west winds and the sea currents in the eastern Mediterranean favoured the outward voyage from the mouths of the Nile so that ships could sail to Carmel in about 96 hours. The return journey, however, took between 8 and 10 days.

The connection between the Lebanon and ships was so fixed in the Egyptian mind that their sea-going ships, even when sailing other seas, were called Byblos-ships. This name was preserved by the conservative Egyptian until the Late Period when it was even given to the Ionian triremes of Apries.[2] The better ships for river traffic and especially the barques of the gods and the boats used for funerals were for the most part built of Syrian coniferous wood. The journal of a royal dock-yard at Memphis in the reign of Amenophis III gives *meru*-wood as the principal ship-building material;[3] and as early as the Middle Kingdom a Coffin Text promises the dead man in the Other World: 'While serving in the barque of Rē' you will punt with a pole 40 cubits long made from cedar wood of Byblos.'[4] In the days when Byblos was under Egyptian sovereignty it would have been undignified to knock together a divine barque out of homely acacia wood. And from that time Egyptian maritime navigation together with much of the Egyptian economy was closely dependent on the connection between Egypt and Byblos.

One advantage of the curious constructional technique of 'fitting together' ships consisted in the fact that boats could thereby be dismantled and transported in sections over long distances. Thus Tuthmosis III tells us that for his crossing of the Euphrates he had built 'many cargo vessels of cedar wood from the mountains of the land of the gods in the dominion of Hathor of Gubli'.[5] 'They were loaded on wagons and drawn by oxen.' Here speaks the voice of ancient experience. The Egyptian State had been compelled to open up in a similar manner another maritime region in earlier times — the Red Sea. The first navigation on the Red Sea was apparently of later date

[1] Palermo Stone, *verso*, l. 6, no. 2.
[2] Stela of Amasis in Cairo, see *Rec. de Trav.*, 22, 2f.
[3] Glanville, *ÄZ*, 66, 105f.; see p. 197 below.
[4] Kees, *Totenglauben*, 422 (on *Coffin Texts*, I, spell 62).
[5] Gebel Barkal stela, l. 17.

than the first voyages to Byblos. The difficulties involved were incomparably greater; for down to the south the African coast had no timber, no means of supporting life and hardly any water that could be drunk. The very same conditions that had rendered this coast useless as a base for conquerors who came from the East in predynastic times (although climatic conditions then were more favourable) impeded the Egyptians to an even greater extent in their attempts to establish a base for their voyages to the 'God's land' of Punt. The lands that were able to supply the much sought after perfumes were given the name Punt. The earliest known voyages to Punt during the Old Kingdom started apparently from the neighbourhood of Suez, which had been discovered in the course of the expeditions to Sinai. Leadership of these voyages was entrusted to the boldest and most successful explorers of the Old Kingdom, the so-called Dragomans of Elephantine, although they lived at the opposite end of the land.[1] They bore the reputation of being specialists on all countries to the south and the south-east. In the Old Kingdom, however, the neighbourhood of Suez was still threatened by Beduin tribes, Egypt's ancient enemies, and one of these nomarchs of Elephantine was forced to report: 'The Majesty of my Lord (Pepi II) sent me to the land of Asia to bring back to him the sole friend, ship's-captain (?) and caravan-leader ('overseer of dragomans') X who had put together there a Byblos-ship to sail to Punt. The Asiatic Beduin had killed him together with the troop of the army accompanying him.'[2] Perhaps this act was the signal for the beginning of the troubles that resulted, after the end of Pepi II's reign, in dangerous raids by nomads into the eastern Delta. The ships represented on the walls of Hatshepsut's temple at Deir el-Bahari are also called Byblos-ships; they took part in the most celebrated of all the expeditions to the lands of incense and here it was shown as one of the great achievements of her reign.[3]

Men from Punt were first depicted in the mortuary temple of Sahurē' of Dynasty V among the types of neighbouring races held in subjection; they bear physically the closest resemblance to the Egyptians. The annals of Sahurē''s reign record that gold and incense were the booty brought back from an ex-

---

[1] See below, p. 312.   [2] *Urk.*, I, 134.
[3] *Urk.*, IV, 323.

pedition to Punt in apparently the thirteenth year of his reign.[1] At the close of Dynasty V under Asosi, the treasurer of the God, Bawardede, reached Punt and brought back a dancing dwarf, an event that was still talked about with admiration a hundred years later. Journeys to 'the incense terraces' became so common, however, towards the end of Dynasty VI that the servant of two successive God's treasurers, the adventurous nomarchs of Elephantine, said that he had journeyed eleven times with his masters to Byblos and Punt and each time had returned safely.[2]

At the beginning of the Middle Kingdom (which owed its foundation to the Thebans) attempts were made to move the ports of departure southwards to a place about forty miles north of Old Qoseir (the Greek Leucos Limen) at latitude 26° 06'. Here at the mouth of the Wadi Gasus el-Fokani and quite close to where the Ptolemies founded the port of Philoteras[3] is a roadstead known today as Mersa Guwesis, at latitude 26° 33'. The traces of an ancient station with a well have been found about five miles up the *wadi*[4] and there can be little doubt that the well determined the choice of this place for the harbour. The harbour itself was called Sawu and inscriptions confirm its continuous use from the days of Dynasty XII to those of the Saite kings. Its upkeep and utilization for expeditions to Punt also necessitated the improvement of the routes in the Eastern Desert. A treasury official called Henu, during the reign of Seankhkarē' Menthuhotpe of Dynasty XI tells us in an inscription in the Wadi Hammamat that he was given this task.[5] He set out from Gebelein to Qena with a levy of 3,000 men from the heart of the Thebaid to build Byblos-ships for Punt and to bring back 'fresh incense'. He constructed water reservoirs to ensure the success of his extensive convoy of materials. A short time later a successor, who styled himself 'Commander-in-chief of the whole land in this desert', extravagantly declared that he had transformed 'the *wadis* into lawns, their heights into waterpools, filled with children'.[6] The stations so set up must have

---

[1] *Urk.*, I, 246 (Palermo Stone).   [2] *Urk.*, I, 140–1.
[3] Cf. Kees' article 'Philoteras' in Pauly-Wissowa, *Real-Encyclopädie*.
[4] Schweinfurth, *Abh. Berl. Akad.* (1885); Erman, *ÄZ*, 20, 203.
[5] Couyat and Montet, *Inscriptions hiéroglyphiques du Ouadi Hammâmât*, no. 114.
[6] *Op. cit.*, nr. 1; see below, p. 120.

resembled Lakeita at the beginning of the Wadi Hammamat route where there is today a post occupied by desert police mounted on camels. The details afforded by the inscriptions in the Wadi Hammamat nevertheless justify the assumption that climatic conditions in the Eastern Desert were better in those days than they are today (Pl. 10. *b*).

After a long interval voyages to Punt were resumed during Dynasty XVIII with an expedition dispatched by Hatshepsut in the ninth year of her reign (about 1495 B.C.). From reliefs in the temple at Deir el-Bahari we learn what the travellers saw in Punt and the things that they brought back with them. The much prized perfumes headed the list and chief of these was one that the Egyptians regarded as the fruit of an 'incense-sycomore'; we distinguish it from ordinary incense and call it 'myrrh' in which scientists today suspect the presence of terebinth resin.[1] From early times myrrh and costly woods were the chief products of the 'God's land', Punt. The expedition even brought back 31 incense-sycomore trees to be planted in the garden of the temple of Deir el-Bahari in honour of the god Amun.[2] These trees were probably specimens of the real incense tree (*Boswellia*) as distinguished from the great heaps of raw incense-resin that were also shipped home. It is impossible, however, to determine whether the Somali myrrh (*Commiphora abessinica*) was included.

Among the animals of the country those whose presence created surprise were the rock-dwelling baboon and the giraffe, both of which avoid the hills. They are most easily met with in the country stretching inland from the ports of Djibuti and Berbera.[3] The Egyptians must therefore have passed through the Straits of Bab el-Mandeb and sailed at least as far as the Gulf of Tadjura. For navigational reasons they would hardly have sailed beyond Cape Guardafui.[4] Punt should then be sought on the African coast. The fact that the Egyptians found there negroes — probably slaves — in addition to the predominant Hamitic race, suggests the coastal districts of Abyssinia and Somaliland. Of the other things brought back — gay

[1] Most recently V. Loret, *Recherches de l'Institut français oriental*, 19 (1949).

[2] Naville, *Deir el Bahari*, III, pls. 78–9; *Urk.*, IV, 329, 334–5.

[3] Hilzheimer, *ÄZ*, 68, 112f. For the baboon, see Naville, *op. cit.*, III, 74–6 and for giraffe, III, 70.

[4] So Köster, *ÄZ*, 58, 128.

9. *a*. Moslem cemetery on the edge of the desert at Zawiet el Meitin.

9. *b*. Landscape in the Delta near Zagazig.

10. *a.* Water-mill in the Fayum.

10. *b.* In the Wadi Hammâmât.

panther skins, ivory, ebony, leopards, greyhounds, gold, eye-paint, the clubs used by the inhabitants of Punt — there was nothing that differed from the articles of normal trade Egypt carried on with the South or from those the Egyptians received as tribute from 'the Southern lands' or even from those mentioned in the tale of the Shipwrecked Sailor as being the products of his Isle of the Serpents. This story, which dates from the Middle Kingdom, tells by way of introduction, of a well-born Egyptian who was sent by the King on a voyage of discovery from which he was returning after meeting with little success beyond reaching Nubia and the barrier of Bigah. A companion, seeking to console him, tells him of his own adventures and how he was wrecked on an island when he was journeying to one of the King's mines. No useful purpose can possibly be served by trying to identify the island of the serpents described in this story with the island of topaz of the classical world of which Pliny tells, which Strabo also calls Ophiades and which seems to resemble the island of Zeberged (St. John's Island) in Foul Bay.[1] It is after all a fairy island that will disappear beneath the waves at the end of the story.

In Hatshepsut's temple-reliefs there are to be seen five ocean-going ships returning from a voyage under the command of the chief overseer of treasure, Nehsi, and berthing at Thebes. In consequence of this representation it has been assumed that there existed at that time a way of communication between the Nile and the Red Sea that was navigable by ships. Yet there is no other evidence nor any inscription to support the existence of such an important work with the sole exception of a very doubtful report by Pliny that the legendary King Sesostris had begun the construction of the canal before Necho. All that is historically true is that Necho started the canal about 600 B.C. and that it was completed by Darius and Xerxes;[2] further, that Ptolemy Philadelphus restored it and reopened it to traffic in 280/279 B.C. According to Herodotus (in Book II, 158) the canal ran from the Bubastite arm of the Nile, branching off a short distance above Bubastis (modern Zagazig), ran eastwards past the village of Patumos (Pithom) and through the Wadi Tumilat. It reached its eastern terminus in the neighbourhood of Lake

---

[1] So Wainwright, *JEA*, 32, 31f.
[2] Posener, *Chronique d'Egypte*, 26 (1938), 259f.

Timsah and the Bitter Lakes, through which Strabo says it passed, so approximately following the route of the modern Freshwater Canal to Suez. It used to be possible to cite as proof of a canal to the Red Sea the report in the story of Sinuhe that during the Middle Kingdom one could travel by boat from Sile on the Eastern frontier of Egypt to Memphis.[1] Now, however, this possibility is lost because it has been established that Sile was not near Ismailiyah but close to el-Qantarah.[2] An ancient canal nevertheless did run from Sile to the Bubastite (or Pelusian) arm of the Nile in the neighbourhood of Defennah. When Diodorus (Book I, 33) says that the canal begun by Necho started at the Pelusian mouth of the Nile he was including within its length the whole Bubastite arm of the Nile which had been developed into a main channel for shipping. All these facts, however, are no proof of the existence of a shipping-canal through the Wadi Tumilat before the Saite Period. Accordingly, in considering the reliefs at Deir el-Bahari one must assume either that the existence of such a canal was passed over in silence or that the arrival of ocean-going ships at Thebes was imaginary. The latter is almost certainly the case when the strongly symbolic character of Egyptian historical depictions is borne in mind.

Succeeding centuries have nothing to say about expeditions to Punt. Possibly they had become everyday affairs at a time when the whole army was transported to Syria by sea; alternatively perhaps trading was transferred to the newly-won provinces of Upper Nubia.[3] Ramesses III is the next king to report that he sent ships over the 'inverted water' of the Red Sea to Punt and that all the goods that were brought back, even the children of the chiefs whom it was customary to bring along as booty, were loaded on donkeys at the coast and conveyed to Coptos.[4] They then travelled downstream to the King's court at Memphis or Tanis (the ancient Piramesse). According to this account there was no canal link with the Red Sea about 1160 B.C. Travellers must have used, as in the Middle Kingdom, the terminal bases in the Wadi Gasus and followed the old Wadi Hammamat route. One can draw the same conclusion from the presentation of tribute by 'the great chiefs of Punt' in the time of

---

[1] E.g. Breasted, *History of Egypt*, 276.   [2] See below, p. 190.
[3] See below, p. 335.   [4] Papyrus Harris, I, 77, 8f.

The Nile and Egyptian Civilization

Horemheb.[1] In general, however, such representations, inasmuch as they were executed as an act of homage, were only of symbolic value, as also in the case of the chiefs of the Keftiu — the geographical opposites of those of Punt.

We know that as a result of the campaigns of Alexander the Great maritime activities were renewed in the Ptolemaic Period and especially under Ptolemy Philadelphus.[2] The constantly repeated establishment of bases on the coast of the Red Sea and the frequent changes of anchorages and landing-places serve to reveal the perils of coral reefs in the dangerously narrow entrances to exposed bays (Pl. 11. *a*). The area of activity extended from Myos Hormos (modern Abu Shar at lat. 27° 23′) in the north to Philoteras (near Mersa Guwêsis? at 26° 33′), Leucos Limen (modern Old Qoseir at 26° 06′), Nechesia (modern Mersa Mubarak near the gold mines of Umm Rûs at 25° 30′) to Berenice on Foul Bay in the south (at 23° 54′).

[1] Wreszinski, *Atlas*, II, pl. 60.
[2] Wilcken, *ÄZ*, 60, 86; Kornbeutel, *Der ägyptische Sud- und Osthandel in der Politik der Ptolemäer und römischer Kaiser* (Berlin dissertation, 1931).

IV

The Desert and Egyptian Civilization

A. THE EASTERN DESERT

In spite of the fact that the valley of the Nile is hedged on both sides by deserts man has in all ages broken through these barriers to reach countries that were not accessible to him by water. Travel along the *wadis* and over the sand is indeed obviously more ancient than travel by boat and in historical times trading interests, particularly the quest for raw materials, sent the Egyptians even further afield into these dangerous thirsty regions.

The 'Way of Horus', the royal road leading from Sile (el-Qantarah) by way of el-Arish to Gaza in Southern Palestine played an important role as a military highway.[1] The migrations of races, following the caravan routes from primitive times pressed on Egypt's frontiers and forced the State to take defensive measures. Conditions differed between the Libyan and the Arabian frontiers; they also changed at different periods in the course of history. Movement in the direction of the desert also changed its methods and aims from time to time. Raw materials and even matters of fashion and taste played their parts in this development.

Two nodal points in eastern traffic were situated on the Arabian side of the Nile; these were the eastern side of the Delta about which something has already been said in discussing the prehistory of Egypt, and the region north of Thebes. The Isthmus of Suez was crossed by two ways of approach to the Delta. The northern has already been mentioned and it was doubtlessly the route by which all Egyptian armies marched into Asia, and which was utilized by all Asiatic conquerors. It

[1] See below, p. 191.

116

crossed the narrow strip of land dividing the seas at Sile (now Tell Abu Sêfe, near el-Qantarah) and then ran over salty flats south of the Pelusian arm of the Nile to reach the north-eastern Delta nome in the direction of Fakûs. From the frontier near Sile the Egyptian canal system was available for further transport. History shows, especially with regard to the Assyrian and Persian invasions, that the conquest of the desert between el-Arish (in Greek, Rhinocorura) and Pelusium beside the lagoons of the Serbonian Lake was no simple matter. The barrier of lakes from the Pelusian mouth up to Lake Balah south of el-Qantarah could easily be defended.

The predetermined southern way of approach, coming from the neighbourhood of Ismailiyah on Lake Timsah, was along the thinly populated Wadi Tumilat. But Lake Timsah in the centre of the isthmus could only be reached from the east along the difficult desert tracks from Syria or from the desert region of the Negeb in Palestine; a watch could easily be kept over the few wells. We learn from the story of the flight of Sinuhe what the state of affairs here was at the beginning of the Middle Kingdom.[1] It was the scene of much activity on the part of Asiatic nomads whose undisciplined mode of life made them the sworn enemies of the Egyptians in the east. It was in order to keep them within bounds that measures had to be taken for safeguarding communications with Sinai. Consequently we find that the early Thinite kings were active in this region; Sememp-ses had a monumental relief carved to celebrate his victories and Snofru, the founder of Dynasty IV, can be regarded as the final conqueror and the tutelary deity of Egyptian rule in that part of the world.[2] It was again the lure of raw materials that brought men to the barren mountain valleys of the Sinai peninsula, in particular the quest for the rich deposits of turquoise from which the mountains of Sinai came to be known as the 'Turquoise terraces'.[3] Under their word for turquoise the Egyptians certainly included all kinds of green stone, malachite, amazonite and green felspar. Although there is no trace today, copper-mining may perhaps also have been carried on.[4] The

---

[1] See below, p. 192.   [2] Gardiner, Peet and Černý, *Inscriptions of Sinai*, I.
[3] Kees, *Kulturgeschichte*, 126f.
[4] Lucas, *Ancient Egyptian Materials*³, 231f.; for malachite, see *op. cit.*, 456, and for turquoise, 460.

existence of the turquoise mines is, on the contrary, proved by numerous Egyptian inscriptions in the Wadi Magharah and at Serabît el-Khâdim, at the latter particularly from the Middle Kingdom when it possessed a sanctuary of Hathor.

The expeditions starting from the regions of Memphis and Heliopolis for Sinai in ancient days certainly took the direct route over the desert plateau between Cairo and Suez, a route followed subsequently by pilgrims from North Africa to Mecca (the Darb el-Hagg), so as to avoid the round-about way through the Wadi Tumilat. To appreciate fully what the ancient Egyptian endured and achieved in his desert travels it must be remembered that all he had in the way of beasts of burden were donkeys and oxen. Judging from a stone vessel in the form of a camel found at Abusir el-Melek,[1] it would seem that during the Second Naqada Period the camel was for a fleeting moment brought to the notice of the Egyptians by the Asiatic beduin, but it was not used generally in Egypt until the Greek Period, as a result of an economic revolution. It is not therefore fair to judge ancient Egyptian expeditions into the desert by the standard of Arab camel caravans. Moreover, throughout the Old Kingdom, expeditions to Sinai had to reckon with the enmity of the beduin,[2] with the result that the labour needed by the expedition had to go along with it. These conditions improved only for the first time during the Middle Kingdom;[3] but in any case the beduin are, and always have been, unsuited for regular work.

The desert tracks leading south on the Arabian side of Suez were used only to a limited extent by the migrations of races. In most cases the people using them could only have been small bands of nomads like those who wander about in the same region today, usually seeking to reach the *wadis* cutting into the limestone plateau and leading down to the Nile. During the reign of Sesostris II the nomarch Khnumhotpe commemorated in his tomb at Beni Hasan the arrival of a band of thirty-seven Asiatic beduin who brought to him an overseer of huntsmen to serve as head of the desert police.[4] This noble of Middle Egypt

---

[1] Scharff, *Abusir el Meleq*, pl. 24, nr. 209.   [2] See above, p. 110.

[3] Černý, 'Semites in Egyptian Mining Expeditions to Sinai' in *Archiv Orientálni*, 7 (1935), 384f.

[4] Newberry, *Beni Hasan*, I, pls. 30–1 = Wreszinski, *Atlas*, II, pl. 6.

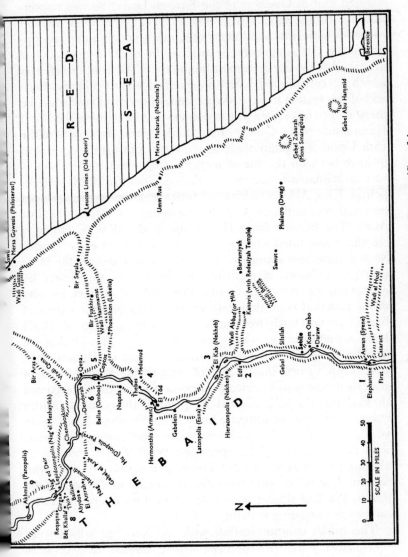

3. Upper Egypt and the Eastern Desert (South)

Map labels:

Siwū
Mersa Gwesis (Philoteras?)
Wadi Gasūs
R E D
S E A
Leucos Limen (Old Qoseir)
Mersa Mubarak (Nechesia?)
Umm Rus
Berenice
Gebel Abu Hammid
Gebel Zabarah (Mons Smaragdus)
Phalacro (Dweg)

Bir Sayāla
Bir Fokhīra
Wadi Hammamat
Phoenikon (Laketa)
Wadi Rina
Bir Artas

Barramīyah
Samut
Kanayis (with Redesiyah Temple)
Wadi Abbad (or Mia)
El Kab (Nekheb)
Sebûa

Qena
Coptos
Qena
Medamud
El Tôd
Thebes
Nagada
Ballas (Ombos)
Dendereh
Hermonthis (Armant)
Gebelein
Latopolis (Esna)
Hieraconpolis (Nekhen)
Edfu
Gebel Silsilah
Kom Ombo
Daraw
Aswan (Syene)
Elephantine
First Cataract
Wadi el Hudi

Akhmīm (Panopolis)
Nag ed Deir
Lepidoconpolis (Nag'el Mashayikh)
Chenoboskion
Hu (Diospolis Parva)
Gebel el Arak
Reqaqna
Girga
Balliana
This?
El Amrah?
Abydos
Bêt Khallāf
Nag' Hammadi
Wadi Gasūs

T H E B A I D

SCALE IN MILES
0   10   20   30   40   50

N

119

claimed that as Overseer of the Eastern Desert he was responsible for its security. Within his nome lay the royal domain Menat-Khufu (literally 'Nurse of Khufu') which, in an inscription of the Theban general Se'ankh at the end of Dynasty XI, is described as the northernmost boundary of the frontier defences which he constructed based on fortified walls.[1] The southern end of this system may, in the absence of certain knowledge, be presumed to have been at the present-day Lakeita on the Wadi Hammamat route. On the other hand, Hebnu the capital of the 16th Upper Egyptian nome which is thought with good reason to have been on the site of modern Zawiyet el-Meitin, south-east of Minia, is mentioned in the testament of the Heracleopolitan King Akhtoy to his son Merikarē' as being the southern terminal of the defences of the north-eastern frontier against Asia: 'The frontier from Hebnu up to the Way of Horus is colonized and filled with people of the best of the entire land.'[2] Such a statement sounds very haughty but it reveals the same principle at work of securing the defence of the desert by occupying the wells with small detachments of hunters. In spite of the fact that conditions today are much worse the camps of beduin are still fairly frequently found at the wells in the Wadi Hammamat country, as at Lakeita and Bir Fuakhir. During the Middle Kingdom the district around Minia or Hebnu must have been turned into a sort of second line in the series of eastern defences although no important caravan route passed through into the Nile valley at this point. Only secondary routes running towards the ultimate branches of the great Wadi Qena which thrusts upwards from the south, lead towards the east, with the exception of the sprawling Wadi Tarfah that opens about 23 miles to the north.[3] The detachments of hunters who were used as police were certainly recruited from the sons of the desert. We find similar 'commandos' in the western oases and on the tracks leading to them.

The routes communicating with the Red Sea which were

[1] See above, p. 111, on Couyat and Montet, *Inscriptions hiéroglyphiques du Ouadi Hammâmât*, nr. 1.

[2] Papyrus Petersburg, 1116A, (ed. Golenischeff), ll. 88–9; see below, p. 191.

[3] At Antinoopolis (Sheikh Abade) in the 15th nome from which the Via Hadriana set out for the Red Sea, Hadrian left indications that the Eastern Desert in this neighbourhood offered no special difficulties.

most frequently used left the valley of the Nile along the stretch of river between Qena and Thebes because, in consequence of the great bend made by the Nile, the stream there ran closest to the coast. Many *wadis* open along this stretch of the river and lead into the eastern desert. On the other hand, after the passage of the limestone plateau great ranges of primary rock rising to over 6,000 feet are encountered (Pl. 10. *b*), necessitating the laborious threading of a way through *wadis* in the course of which the track, as in the case of the Hammamat route, climbs to a height of 2,500 feet in order to gain the watershed between the Nile and the Red Sea. Nevertheless these masses of primary rock reward so much labour by concealing in their midst more springs and green places than are to be found in the northern region. What especially attracted the inhabitants of the Nile valley to these mountains from the days of the predynastic hunters and cattle-breeders onwards were the wonderfully coloured hard stones used for arts and crafts,[1] the gold and the semi-precious stones which the primary rocks conceal in their veins. In the Hammamat was found greywacke or schist, a sort of greeny slate which was used for cosmetic palettes in the Pre-dynastic and Early Dynastic Periods and which was much favoured by sculptors in the Late Period because of the mirror-like polish it could take. The Egyptians called this stone 'the beautiful *bekhen*-stone'.[2] Earlier volcanic rocks were also to be found there, such as grey granite (on Gebel Fatiri, the Mons Claudianus of the classical world) and diorite (near Fuakhir in the Hammamat) which were coveted from time immemorial for architectural and sculptural purposes. The obvious point of departure for the Wadi Hammamat and the route to Qoseir (Leucos Limen) 107 miles away (Pl. 11. *a*) was Coptos. By using this route it was possible to reach the port of Sawu at the mouth of the Wadi Gasus (and the Ptolemaic port of Philoteras) either by travelling along the coast northwards or by turning north-wards at the wells of Bir Seyala, 82 miles from Coptos.[3] Alterna-

---

[1] See above, p. 35.

[2] The word occurs in the Wadi Hammâmât from the time of Sesostris III, cf. Couyat and Montet, *op. cit.*, nr. 47. On the stone see Lucas and Rowe, *Annales du Service*, 38, 127f.

[3] On the stations and routes see G. W. Murray, *JEA*, 11, 138 with figure and map; also D. Meredith, *JEA*, 38, 94f., and 39, 95f.

tively the broad Wadi Qena could be followed northwards from Qena to Bir Aras (13 miles distant) at which point the track turned north-eastwards into the Wadi Atrash in the direction of Gebel Dukhan (5,400 feet), the Mons Porphyrites of Imperial Roman times (Pl. 12. *b*), where the track wound between this mountain and Gebel Qattar (6,400 feet) to the south before finally reaching the Wadi Abu Shar and the port of Myos Hormos (a distance of 113 miles). From Qena it was also possible to reach the heart of the Wadi Gasus, the outlet to the port of Sawu, by travelling straight across the mountains. The decisive factor in the choice of these routes was their ease of access to the mines of gold, iron and precious stones. It must be pointed out in this connection that the magnificent porphyry of Gebel Dukhan did not attract the attention of the ancient Egyptians until the Romans came.

When Ptolemy Philadelphus directed the principal traffic on the Red Sea south to Berenice (Sikket Bender) on Foul Bay, which lies on the same latitude as Aswan (23° 54′) he allowed the route to the Nile again to run to Coptos. The new route branched off from the Qoseir road at Phoenikon (modern Lakeita) and ran southwards through ten more stations that are noted in the late Roman *Itinerarium Antonini* to reach Berenice. This was a distance of 259 Roman miles or 236 English miles, with 24 Roman miles to Lakeita.

The Egyptians have left no records of the travelling times for the various routes. Camel caravans have been available for these journeys since Greek times but they were not known to Pharaoh and his servants. It is therefore only to a limited extent possible to estimate, from the known distances between the ancient wells or from modern journeys dependent for water on these wells, the times taken for these journeys in ancient days. Today the journey to Qoseir takes four or five days, from Qena to Abu Shar (Myos Hormos) five to six days, and from Coptos to Berenice about twelve days. It is therefore all the more surprising to find with what perseverance and how successfully the explorers of the ancient world penetrated to the most distant corners of the eastern desert. In the area of the Wadi Hammamat, frequently in resting places where prehistoric hunters had already left rock-drawings, innumerable inscriptions commemorate these expeditions and their leaders. The dated texts begin in the reign of Asosi at the close of Dynasty V and reach their first concentration in Dynasty VI. Apart from man-power (which was ruthlessly expended) donkeys were used for the carrying of supplies and oxen as draught animals for dragging away stone. Provisioning created a serious problem. Thus the leader of an expedition dispatched towards the end of the Old Kingdom from the court at Memphis to quarry stone in the Wadi Hammamat reports that the king placed at his disposal daily 50 head of cattle and 200 goats to feed 100 stonemasons and 2,200 men of the labour service whom he took with him.[1]

At the departure points in the Nile valley the great lords boasted of their offices as supervisors and the ancient gods lost no chance to enhance their fame. It is easy to see how the nomarch of Coptos in the feudal period, being 'Overseer of Upper Egypt' could also call himself 'Overseer of the western and eastern deserts' with more justification than his Middle Egypt colleague at Beni Hasan of whom mention has already been made.[2] For it was Coptos, which was subsequently superseded by the neighbouring Qus and then Qena, that owed its importance in ancient times chiefly to the routes to the east. The ancient name of the town of Ombos (near Ballas) on the west bank of the Nile opposite Coptos was *Nebet*, literally meaning 'the Golden (town)' and it too reflects the wealth derived from the treasurehouse of the eastern desert, notably so in the place that was the centre of the predynastic Naqada culture of Upper Egypt. The gold clearly came from the 'desert of Coptos', as the Egyptians said in order to distinguish it from the Nubian gold of Kush;[3] most of it came from the Fuakhir mine in the Wadi Hammamat. It has been assumed that the unique map of Ramesside date preserved on a papyrus in Turin is concerned with the neighbourhood of the Fuakhir mine together with the routes leading through the Wadi Hammamat to it and the road proceeding to the Red Sea. It shows not only a 'well of Sethos I,' 'the mountains in which gold is mined,' two tracks leading to the Red Sea and a temple of Amun in the centre of the labour camp, but also, at some distance from the camp of

[1] Couyat and Montet, *op. cit.*, nr. 206 = *Urk.*, I, 149; cf. Kees, *Kulturgeschichte*, 104f.
[2] Cairo, 1442.　　[3] So, *Urk.*, IV, 931 (under Tuthmosis III).

the gold mines, the 'mountain of the *bekhen*-stone', the coveted greywacke or schist of the Wadi Hammamat.[1]

The routes that led eastwards from the southern Thebaid from the district opposite Edfu (from Redesîyah) and from el-Kab and Kôm Ombo, were never of any importance for through-traffic but were mainly used as means of access to the goldmines. The rock-temple of Kanayis in the Wadi Mia (Wadi Abbad) about 42 miles east of the Nile valley was built by Sethos I about 1305 B.C. at what is clearly an advanced post, and inscriptions there mention the exploitation of what was certainly the most productive mine on Egyptian soil at Barramiyah some thirty miles further east.[2] It was possible from Barramiyah, by using the Wadi Beiza and cutting across the route from Coptos to Berenice at Bir Beiza (the ancient wateringpoint of Jovis in the *Itinerarium Antonini*) to reach the mines of Umm Rûs near the coast of the Red Sea and also the anchorage of Nechesia (modern Mersa Mubarak); although to reach the latter necessitated the use of a difficult desert track for more than sixty miles. Another well-known goldmine, that of Sukari, north of the Emerald mountain (Gebel Zabarah, 4,250 feet), could also be reached from Bir Beiza. Furthermore the goldmine at Samut, seventy miles from Sethos I's rock-temple at Kanayis, was accessible by following an ancient gold-road further southwards through Abu Kreyah;[3] beyond Samut, travelling eastwards the Coptos-Berenice road was reached at the station of Dweg (Phalacro in classical times).[4]

Sethos I donated the revenues of what was in his time undoubtedly the most profitable mine to the Temple of Osiris which he built at Abydos.

Egyptian records say nothing about mining methods, labour forces or the certainly very high loss of life apart from a single instance in Nubia in the reign of Ramesses II.[5] In the Roman Period the workers in the mines and quarries of the eastern desert were the *damnati in metallum* of whose terrible lot Agath-

[1] Erman and Ranke, *Ägypten*, fig. 234; more completely now in G. Goyon, *Annales du Service*, 49, 337f., with 2 plates and many figures.

[2] Gardiner and Gunn, *JEA*, 4, 244f.

[3] The Dunkash goldmine lies rather to the north-east of Samut, in the direction of Barramiyah.

[4] Baedeker, *Ägypten*, 390–1, after Golenischeff, *Rec. de Trav.*, 13, 75f.

[5] See below, p. 322.

archides of Cnidus, who lived about 130 B.C., gives us some idea in his description of the labourers washing out gold from the crushed quartz in the mountains during the Ptolemaic Period.[1] We can also count on the fact that from the New Kingdom large numbers of prisoners-of-war were employed in Egyptian mines. Before that time reliance had to be placed on conscripted labour and on the recruitment of nomads who were little suited for such work. The guarantee given by Sethos I that workmen for the goldmines would be provided solely out of the labour force attached to the Temple of Osiris at Abydos did not exclude the use of prisoners-of-war because large numbers of them were to be found among the temple slaves. In addition there were convicts of all kinds. Egyptian decrees of this period, especially those of Horemheb which have been frequently mentioned already, often threaten evil-doers with transportation and forced labour in the frontier zones — Sile, Kush or the Libyan oases.[2] Many ancient camps still stand in the most distant corners of the desert complete with stalls for cattle, barracks for guards and miserable stone huts on the mountain slopes for the workmen. A good example is the Roman encampment for workers in the porphyry quarries which stands in magnificent isolation on the slopes of Gebel Dukhan (Pl. 12. b). The mines in the eastern desert opposite the southern Thebaid (the district known in ancient times as the 'Head of Upper Egypt') came, during the New Kingdom, under the control of the high official known as 'King's son of Kush' (the Viceroy of Nubia); but their discovery and exploitation was by no means the achievement of the New Kingdom or indeed of the Ramesside Kings. The wealth and fame of the oldest capital of Upper Egypt, Hieraconpolis (modern Kôm el-Ahmar) and of its sister city on the eastern side of the river, Nekheb (modern el-Kab), the city of the tutelary goddess Nekhbet, already depended on the gold from the desert. Local conditions were similar to those at Coptos and Ombos. At el-Kab a *wadi* runs eastwards and at its entrance stands a sanctuary of Hathor 'Mistress of the desert-valley', while further inland is a speos similar to the shrine of the lion-goddess Pakhet near Beni Hasan. It was dedicated, in addition to Nekhbet, to

[1] Diodorus, III, 12–14.
[2] See above, p. 104; below, p. 131.

Hathor-Tefnut as 'Mistress of the valley-entrance';[1] behind this dedication there certainly lies an ancient animal cult either of a lioness, as at Beni Hasan, or of 'the great wild cow that is a visitor in el-Kab', which appears in the Pyramid Texts. In the mortuary temple of Sahurē' there is a representation of Nekhbet offering the King gold and, what was still more rare (though extracted from the same veins of quartz) silver.[2] The title 'Guardian of silver and gold' borne by the nomarchs of el-Kab during the Middle Kingdom was undoubtedly inspired by duties dating from early times.[3] Herein perhaps lies the explanation of the remarkable fact that the unifiers of the two kingdoms of Egypt came apparently from the extreme south of the country where agricultural land was scarce, a district which almost bordered on the Nubian nome (that of Elephantine). Was the precious metal already their source of power?

Other gifts that the eastern desert had for its visitors were those semi-precious stones that from the Thinite Period onwards and even to some extent during the Predynastic Period, render Egyptian trinkets and jewellery so attractive. There are garnets, felspar, onyx, chalcedony, agates, jasper, rock-crystal, amethysts, turquoises and carnelians. Stones like steatite and turquoise were used as early as the Badarian Period in Egypt,[4] and such use presupposes the beginnings of an extensive system of barter. The favourite coloured stones used by the Egyptians were green turquoise, dull-red carnelian and blue lapis-lazuli, but the last had, at all periods, to be obtained by barter from abroad, if the genuine stuff was wanted. It probably came from far afield, even Asia. Green-stone and turquoise came from the Eastern Desert and from Sinai; carnelian and other reddish stones such as garnets were found in the neighbourhood of the cataract at Aswan while the violet-coloured amethyst was found in the Nubian Desert.[5] Many names of stones in Egyptian texts have not yet been identified. The use of such stones was not decided wholly by chance; fashion, that changes its favourites from time to time, undoubtedly had much to say in this matter. We shall return to this question when we come to describe

---

[1] L. *D.*, Text, IV, 39; the existing plan is Ptolemaic.
[2] Sethe in Borchardt, *Grabdenkmal des Königs Saȝḥure*, II, 93 on pl. 18.
[3] L. *D.*, III, 13b (Dynasty XIII).
[4] Brunton, *Badarian Civilisation*, 41.   [5] See below, p. 322f.

Nubian conditions. Furthermore, Pharaonic Egypt made no use of several stones among those most highly valued today, although found within her borders, such as the exceedingly precious emerald and the transparent many-coloured beryl. The former is found in the Gebel Zabarah (4,464 feet) known to the classical world as *Smaragdus Mons*; the latter in the mountains by the Red Sea.[1] Their beauty was first appreciated in the classical period.

B. CARAVAN ROUTES IN THE WEST — THE LIBYAN OASES

The conditions that prevailed on the caravan routes in the West were essentially different from those in the East. The men who travelled them from Egypt were not looking for raw materials on the frontiers of their own cultural area nor did they go as hunters in search of game. The goals in this instance were far-distant and between them and the Nile valley lay a stony desert waste of sand dunes with few noticeable areas of high ground for hundreds of miles. The Libyan oases were pivots; they are depressions in the desert plateau which lie considerably below the level of the Mediterranean and which in places fall by steep slopes so abruptly from the edge of the desert that they are spotted only when one is right upon them. The Egyptian name for oasis was *wahe* and it is from it that the Greek 'oasis' is to be derived; *wahe* actually means 'basin' and it was therefore used for oasis with singular appropriateness. The oases contain water derived from natural springs or wells in which the water is replenished underground from the marshes of the Sudan. The theory that the oases lie on the line of a primeval branch of the Nile called Bahr Bilama has been proved false. The largest and most important oasis is el-Khargah ('the inner one') known to the ancient Egyptian as the 'southern oasis'; it is about 125 miles from north to south with a breadth varying between 13 and 30 miles. About 45 miles to the west of el-Khargah lies el-Dakhlah ('the outer one'). Khargah is about 100 miles from the Nile valley and the natural ways of approach start from the neighbourhood of Abydos and Hu (the classical Diospolis Parva). Consequently in ancient times the oases were for purposes of administration under the authority of the 8th (Thinite)

[1] Lucas, *Ancient Egyptian Materials*[3], 445f.

nome or 7th (Diospolis Parva) nome and occasionally under that of the 9th (Panopolite) nome.[1] We have already mentioned Khargah as being the district containing royal vineyards in the Thinite Period.

The fact that during the New Kingdom, as we learn, for example, from scenes in the tomb of the Second Prophet of Amun Puyemrē' who lived during the reign of Tuthmosis III, the 'Great ones of the southern and northern oases' brought tribute, including wine,[2] indicates that in the oases the endowment estates of Amun were in many cases the successors of the old royal domains. In this way Amun himself became Lord of the Oases. In ancient times the desert tracks and the oases were under the protection of Seth or of a god akin to him in character called Ash whom we find in the likeness of Seth on the jar-sealings from the Thinite royal tombs at Abydos. In the Old Kingdom he was called Lord of Libya. From Asyut by way of Khargah runs the famous Road of Forty Days (Darb el-arba'in) to Darfur (el-Fasher); leaving Khargah it first passes by the desert wells of Bir Murr and Bir Kasaba and then by the small oases of Selime, Lakiza and Bir Natrun (which are only occasionally visited by beduin of the tribe of the black Goran or Tibbu) before reaching its destination. It avoided the whole area of the cataracts and led directly into the land of the negroes. The great days of this route were those of the Arab slave-traders and with such routes is closely associated the camel, the means of transport for men and goods. Nevertheless it must be remembered that even today cattle-breeding nomads like the Tibbu cross vast waterless stretches of desert with their cattle from the uplands of Tibesti or the oasis of Kufra to the pastures on the Gebel Uwenat and in Gilf Kebir just like their ancestors who tended their herds under much better conditions of climate and who left behind them drawings on the rocks.[3]

The struggle for the few pasturages was not, however, one with Nature alone. The population of the oases possesses a characteristic intermixture of races with divisions into ruling and slave classes which afford clear proof of continuous strife between different racial groups. In ancient times the Libyan tribes from the northern fringe of Africa spread down into the southern

---

[1] See Kees' article 'Oasis' in Pauly-Wissowa, *Real-Encyclopädie.*
[2] Davies, *Tomb of Puyemre*, I, pl. 31.   [3] See above, p. 22.

11. *a.* Roadstead at Old Qoseir on the Red Sea.

11. *b.* Desert plants after rain.

12. *a*. Sand-dunes and tamarisks in the Northern Sudan.

12. *b*. The quarrymen's village at Gebel Dushan.

oases and consequently came into conflict with the Nubian tribes of the Nile valley. The nomarch Harkhuf who lived in the reign of Merenrē' of Dynasty VI left an account of one such conflict.[1] He himself had set out from the Nile valley, starting probably from the neighbourhood of Abydos, but certainly from somewhere north of Aswan 'on the road to the oasis' with the intention of travelling perhaps by way of Khargah and the small oasis of Dunkul to the Nubian land of Yam, a district south of the Second Cataract. On the way he encountered the chief of Yam making a foray into the 'land of the Libyans . . . as far as the western corner of heaven'. The cunning Egyptian fell on him from the rear, clearly not from the direction of his intended march southwards, and restored order; in short, he deprived him of his booty! Such conflicts arose chiefly over the seizing of men and animals and over rival claims to the ownership of individual oases.

The ancients clearly understood the necessity for the construction of reservoirs to supplement the few natural springs so that detachments of troops could be sent over vast waterless stretches of desert. A modern desert expedition discovered in 1917 an ancient storage depot of hundreds of pottery jars at Abu Ballas far to the south-west of Dakhlah. It was situated on the old caravan route that by-passed the Sahara to the south and went north by way of Gilf Kebir to Kufra. Stories were still current at Dakhlah that in former times the oasis had frequently been attacked by bands of negroes for whom this water depot had served as a spring-board for the assault.[2] In this connection it may be recalled that there is historical proof for frequent raids on the Libyan oases, particularly Khargah, by Nubian robber-bands in the late Roman Period (about A.D. 440).[3] On such dangerous expeditions disasters often occurred especially when they were undertaken by raiders unused to desert travel. The greatest catastrophe of this kind known to history was the destruction of Cambyses' army which lost its way among the sand dunes of the Sahara while marching to Siwa, the oasis of Amun.[4]

---

[1] *Urk.*, I, 125–6.   [2] Almásy, *Unbekannte Sahara*, 72f., 179.
[3] Kees' article 'Oasis', see n. 1, p. 128.
[4] Investigations after traces in the area of sand-dunes south-west of Bahrein, described by Von der Esch, *Weenak — die Karawane ruft*, p. 280f., with maps.

The ancient Egyptians considered the maintenance of communications with the Libyan oases of such great importance that the supervisory control of the oases was during the Middle Kingdom entrusted to the vizir, the highest royal official, who might be a feudal lord from Middle Egypt like Ahanakhte, the nomarch of Hermopolis; he might be a courtier like Menthuhotpe, the vizir of Sesostris I.[1] Both men bore the title 'Overseer of the Western Desert' just as the corresponding official on the other side of the Nile was the 'Overseer of the Eastern Desert'.

It was natural that the oases became the resorts frequented by many kinds of doubtful characters who tried to escape official supervision. One overseer of hunters, who also calls himself overseer of the Western Desert, commemorates on a stela the police chase after a fugitive from justice during the Middle Kingdom: 'I reached the Western Oasis (certainly Dakhlah), explored all its tracks and brought back the fugitive that I found there. The detachment was in good shape and suffered no losses.'[2] The 'detachment' was a troop of hunters similar to those we have already come across serving as a frontier defence force under a nomarch of Beni Hasan. During the New Kingdom these detachments were recruited from desert tribesmen, probably Libyan in origin, as their names show, e.g. the Tjukten of the Oasis and the Niau. They were stationed in the oases and were the predecessors of the Ptolemaic desert police, ἐρημοφύλακες. They also served as guides for hunting expeditions in the country surrounding the oases. A model letter used in the training of Civil Service candidates during the Ramesside Period, written in the form of an admonition to an official of the frontier service, deals with this type of person: 'When this dispatch of Pharaoh reaches you, you shall write a letter to this scribe whom you sent to the oasis, to say: "Beware of meddling with the Tjukten by removing even one of them, or else it will be reckoned against you as a capital offence." '[3] Merenptah's hymn of victory after the Libyan War characterizes the peace that followed as being such that the Tjukten and the Niau were now working in the fields while the Medjay (the Bedja) slept.[4] Here the reference is certainly to the military detachments.

[1] *El Bersheh*, II, pl. 13; Cairo 20539, l. 16.
[2] Anthes, *ÄZ*, 65, 108f. (Berlin 22820).   [3] Papyrus Anastasi, IV, 10, 8.
[4] Ll. 23–4, cf. Erman, *Literatur der Ägypter*, 345.

The Desert and Egyptian Civilization

The oases, and particularly Khargah, were also used as places of exile. During the period of the God's State at Thebes in Dynasty XXI members of an unpopular party were exiled to the oases, while in the Christian Periods recalcitrant bishops like Athanasius and Nestorius (A.D. 435) met the same fate. Even in quite modern times, under the law of the 4th July 1909, a number of 'notoriously dangerous persons' were deported to the oases for political reasons. The oases shared this fate with other frontier regions and, in the Ptolemaic Period, the Upper Thebaid south of Coptos was regarded as a suitable place of exile. Moreover the oases proved themselves suitable centres for anchorites. During the Roman Imperial Period Khargah or the Oasis of Hibis, as it was called from its capital, was reckoned to be the particular area or νομός for anchorites, and the Christian monuments there are extraordinary for their grandeur. One of the most inhospitable oases, the Wadi Natrun, on the north-west border of Lower Egypt, became known as the land of Monks because of its monasteries. Its Egyptian name was Shiet, in Greek Scetis. This oasis, which was known to the Egyptians as the 'field of salt' had little to offer apart from 'Lower Egyptian natron' which was used for purifying and in the process of mummification. The instructive story of the Eloquent Peasant which dates from the early Middle Kingdom begins with an account of how a poor peasant from this oasis travelled from the 'field of salt' to the market at Heracleopolis which was at that time the royal capital. He took with him on his ass all kinds of plants, wooden articles including rods from the Land of the Cow (i.e. the Oasis of Farafra), skins, furs and minerals which he hoped to barter for food. But this enumeration of products which are typical of most oases is surely excessively optimistic when applied to the Wadi Natrum.

The 'northern' oasis which is still today known as el-Bahriyah (Arabic for 'northern') was of far less importance than the great southern oasis. It was sometimes called by the ancients the oasis of Behnesa or Pimedjay after the town in the valley of the Nile which was the most important starting point for the oasis. Its ancient Egyptian name was Djesdjes which was certainly derived from a legend. In the nome lists in Ptolemaic temples it is listed with Khargah as a source of wine. It was, nevertheless, of

little economic importance except as a supply base for caravans.[1]
During Dynasty XXVI, in the reign of Amasis, a small
sanctuary was built there by Djedkhonsiufankh, a Governor of
the Oases who was certainly of Libyan descent. South-west of
Bahriyah and not far from the eastern edge of the Sahara lies
the unimportant oasis of Farafra, about seventy-five miles from
Dakhlah; a road runs through it from Dakhlah to Bahriyah.
The Egyptians called it oddly the 'Land of the Cow' which
possibly contains an allusion to Hathor, the cow-goddess whose
worship was characteristic of the Libyan frontier region.
During the reign of Merenptah, about 1230 B.C., groups of
Libyans filtered into Egypt along the caravan route through
Bahriyah and Farafra, at first apparently unopposed and
hardly noticed;[2] then, from the close of the Ramesside Period
with ever increasing success until ultimately their incursions
attained the proportions of a large-scale invasion which resulted
about 950 B.C. in the conquest of the Nile Valley and the setting
up of the Libyan Dynasty XXII. It is no surprise to find that
the first foothold gained by the Libyan chiefs was at Heracleopolis (modern Ihnasyah) for the Libyans entered the valley by
way of Lake Mareotis and the Fayum.[3]

Bahriyah acted as a link between Middle Egypt and the Oasis
of Amun, Siwa, that first came under Egyptian control at the
beginning of the Late Period. The fortress-temple of Aghurmi,
the famous sanctuary of the oracle which was visited by Alexander the Great, was apparently not of Egyptian origin.[4] There
is no doubt that the holy places in Siwa have been held in
veneration from time immemorial by the Libyans and the
dwellers in the oases. 'The gods of Libya and the gods of the
field of Palms come to you', was the address to Isis who in Siwa,
as in the whole frontier region of Libya, was regarded in the
Late Period as the chief deity in succession to the cow-goddess
Hathor. The advancement of Amun, on the other hand, was
certainly connected with the establishing of Theban temple
domains in the Libyan oases. Egyptian sovereignty was first
acknowledged by the reigning chief in Siwa apparently in the

---

[1] For Bahriyah and Farafra, see Fakhry, *Bahria Oasis*, 2 vols., and *Annales du Service*, 38, 397f.; 39, 627f.; 40, 855f. Earlier literature is quoted there.

[2] Inscription at Karnak, see Breasted, *Ancient Records*, III, § 580.

[3] See below, p. 217.   [4] Steindorff, *ÄZ*, 69, 1f.

reign of Achoris in the Fourth Century B.C. Under Nekhthorheb, the last native King of Egypt who came from Sebennytus
in the Delta, a prince of the oasis with the Egyptian name
Wenamun built the valley temple at Umm-'Ebeida. Political
intercourse in earlier periods was prevented by the remoteness
of the oasis which lay fifteen days' march from the Wadi Natrun
on the west side of the Delta. It lay, furthermore, in a district
that was always inhabited by an insubordinate people hostile to
the peasants of the Nile Valley. There was consequently little
departure throughout the centuries from the regular practice of
trading by caravan. Apart from a small strip of land in the
Marmarika to which the Ramesside kings held fast, Egypt up to
the Late Period revealed little ability to expand on the north-
west frontier against Libya beyond the point where the battles
for the unification of the land ended at the beginning of the
Dynastic Period. The frontier here in contrast to that on the
east was organized purely for defence. The Egyptians therefore
had no special name for Siwa which was included under the
collective term 'Field of Palms', like the other Libyan oases.
Date-palms were in fact the principal source of wealth for the
inhabitants and dates were their chief article of commerce.
Siwa dates are famous even today.

The part played by the Libyan oases can best be expressed by
claiming that as long as Egypt ruled at the Second Cataract or
indeed as far down the Nile Valley as Napata the most valuable
products from the centre of Africa were obtained by way of
these centres of commerce.[1] Whatever was to avoid the strict
Egyptian frontier control, both men and goods alike, took the
roundabout route through the oases. Horses and carts were
excluded as means of transport for desert tracks. Both became
known to the Egyptians at the time when the great racial migrations from the mountainous regions of Asia precipitated the
Hyksos invasion about 1700 B.C.; but they knew them only as
aids to warfare. Light horse-drawn wagons and chariots effected
a complete revolution in military tactics because they made
possible the organization of swiftly moving fighting units with
great striking power. From the beginning of Dynasty XVIII
the Pharaoh used his chariot to drive to the temple, his officials
used them for inspections and the military charioteers for their

[1] See below, p. 317f.

manoeuvres on the desert's edge. But when an official had to make a journey, as when the Viceroy of Kush went to Thebes, chariot and horses were loaded on a big travelling-vessel.[1] A horse-chariot was quite useless on the long waterless desert tracks.

[1] Davies, *Tomb of Huy*, pl. 31.

V

Raw Materials and Foreign Relations

The Egyptians were never a conquering people like the Hittites, the Assyrians, the Persians, the Arabs or the Mongol tribes of the Asiatic steppes. In remote antiquity they gained their home-land by colonization rather than by conquest; and in historical times when they crossed their borders they did so, in the vast majority of cases, in search of raw materials that they lacked and to assure their supply. Their approach to international relations was coloured by this point of view. The Egyptian preferred to obtain what he wanted by trading rather than by permanent military occupation. Nevertheless this policy had its disadvantages and these are particularly apparent in the history of Egypt's relations with the Nubian countries.

We have already seen that Egypt lacked timber and that in consequence communications were soon built up with the Phoenician coast in order to obtain pinewood from the Lebanon. Without this timber it would have been impossible for the Egyptians to construct the vast wood substructures of the royal tombs of the Thinite Period,[1] the doors of Snofru's palace, the interior woodwork of the great pyramids of the Old Kingdom, coffins for mummies, ships, or even the tall flag-staffs rising up in front of the pylons of the temples of the New Kingdom. When Egypt had an Empire Syrian supplies were supplemented by timber from Asia Minor, such as oak, ash, oriental beech, birch and other woods used in the manufacture of war-chariots.[2]

---

[1] Schweinfurth, *Voss. Zeitung*, 5, 6 (1898) (Supplement): 'Well-preserved pieces of coniferous woods have been found in most of the ancient royal tombs.'

[2] Schäfer, *Sb. Berl. Akad.* (1931), XXV; Lucas, *Ancient Egyptian Materials*[3], 496.

These woods were certainly exported through Phoenician ports. Countries to the south of Egypt, because of the difficulties of transport, were obliged to use overland routes to a large extent and, because of the paucity of timber along the coastal regions, restricted exports to choice and valuable woods specially needed for the arts and cabinet-making, particularly ebony. They also exported those fragrant woods so much favoured in the East.

The Near East supplied Egypt with other raw materials also. 'Asiatic copper' is mentioned time and again in Egyptian inscriptions from the Old Kingdom onwards. Egypt possessed only small deposits of copper-ore and then mostly mixed with malachite. They were to be found mostly in very inaccessible parts of the country south of the Barramiyah goldmines and in the country of the Bedja, as far down as Abu Seyal in the neighbourhood of Wadi Alaki in Nubia.[1] Copper may also have been extracted from malachite ore in the mines of Sinai. Ramesses III boasted that good supplies reached Egypt partly by ship and partly overland, from Atika;[2] but what he means here is probably not Sinai but one of the workings close to the Red Sea, such as the mine in the Gebel Abu Hammid. In the time when Egypt was a world power and possibly even in the Middle Kingdom also, the chief source of supply for copper was Cyprus and next to it the kingdom of Mitanni after Tuthmosis IV had entered into alliance with it. The Phoenician ports again played an intermediate role in the trade with Cyprus at least up to the time when Tuthmosis III brought the island directly under Egyptian control.

Silver, the second precious metal, which the Egyptians extracted from the same veins of quartz of the primary rock from which they obtained gold, came chiefly from the south-east corner of the land; it was also imported in large quantities from the Near East. We learn this fact indirectly from its economic value. In the Old Kingdom silver, reckoned as a rarer 'white' kind of gold, was valued more highly than gold proper or the well-known mixture of silver and gold that the ancients called

[1] Lucas, *op. cit.*, 235–6. An ancient vein of copper in the Gebel el Hudi, with an alleged copper content of 60 per cent, described by Von der Esch, *Weenak*, 124 f.; contested from information from G. W. Murray, *Annales du Service*.

[2] Papyrus Harris, I, 78.

electrum.[1] At least silver is quoted before gold. From the Middle Kingdom, however, the value of gold to silver was fixed at 2 : 1 and so it remained until after the Ramesside Period with minor variations due in part to differences in the quality of the gold; thus in Dynasty XX 'good gold' stood at $3\frac{1}{2}$: 1. Unfortunately we do not know with any certainty the places from which the imported silver came.

The ratio in value between copper and silver during the New Kingdom varied between 60 : 1 and 100 : 1, being subject to considerable fluctuation.[2] We have more exact figures only for the Late Period.

The source of tin is as yet unknown; but it was indispensable for alloying with copper to make bronze. Archaeological evidence proves that genuine bronze alloys with a 10–14 per cent content of tin are known first only in the Middle Kingdom[3] when they were used for figures and for other objects such as the blade of the razor from the Treasure of el-Lahun that has a gold handle.[4] Here again we can point to the ports of Phoenicia such as Byblos as the places through which the metal was obtained.

To pay for these imported metals Egypt had especially the gold from her mines; and the possession of these mines, more than any military power, assured for Egypt up to the Amarna Period unquestioned superiority as the richest country in the Near East. This superiority extended much further than the immediate sphere of direct influence which at that time went as far as North Syria. We learn from the foreign correspondence of Amenophis III and Akhenaten the effect produced by the wealth of the Egyptian court upon both friends and rivals among the powerful Asiatic kings. The request for gold from Egypt is repeated time and again by Mitanni, Ashur and Babylon: 'My brother will please send me much beautiful gold that I can use for my work'.[5] Again, Tushratta of Mitanni wrote to his son-in-law Amenophis III: 'My brother, pray send gold

[1] Kees, *Kulturgeschichte*, 132; examples given there for what follows.

[2] *Op. cit.*, 133; the maximum value occurs in Cairo Papyrus 65739 of the sixteenth year of Ramesses II, see Gardiner, *JEA*, 21, 146: 10 *deben* of beaten copper = 1 *kite* ($\frac{1}{10}$ *deben*) silver.

[3] Lucas, *JEA*, 14, 97f.   [4] Winlock, *The Treasure of el Lahun*, 62, 74.

[5] Burraburiash to Amenophis IV, letter nr. 7, according to Knudtzon's numbering; similarly Assuruballit, see letter 16.

in very great quantities, such as cannot be counted; my brother may send me that; and my brother may send me more gold than my father got. In the land of my brother is not gold as the dust upon the ground?'[1]

When Egyptian kings from Tuthmosis IV onwards became tired of marching their armies into Asia and of fighting always the same opponent, gold became the instrument of power-politics and allies were bought over with it in Asia. This policy of alliances broke down, however, during the last years of the reign of Amenophis III owing to the selfishness displayed by Egypt's princely neighbours under pressure from the Hittite invasion of Northern Syria. The process of disruption was furthered by avarice and by the bad diplomacy of the sun-king Akhenaten. Egypt's old allies now complained bitterly of Egyptian negligence, for during the Amarna Period there was still gold enough in the treasury in spite of maladministration, a fact that is confirmed by looking at the gold found in the tomb of Tutankhamun, Akhenaten's son-in-law (Pl. 25. *b*). On the other side of the picture, however, many of the Asiatic states had prospered exceedingly under Egyptian protection, especially during the Middle Kingdom. A good example is Byblos;[2] in the tombs of her princes of this date were found gold-rimmed obsidian vessels which had held the finest oil, undoubtedly the customary gifts from the King to the Prince on the occasion of his investiture.[3] There were also ornaments of gold and weapons in Egyptian style and with hieroglyphic inscriptions, although made on the spot, among them a scimetar; all such things clearly demonstrate the extent of Egyptian influence. The scimetar was a Syrian weapon which became during the New Kingdom the characteristic victory-sword of the Egyptian king. With its singular shape it illustrates how the Egyptian was able to learn from foreign craftsmen and that they had in fact learned. This process is seen in new techniques also, as in metalwork with polychrome inlays and also in gold and silver vessels the shapes and decorations of which (particularly the spirals)[4]

[1] Knudtzon, nr. 19.
[2] Montet, *Byblos et l'Egypte*, and *Monuments Piot*, 25, 237f., with pls. 19, 20; 27, 12f. with pls. 1–2.
[3] Montet, *Byblos*, pls. 88–89 (nr. 610) =*Syria* (1922), pl. 67.
[4] Montet, *op. cit.*, pl. 111 (nr. 748) =*Syria* (1922), pl. 64.

were obviously influenced by Aegean art. The Phoenician ports were also the places where the Egyptians came into contact with the civilization of the Aegean islands and Crete.

The knowledge gained from the finds at Byblos was much augmented by the hoard of treasure found in the temple of Monthu at el-Tôd, south of Luxor. A whole consignment of presents sent from Syria during Dynasty XII was found here sealed up in the foundation of the temple wall. There were all kinds of silver bowls decorated with 'Aegean' motifs together with cylinder seals of the Mesopotamian kind.[1] In addition to metals Egypt imported from Syria wine and oil also in early times as is shown by finds of pottery in the royal tombs of the Thinite Period. They came sometimes in their original vessels, characteristic of their country of origin,[2] and such consignments doubtlessly included the olive oil that was lacking in Egypt and the 'finest cedar oil' (made from the resin of coniferous trees) that is so well known from the offering lists of the Old Kingdom. Egypt, for her part, exported fine linen fabric and rolls of papyrus, that writing material made of strips of papyrus-pith pressed and glued together in lattice-fashion the discovery of which led to a revolution in the development of writing in the ancient world. Such rolls met with a correspondingly good sale in the Syrian markets. Egypt also exported surplus food such as salted fish and, occasionally, corn.[3]

Trade was a royal prerogative and it is true that the great wholesale merchants of the East in ancient times were the kings because they alone controlled the necessary articles of barter. Trading expeditions by land and sea were therefore led by royal commissioners, the 'Treasurers of the God', or whatever else they were called, acting under royal authority. A large part of the diplomatic mail during the Amarna Period was actually concerned with commercial transactions between princely and royal partners. Business was business even if its subject was a king's daughter and her dowry, as happened in one case during the reign of Amenophis III. The correspondence occasioned by such transactions was often conducted with the utmost frankness. A royal commissioner, escorted by a military detachment

[1] Vandier, *Syria*, 1937, 174f., with pls. 28, 29.
[2] Frankfort, *Studies in the early pottery of the Near East*, I, 106f.
[3] See above, p. 76.

for prestige purposes was attached to the expedition sent by Hatshepsut to Punt so that he might negotiate and conclude business transactions with the native princes. The royal monopoly over trade was, however, gradually broken by the progressive granting of trading concessions and especially by the steady transfer of real-estate (which provided the foundation for trading) to officials in the feudal period, who then became settled, and to temples; in this way independent economic entities were evolved. The cession by the king of transit dues and customs privileges also contributed to this development.[1] Compromise arrangements were likewise made in this connection but their results in detail are difficult for us to ascertain.

The establishment of trade relations with Crete must have proceeded along lines similar to those that have been described for the Near East. All attempts to prove the existence of an ancient Minoan trading base in the area of the harbour district of Alexandria have so far proved fruitless.[2] There can be no question, however, that after the expulsion of the Hyksos from Egypt and Southern Palestine about 1580 B.C., associations revealed themselves, as in the sphere of arts and crafts where Cretan influence shows itself in the ornamentation of the weapons and jewellery belonging to the Queen-mother Iah-hotpe and her son Kamose. They are revealed also in the field of politics. Iah-hotpe assumed the boastful title 'Mistress of the shores of *Hau-nebet*', the latter being the age-old Egyptian name for the Aegean and its islands.[3] These associations took definite shape in the embassy of Keftiu (Cretans) to Egypt in the reign of Hatshepsut which is depicted in the tomb of her favourite Senenmut.[4] What they brought with them the Egyptians naturally called 'tribute', but what was actually happening was the starting of trade relations through diplomatic channels in the manner characteristic of Hatshepsut's reign. The importance of this exchange of products should neither be ignored nor exaggerated. Eduard Meyer exaggerated it when he argued in favour of the existence of a political alliance between Egypt and Crete against the Hyksos;[5] he even went so far as to make

[1] See below, p. 208.   [2] Kees, *Kulturgeschichte*, 109.
[3] *Urk.*, IV, 21.
[4] Often illustrated; best reproduced in Nina Davies, *Ancient Egyptian Paintings*, pl. 14.   [5] *Geschichte des Altertums*, II, 1, p. 54.

Queen Iah-hotpe the wife of the Cretan king. It is indeed possible that in the course of the struggle against the Hyksos Cretans encountered Egyptians in Syria and that this meeting prepared the way for the establishment of direct relations. The initiative, however, would surely have come from the side of the adventurous Cretan seafarers. At all events, at this time Egypt came to know the Kefti-ship at sea and, from the reign of Tuthmosis III, Kefti-ships were numbered along with Byblos-ships among the sea-going vessels built in Egyptian ship-yards in Lower Egypt.[1] Furthermore, representations showing the Keftiu bringing tribute became, from the time of Senenmut, common subjects among the paintings in the tombs of senior Egyptian officials and high-priests. We must not, however, assume that embassies of this kind came regularly to Egypt from this time onwards; for the objects that the men carry as gifts[2] are in part so clearly the creations of Syrian metal-workers and so precisely the same as articles of tribute coming from Syrian lands that the country of the Keftiu which the inscriptions on such scenes mention as the source of these gifts, was with some reason placed by early scholars on the Asiatic continent.[3] This fact also serves to confirm the view that the largest part of what Egypt derived from the Aegean civilization found its way to Egypt by way of the Phoenician court or the Syrian colonies especially from the time of the Amarna Period when the splendour of the Cretan palace-culture had already passed away. The Egyptians, likewise, without distinguishing between the original article and the imitation derived from mixed sources, called these particular creations 'Keftiu-ware' simply because that was the popular designation. Such articles, and especially those in metal, were in reality increasingly being made in the workshops of Byblos and in those of other mainland cities allied to or commercially associated with Egypt.

The Egyptian peasant was never at heart a soldier. He hated and feared foreigners and foreign lands. The Pharaohs, there-

---

[1] *Urk.*, IV, 707 (instructions for the preparation of the Phoenician harbours); *ÄZ*, 66, 116 (journal of the time of Amenophis II).

[2] Typical examples illustrated by Davies, *Bulletin of the Metropolitan Museum of Art*, 1926, Part II, 42f.

[3] Wainwright, *JEA*, 17, 26 for Cilicia. The criticism of E. Meyer, *Geschichte des Altertums*, II, 1, 108, n. 4, misses the mark.

fore, had to take into their service the men of neighbouring Hamitic tribes in whom the warlike virtues of primitive times still survived. First among these were the nomadic Bedja tribesmen of the south-east, known to the Egyptians as the Medjay. As early as the reign of Merenrē' in Dynasty VI we find Nubian contingents accompanying Weni on a punitive expedition against the Palestinian beduin, and by that time too 'pacified Nubians' seem to have been employed as police just as Sudanese are in modern Egypt.[1] Such foreigners were rewarded with land in Egypt and they became settlers just like those Medjay and Kushites who served in the army of Kamose against the Hyksos in 1580 B.C. That these people remained in Egypt is proved by their miserable cemeteries situated in the narrower part of the Thebaid as far north as Asyut.[2] They were buried in shallow graves, known today as 'Pan-graves'. During the New Kingdom the word Medjay became the official name for the whole police force of Egypt including that of the capital city, Thebes.

In the description of the frontier regions in the south some account has been given already of the Egyptian policy towards the southern lands. In conclusion, however, a few remarks about Egypt's eastern policy may not be out of place. After the Hyksos Period it seemed as if Egypt intended to pursue a policy of naked conquest in Asia. Tuthmosis I and Tuthmosis III set up victory inscriptions on the Euphrates and there drew the frontier of their empire. In doing so they were clearly labouring under the false belief that the defence system built up laboriously during the Middle Kingdom was not capable of warding off a catastrophe like the Hyksos invasion. The counter-blow was to destroy on Asiatic soil the centre of the enemy forces threatening Egypt. This strategic plan was put into operation in Northern Syria about 1500 B.C. It was directed primarily against the Kingdom of Mitanni beyond the Euphrates and it took the form of crucial new political formations. In this widespread defensive area the Tuthmosid Kings established an administrative system that depended for its strength on the native princes who had become Egyptian vassals and on numerically weak contingents of Egyptian troops under the command of royal com-

---

[1] See above, p. 73; below, p. 314.
[2] Survey by Säve-Söderbergh, *Ägypten und Nubien*, 135f.

missioners. These contingents were largely composed of Asiatic mercenaries. Similarly Akhenaten's guards at Amarna have the same international appearance.[1] Besides the members of the southern tribes, willing mercenaries were also found from the unruly beduin of the highlands and possibly also from the migrant sea-peoples of the Aegean.

The same state of affairs is found during the Ramesside Period (about 1300 B.C.) in the wars Egypt waged as an imperial power against the Hittite Empire pushing forwards across Northern Syria. The kernel of the Egyptian army was always made up of foreign mercenaries;[2] in addition to the Kushites there were the heavily armed Shardan guards of Ramesses II (possibly Sardinians). From the time of Merenptah such guards were increasingly recruited from Libyans who left districts that had become overpopulated by racial movements and who sought military service in Egypt. There were also former prisoners-of-war and volunteers in the army, and eventually, as a result of ordinary racial infiltration, the presence of prisoners-of-war and the numbers of settled, foreign ex-servicemen, the foreign element so outweighed the native in Egypt that the government of the country passed into the hands of its chiefs in the Tenth Century B.C. In the Eighth and Seventh Century B.C. Ethiopian kings with troops recruited in the southern lands fought against these Libyan kings and their Egyptian supporters. Then, during the Late Period Egypt's freedom depended on the resistance put up by her Ionian and Carian mercenaries against the Asiatic menace. The last epochs of Egypt's history are filled with the struggles between peoples on the frontiers for the mastery of the Nile valley. The wanderings of such peoples in primitive times had kept them separate and their harsh conditions of life had condemned them to a low level of civilization; the peasant in the Nile valley, on the other hand, had been more favoured by Nature and had consequently achieved a high level of civilization. The movement during the Late Period was as if the events of remote antiquity were happening again. The struggle for room to live in was begun anew, but in the meanwhile the land sought after had already been populated. Nevertheless, all these racial streams from outside, after running fiercely in spate, eventually drained away into the soil of Egypt.

[1] See below, p. 295.   [2] Kees, *Kulturgeschichte*, 237f.

PART THREE
Cities and Districts

VI

Memphis and Heliopolis

The names of Memphis and Heliopolis dominate the Old Kingdom. Their principal deities, Ptah of Memphis and Rē'-Harakhte of Heliopolis, remain as rivals or, if one so prefers to put it, complements of each other in the New Kingdom, particularly so in the period following the Amarna Age.

This distinct antithesis originated in early historical times. Memphis was a political foundation, its position determined by the unification of Upper and Lower Egypt, and it was in Egyptian eyes therefore a young city.[1] Heliopolis acquired its fame from its religion and its myths; it also looked eastwards in the direction of the overland route to Asia. In addition to the fact that the Nile separated them, these two cities lie further apart than is often thought, a misconception largely due to the fact that the sprawling mass of Cairo comes between. Ancient Memphis, lying about 16 miles south of the apex of the Delta, is about 20 miles from Heliopolis as the crow flies; by road it is a good deal further.

Legend ascribed the foundation of Memphis, or at least of the original fort there, to Menes, the unifier of Egypt. Herodotus was told (Book II, chapter 4; and see also chapter 99) that before the time of Menes all the land from the southern boundary of the Memphite nome northwards was marsh, the Nile flowing to the west of the site of the city, close to the desert, approximately in the bed of what is now the Bahr el-Libeini. There may be a grain of truth in this assertion. Excavations in the area of Memphis, particularly in the necropolises of Saqqara and Abusir have yielded finds apparently dating only from the

[1] Article 'Memphis' in Pauly-Wissowa, *Real-Encyclopädie*; Porter and Moss, *Topographical Bibliography*, III (Memphis).

147

historic period. The only predynastic remains in the area have been found on the eastern bank of the river which in the Old Kingdom belonged to the Memphite not the Heliopolitan nome. Here have been uncovered the great peasant settlement of Ma'adi and near it that of el-Omari.

The Memphis that was subsequently established was centred round the royal palace of the Thinite kings. It probably stood where the palace of the Late Period was built, to the north of the temple of Ptah (a place now called Kôm Teman) and it may have been a building something like those of a somewhat later date the ruins of which are to be seen at Abydos and Hieraconpolis (Pl. 20. *b*).[1] It would therefore have consisted of a rectangular enclosure surrounded by a double wall of sun-dried mud bricks, the inner one being probably thicker than the one at Hieraconpolis, being panelled and niched on the outside and whitewashed. The place was called 'the White Walls' and by extension later the whole Memphite nome likewise. In the case of Memphis itself this name had no architectural significance but it bore some political meaning. White was the colour of the Upper Egyptian crown, red (originally green) that of the Lower Egyptian crown. From the very beginning the unification of the two lands was intimately connected in people's minds with the royal palace of Memphis and far less with a fortress watching over conquered Lower Egypt. The palace and the temple of Ptah were the places where the king traditionally received the double crown of the two kingdoms and where the coronation was re-enacted on the occasion of the thirtieth anniversary of the king's accession, the so-called *sed*-festival. On such occasions all the gods of the country and 'the great ones of Upper and Lower Egypt' came together there to do homage to the king and afterwards to receive gifts from him. At a very early period the local festivals of Memphis became elevated into the number of the great state festivals.

One of the coronation ceremonies was the 'circling of the walls' which symbolically represented the king's entry into the possession of the palace and the land. It also formed part of the agricultural festival of Sokar, the god who dwelt in the earth and who, accompanied by the herds, circled the walls at the beginning of the season of ploughing to awaken the soil to life.[2]

[1] See below, p. 238.   [2] See above, p. 56.

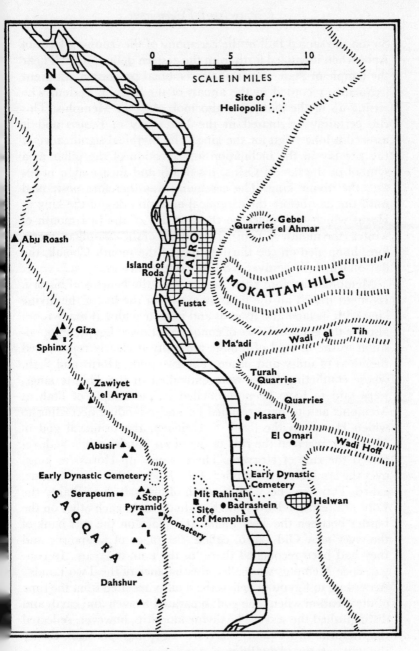

SCALE IN MILES

0   5   10

N

Site of
Heliopolis

Abu Roash

Gebel
el Ahmar

Quarries

Island of
Roda

CAIRO

MOKATTAM HILLS

Fustat

Giza

Sphinx

Ma'adi

Wadi el Tih

Zawiyet
el Aryan

Turah
Quarries

Quarries

Masara

Abusir

El Omari

Wadi Hoff

Early Dynastic Cemetery

Serapeum

Step
Pyramid

SAQQARA

Mit Rahinah

Monastery

Site
of Memphis

Badrashein

Early Dynastic
Cemetery

Helwan

Dahshur

4. Memphis and Heliopolis

149

So too the sacred bull in the ceremony of the 'running forth of Apis' when it was led forth from the eastern door of its stall near the temple of Ptah, to join the ceremonial procession, an event frequently recorded in the annals of the Thinite Period. The setting-up of the *djed*-pillar also took place in Memphis. This rite certainly originated in the Delta city of Busiris and it assured a long reign for the king. The mythical significance of the rite lay in the inclination and erection of the pillar as a symbol of the fate of Osiris, his death and incarnation in his son, the divine king. The ceremony was therefore postponed until the day before the canonical accession day of the king as Horus which took place on the first day of the first month of winter (the month of Tybi). The raising of the *djed*-pillar, therefore, happened on the thirtieth day of the month Choiak, the day on which the festival of Sokar came to an end.

Memphis therefore knew how to reap the benefits of history. Its myth linked all the decisive events in the life of the divine king with its land and its gods and in its teaching it made room also for the gods and rites of conquered Lower Egypt. In opposition to the discord of remote antiquity it clearly represented the ideas of unity and peace. The two gods, Horus and Seth, whose conflicting forces were embodied in the Thinite kings, were said to have been reconciled in the temple of Ptah at Memphis and to have reached an understanding according to which Horus, in the form of Tatjenen, the primeval god of Memphis, received the rule of the 'Two Lands', while Seth received the rule of Heaven. 'There stands up Horus (as king) over the land. He is the unifier of this land, with the great name, called Tatjenen, he who is south-of-his-wall (i.e. Ptah), the Lord of Eternity.' Horus and Seth had fought each other on the border between the Two Lands at a place on the east bank of the river near Old Cairo, called 'the place of weapons'; and they had been reconciled there 'in the land of Ayan'. In consequence Memphis was called the 'balance of the Two Lands'. According to Egyptian beliefs the duality resulted from the time of the creation when 'one god' separated heaven and earth and distinguished the sexes. The divine kingship, however, reflected the natural order and therefore Egyptian political theory thought in terms of dualities.

It was also thought that the body of the great god, Osiris,

who came originally from Busiris in the Delta, rested in Memphis. Osiris was the image of the dead king and his grave was identified in the cave of Sokar, that god whose autumn festival we have already mentioned. Consequently Memphis became the 'granary' of Egypt, for there slept the great fertility god who lost his life in the new waters of the inundation to become the fertiliser of the land; like him too died the corn when it was cut and threshed.[1] In this way Memphis established its claim to be both the Residence of the King of the Two Lands and the central granary of the kingdom.

The religious teaching now known as the Memphite Theology has been preserved for us by the Ethiopian King Shabaka who had the text transcribed on to stone from an ancient tattered document.[2] It contains the theological reasoning that explains that the primacy of Ptah as a creator was due to his power over the heart (judgment) and tongue (commanding will). With this power he can judge all gods and all creation and assign to each thing its place. To judge by its language this noble body of doctrine was composed in the early Old Kingdom at a time when on the eastern bank of the river Heliopolis, the city of the sun, preached the teaching that Atum 'he who has not yet achieved perfection, yet perfects himself' was the creator of the world. At the same time the Heliopolitans declared the sun-god Harakhte to be the divine king of the existing world, born of the earth-god Geb and Nut the goddess of heaven, who daily rises regenerated from the primeval ocean and the underworld. The 'King's House' in the Memphite myth of Ptah-Tjenen found its exact counterpart in the 'House of the Princes' in Heliopolis — the place in which the council of the gods assembled under the chairmanship of Geb, the successor to the throne of Atum and in which Geb, after the death of Osiris, will deliver judgment on Horus and Seth and declare the inheritance of Geb.

The monument bearing the Memphite Theology reveals clearly this rivalry between Memphis and Heliopolis in its subordinating Atum and his ennead to Ptah of Memphis. Furthermore it seems that important parts of the legend that served to interpret and to give symbolic value to the ritual ceremonies of

[1] See above, p. 59.
[2] Kees, *Götterglaube*, 289f.; Junker, *Die politische Lehre von Memphis*.

the great royal festivals were fashioned in Memphis in that typically Egyptian way of selective compromise which likewise accorded with the political role of the capital city of a united Egypt.[1]

The search for historical proofs for this state of affairs by means of archaeology has not yet, however, been successful. The Early Dynastic cemetery on the edge of the desert plateau beginning above the village of Abusir and extending to the neighbourhood of Zoser's Step Pyramid, which is perhaps the most important cemetery in Egypt, has not yet fully yielded up its secrets. The oldest buildings are great brick mastaba-tombs that rival those in the royal cemetery at Abydos and among them is the oldest dateable tomb in which were found offerings with the name of the Horus (King) Aha, 'the Fighter', in whom may be seen the historical original of Menes, the unifier — unless that legendary name covers a number of persons.[2] The excavators claim that they have discovered real royal tombs but it is possible that only the viceroys of the Thinite kings were buried there. These men, nevertheless, must have been relations of the royal family in accordance with the ancient idea of the State. One among them whose identity is certain is the canal-master Hemaka who was Seal-bearer of the King of Lower Egypt in the reign of Udimu of the I Dynasty.[3] It should also be remembered that mastabas no less pretentious and belonging to members of this same ruling class have been found outside the Early Dynastic cemetery of Saqqara, at Abu Roash (north of Giza), at Giza itself and at Tarkhan, some seven miles to the south of Lisht and therefore in Upper Egypt. In recent years somewhat smaller mastabas have been found at Helwan on the east bank of the Nile opposite Memphis.

The proximity of the royal residence also exercised an extraordinarily benificent influence in this part of Egypt. There was here undoubtedly a concentration of power that both confirms and explains the historical tradition that the political centre of gravity in Egypt was transferred from Upper Egypt to Memphis at the close of the Thinite Period, that is, at the end of Dynasty II.

At Abydos the only royal tombs of Dynasty II that can

[1] Schott, *Myth und Mythenbildung*, 25f.   [2] W. B. Emery, *Hor-Aha*.
[3] W. B. Emery, *The Tomb of Hemaka*.

be identified with certainty are those of Peribsen, the remarkable worshipper of Seth whose name was subsequently misread by the transcriber of the list of kings in the hieratic script as Tlas (Wadjlas), and also of Khasekhemui, the last king of the Dynasty.[1] In the soil of Memphis, on the other hand, the indications of the presence of the kings of Dynasty II and their tombs multiply; this is partly revealed in the continuance of the service to the dead, as in the case of Peribsen's successor, Sethenes,[2] and partly by other monuments. And yet many of these royal tombs are still to be found and they may have been covered by later constructions. The information contained in the surviving annals of these kings, particularly so in the case of Binothris (whose ancient name was Ninetjer) a predecessor of Peribsen, reveals in the designations of years by means of festivals and pious activities ('foundations') that an organized system of government existed.[3] It was only at the end of Dynasty II that a crisis occurred and the memory of it has been perpetuated by the masses of slain Lower Egyptians commemorated on two statues of Khasekhemui which were set up in Hieraconpolis in Upper Egypt. The King Nebka, whose name lived on in popular legend along with those of Zoser, Snofru and Cheops, must have been the successor of Khasekhemui because he recorded in the annals the making of a copper statue of Khasekhemui.[4] It was he apparently who began the construction of a vast pyramidal tomb at Zawiyet el-Aryan between Giza and Abusir. In spite of a reign of 18–19 years he only completed the subterranean sarcophagus-chamber which was faced with Aswan granite and contained an oval granite sarcophagus.[5] This situation points to the coming of troubled times at the close of his reign.

The historian Manetho begins a new dynasty with Zoser, the successor of Nebka. This is Dynasty III, the first Mem-

---

[1] See below, p. 237.

[2] For the funerary cult of Peribsen in the chapel of Sethenes, see Mariette, *Mastabas*, B.3 (of Dynasty IV date).

[3] Palermo Stone, *recto*, l. 4, nrs. 1–16 (a twenty-year period of rule).

[4] Palermo Stone, *recto*, l. 5, nr. 4 (in the 15/16th regnal year).

[5] The Royal Papyrus of Turin gives Nebka nineteen years; according to the Palermo Stone, *recto*, l. 5, nr. 7, it was in the last, uncompleted regnal year that the ninth occasion of numbering (of cattle) took place (possibly year 18?).

phite Dynasty and that with which the Old Kingdom begins. Two events indicate that a profound change took place about this time. Recent discoveries in the Memphite area dating from early in Dynasty I[1] show that at this time the so-called Giza-race came permanently into prominence as the future bearers of the civilization of the Old Kingdom (see Pl. 23. *a*). The more delicately formed Upper Egyptian race was consequently de-prived of the leadership. Secondly, the Heliopolitan sun-worship began to influence the monarchy at Memphis. Zoser was now king and his chief architect, Imhotep, was the first high priest of Heliopolis known to history; his title was 'Greatest of Seers'. The Heliopolitan religion first made its appearance during Dynasty II, as is suggested by certain royal theo-phorous names like that of Nebrē' — 'Rē' (the sun god) is Lord' — who was a predecessor of Binothris.[2] We know nothing of the origin of this Imhotep who was able to com-memorate himself on the base of the statue of Zoser placed in the *serdab* of the Step Pyramid at Saqqara. Such an act is unique in Egyptian history and here we find him inscribing all his titles, which elevated him to the position of being an heir to the throne or a royal deputy. In the Late Period he was deified, and the things that were then said about him were legendary.[3] Nevertheless, in conformity with the contemporary ordering of society, he must have been a member of the royal family or have been made a member of it by his sovereign. Then only could he participate in the ruling powers of a 'great God'. And this Imhotep not only created the royal tomb as a stone structure (built of limestone) but he designed in it the most remarkable building on Egyptian soil. He raised up the superstructure of the royal tomb to form a step pyramid that is to this day the outstanding feature of the landscape at Saqqara. He surrounded the pyramid with a replica of the court in which was celebrated the jubilee of the King of the Two Lands and this court con-tained copies of the traditional booths, usually built of wooden frameworks with matting and with wooden flower-bedecked columns, but here at Saqqara built entirely of limestone with

[1] See above, p. 27.
[2] So, according to the order of the three royal names on the statue from Saqqara (Cairo nr. 1); cf. Petrie, *Royal Tombs*, II, pl. 8, 12 (palimpsest).
[3] Sethe, *Imhotep*.

false façades and stone representations of wooden doors. The purpose of the whole apparently was to allow the king eternally to celebrate *sed*-festivals.[1] This court and the pyramid were enclosed by a massive stone wall with false gate-towers and pilasters, an imitation in white stone of the 'white walls' of the royal palace in Memphis. Everything was intended by imitation to serve the dead.

A small shrine of Zoser from Heliopolis, however, gives us the oldest representation of the Great Ennead of Heliopolis. In Heliopolis too there flourished many kinds of cults connected with natural things, such as sacred trees, the Mnevis bulls, and the pair of lions who had their own proper place of worship in Leontopolis (modern Tell el-Yahudiyah), north of Heliopolis. The particular worship peculiar to Heliopolis was, however, that of the stars.

The principal Heliopolitan festivals were the festivals of Heaven, the divisions of the lunar month, the New Moon, the 6th day of the month (being the start of the second week), Full Moon and the Last Quarter; these festivals remained unaltered through the ages. From the worship of the stars evolved the worship of Rē' in the form of 'Horus of the Horizon' (in Egyptian Harakhte), the god of the morning sun. This conception must have been developed at a time when Horus, the god of the Egyptian king, played a dominant role.

As few remains of the House of Rē' in Heliopolis now exist as of the earlier temple of Atum. We can get some idea of it, therefore, only from the surviving account of a visit paid to it by the Ethiopian King Piankhi about 730 B.C.[2] Perhaps more, however, can be learned from the sanctuaries erected by the kings of Dynasty V near their Residence in Memphis, to serve for the worship of Rē', which had become the state religion. The chief Heliopolitan sanctuary was situated on the 'high sand' north of Heliopolis, an artificial mound that mythology regarded as the primeval hill 'the place of the first becoming' which rose out of the primeval waters of chaos. In the same system of symbolization stress was laid on the *benben*-stone that stood in the open court as the cult-image; it was the forerunner of the obelisk. At sunrise every day when the sun's rays touched

---

[1] Lauer, *La Pyramide à degrés*; H. Ricke, *Bemerkungen zur ägyptische Baukunst des alten Reiches* I, (1944).   [2] *Urk.*, III, 37–40.

the gilded tip of the stone the sun god took his seat there, an act that was the never-ending repetition of the first rising of the sun at the time of the creation of the world. Associated with this system also was the myth of the phoenix whose return to the sanctuary from a far-distant land of the gods symbolized the appearance of the primeval god on the primeval earth. The House of the Phoenix and the House of the Obelisk were of equal importance in the eyes of the Egyptian theologian; the Egyptian words for phoenix and obelisk (more exactly, the *benben*-stone) were formed from the same root which meant 'rise up' or something similar.

In front of the base of the obelisk in the court stood the great sacrificial altar on which veritable hecatombs were sacrificed to the sun-god. The royal annals of Dynasty V inform us that the kings of that time gave everything to Rē' and his companion-gods in the sun-temples,[1] and confirmation of this fact is provided by what we read in the lists of donations recorded on stone in the sun-temple of King Niuserrē' in celebration of his *sed*-festival in the thirtieth year of his reign.[2] The immense sacrificial offerings include the provision of more than 100,600 meals of bread, beer and offering-cakes on New Year's Day and 30,000 for another festival.[3] Quite clearly these colossal offerings were not intended solely for the priests and the court, but also for the population of the royal residence. This system of meals for the masses which enabled the poor man occasionally to eat something better than his daily bread and even to drink wine instead of beer, was continued at least until the New Kingdom, as we know from the great offering lists of Ramesses III in his temple at Medinet Habu. For the great state festivals celebrated by the king and gods together the principal participants were the great nobles of the land and the representatives of the priesthood; but in the festivals of the gods opportunities occurred when the temple courts were thronged with 'all the people'. For in the Ancient East festivals of the gods were popular festivals. This was also true in respect of the king in his special position of 'son of Rē'' in the sun-temples of the Old Kingdom; it was not true, however, for the king in the royal pyramid temple near the Residence.

[1] See above, p. 89, 94.   [2] Borchardt, *Das Re-Heiligtum des Ne-woser-Re*, I.
[3] Von Bissing and Kees, *Re-Heiligtum*, III, 54.

Memphis and Heliopolis

When we talk of Memphis as being the royal residence in the Old Kingdom we have to include a larger district than the settlement surrounded by the White Walls. Each king built his own palace but these changes did not involve great difficulties as they were built of sun-dried bricks and wood. It has been supposed that this practice in the Old Kingdom was inspired by the eternal city of stone, the actual pyramid city. Even today Eastern potentates consider that it is due to their rank and manner of living to build palaces for themselves. Nevertheless, we must not judge by a wrong set of values; for in Egypt wooden pillars could cost more than stone columns — timber had for the most part to be imported from abroad and if the wooden pillars were decorated with gold-mounted composition inlays they could be more costly than granite columns.[1]

The tombs of Dynasty III were built close to the Early Dynastic cemetery at Saqqara and they extended in a southerly direction. Tombs of Dynasty IV, starting with that of Snofru, were built at Dahshur (Pl. 15. *b*) and simultaneously at Meydum in the most northerly Upper Egyptian nome. Cheops, Chephren and Mycerinus, the great kings of this dynasty, had their residences near Giza while Shepseskaf and the kings of Dynasty V devoted to sun-worship, returned closer to Memphis, to Abusir. Isesi built further south in the District of Sokar, and here the kings of Dynasty VI from Pepi I onwards continued. Consequently, by an historical accident, the relatively unimportant Pyramid city of Pepi I, which was called Men-nefer, gave the capital city its historical name of Memphis. The history of names is full of peculiarities. Memphis acquired from its chief temple the sacred name of Hikuptah which means 'House of the *ka* of Ptah'; foreigners used this name for the whole land of the Nile and it eventually became the Greek Aigyptos. In just the same way the Roman poet used *memphiticus* for 'Egyptian'. Hikuptah or Aigyptos, when it became arabised, provided the Christian inhabitants of the country, in distinction from their Islamic conquerors, with the name 'Copts'.

It would be a mistake for us to imagine that these Pyramid cities were very grand. A literary composition depicting conditions during the Heracleopolitan Age claims that Djedisut,

[1] See below, p. 299.

the Pyramid city of Teti, which lay not far from the Step Pyramid of Zoser close to the eastern edge of the desert plateau, had 10,000 inhabitants exempt from taxation and compulsory services because they were priests.[1] Such a claim is a gross exaggeration. Yet at that time Djedisut formed the actual centre of Memphis and somewhere in the neighbourhood must have been the tomb and Pyramid city of Merikarē' the only king of the Heracleopolitan Dynasty certainly to have such monuments. Some idea of what a Pyramid city was like can be gained from the excavations carried out by the Fuad University of Cairo at Giza, to the east of the tomb of Khentkaus, the daughter of Mycerinus and the ancestress of the legitimate line of Dynasty V (Pl. 15. *a*). We can see a district made up of sun-dried mud-brick houses built close together, rather like those of the Pyramid city of Sesostris II at Illahun, near the entrance to the Fayum, those of the workers' village at Amarna and those built for the state necropolis workers in the Theban City of the Dead (Pl. 19. *b*). During the age that saw the building of the pyramids there had also to be barracks for the stone-masons who worked all the year round. Traces of such barracks can be seen behind the Pyramid of Chephren.[2] The people needed to maintain the Pyramid cities were recruited by conscription and organized through a 'workhouse' which was called, traditionally in agricultural Egypt, the 'farmhouse'. The workers were divided up into gangs or phyles and were employed more generally in labouring tasks than in priestly duties.[3] This organization of labour was based on that used in the state labour service. It is true that the employees of the Pyramid cities were protected by royal privileges from having to undertake other forms of compulsory labour or 'hourly services', as they were called, but it is equally true that they were required not only for the carrying out of ritual duties; the whole economic activity of the privileged area depended on them. They were, however, looked upon as 'clean' and had to satisfy the priestly regulations concerning cleanliness when called upon for service in the sanctuaries. Their overseers had also to perform administrative tasks and there were few regular priests, lector-priests and

[1] Papyrus Petersburg, 1116A, ll. 100–1.
[2] Hölscher, *Grabdenkmal des Chephren*, p. 70.
[3] Kees in *Orientalia*, 17 (1948), 71f.; see above, p. 55.

masters of ritual among them. In the Middle Kingdom the men subject to the hourly compulsory service were organized into four gangs which succeeded each other for monthly periods. During the Old Kingdom the number of gangs is not known with certainty. In general recruitment was made from the rising members of the families already engaged in the work,[1] but in some cases it was purely a question of social welfare. 'Recruitment, employment and removal' are words that constantly occur in the contents of decrees for the organization of labour.

After the completion of the main buildings an unpretentious Pyramid city could consist simply of a few brick houses. Cities of this kind can still be seen, for example, at Saqqara near the mortuary temple of Queen Neith who was one of the wives of Pepi II, and also at Dahshur around the recently discovered valley temple of the Bent Pyramid, built by Snofru. We can thus visualize the desert plateau dotted with a string of small settlements which had their farms, gardens and plough-lands on the edge of the cultivated area in the valley below. This land was, for the most part *sharaki*-land and hence, the term used by the Egyptians for someone who cultivated such exempted land was 'Garden-(owner)'. In places, however, it was poor pasturage on which flood-water remained in pools as is seen today near Saqqara and Abusir. Naturally there was also some land that could be rendered fertile by means of clever cultivation, but in the main the problem was one of working undeveloped land. So that they could devote their energies entirely to this hard task the citizens of the Pyramid cities were exempted by royal decree from other compulsory labour.

As far as their limited measure of self-government was concerned these settlements can be compared with the monasteries of the Christian Era. In a position very much like that of a Pyramid city we find at Saqqara the monastery of Apa Jeremias which was founded in the second half of the Vth Century A.D.[2] It shelters within its precinct — which is an irregular rectangle barely 650 feet long by 325 feet wide — a large number of mud-brick houses and tiny alleys and many communal services such as wine-presses, oil-presses and bakeries that pro-

[1] See above, p. 63.
[2] Quibell, *Excavations at Saqqara*, III (1907–9).

vided for the needs of the monks and their dependants. Fresh produce came from the monastery estate on the neighbouring agricultural land. In typical Egyptian fashion the monastery lies on completely sterile ground in a sheltered position from which there is a most beautiful view of Memphis and the whole Nile valley. It was placed in the middle of the ancient mastabas, just to the south of the causeway leading up to the Pyramid of Unas. Living in similarly unfavourable situations, the inhabitants of the Pyramid cities will have been induced to devote themselves to crafts, particularly stone-masonry. It is not surprising therefore that we mostly hear about the gangs of the Pyramid cities, even during the Middle Kingdom, in connection with the restorations of the sanctuaries or the maintenance of the temple inventories which were handed in writing to the leaders of the gangs engaged in the monthly service. This organization, which in origin was wholly priestly, in fact displayed a very unecclesiastical manner of life. It was during the New Kingdom that specialists for the various sides of life, both spiritual and economic, were developed to meet the new needs of the time.

A whole complex of sanctuaries in addition lay around Memphis on the edge of the desert, but little has survived. We have already frequently spoken of Sokar who was called Lord of the Curved Pond in the Pyramid Texts and whose name lives on in that of Saqqara. Outside the city too, perhaps some distance away to the south at Dahshur, lay the sanctuary of Hathor of Memphis, Lady of the Southern Sycomore. Ptah was accustomed to visit her, travelling from his temple by boat along a canal.[1] Possibly the goddess possessed another temple within the city boundaries, to the east of the Temple of Ptah, on the modern Kôm el-Kala. In accordance with her nature, the lion-goddess Sekhmet, 'the mighty one' and 'she who lives in the desert-valley', dwelt on the edge of the desert. Already in the Old Kingdom she had been identified with the form of Bastet, the cat-goddess, specially favoured in Ankh-tawy, the western quarter of the city. Unfortunately the name Ankh-tawy, like Memphis itself, was used generally for the whole city at such an early period that it is impossible to locate it to its particular quarter. Certain things like the late cat cemetery in an enclosure

[1] Papyrus Harris, I, 49, 1–3 (Ramesses III); on the situation, see *Urk.*, I, 247, 16.

13. Desert animals in the sun sanctuary at Abusir.

14. *a*. Desert animals and a huntsman of the Predynastic Period.

14. *b*. Sunrise at the Pyramid of Chephren.

near the east building of the Ptolemaic Serapeum, distinguish that part of the Memphite necropolis; we know this area rather better because of the Serapeum Greek papyri.[1] Here was one of the best known and most famous sanctuaries of the Ptolemaic Period, the 'great Asklepieion near Memphis' in which was worshipped the deified Imhotep (identified with Asklepius), the architect of the neighbouring Step Pyramid. It was constructed on the supposed site of his tomb and it therefore should be sought to the south of the *dromos* of the Serapeum. Within the precincts of the Serapeum, which itself was the burial-place of the Apis bulls, stood a subsidiary of the main municipal temple, an Astartieion, in the priestly quarters of which hermits dwelt under the asylum of the Serapeum. This too must have lain in the eastern part of the Serapeum, near the Pyramid of Teti and the sharp slope of the desert plateau. Here were found rooms containing pictures of the god Bes and phallic figures that can be connected with the worship of Astarte. Somewhere in the same area there remains to be found the Anubieion, the shrine of Anubis 'who is upon his hill, the Great God'; in the Ptolemaic Period it served as the police station and court-house for the necropolis. It is not certain whether it is to be identified with the shrine of Anubis-Imiut which is mentioned in Ramesside lists as being in the district 'outside the walls, northern half'[2] or with that of Anubis 'at the northern gate'.

The citizens of Memphis evidently had a predilection for religious names based on topography; but unfortunately such names are only of limited assistance to us. The central point of the town of Memphis was the Temple of Ptah 'south of his wall', the site of which is fixed by its remains directly south-east of the modern village of Mit Rahînah (Pl. 16. *b*). The royal palace of the 'White Walls' lay to the north of the temple, probably on the other side of the depression that may correspond to the ancient Sacred Lake. It was still so described by Strabo in the days of the Roman Empire. According to ancient sources the royal gardens also lay in this area. South of the Temple of Ptah and opposite its southern door stood the shrine of the Apis, his stall with a court in front and near it a room for the mother of the Apis. Recent excavations at Kôm el-Fakhry on the road

[1] Kees' article 'Memphis' in Pauly-Wissowa, *Real-Encyclopädie*.
[2] Kees, *Rec. de Trav.*, 37, 76, nr. 45; cf. Mariette, *Abydos*, I, 45a, l. 36.

running south from the Temple of Ptah to Saqqara have brought to light the hall of the embalmment of the Apis which could hardly have stood too far from his shrine. It contains huge alabaster basins used in the process of mummification and it dates from the time of Sheshonk I to that of Necho.[1]

The 'walls' also serve to identify locally the cults of Neith, the opener of the ways, so often mentioned in the Old Kingdom, who was also called 'north of the wall'; so too the districts mentioned in Ramesside lists of cults — 'outside the wall (behind the wall), southern half', and 'northern half' and 'southern and northern court'. Districts were also named after shrines, e.g. 'Seat of Ptah', 'House of Sokar', another under its cult name 'Hoe' (*henu*), 'House of Nefertum' and 'the Upper Houses'. Innumerable divinities are listed of whom we know the names of some from priestly titles; others are wholly unknown to us. In addition to Tjenen, the well-known god of the exalted places, there were the *djed*-pillar, Nefertum the god of ointments, in the form of the lotus flower, whom the theologians made the son of Ptah and Sekhmet, Sekhmet herself and other gods connected with animals or plants, 'he under his olive-tree', 'Horus on his papyrus', the ram-worship of Khnum 'before his wall,' who was also called 'in front of his sycomore', divine personifications like Nepre, the corn-god, and Hapy, the inundation. There were also the gods of the great theological system, Shu and Tefnut, Isis and Nephthys; there were even particular religious identifications like 'Horus on the corner of the southern door' and even 'the southern and northern boundary-stones'.[2] Other well-known gods are absent from the lists; such a one is Hathor, 'Lady of the (Southern) Sycomore' whom the ladies of the court served as priestesses in the Old Kingdom. These lists nevertheless afford some idea of the extraordinary multiplicity of local cults that acquired a new vigour in Ramesside times; in them poor people found an outlet for their religious feelings. It does not follow, however, that an enormous number of priests served these special cults. Even in religious matters the Egyptian was too economically minded for that to be the case. We know that the contrary was the case and from the series of titles held by Old Kingdom priestly officials we learn that many of these

[1] *JEA*, 34, pls. 15–17 and Brugsch, *Thesaurus*, 817.
[2] *Rec. de Trav.*, 37, 57f. (the Abydos Temple).

particular cults and among them even one so esteemed as that of Sokar, were simultaneously served by the High Priest of Ptah. By this it is not meant that one man enjoyed a multiplicity of benefices but that the small cults were dependent on the shrine of Ptah, just as we find happening in the New Kingdom with the statue-chapels of the king. These little temples received their share of the divine offerings at the Temple of Ptah by the procedure of 'circulating benefits' approved of old. It permitted the inclusion of two or even three beneficiaries between the principal deity and the ultimate beneficiary. Priestly titles held jointly therefore indicate for the most part joint shares in the divine offerings. The endowments, in spite of the fact that they were large in comparison with the economic strength of the country, did not surrender anything more.

The earliest known High Priest of Ptah was called Ptah-shepses; he was the son-in-law of King Shepseskaf, was reared in the royal harîm and apparently became high priest in the reign of Userkaf.[1] The high priest bore the title 'Chief of the craftsmen' and the Greeks identified Ptah with Hephaestus; but crafts belonged to him only inasmuch as he was Lord of the Earth. The association of Ptah with crafts was therefore founded less on religious than on economic grounds. Works in everlasting materials like gold or stone belonged by right only to the gods and to the king as the Great God. For this reason the organization of sculpture workshops which the Egyptians generally included in the term 'House of Gold', was associated with the Temple of Ptah. In addition, under Dynasty IV only the king's sons could occupy the office of high priest and that dignitary therefore became the obvious controller and organizer of public works. It is scarcely fortuitous that we also find that the oldest-known high priests of Heliopolis — the Greatest of Seers — combined in themselves the offices of Masters of Works and Leaders of expeditions to obtain raw materials along with that of directing the temple. We have already seen this arrangement in practice in the case of Imhotep, the architect and master sculptor in the reign of Zoser. We find it again in the reign of Snofru: Kanufer, his eldest son, who later became vizir, Captain of the royal ships and Treasurer of the God. Similarly Meryib,

[1] *Urk.*, I, 51–2 (= Mariette, *Mastabas* C.1); earlier, but without name, *Urk.*, I, 20 (under Mycerinus).

the natural son of Chephren, who is buried in the cemetery surrounding the Pyramid of Chephren, styled himself Chief Architect and General (leader of the gangs of workmen) at the time when Dynasty IV was coming to an end.[1] Rahotpe, another general whose tomb is at Meydum and who was also certainly a son of Snofru (Pl. 23. *a*) belonged to this tradition as a leader of shipping and of youth organizations. It may be reasonably supposed that, like Kanufer, he was one of those men of action who established Egypt's rule over Sinai. Kanufer, Meryib and Rahotpe all bore the title 'Greatest of Seers', like Imhotep. The explanation of this fact is not that these men were given the office of high priest as a reward for services abroad, but that they were appointed to an office centred in a place that was crucial for foreign commerce, that is, Heliopolis, the starting place for traffic to Sinai and Asia.

The economic duties of the high priests of Heliopolis are revealed in the titles they bore in the closing years of the Old Kingdom; in a parallel manner to that of the Upper Egyptian nobles, in particular the nomarchs of Elephantine, they called themselves 'Privy councillor of the Southern and Northern Gate' and also let it be known that they were royal scribes.[2] At times naturally the king appointed his own officials to act along with them, even in Heliopolis; such were 'overseers of the barriers, the deserts and the royal forts'.[3] Furthermore, the Palermo Stone tells us that during Dynasty V the office of greatest of seers in Heliopolis was administered jointly by two men, and we find the same dualism occurring at Memphis in the office of chief of the craftsmen for the administration of the limestone quarries at Tura.[4] In point of fact, the moving of the site for royal pyramids from Giza to Saqqara at the beginning of Dynasty V presented great problems for the chief of the craftsmen in Memphis and led to the enlargement of the organization of the limestone quarries at Tura and Masara on the east

[1] British Museum stela 1324, probably from a tomb at Dahshur; L. *D.*, II, 18–22 = *Ägyptische Inschriften aus Berlin*, I, 88f. (nr. 1107).

[2] Daressy, *Annales du Service*, 16, 195, 204 (probably Dynasty VI–VIII).

[3] So, Nesunefer, the royal kinsman buried in the Chephren cemetery, see Kees, 'Beiträge zur altägyptische Provinzialverwaltung' in *Gött. Nachr.* (1933), 588–9; Junker, *Giza*, III, 172f. (mid-Dynasty VI).

[4] *Urk.*, I, 247, 3 (Palermo Stone, *verso*, 4, 2), cf. *Urk.*, I, 20, 7; 38, 15.

bank of the Nile. It was now that sculpture in limestone experienced its greatest age. At Helwan on the east bank of the Nile opposite Memphis are to be found the earliest tombs in which monumental limestone blocks were used for the construction of the subterranean burial chamber.[1] These tombs were built at a time when at Abydos in Upper Egypt a royal tomb such as that of Usaphais was floored with gravel. During Dynasties II and III at Saqqara the archaic statuary made for the tombs of important private persons was in preference and in the best cases made out of hard granite in spite of the fact that a good technique for the dressing of the stone was still lacking.[2] A change to limestone came with the sculpture produced for Zoser and Imhotep, and a similar fashion flourished at Meydum in the time of Snofru (Pl. 23. *a*). The pyramid builders at Giza returned to the use of hard stones for their sculpture and it was not until Dynasty V that sculpture in limestone reached its height, due largely to the help of the workshops of the Temple of Ptah. With sculpture we must here associate low-relief work which became the perfect and unsurpassed successor to the soft rounded relief of earlier carving in wood. At the same time the artist's creative task was unexpectedly enriched by the deepening of thought and feeling inspired by the sun-worship of Heliopolis. The creative sphere of the sun-god embraced everything, gods, men, animals, plants, and this fact is portrayed in art in the so-called representations of the seasons in the Sun-temple of Niuserrē' at Abusir (Pl. 13).

The lay-out of the necropolis near Memphis did not follow a regular plan such as can be found in cemeteries by the pyramids of Cheops and Chephren at Giza (Pl. 14. *b*). We can speak of streets of mastabas in the Memphite necropolis only in respect of the early dynastic cemetery and of tombs up to the beginning of Dynasty IV. Graves that were built subsequently, after the Giza Period, were certainly for the most part grouped near the pyramid of the king in whose reign their occupants had lived, but some were also constructed in groups elsewhere. It is often difficult, therefore, to establish the chronology of these tombs and particularly so for those of Dynasty V up to about the reign of Niuserrē'. Much of the blame for this state of affairs rests upon

[1] Z. Y. Saad, *Royal Excavations at Saqqara and Helwan* (1941–5), 162f. and pl. 61f. [2] Schäfer-Andrae[3], 224–5.

the methods of excavation used during the period when Mariette controlled work at Saqqara (1851–81). It was the practice then to search chapels and grave-shafts for museum-pieces without making exact records of where the finds were made. What was left behind fell prey to the spoliation by which the necropolis furnished material for local lime-kilns, a form of plundering that continued down to quite recent times. In the light of this plundering the carrying away of whole rooms from mastabas to be re-erected in museums is regrettably justified, even if it has injuriously affected the appearance of the whole necropolis.

The high-water mark in the artistic decoration of private tombs with sculpture and reliefs was reached in the period following the reign of Niuserrē', particularly in the years of the reigns of Isesi, Unas and Teti, the last of whom was the first king of Dynasty V. The famous mastabas of Ti (Pl. 4), Akhtihotpe and Ptahhotpe date from the beginning of this period and those of the viziers Kagemni and Mereruka (Pl. 8) near Teti's pyramid, mark its close. It was a time when the supremacy of Heliopolitan sun-worship was waning. None of the kings from Isesi onwards erected a sun-temple in honour of his father Rē' near his palace and consequently forces were released that formerly were exclusively at the disposal of the endowments established on behalf of the state religion. They were now employed not so much on royal tombs like those of Dynasty IV, but on those for a class of person surrounding the king who were frequently connected with the royal house by political marriages. Children who had been brought up in the royal harîm, real or alleged royal descendants, princes of the second or third grade, filled the ranks of this class and they now occupied the principal offices of state as viziers, chief architects and High Priests of Ptah. In response to the demands of the times the circle of the privileged became enlarged far beyond the narrow limits of the Giza Period. The courtiers who served the sacred person of the king, the palace officials and naturally the overseers and foremen of works also were one and all honoured by the king. Unas, the last king of Dynasty V, did carry on the tradition of the sun-sanctuaries of his predecessors by including among the scenes on the walls of the causeway leading to his mortuary temple, reliefs depicting the seasons. At the same time he was the first king to have the royal spells for the dead inscribed on the walls of his burial chamber, as if to perpetuate by the written word the idea that in the company of the sun-god, he, the son of Rē', would enjoy a heavenly hereafter, being the heir of an age that had seen a solar state religion, but which was now gone. He did it again as if to perpetuate this solar tradition for a world that was stripping the god-king of his ancient privileges one by one. In this period too we find in the tombs of the highest officials indications of their increasing authority. Thus, in the tombs of some viziers (and among the viziers were members of the powerful family of Ptahhotpe) we find representations of the so-called obsequies of Buto,[1] burials conducted in the ritual form of a pilgrimage to the sacred shrines of predynastic times, in particular Buto and Sais, places in which, according to the Pyramid Texts, the worship of Osiris was already firmly established. Such practice was an infringement of royal rights and privileges and parallel to it was the taking over by others than the king of the mythical significance of the ritual ceremonies for burial and offerings.

More regular streets of mastabas belonging to the highest dignitaries are to be found in the cemetery around the Pyramid of Teti and in the area to the north of the causeway of Unas. The increased demands on the limestone quarries on the east bank of the Nile necessitated the enlargement of the labour gangs. These had to be made up mostly of trained stone-masons and could not be recruited simply by making use of the villagers conscripted for the hourly or monthly service. The gangs were organized along military lines and were divided into troops, each of which bore a special name. The principal tasks of the generals, as the foreman were called, and their detachments were public works rather than military missions. The permanent cadre of skilled workmen was augmented by levies when required as, for example, for the conveying of material from the quarries. One advantage enjoyed by the labour corps was that the families of its members were looked after by the State as far as food and clothing were concerned. A sheet of papyrus of the late Dynasty VI which was found on the floor of the temple of Zoser, lying loose with scraps of other documents, contains the complaints of one of these commanders of the labour corps over a characteristic piece of oriental negligence: 'The General says:

[1] Junker, *Mitt. Dt. Inst. Kairo*, 9, 15.

This servant was brought a letter from the vizir about the bringing of the companies of skilled workmen from Tura in order to be clothed in his presence at the very beautiful door of the palace. Now this servant spoke from the furthest corner when the letter-carrier came to Tura with the barge. Now this servant spent six days in the Residence (Memphis) together with this detachment without its being clothed. That is an injuring of the work of this servant since *one* day was allowed for this detachment to be clothed. This servant says: Let the letter-carrier be informed.'[1] Here the complaint may have been concerned with some question of overtime payment since the vizir himself was concerned in the matter. Time, however, is of no importance to oriental officials. All the evidence we have on this subject shows a preoccupation with the same things: those in authority extol the excellence of the care shown by the king and his officials for the state labour corps; those who suffer give voice to enraged complaints about delays.[2]

Heliopolis lay close to the quarry district and in the immediate neighbourhood was one quarry hardly less famous than the granite quarries at Aswan or the alabaster quarry of Hatnub in Middle Egypt. It was that of the 'Red Mountain' (Gebel el-Ahmar) on the northern spur of the Mokattam Hills, a point that was passed by the hero of the Story of Sinuhe in his flight from Egypt. This quarry produced a dark yellow quartz, the hardest stone in Egypt, which was highly valued for statues and sarcophagi including those of kings and particularly from Dynasty XII onwards. The burial chamber of the Pyramid of Ammenemes III at Hawara was hewn from a single block of this quartz weighing about 110 tons; but even this immense monolith is exceeded in weight by a similar burial chamber in a late Middle Kingdom pyramid at Saqqara that has been estimated to weigh 150 tons.[3] Similarly the great Memnon colossi of Amenophis III strayed from the Gebel el-Ahmar to Thebes, from the 'Lower Egyptian Heliopolis to the Upper Egyptian', as it was realistically said.[4] Ramesses II erected a

---

[1] Gunn, *Annales du Service*, 25, 242f. dated in the 11th occasion (of numbering), the 23rd day of the 1st month of the Inundation Season, with no royal name.   [2] See below, p. 277.

[3] Petrie, *Kahun, Gurob and Hawara*, 16; cf. Jéquier, *Deux Pyramides du Moyen Empire*, 64.   [4] See below, p. 263.

stela when he visited the quarry in the eighth year of his reign
and on it he praised himself for his concern for the labour corps
working there.[1] He rewarded the overseer with gold as a mark
of honour for finding out a block and preparing it for its purpose; he also assured the workmen that he had filled up the
storehouse in advance so that 'each one of you will be cared for
monthly. I have filled the storehouse for you with everything,
with bread, meat, cakes, for your food, sandals, linen and much
oil, for anointing your heads every ten days and clothing you
each year.' Current requirements were therefore distributed
every ten days while linen was apportioned annually. Such
conditions were infinitely better than those of the *fellaheen* and
labourers today. Stone-masons and sculptors were also paid
their wages in kind. For the duration of a job like the decorating
of a tomb, their overseer was received into the household of the
employer as 'one who received gifts'.[2] Old Kingdom inscriptions,
the express purpose of which was to establish the fact that the
materials for the tombs concerned had been obtained legiti-
mately and not plundered from earlier tombs, or to maintain
that the manual labourers had not been cheated, clearly say: 'I
never brought the property of anyone to this tomb in remem-
brance of the judgment in the West. I made this (my) tomb in
return for the bread and beer that I gave to all the manual
labourers who made the tomb. I also gave them very much payment in all sorts of linen that they asked for and for which they
returned thanks to god.'[3] Another says: 'They made this for
bread, for beer, for linen, for ointment and for much barley and
emmer.'[4] In private affairs the same practice obtained as in
state undertakings but on a smaller scale. We do not know,
however, to what extent stone-masons and sculptors in earlier
periods were obliged to perform monthly and hourly services on
public works such as mortuary temples and shrines, or to what
extent they were at liberty to hire themselves out. It is hardly
possible to assume that such people had complete liberty of
movement during the Old Kingdom.

The title 'Greatest of Seers' was also borne by the same

[1] Cairo, J.34504, see Hamada, *Annales du Service*, 38, 218f., ll. 14–15.
[2] Kees, *Kulturgeschichte*, 163–4.
[3] Selim Hasan, *Excavations at Giza 1930–1931*, 173.
[4] *Urk.*, I, 50 (time of Niuserrē').

Kagemni who was vizir under Teti. We cannot tell, however, whether he held this office as a sort of old-age pension, or whether it was a fully administrative post as in earlier times. But we do notice that it was Kagemni who was honoured as a god in his tomb near the Pyramid of Teti[1] just like his predecessor Isy, a retired vizir who ended his days as nomarch of Edfu and was buried there.[2] Both men incorporated the idea of the life filled with achievement; their success proved that their careers had followed the desirable 'way of God'. Nevertheless the structure of the State that they had accepted as the foundation on which to build their lives and careers had collapsed at the close of Dynasty VI. For that very reason perhaps, the subsequent period of depression evoked their memories and put into their mouths the worldly wisdom of their teaching. The Egyptians, however, paid no attention to historical accuracy. Thus Kagemni, under whose name circulated such sayings as are found in the Papyrus Prisse, was said to have been the vizir under Snofru, undoubtedly because this conferred greater distinction on him, although he had in fact lived some two hundred years later. Similarly the Ptahhotpe who was the author of the best-known collection of ancient sayings was not identified personally as one of the famous family of vizirs of that name who lived at the close of Dynasty V. The one important thing was to link the sayings with famous names from the Golden Age of the highly developed Memphite civilization. In this way the names were immortalized just like those of Imhotep of the time of Zoser and of Djedefhor, the son of Cheops.

The peculiar Egyptian conception of history is usefully illustrated by the fact that Pepi II, the king whose reign of ninety years brought the Old Kingdom to a close, had copied in his mortuary temple at Saqqara reliefs portraying the victories of Sahurē' a century earlier in which even the names of the defeated Libyan princes were repeated. What had once been an historical deed now took its place in the repertoire of achievements claimed by a model and successful ruler. The example became stereotyped. In the Old Kingdom this process was true of the Libyan war waged by Sahurē'. Similarly in the New Kingdom the list of cities captured by Tuthmosis III was

[1] Firth and Gunn, *Teti Pyramid Cemeteries*, 126, cf. Otto, *ÄZ*, 78, 30f.
[2] Alliot, *BIFAO*, 37, 93f.

170

adopted by his successors for themselves. Even the reliefs of the battle of Qadesh, won by Ramesses II, were used to some extent as models by Ramesses III a century later.

Memphis and Heliopolis are both some distance away from the Nile, but ship-canals connected the town-centres with the river and its traffic. Memphis was probably always enclosed on the east and the west by canals, as it is today. The account of the capture of the city by Piankhi who made use of the waters of the inundation to surmount the city walls, suggests a rather insular position.[1] There was certainly a harbour district near the modern railway station of Badrashein. The Cairo city canal that became silted up only in modern times ran from the Nile to Heliopolis. 'The House of the Nile' was the name given to the harbour of Heliopolis on the Nile near the modern Atar en-Nabi at the southern end of Old Cairo (Pl. 1. *b*), because near here was the Nilometer on which official measurements of the height of the river were made.[2] A little to the north was an old shrine of the holy Sepa, the One of a thousand feet, who was invoked as the dispenser of the waters of the Nile from the depths of the earth. There too, on soil belonging to Heliopolis, was the opening from which was said to come the Lower Egyptian Nile. An ancient fortress, known only from its name 'Place of Weapons', which guarded this important harbour on the Nile, stood near on the frontier between Upper and Lower Egypt, probably on the same spot as that where the Romans built a camp for their legions and which they called the Egyptian Babylon; it is now the heart of Arab Old Cairo. At this point the regions of Memphis and Heliopolis touched, on the frontier between Upper and Lower Egypt, and whoever ruled here held the key to the Nile valley in his hand. A processional way known as the Road of Sepa[3] ran from Old Cairo and the House of the Nile (Nilopolis in classical times) east of the Heliopolitan canal over the desert plateau to Heliopolis, the city of temples.

The kings of Dynasty XII who came from Thebes did not have their Residence at Memphis but further to the south at Lisht, near the entrance to the Fayum. The art and civilization that flourished under these kings reveal characteristics so much more Memphite than Theban that it is sometimes difficult in

---

[1] *Urk.*, III, 33–4.　　　[2] See above, p. 50.
[3] *Urk.*, III, 37, cf. *Annales du Service*, 37, 233.

the case of the delicate low reliefs from Lisht to decide whether
they are Middle Kingdom copies or actually loot from Old
Kingdom buildings. The same is true of the administrative
system. The ancient instructions to the vizir which were still
inscribed in the tombs of the Theban vizirs during Dynasty
XVIII called on the Memphite ritual.[1] The necropolis of
Memphis, therefore, had little to communicate to the Middle
Kingdom; temples throughout the country were still for the
most part built of sun-dried mud brick with monumental stone
doors and chapels. A recently discovered chapel built by Pepi I
of Dynasty VI at Bubastis and apparently meant to house a
statue of the king, had a holy of holies built of mud brick. We
should also note the building of the monumental gateways of
stone in Memphis, as in the Temple of Ptah. Herodotus (in
Book II, chapter 101) reports that of the four gateways of this
temple the northern was erected by Moeris and, according to
Diodorus Siculus (Book I, 51) it was renowned for its magnificence. This gateway was probably built by Ammenemes III and,
if not by him, possibly by Amenophis III, an alternative not
altogether impossible in view of the similarity of the prenomens
of these two kings; that of Ammenemes III is Nima'atrē', that
of Amenophis III is Nebma'atrē'. No trace now remains of this
gateway. It is practically certain that every ruler of the Middle
Kingdom from Ammenemes I to Khaneferrē' Sebekhotpe of
Dynasty XIII (who was one of the last kings to rule over the
whole of Egypt before the Hyksos domination) erected sculptures in the forecourt of the temple, including seated figures
greater than life-size and royal sphinxes. Most of these pieces
were carved out of grey granite from Upper Egypt and such as
survive are counted among the finest creations of Egyptian
art.[2] In addition to the classical quality, such as is revealed in
the limestone reliefs at Lisht, we find in these sculptures a
touching attempt to achieve in a representation modelled in the
old age of the subject an insight into the personality of the
strong-willed ruler who had known much human disappointment. The Hyksos ruler Apophis carved his name on some of
the particularly impressive sculptures, such as the unique
sphinx from the time of Ammenemes III which has the king's

[1] *Urk.*, IV, 1089, 7, cf. Sethe, *Untersuchungen*, 5, 2, p. 13.
[2] The majority illustrated in Evers, *Staat aus dem Stein*.

face surrounded by the lion's mane, and also on some imposing colossi.

The old but not very impressive temple of Atum at Heliopolis was rebuilt by Sesostris I who, in the course of the *sed*-festival in the thirtieth year of his reign, erected two obelisks of Aswan granite in front of it. These two were the earliest of their kind in Egypt and one of them, rising to 66 feet in height is today the only clear indication that Heliopolis ever existed on that site. Another pair of obelisks erected in the same place by Tuthmosis III on the occasion of his third jubilee and dedicated to Atum or Rē'-Harakhte, now stand far apart, one in London and one in New York after they had been conveyed from Heliopolis to Alexandria by Augustus.

A new age began for Memphis with the New Kingdom, in the course of which the city rose to be the second capital of an empire. The weak kings of Dynasty XIII who had come close to destroying utterly the unity of the Two Lands, had introduced a division between the southern capital, Thebes, and Memphis which was the administrative centre for Lower Egypt. Each received a vizier as head of the administration. This innovation stimulated activity at Memphis during the widening circumstances of the Empire. Furthermore, there was the additional fact that in the reign of Tuthmosis I, at the time of the first great Syrian campaign, the crown-prince resided at Memphis as Commander-in-chief of the army, and particularly of the chariot guards who were organized on Asiatic lines and equipped with Asiatic horses. The broad and level stretches of land on the edges of the desert between Saqqara and Giza were available for the manoeuvres of the horse-drawn units. A favourite place for excursions was the point where the Great Sphinx stood just below the Pyramids at Giza; there was probably a rest-house of some kind there and the king and crown-prince honoured it with their presence when archery practices were held. The first to give us this information was Amenmose, a son of Tuthmosis I.[1] Amenophis II, who loved to show off as a bowman of unequalled strength and accuracy, commemorated these shooting matches in great detail on a memorial stela.[2] It

[1] *Urk.*, IV, 91.
[2] Selim Hassan, *Annales du Service*, 37, 129f.; A. Badawy, the same, vol. 42, 12f.

was this king too who described himself on a commemorative scarab as 'born in Memphis'.[1] The custodian of his estates, Kenamun,
played a prominent role as overseer of the crown estate at
Perunefer, which was apparently under the control of the
crown-prince and comprised workshops of all kinds, including,
in particular, a ship-yard. Tuthmosis IV, when still crown-
prince, rested once in the shade of the Sphinx and saw a vision
in which he was commanded to clear away the sand that the
wind had piled up round the Sphinx.[2] The Sphinx, now considered the likeness of Chephren, was at that time thought to be
a representation of Rē'-Harakhte, the sun-god of Heliopolis. It
was also called after the falcon god of the Syrian provinces,
Hurun or Hul, of which an echo may be heard in Abu el-Hôl,
the popular Arabic name for the Sphinx. The Egyptian army
brought this god back with them from Syria and, as a tutelary
deity of the king, he is later to be found in the Tanis of Ramesside times.[3] Colonies of foreigners were to be found especially in
Memphis on the estates and in the workshops. Most of these
foreigners were settled prisoners-of-war and hence the colonies
were later often called camps. It was at this time that the core of
the district known as Tyre Camp was established. In the
Ptolemaic Period its inhabitants were described as Phoenician
Egyptians[4] and their god was Astarte, the original of the
'foreign' Aphrodite described by Herodotus (Book II, 112). In
the early years of the reign of Amenophis III this same Astarte
was appointed the goddess of the royal estate Perunefer[5] and
this was just the place where foreigners were put to work. It is no
surprise, therefore, to find that in the reign of Amenophis IV
(Akhenaten) a Semite was High Priest of Amun, Baal and
Astarte in Perunefer.[6] Memphis had just begun to be a cosmopolitan city and it was so to a far greater extent than far distant
Thebes. As with the mercenaries of the army, so with the
foreigners there came foreign gods. The patron gods of the
chariot troops were the Syrian Reshef and Astarte, as we learn

[1] Petrie, *Scarabs and Cylinders*, pl. 30, 1.
[2] Erman, 'Die Sphinxstele' in *Sb. Berl. Akad.* (1904).
[3] See below, p. 199.
[4] Article 'Memphis' in *Real-Encyclopädie*, col. 668–9.
[5] Inscription of the Chief Architect Minmose in the Quarries of Masara,
Annales du Service, 11, 258.
[6] Berlin 1284, cf. *ÄZ*, 68, 26.

from the stela at the Sphinx; and this fact throws significant light on the composition of these troops. The association of the Great Sphinx with the sun-god was principally based on the ancient legend that the kings of Dynasty V were borne as sons of Rē' by the wife of a priest from a place called Sahebu which was apparently near Giza. Its local god was in consequence readily invoked on the monuments erected near the Sphinx. Yet the Sphinx, the image of Chephren, dating from a time when the kings of Egypt despised the Asiatic nomads as their enemies and defeated them in battle, allowed the name of a Syrian god to be given to it. To such an extent had the focus altered with the advent of the Empire.

The kings of Dynasty XVIII erected in Memphis, as at Abydos, chapels for their cult of the dead which contained statues of themselves. For reasons of economy they were associated with the Temple of Ptah and were probably situated in its neighbourhood. Their property, however, was administered by their own steward. This is attested fortuitously in the cases of the chapels of Tuthmosis I and Tuthmosis IV by inscriptions in the neighbourhood;[1] for the exceptionally well-endowed chapel of Amenophis III we have the decree governing the special endowment for a steward for this purpose. Amenophis III at times seems to have favoured Memphis before Thebes. He sent the prince Tuthmosis there to be High Priest of Ptah, which was an exceptional procedure for that time; the Apis bull that died during his reign was buried in its own chapel near the place where the Serapeum ultimately stood. A complicated theological system grew up round the figure of the Apis bull[2] that was designed to associate it with the chief divinities as 'the living Apis-Osiris, Lord of Heaven, Atum whose two horns are upon his head', and which made it what it was later called: 'King of all the sacred animals'. The growing animosity of the kings towards Thebes and to the pretensions of the priests of Amun stood Memphis in good stead. The balance dipped increasingly in its favour as more Memphite families secured leading positions, even in Thebes itself, and as more dependants of the army gained control of the State. Moreover the persecutions of the Amarna Period affected Memphite families far less severely

[1] Stela of Ay from Gîza, see *Rec. de Trav.*, 16, 123.
[2] Otto, *Beiträge zur Geschichte der Stierkulte*, 23f.

than those of Thebes. Consequently when Horemheb, who had been Commander-in-chief under Tutankhamun and Ay, started from Memphis and seized the royal power, Memphite art moved into the first place, consciously replacing what the reforms of Akhenaten in Thebes had removed. Many Theban craftsmen at that time evidently migrated to Memphis; for at Memphis one finds overseers of craftsmen who own tombs with the like of which Thebes had at that time nothing to compare. Unhappily none of these tombs survive undamaged; the New Kingdom tombs for the most part lay on the edge of the desert plateau near the Pyramid of Teti and further south where the Monastery of Jeremias later stood. Their reliefs were therefore the first to disappear into the lime-kilns of the villagers with the exception of a few pieces that are scattered through the museums of the world. The splendid tomb of the viceroy Horemheb is the best known among many.

The more that foreign policy demanded the presence of the king in the north, the more Memphis fulfilled the role of second capital. And this role Memphis continued to fill throughout the Ramesside Period, although Ramesses II built a new Residence at Piramesse in the Delta.[1] Many decisive councils of state and royal decrees are dated from Memphis, and all that remains of the city area dates from this time. Then too the great temple was rebuilt completely. From the Temple of Ptah south-east of Mit Rahînah can still be seen a forecourt facing westwards (Pl. 16. *b*) and the foundations of a hypostyle hall which look like an extraordinary patchwork, although very choice materials were used, an alabaster pavement in the forecourt and basalt and granite column bases. Much of the material for this building was obtained by pulling down older structures; some came from the sun-temple of Niuserrē' at Abusir and some from the Pyramid of Teti.[2] The colossi, however, which Ramesses II liked to set up everywhere to parade his greatness were certainly the idea of that king himself (Pl. 19. *a*). Two of them still lie beneath the palms in front of Mit Rahînah at the spot where perhaps the south gateway of the Temple of Ptah stood. The smaller, which is of granite, is 26 feet high; the larger, which is of fine limestone, was originally over 42 feet high. Merenptah who continued the rebuilding of the Temple of Ptah also built a palace to the east

[1] See below, p. 196. [2] Petrie, *Memphis*, I, pl. 3.

15. *a.* Excavation of the Pyramid City to the east of the Pyramid of Chephren at Giza, 1933.

15. *b.* The Pyramids of Dahshur.

16. *a. Sebbakhin* working on the ruins of ancient Memphis, 1909.

16. *b.* Ruins of the Temple of Ptah, Memphis, 1952.

of it for his use when he visited Memphis for the great festivals.[1]
Perhaps there was also at that time on the modern Kôm el-Kala
a shrine of Hathor, Lady of the Southern Sycomore, whose cult
next to that of Ptah was certainly the most highly regarded
among the ancient cults of Memphis.

Ramesses II sent his favourite son Khaemwese to Memphis
with the title of High Priest of Ptah to direct the building work.
He specially devoted his attention to the cult of Apis and to the
enlargement of the necropolis of the sacred bulls; several died
during the long reign of this king — one in the sixteenth and
another in thirtieth year — and they were buried in separate
tombs under the direction of Khaemwese. After the burial of the
one that died in the thirtieth year Khaemwese had a common
burial place constructed for those that died subsequently and
this was the beginning of the famous catacomb of the Serapeum.[2]
Above it was built a shrine of the 'living Apis'. The prince's
second great task consisted in the preparation and holding of a
great number of *sed*-festivals which were celebrated from the
thirtieth year of his father's reign onwards, usually at intervals
of three years. These festivals were placed under the protection
of Ptah-Tjenen, so conforming with the tradition of the time
when the Lands were unified; and thus the importance of
Memphis was firmly established as a city where the festivals of
the unification of the kingdoms were celebrated. Nevertheless,
no matter how strongly the king sang the praises of his new
buildings and no matter how often Khaemwese perpetuated
his own memory as the restorer of sacrifices to the ancient gods
by means of inscriptions on ancient buildings such as the Pyramids of Unas and Sahurēʿ and the sun-temple of Niuserrēʿ, the
truncated obelisk of which he perhaps took to be an old Pyramid,[3] the rebuilding was for the most part effected at the cost
of ancient monuments. The architects made use of them as
quarries, tearing down the casings of the Pyramids and pulling
out granite pillars wherever they found them. They were then
carted away, some to form the foundations of the Temple of
Ptah, but most to go to Tanis in the Delta. To Tanis also went
the wonderful royal statues and the granite sphinx that had

[1] Borchardt, *Zeitschrift Dt. Architekten*, 22 (1922), nr. 25.
[2] Otto, *op. cit.*, 20–1.   [3] Drioton, *Annales du Service*, 37, 201f.

filled the forecourt of the old Temple of Ptah and that had to be removed to make room for the new building. They were carried off[1] and had the names of the new kings inscribed upon them. It probably never occurred to the Egyptians that in doing this work of 'restoration' they were disfiguring monuments. On the contrary, the old half-forgotten monuments experienced a renewal of life through being identified with the fame of the *living* Pharaoh. The older royal teachings were certainly inspired otherwise in respect of matters such as these.

The shadow of doubt is therefore cast on Khaemwese's actions. We today are sensible of the destruction of valuable ancient buildings and regret it, but he and his age regarded it otherwise. Khaemwese nevertheless became for posterity the exemplar of a pious and learned son of a king whose legendary figure lived on in the tales of Egyptian popular literature. What actually survived in the way of ancient cults is to be found in humble, popular cults such as that associated with a statue of Sekhmet of Sahurēʿ in the mortuary temple of that king,[2] or in that of a 'Hathor of the Field of Rēʿ', the companion goddess in the sun-temple of Sahurēʿ. In the same class is a supposed 'Ptah of Menes', a statue of Ptah that certainly did not have as its model the legendary founder of Memphis.[3]

If we turn for comparison to Heliopolis it can be established that as far as the gifts made by Ramesses III to Thebes, Heliopolis and Memphis, the three stars of Egypt, are concerned, it was Memphis that received the smallest share. The temple at Memphis received only about 10 square miles of land compared with nearly 925 for that at Thebes and about 170 for that at Heliopolis. Further, Memphis received 3,079 slaves as against 12,963 for Heliopolis and no less than 81,322 for Thebes. Yet it is remarkable that during the New Kingdom Heliopolis was continually being placed under Memphis administratively. We know cases as early as mid-Dynasty XVIII of the same person being high priest both in Memphis and Heliopolis[4] and this merging of offices was repeated in regard to the worship of the sacred bull of Mnevis at Heliopolis and that of Apis at

[1] See below, p. 198.
[2] Borchardt, *Grabdenkmal des Königs Saȝhure*, I, 41, 101.
[3] Erman, *ÄZ*, 30, 43, from a Theban monument of the time of Ramesses II.
[4] Sennufer, cf. Petrie, *Sedment*, II, pl. 50.

Memphis.[1] The service of the Apis clearly profited from this union, especially the organization set up to deal with the bull's costly burial. In this connection it should be remembered that the whole country had to contribute towards the cost of the burial of the Apis in accordance with the memorandum drawn up by the *idiologos*, the Roman prefect of Egypt in imperial times. In earlier times this expense had been a royal obligation that not even the Ptolemies could escape. We learn fortuitously from one of the Zenon letters written in the time of Ptolemy Philadelphus that Apollonius, the finance minister, had to pay out at the king's command 100 talents even for the sacred cow of Atfîh. 'You must know that the Hesi is Isis', declared the writer.[2] According to Egyptian theology the white cow of Atfîh was reckoned the mother of the black Mnevis-bull of Heliopolis.[3] She was indeed his neighbour in the nome to the south. The corpus of myths of the Osiris cult even embraced them all, the Mnevis and the white cow that became Isis.

We have already noticed that Memphis became a cosmopolitan city with the growth of the Empire. The oldest historical example of a whole settlement of prisoners-of-war named after their origin seems to have been the 'Field of the Hittites', established in the reign of Ay and therefore long before the great wars against the Hittites waged by the Ramesside kings.[4] The best known of the foreign city-quarters of Memphis were Syropersikon (for Syrians and Persians) and Karikon (for Carians) during the Late Period. They cannot now be located. The Tyrian camp that is mentioned by Herodotus was situated around the shrine of Astarte to the south of the Temple of Ptah. Small finds of all sorts both in the necropolis and in the city itself testify to the presence of these types of foreigners who actively engaged in trade and wrote in Aramaic. The individual racial types were commemorated for posterity during the Graeco-Roman Period by strikingly characteristic terracotta heads.[5]

The city of Memphis covered an area about one and three-quarter miles in length and three-quarters of a mile in breadth.

[1] Otto, *op. cit.*, 36, especially for the Mnevis bull buried in the twenty-sixth year of Ramesses II.

[2] *PSI*, IV, 328 (257 B.C.); Hesi = Egyptian *ḥs3t*; the name could have denoted the wild cow or the 'fruitful one'.

[3] Otto, *op. cit.*, 35.   [4] *Rec. de Trav.*, 16, 123.

[5] Petrie, *Memphis*, I, 35f. (predominantly Roman).

At the beginning of this century the brick walls of the ancient occupation levels still rose up in ten *kôms* as picturesque mounds (Pl. 16. *a*.) The work of native diggers called *sebbakheen* who dig ancient remains to collect disintegrated brick as fertilizer, has resulted in the course of recent years in the almost total removal of these last traces of the existence of the one-time cosmopolitan city, with the exception of a few architectural remains in stone that have escaped destruction. Memphis has shared the fate of Heliopolis and nothing is left even of buildings erected in the Late Period and Ptolemaic Period. Whatever could be used has disappeared into the mosques and fortifications of more recent towns such as Fustat and el-Kahira, or into the lime-kilns; for the Arabs, as pupils of the Syrian builders of castles, were not content with walls built of sun-dried mud bricks.

In spite of its walls Memphis was never a real fortress. In all the many wars the Egyptians waged with Ethiopians, Assyrians and Persians up to the arrival of Alexander, this important key-point almost invariably fell into the hands of the conquerors without any great resistance or long siege. The sole exception is the successful defence by the Persian garrison of the quarter containing the fortress during the rebellion of Inaros, as recorded by Thucydides (Book I, chapter 104). The defence of the extensive suburbs of the city was clearly a problem beyond the capacity of the Egyptians. In spite of all the blows rained on her by fate Memphis yet knew how to maintain her importance as the real capital of Egypt. Memphis became the centre of the opposition raised by the petty princelings of Lower Egypt to the Ethiopian kings, while the Saites who followed the Ethiopians and Assyrians moved the Residence in the time of Amasis back to Memphis and with it the Greek mercenaries who formed the pick of their guards. Egypt could not be properly governed from Sais in the Delta. It was in the Temple of Ptah in Memphis that the high priest, speaking in the name of Egypt, welcomed the victorious Alexander as the liberator of Egypt and sovereign of the country. From the time of Ptolemy Epiphanes the Egyptian priests obliged the Ptolemaic kings to be crowned in the Temple of Ptah, an outward acknowledgment at least of the city's royal tradition. And from the reign of Ptolemy Philopator one of the royal titles was 'chosen of Ptah', just as 'beloved of Ptah' had been among those of the Ramesside kings.

Traces of the Late Period have, however, to be sought chiefly in the necropolis. Near the Pyramid of Unas and south of the Pyramid of Userkaf lies a number of splendid tombs dating from Dynasty XXVI and the Persian Period, made for generals, court physicians, captains of royal ships, chamberlains and men occupying positions of similar importance.[1] Such people clearly wished to be buried near the Pyramid of Zoser for whose mortuary cult new priests were appointed in the Late Period,[2] and near the supposed tomb of Imhotep who had by that time become deified. They also copied the ancient reliefs in the subterranean chambers beneath the Step Pyramid that so closely resembled earlier wood carving in their subtle modelling.[3] To help them in their work of copying they superimposed grids on the ancient reliefs. In his excavations on the Kôm Teman at Memphis Petrie thought that he had found the palace of a Saite king, and there he discovered a monumental door on which were fine reliefs clearly executed after some such ancient pattern.[4] It is not surprising therefore that the artistic renaissance started by the Saite Dynasty revealed Memphite traits and was quite different from that instituted by the Ethiopian kings at Thebes. The Saites indeed had the monuments of the Old Kingdom before their eyes and they adopted the titles of the ancient court offices as well as the artistic style of that time. There is good reason, therefore, why this Late Period style which continued in use down to the Ptolemaic Period is called Neo-Memphite, in spite of the fact that the flourishing towns of the Delta played as much part in its development as Memphis. Distinctly Memphite in character also were the products of the minor arts, in glazed composition, small statuary and glass. Finally there was the continuing fame of the Apis whose mausoleum and temple were enlarged by the kings of the Late Period down to Nectanebes II of Dynasty XXX, into the grandiose catacomb the discovery of which in 1851 established the fame of Mariette. Even Roman emperors were attracted by the sacred bull and its oracle as a curiosity. Julian the Apostate instituted a search for a new Apis and in

[1] *Annales du Service*, I, 161f.; 40, 693f.; 41, 381f., 51, 469f.
[2] Erman, *ÄZ*, 38, 114.
[3] Von Bissing, *Archiv für Orientforschung*, 9, 35f.
[4] Petrie, *Memphis*, II (*Palace of Apries*), pls. 2–9.

A.D. 362 had coins minted bearing its effigy. Again, in the reign of the Emperor Arcadius (A.D. 398) an account was composed of the procession of the Apis — the ancient 'running forth of the Apis' known in the Thinite Period.[1]

In the Vth Century A.D., however, monks built the Monastery of Jeremias from the ruins of the City of the Dead and thus became the spiritual successors of the hermits of the pagan Serapeum.

[1] Claudian, *De quarto consulatu Honorii Augusti*, 574.

VII

The Delta: Fortresses and Harbours
(Sile, Tanis and Naucratis)

Anyone who travels by railway across the wide expanses of the Delta sees endless fields and isolated clumps of trees that mark villages or embankments running beside water (Pl. 9. *b*), but he senses the virtual absence of boundaries. The canals are noticed only when a tall white sail suddenly rises in the middle of the fields. Everything seems to have been created for agriculture on a large scale, such as is represented here by the extensive cotton plantations.

The impression is quite different if you travel by car. The strong dykes running along the arms of the Nile or along the canals are the obvious routes for communication for man and beast, but they run principally in a north to south direction towards the apex of the Delta near which lies the capital of the country, Cairo. To cross the Delta from east to west is, even today, a complicated business because of the scarcity of sound bridges. The best way to travel from Fakus or Tanis in the north-east to Alexandria in the north-west is to go by the round-about route south to the level of Mit-Ghamr-Ziftah or even as far as Benha (ancient Athribis). It has always been the same throughout the ages. All the great conquerors from the East, like the Egyptian kings returning to their country from abroad, made use of the Bubastite arm of the Nile from the Egyptian frontier posts onwards. They therefore appeared in Egypt at Memphis and not in Lower Egypt itself. The first mention of a lateral route across the Delta occurs in the late Roman *Itinerarium Antonini*; this route, crossing the principal branch of the Nile, ran from the eastern frontier near Pelusium, via Tanis and

Thmuis (modern Tema el-Amdid) to Cynopolis (near Busiris, the modern Abusir Baa) and Taba (modern Taua) in the middle of the Delta, whence it turned north-westwards to cross the Canopic branch of the Nile to make for Alexandria via Hermopolis (near Damanhur). This route, therefore, turned from the Damietta branch of the Nile sharply to the south as far as the level of modern Tanta.

If we leave out of consideration the navigable arms of the Nile, the Delta as a whole was difficult of access and especially so the northern districts and the area lying between the two principal arms of the Nile.[1] It was in ancient times quite unsuited for agriculture on the large scale for which today it is the outstanding region of Egypt. In very ancient times in fact we hear very little about the Delta except in one respect — the gods and shrines of the 'Land of the Papyrus', an echo of the fame of which comes down to us in the ritual and religious texts of the Old Kingdom with its traditions derived from the Thinite Period. There is Buto, the 'place of the Throne' (ancient Pe), the old capital of the kingdom of the West Delta, situated deep in the marshes of the Delta (modern Tell el-Fara'in), with its mistress, the papyrus-coloured cobra goddess Edjo; further to the south and near the Canopic arm of the Nile was Sais (Sa el-Hagar), the home of the arrow goddess Neith; Busiris (Abusir) in the middle of the Delta, almost on the Damietta arm of the Nile, the home of Osiris and the *djed*-pillar; and further to the north in the neighbouring Sebennytic nome, the city of Isis (Behbet el-Hagar) that acquired its name 'the divine' from the sacred lake from which, according to the ancient rituals, water for purification was drawn, as from the alleged source of the Nile at Elephantine.[2] These divinities dominate the myths and rituals of the Memphite Kingdom and it was to these places that the privileged dead wished to make pilgrimages to take part in the festivals and to be greeted by their ancestors of blessed memory.[3] These places were early won over to the worship of Osiris and their festivals still survived into late times to be described for us by Herodotus. We find Neith of Sais 'north of the wall' in Memphis during the Old Kingdom as well as the sacred *djed* and Osiris. Osiris and Isis likewise occupied leading

---

[1] See above, p. 32.   [2] *Pyr.*, 1293a, 1902c, *et. al.*

[3] See above, p. 167.

positions in the ennead of Heliopolis early in the Old Kingdom. The appropriation and transplanting of gods in this manner was typically Egyptian.

In trying to complete the picture with examples from the fields of economics and administration we find that there was a great dependence on the royal seat of government; but this does not altogether mean that there was a centralized administration. From the part of the Early Dynastic cemetery at Saqqara dating from the time of the kings Zoser and Snofru we have the inscriptions from the funerary chapels of several men who acted as royal administrators in Lower Egypt.[1] With the offices of 'Overseer of Commands' and 'Canal-master', the oldest titles used for the Lower Egyptian nomarchs, they changed from nome to nome. Metjen, who has been mentioned before, sang his praises in this connection for having been overseer of the principal royal estates in the Lower Egyptian nomes of the Haunch (the 2nd or Letopolite), the Arrow (4th and 5th, Prosopite and Saite) and the Desert Bull (6th or Xoite); he also 'founded' 12 villages which were given to him as his own property for his exemplary development work. When he served in the frontier nomes to the west he became 'Controller of the Door of the West', 'Master of the Desert and Leader of the Hunters' and was faced with important duties arising from the defence of the frontier against the unruly Libyan tribes in the Mareotis and Marmarika. The economic activities in which he was principally engaged were the care of vineyards and orchards, characteristic of the peripheral areas of the Delta, and the cultivation of flax.[2]

At the height of the Old Kingdom the estates of the Delta are often represented as the sources for the funerary endowments of Memphite notables. From the description of estates it is remarkable to notice how dispersed landed property was, due principally to the steady accumulation of royal gifts. The chief share of these gifts fell to the clearly defined circle of metropolitan officials in Lower Egypt. In addition there were the reserves of land belonging to the royal domains which offered great opportunities for reclamation and the winning of new cultivable land by the building of dykes and canals and the

---

[1] *Urk.*, I, 1–7 (Berlin 1105–6), see Junker, *ÄZ*, 75, 63f.
[2] See above, p. 81.

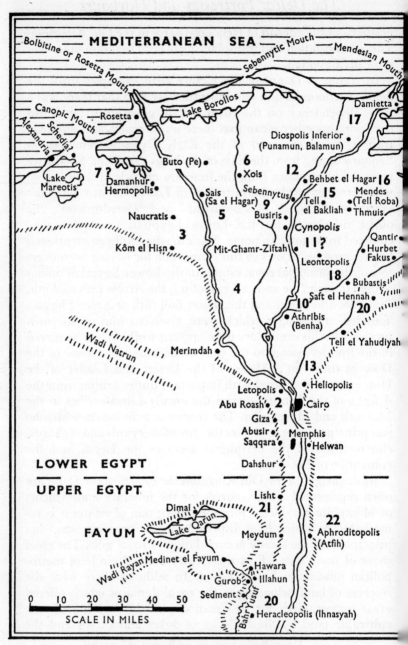

MEDITERRANEAN SEA

Bolbitine or Rosetta Mouth

Sebennytic Mouth

Mendesian Mouth

Canopic Mouth

Alexandria

Schedia?

Lake Mareotis

Rosetta

Lake Borollos

Damietta

17

Diospolis Inferior
(Punamun, Balamun)

Buto (Pe)

6

12

Xois

Behbet el Hagar 16

Damanhur
Hermopolis

7 ?

Sais
(Sa el Hagar)

Sebennytus

15

Mendes
(Tell Roba)

Tell
el Bakliah

Thmuis

Naucratis

5

9

Busiris

Cynopolis

Qantir

Hurbet

Kôm el Hisn

3

Mit-Ghamr-Ziftah

11 ?

Leontopolis

Fakus

18

Wadi Natrun

4

Saft el Hennah

Bubastis

20

Merimdah

10

Athribis
(Benha)

Tell el Yahudiyeh

13

Heliopolis

Letopolis

Abu Roash

2

Cairo

Giza

1

Abusir

Memphis

Saqqara

Helwan

Dahshur

LOWER EGYPT
— — — — — — — —
UPPER EGYPT

Lisht

Dimai

21

FAYUM

Lake Qarun

Meydum

22

Aphroditopolis
(Atfih)

Wadi Rayan

Medinet el Fayum

Hawara

Gurob

Illahun

Sedment

20

0   10   20   30   40   50

SCALE IN MILES

Bahr Yusuf

Heracleopolis (Ihnasyah)

5. The Delta and Lower Egypt

186

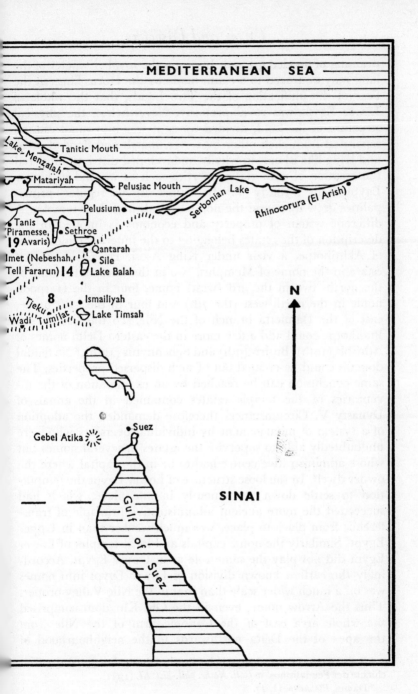

draining of flooded ground. In origin the royal character of the land may be traced to a claim made by the Horus kings at the time of the unification of the Two Lands, that the whole of Lower Egypt was royal property. Nevertheless, the physical structure of the land, divided up as it was into small estates, separated from each other by water, marsh and flooded areas and lying like islands in wholly undeveloped districts, hindered the creation of manorial properties such as we find in Upper Egypt from Dynasty V.[1] In Upper Egypt regular principalities grew up round the nome capitals and their temples. A different system of property and economy is implied in the description of the estates belonging to the funerary endowment of Akhtihotpe, a vizier under King Asosi. He possessed one estate in the nome of Memphis, two in the Letopolite nome to the north, two in the 3rd (west) nome, four in the Harpoon nome in the north-west (the 7th) and four in the 11th nome, east of the Damietta branch of the Nile. To this list his son Ptahhotpe could add a few more in the eastern Delta nomes of Athribis (10th), Busiris (9th) and Sebennytus (12th).[2] No feudal domain could be created out of such dispersed properties. The same conclusion can be reached by an examination of the inventories of the temple estates contained in the annals of Dynasty V. Circumstances therefore demanded the adoption of a system of management by individual overseers who were undoubtedly able to supervise the estates in several nomes but whose administrative centre had to be in the capital where the owner dwelt. In the loose structure of Lower Egypt the temptation to settle down permanently in one place, which had succeeded the more ancient administrative principle of transference from place to place, was much weaker than in Upper Egypt. Similarly the nome capitals and local temples of Lower Egypt did not play the same role as in Upper Egypt. Accordingly the earliest known division of Lower Egypt into nomes was on a much wider scale than that in the Nile Valley proper. Thus the Arrow nome, even in the Old Kingdom comprised the whole area east of the Canopic arm of the Nile from the apex of the Delta northwards to the neighbourhood of

[1] Kees, 'Beiträge zur altägyptische Provinzialverwaltung und der Geschichte der Feudalismus' in *Gött. Nachr. phil.-hist. Kl.* (1932).

[2] Davies, *Ptahhetep*, II, 27.

Buto.[1] Its southern part consisted of what the classical world called the Prosopite Island; it corresponded with the modern province of Menufîyah which has 1,168,777 inhabitants (according to the 1947 census) living on about 600 square miles; the density therefore is nearly 2,000 to the square mile, making it one of the most densely populated areas of Egypt. How profoundly have the conditions in the Delta changed with the passage of time! The character of the Delta in early days was one of a large-meshed network of domains, an agricultural economy of the kind found in new colonial areas and this character lasted well after the New Kingdom until the Libyan and Saite kings of the Tenth to Sixth Century B.C. instituted great internal schemes of colonization. What we have already said about the Delta fits into this picture: the maintenance of great herds of cattle in the Delta,[2] the vineyards, even the highly characteristic case of the royal chief steward of Ramesses III (about 1170 B.C.) who created an estate for the growing of fruit on the 'Western river' (Canopic arm of the Nile) from newly reclaimed land that formerly had been *birket* or flood-land and donated it as the estate of No-amun to Amun of Thebes.[3] The situation in the New Kingdom differed from that in the Old Kingdom principally in the fact that as a result of progress in cultivation there arose a predominance of temple estates, particularly of those belonging to Amun of Thebes.

It is impossible to determine whether the people who cultivated these estates in the Delta collected themselves into settlements in the manner of those who inhabited the predynastic settlement at Ma'adi in what were admittedly the quite different circumstances of the district between Heliopolis and Memphis. Lower Egypt certainly offered, as the result of planned development, far more room for the reception of far greater numbers of people than the valley of the Nile. We cannot moreover doubt the populousness of the Delta towns in later times even if the remains of these towns have for the most part been destroyed by the *sebbakheen* with the exception of a few such as Tanis, Thmuis and Bubastis. We have chosen for con-

[1] Still undivided in the nome list in the Sun Temple of Niuserrē' (in Cairo).
[2] See above, p. 30, 88.
[3] See above, p. 69; wine jars marked 'No-Amun' are, moreover, found in the cellars of the Ramesseum in Thebes.

sideration three places from this patchwork of land, Sile and
Tanis in the north-east and Naucratis, the later Greek city in
the north-west. Alexandria, a purely Greek foundation, does
not enter into the picture of Pharaonic Egypt.

Tanis and Sile are both situated in the eastern Delta, an area
that suffered peculiarly great changes in its administrative
divisions and certainly in its composition. The list of nomes in
the shrine of Sesostris I at Karnak lacks nomes 18 to 20 of the
east Delta and also the 17th nome north of Sebennytus. The
organization of these additional nomes clearly followed the expulsion of the Hyksos and it suggests a general administrative
reorganization at that time. Previously the 13th Heliopolitan
nome in the east Delta must have extended northwards beyond
Bubastis. To the north was the 10th nome of which the principal
part belonged to the middle Delta (the area of Athribis), and
north of the Bubastite arm and east of the Damietta branch lay
the 11th nome of the 'dismembered bull'. Finally there were
two nomes in the marshy districts lying rather close together
for the Delta, the 15th or Ibis nome with its capital near the
modern Tell el-Bakliah and the 16th nome of Mendes around
Tell Roba to which the whole lowland area between Damietta
and Lake Menzalah originally belonged. The rest of the country
to the east and the north-east was in the Old Kingdom apparently called, simply, 'the East,' to correspond with 'the West'
on the Libyan side,[1] just as the Greeks called the eastern side of
Egypt Arabia; or the area was more precisely divided into what
was called 'Further East'[2] and 'Near East'.[3] The latter designation remained in use as the title of the Asiatic frontier nome (the
14th). In the list of Sesostris I its capital is given as Sile, the
place that is known to us as a frontier fortress at the eastern
entrance to Egypt. It lay on the site of the unimportant modern
town of Tell Abu Sefah about one and a half miles east of
Qantarah[4] and therefore at that strategically important point

[1] Cf. Palermo Stone, *verso*, 3, 1; 4, 3; *Urk.*, I, 244, 246. It is not clear
whether the reference here is to a Crocodile nome (*Urk.*, I, 2, 6) so named
only at the beginning of Dynasty IV.

[2] *Urk.*, I, 17 (Dynasty IV).

[3] So already, Palermo Stone, *verso*, 3, 14 = *Urk.*, I, 245, 2 (Sahure); and
verso, 4, 3 = *Urk.*, I, 247, 2 (Neferirkareʿ).

[4] For the trifling remains, see Griffith in Petrie, *Nebesheh and Defenneh*, 96f.;
Annales du Service, 12, 69f.; *BIFAO*, 11, 29.

where the lagoons south-east of the modern Lake Menzalah and south of the ancient Pelusian arm of the Nile (which ran north-eastwards from the Bubastite or principal arm of the Nile near Tell Defennah — the Greek Daphnae) leave a narrow tongue of land on the other side of the Bitter Lakes, which is consequently called el-Qantarah or, more precisely, Gisr el-Qanatir, 'the crossing by bridges'. From this point the 'Ways of Horus', the Pharaonic road, led by way of el-Arish to Gaza.[1]

Here in ancient times was Egypt's most threatened flank in spite of the fact that Nature had protected this eastern gateway with brackish waters and a frontier river, the channel that the ancients called *She-Hor*, 'the Canal of Horus'.

At the start of Tuthmosis III's wars of conquest the name of Sile rang out like a clarion call: 'In regnal year 22, day 25 of the 4th month of winter His Majesty passed the fortress of Sile on his first campaign of victory.'[2] There is evidence to show that Sethos I and Ramesses II also set out from Sile on their Asiatic campaigns. In the reliefs of Sethos I's campaigns in the Temple of Karnak we can see at Sile, protected by advance fortifications, the bridge over the canal, in which crocodiles sport.[3] In the background stands the fortified town. There stand deputations of Egyptian priests bearing life-giving bouquets, and of officials waiting for the home-coming king — a delicate form of congratulation which is also to be seen in the case of the Ptolemaic king returning to Memphis as victor after winning the battle of Raphia in 217 B.C.[4] Akhtoy II, the Heracleopolitan king in his instructions to his son, written about 2060 B.C. expressly mentions the defence of the frontier along the Ways of Horus.[5] More vigorous measures were taken there after the bitter experiences at the end of the reign of the aged Pepi II when disturbances in the capital coincided with incursions by Asiatic hordes into the Eastern Delta. Nevertheless, defensive measures for the eastern frontier were certainly taken during the first half of Dynasty V, as is proved by the title 'Overseer of the barriers, the deserts and the royal fortresses in the

---

[1] Gardiner, 'The ancient military road between Egypt and Palestine' in *JEA*, 6, 99f.

[2] *Urk.*, IV, 647.   [3] Gardiner, *loc. cit.*, pl. 11 = Wreszinski, *Atlas*, II, 40–1.

[4] Spiegelberg, *Sb. bayr. Akad.*, 1925, 4; 1926, 2; cf. above, p. 79.

[5] See above, p. 120.

nome of Heliopolis' which was held by the Overseer of Commands at that time.[1]

This defensive organization has already been discussed in the description of the eastern caravan routes with special regard to the route to the Red Sea through the Wadi Hammamat. In actual fact all that was necessary was the occupation and defence of the few wells upon which travellers depended. From the description of the flight of Sinuhe we gain an idea of how effective were these defensive positions which started at el-Qantarah on the Ways of Horus and covered the whole arid eastern flank as far as Hebnu (Kôm el-Ahmar) in Middle Egypt. We also learn that apart from the fortress of Tjeku (modern Tell el-Maskhutah) in the Wadi Tumilat and the so-called Walls of the Ruler further to the east in the neighbourhood of Ismailiyah, the most southerly way was also defended by watchtowers at the wells. The instructions prepared for the Crown-Prince Merikarē' contain the most striking description of the Arabian Beduin as the hereditary enemy of Egypt: 'The wretched Asiatic, evil is the land wherein he is, with bad water, inaccessible by reason of thickets and the paths thereof are bad by reason of the mountains. Never does he dwell in one place and his feet wander. Since the time of Horus he fights and never conquers, but likewise is never conquered. . . . Although he may plunder a lonely settlement he never captures a populous city. A wall is set at his side, its (other) side is covered with water up to the Bitter Lakes. Its walls are strong against attack. . . .'[2] Such is the description of the Walls of the Ruler and the fortifications of the Bridge of Sile. Nebhepetrē' Menthuhotpe, the Dynasty XI unifier of the land from Thebes also carried out a punitive expedition against these Asiatic Beduin to render safe the vital traffic between Egypt and Sinai, to judge from the reliefs in his mortuary temple.

Every traveller was checked at the frontier posts. Each incomer was compelled to wait until his entry had been approved. The homecoming Sinuhe was detained at Sile until he was sent for and conducted to the Residence of Sesostris I at Lisht. The same system was operated on the southern frontier.[3] Compared with this ancient southern frontier at Elephantine, Sile retained

[1] Kees, *Gött. Nachr. phil.-hist. Kl.* (1933), 588–9; Junker, *Gîza*, III, 172f.
[2] Papyrus Petersburg, 1116A, l. 51f.   [3] See below, p. 317.

far more strongly, even in the New Kingdom, the character of a true frontier post. Amenhotpe son of Hapu, 'Chief recruiting officer and Overseer of public works' under Amenophis III, specified the organization of the frontier control in the Delta as being his principal task next to recruiting: 'I stationed troops in the marshland in order to keep foreigners within their places; both sides (of the Delta) were guarded to watch over the movements of the Beduin. I was at the same time the actual leader at sea; the mouths of the Nile were closed by my troops except to units of the King's navy.'[1]

It was just at this time that the threatening invasion of the Khabiru from Transjordan brought fresh unrest close to the Egyptian frontier. Caution was required. In another respect also are these reports of interest; they reveal the linking up of the defence of the mouths of the Nile with that of the eastern frontier. The former was really based on the Tanite and Pelusian mouths of the Nile, both of which gave access higher up to the principal or Bubastite arm of the Nile; it supervised, therefore, the maritime traffic with Asia. This control, however, had nothing to do with overseas traffic to the Western Delta. This association between the eastern mouths of the Nile and the defence of the eastern frontier continued in force in the Ramesside Period when everything was overshadowed by the international quarrel with the Hittites over Northern Syria.

At this time we find men of the highest rank serving as commanders of the fortress of Sile and as overseers of the mouths of the Nile; Piramessu, the later king Ramesses I and his son Sethos I held these posts themselves.[2] Sile and the rising seaport of Tanis which stood under its protection, developed a connection based on strategic grounds that can be traced down to the Late Period, a connection between a town on the sea and a town inland, both of which looked towards Egypt's Asiatic provinces. A fragment of a diary kept by an official obviously stationed in Sile and dating from the third year of the reign of Merenptah (about 1222 B.C.), contains entries about all passers-by and, of especial interest, about the official journeyings of officers and couriers leaving the country. It even contains notes of how many letters they took with them and to whom they

[1] Cairo Statue 583, cf. Helck, *Militärführer*, 22f.
[2] Kees, *Kulturgeschichte*, 109; Helck, *op. cit.*, 84f.

were addressed. For the rest the work was like that at an army base: 'Regnal-year 3, first month of summer, day 17: Arrival of the Captain of troops of the wells "Merenptah-is-contented-with-truth" which are in the hills, in order to investigate (matters) in the fortress that is in Sile.'[1] When it is realized that these auxiliary troops consisted for the most part of non-Egyptians it is possible to understand that a posting to Sile or to any garrison on the military road to Syria was anything but attractive to the educated Egyptian and that a soldier's life on foreign service was painted in the most frightful colours to civil service candidates in the class-room. For this reason convicts were sent to do hard labour in such districts — in Kush, where it certainly meant work in the gold mines, in the Oases and, during the New Kingdom, in Sile. We have already mentioned the decree of the dictator Horemheb that ordered this punishment together with the severance of the nose for the unjustifiable requisitioning of ships.[2] Penal settlements made up of such mutilated prisoners must have been common sights along the Ways of Horus, as is confirmed by the Greek name Rhinocorura ('the cut-off noses') for the modern el-Arish. The Egyptian civil servant, however, longed for Memphis: 'Behold! My heart has gone forth furtively and hastens to a place that it knows. It has gone down-stream to see Memphis. But I sit and wait for (a messenger) to tell me how things are in Memphis. No task can I do because my heart is separated from its place.'[3] Another sits somewhere on the frontier at a well garrison; 'Punishment of the Two Lands' is the name he ironically calls it.[4] There was certainly in this place a settlement of forced labourers for whom no-one cared a thought: 'There are no men to make bricks and there is no straw in the district. . . . Are there no donkeys there? They are stolen. All day long I sit and watch what is in the sky as if I were a birdcatcher. . . . There is the gnat at sunset and the midge at noon . . . and they suck every vein.' There are dogs, however, packs of dogs and the only consolation of the royal scribe in his solitude is the little jackal he owns. This is what the Egyptian official thought of life on the frontier.

[1] Papyrus Anastasi, III, *verso*, col. 6 and 5, cf. Wolf, *ÄZ*, 69, 39.
[2] See above, p. 104.
[3] Papyrus Anastasi, IV, 4, 11f., cf. Erman, *Literatur der Ägypter*, 260.
[4] Papyrus Anastasi, IV, 12, 5, cf. Erman, *op. cit.*, 258.

Sile had little to offer that was peculiar to itself, not even in its cults. The local legend did, however, claim that from Sile came the 'phoenix (heron) who comes forth from the divine heart of Osiris'; the phoenix in its return from the eastern land confirmed the mighty death and resurrection of the universe. At Sile the phoenix's earthly territory was called 'Phoenix District' on 'the Horizon of Egypt'.[1] The principal deity of Sile was Horus, surnamed Lord of Harpooning, a conception derived from the legend of the royal huntsman which was localized chiefly on the Western Delta. This myth lays especial stress on the slaying of Horus' enemy Seth and his followers. At Sile this idea was interpreted as the hunting down of Seth as the god of the inimical easterners who, according to the New Kingdom conception, was in the chase expelled from Egypt over the boundary towards Asia; it is described in a ritual text of later times: 'They banish you, you of evil inclinations, and hurl you and all your abominations into the land of the Asiatics. Egypt that is dedicated to Horus prepares your slaughter.'[2] The myth also occasionally invests Horus with the form of the lion, the king of the desert, tearing its enemies to pieces. The king especially liked to compare himself with him 'who protects the fortress from the foreign lands of the Phoenicians', 'who drives out Seth into the red land (the desert)'. Nevertheless strained relations must have developed over this hostile attitude towards Seth, for Seth was the family deity of the Ramesside kings and he was worshipped at Tanis in the territory of which the dynasty of Ramesses II certainly had its origin. Egypt overcame this conflict of belief in its own individual fashion: it accepted both attitudes and ignored the conflict between them.

Sile owed its position as capital of the Eastern nome to its strategic position, for it was not a natural centre for trade and industry. All the district could offer apart from its own poor pasturage was good conditions for the growing of vines. The same was true of the district around Pelusium. The vineyards on the borders of Lake Menzalah had long been famous.[3] Taxes derived from the Ways of Horus were what a chief gardener brought for the offerings for Amun to the Second Prophet of Amun, Ipuemrē'; and wine of Sile was well-known to the royal

---

[1] Brugsch, *Dictionnaire géographique*, 1366, 1389.
[2] Schott, *Urk.*, VI, 12.   [3] See above, p. 81.

butlers in Thebes and Amarna.[1] The same was true of the district around Tanis and particularly so of Imet, the capital of the Lower Prince nome, which was known as an ancient city already in the New Kingdom. In the tomb of the High Priest Petosiris at Hermopolis it is written: 'Imet was given to you that you might be rich in wine when your festival is celebrated.'[2] Petrie discovered the site of this town on a hill covered with ruins known today as Tell el-Fara'un, but which he called Tell Nebeshah; as a settlement it had made use of a sand-dune island (in Arabic *gezira*) as was usual in the marshy districts and it lay about eight miles south-east of Tanis.[3] It can never have been an important town because by the time that history conferred importance on this lost eastern corner of the country, the leading role devolved upon Tanis. Tanis owed its name to the Field of Tanis (Zoan in the Old Testament), the salty plain on the southern border of Lake Menzalah which has now become even more desolate than it was in ancient days through invasion by the sea, particularly in the Fourth Century A.D. and the erosion of the coast.

The Tell or mound of Tanis rises out of a flat lowland with the brackish waters of Lake Menzalah glistening in the distance; to the south-west the navigable Muizz canal that has superseded the ancient Tanite arm of the Nile, draws near the poor fishing village of San el-Hagar. Whoever crosses the desolate waste between Tell el-Fara'un and Tanis immediately appreciates that Tanis was established there not as the economic centre of an agricultural area but as a strategic base on the arm of the Nile most suitable for the traffic with Asia; on the seaward side protected by a broad lagoon and on the landward side virtually unassailable across exposed flats, that were at times flooded by high water. Tanis is the Egyptian Venice.[4] Yet its fame as a town and a harbour was late in developing and dated only from the time when Ramesses II decided to build a new Residence there called Piramesse.

[1] *Urk.*, IV, 523 and Hayes, *JNES*, 10, nrs. 51, 74–6 (from the Palace of Amenophis III); or *City of Akhenaten*, I, pl. 63, nr. 553.

[2] Lefebvre, *Tombeau de Petosiris*, Text, nr. 58b.

[3] Petrie, *Nebesheh and Defenneh* (*Tanis*, II); Kamal, *Annales du Service*, 3, 8.

[4] Kees, 'Tanis' in *Gött. Nachr. phil.-hist. Kl.* (1944) and article 'Tanis' in Pauly-Wissowa, *Real-Encyclopädie*.

The Delta: Fortresses and Harbours

The origins of the town are shrouded in darkness. The Hyksos who gained power in Egypt about 1700 B.C. apparently found here a cluster of buildings called *Hut-waret* 'House on the Dunes' or something similar, the Avaris of classical times. It was perhaps a customs- and guard-post on a sand-dune on the Tanite arm of the Nile; but it could scarcely have been a place of any size. Egyptian ports lay far up the arms of the Nile because of the shallow mouths of the river and the flat unprotected coastline. Ocean-going ships sailed with their cargoes as far as possible inland for technical reasons. No-one wanted unloading-places in an area of lagoons only to be reached with difficulty from the landward side. Goods from abroad were destined for the seat of government and the state warehouses. Ports on or close to the sea, acting as points for the reshipment of cargoes between inland and overseas traffic were only developed during the New Kingdom when Tuthmosis III had made the Phoenician ports serve as deployment bases for his campaigns, sending his troops there by ship in order to avoid wasting time by marching them overland.

From the diary of the dockyard at Peru-nefer we learn, however, that the equipping and manning of the fleet used for the decisive campaign of year 30 of Tuthmosis III were carried out precisely at Peru-nefer which was close to Memphis, and not at some other place nearer the coast.[1] The decisive factor in favour of Peru-nefer was the availability of material and labour. The Hyksos, although they possessed Memphis, yet constructed their chief base at Avaris in the extreme north-east. In doing so they were looking for support to Asia. The Hyksos took this step moreover although Avaris and the neighbouring plain of Tanis offered no good testing-ground for the miraculous new weapon of the time, the horse-drawn fighting chariot. Unhappily the poor sources we possess for the Hyksos Period render many things of that age problematic for us. One thing that is certain is that the name Seth of Avaris appears for the first time on Egyptian monuments about the time of the Hyksos invasion; and Seth was the very god whom alone, according to tradition, they worshipped. An attempt has been made to prove that the cult of Seth existed in more ancient times in the north-east

[1] Säve-Söderbergh, *The Navy of the 18th Egyptian Dynasty*, 37; on the Journal, see *ÄZ*, 65, 105f.

Delta and the priestly title of an official of early Dynasty IV has been adduced as evidence.[1] The case here, however, is not of a Seth of the later town Sethroe in the north-east Delta but of a priest of 'Seth at the head (of the place: the King NN) who defeated the Asiatics', a name that at the most tells us something about the earlier importance of Seth as god of the Asiatic foreign land (Sinai). The Egyptian tradition was itself quite different. The Ramesside royal family was certainly in possession of the best local sources and at the time of the celebration of the fourth centenary of the town of Tanis they must have accepted the date 1700 B.C. as approximately that of the foundation of the town and the introduction of the worship of Seth; that is at the time of the Hyksos invasion or shortly before.[2] An Egyptian Seth of more ancient date was not known in this neighbourhood.

Montet, the French excavator of Tanis, has nevertheless maintained that in the Old Kingdom Tanis far from being a place of no consequence was already a town of many temples built of granite and limestone,[3] which, if it were true, would say a great deal for a town in the north-east Delta. In this contention, however, he has allowed himself to be misled by the peculiar building methods of Ramesses II. His architects and builders carried off masses of fallen stones, especially blocks of granite, and perhaps columns from the pyramid temples at Giza, Abusir and Saqqara and even from Hawara, Illahun and Gurob, to be used for their buildings at Tanis.[4] Further, Ramesses II had very many royal statues, usually of granite, brought from all possible temples, and particularly from those in Memphis, to fill the forecourts of the temples at Tanis so that these temples would not be at a disadvantage in comparison with the famous ancient temples of the country. It was enough that he or his son Merenptah should have his name carved on the statues. In some cases this fate had already been suffered, notably in the case of the famous Hyksos sphinx, at the hands of the Hyksos king Apophis at a time when he wanted no doubt to perpetuate his rule over Memphis. Proof of the origin of the various usurped pieces is afforded by the preservation of the texts of dedication mentioning the shrines at which they were

[1] Junker, *ÄZ*, 77f. (with impossible translation).
[2] Sethe, *ÄZ*, 65, 85f. (the so-called Stela of Year 400 from Tanis).
[3] Montet, *Tanis* (1942).   [4] See above, p. 178.

dedicated; and the chief among these is the Temple of Ptah at Memphis.[1]

Ramesses II built the new town on ground belonging to an estate of Amun so that it was regarded as the possession of the Theban god. This land could have been the Field of Tanis when the Theban kings drove out the Hyksos and confiscated the property of the petty princes who had ruled there as vassals of the Hyksos. Ramesses II was obliged to pay regard to its character as an estate of Amun inasmuch as he dedicated the chief temple of Tanis to Amen-Rē'. Later royal dynasties established a theocracy at Tanis based on the Theban model. Ramesses II, however, came from a family that looked on Seth as its patron deity; when Piramessu, the father of Sethos I was viceroy the family paid great honour to Seth by sending Sethos, the heir to the throne, to be director of the festival celebrating the fourth centenary of the founding of Tanis and the establishing of the worship of Seth there. Consequently Seth received his traditional apartments in the new Residence, but his nature suffered, as it were, a recoinage. In Tanis, or Piramesse as it was then called, Seth bore the insignia of a Syrian god — a fate that had also overtaken Sopdu of Saft el-Hennah in the Eastern Delta when he was called 'Lord of the Foreign Lands' in the Old Kingdom. Seth now became the tutelary deity of Egyptian rule over Asia and contemporary myths emphasize his importance as a powerful god of heaven and as 'one rich in magical lore', the helper of the sun-god Rē'.[2]

The new town opened its shrines to other Asiatic divinities. A temple was built for Anat who was regarded as the 'milch-cow of Seth' and hence as the mother of the gods; further, a colossal statue has been found in Tanis of a falcon who acted as the king's tutelary deity under the name of Horun[3] of whom we have already heard something in connection with the Great Sphinx of Giza.

The court poets sang the praises of the new town: 'Its western part is a temple of Amun; its southern part a temple of Seth. Astarte (i.e. Anat) is to be found in its eastern quarter and Edjo in its northern. The fortress that is in its centre reaches to

[1] Daressy, Annales du Service, 17, 164f.; Kees, Tanis, 158f.
[2] Kees, Götterglaube, 237f.
[3] Montet, Tanis, 96f., pl. 4; cf. Posener, JNES, 4, 240f.

the horizon of heaven.'[1] If this description is compared with the results of the excavations it is difficult to make them agree. It offers no true guide to the plan of the city; and this is typically Egyptian. In fact the temple of Amun dominated the townscape so clearly that it could to all appearances emulate the ancient imperial temple. It possessed no fewer than 10 obelisks, 2 each before the first and second pylons, 4 before the third pylon and 2 more in the back court; some reached a great height. The forecourts, especially the second, were filled with magnificent old royal sculpture among which were the famous Tanis sphinxes and offering bearers that were probably brought from a temple in the Fayum. They formed a very noble company in which the colossal statue of Ramesses II occupied the place of honour. Here was collected everything that characterized Egyptian history from the time of Ammenemes I and Sesostris I onwards, including a grey granite colossus of the ephemeral king Mermesha and four statues of Khaneferrē' Sebekhotpe, one of the last kings of Dynasty XIII to rule over the whole of Egypt. There was a gap only from the period of the Hyksos up to the time of Ramesses II himself. It seems as if Ramesses II and his son wanted to apply to the kings the saying that was applied to the new foundation of the town: 'All peoples leave their cities and are settled on your domain.'

This resettlement programme of Ramesses II had, however, a remarkable result. The principal temples of Tanis lack the dedicatory statues of high officials that are so characteristic of the great temple of Amun at Thebes and the other great provincial cities. Could it be that the king wanted no-one else there apart from himself (which was probably the answer)? Or was it that the officials that were summarily brought there felt themselves merely as visitors in their new home? Thus the Lower Egyptian vizir Rahotpe who was obliged to change his abode from Memphis to Tanis yet had himself buried in his home at Heracleopolis.[2] Honorific dedicatory statues are first found for the *strategi* in the Ptolemaic Period who had their seat of office in Tanis. Private tombs are also lacking in Tanis and there seems to have been no regular necropolis. The old families of Thebes and Memphis therefore regarded Piramesse as half

---

[1] Papyrus Anastasi, II, 1, 4f.
[2] Petrie, *Sedment*, II, pl. 72f.; Scharff, *ÄZ*, 70, 47f.

The Delta: Fortresses and Harbours

abroad both from a religious and cultural standpoint. We have already encountered this frontier atmosphere at Sile.

In spite of lavish expenditure Ramesses II's city remained a new town, the 'House of Rē', the beginning of the foreign land and the end of Egypt, with beautiful windows and rooms ablaze with lapis-lazuli and turquoise, the place where war-chariots are exercised; the place where infantry is reviewed; the place where sailors land when they bring him gifts'. This poem must, however, be corrected in two important particulars to prevent its making a false impression. Tanis constituted only the kernel of a far-flung system of settlements to which the Residence gave a unity. Royal palaces lay scattered around Tanis like the summer palaces of modern pashas. From excavations we know of one such palace built apparently as early as the reign of Sethos I at Qantir, north of Fakus[1] and at such places the king spent more time than in Tanis itself.

In thinking of Tanis it is also necessary to disabuse oneself of the notion of a great central stronghold. Apart from ceremonial occasions or inspections the garrisons were divided up among camps across the whole East Delta. The presence of military detachments with their inevitable train of military scribes in Hurbet near Abu Kebir, west of Fakus, can be deduced from the innumerable dedications there from the time of Ramesses II, indicating the existence of some sort of cult of the reigning king.[2] Egyptian reserves were clearly stationed in readiness there. The doubts we mentioned in speaking of Avaris in the Hyksos Period with regard to its suitability as a garrison for the horse-drawn detachments do not arise therefore for the Ramesside kings who came later.

In Tanis and Pelusium, besides the summer-palaces and military camps, the estates of Amun formed the centre of economic life. Orchards and vineyards were their pride. The court poet of Ramesses II describes for us the model estate of Kaenkeme, 'Preserver of Egypt', as a domain of Amun of Thebes that in all probability had to furnish supplies for the king's mortuary temple. At least, wine dockets from Kaenkeme are very common there.[3] Ramesses III celebrated his jubilee as

---

[1] Hamza, *Annales du Service*, 30, 41f.; Hayes, *Glazed Tiles from a Palace of Ramesses II at Kantîr*.   [2] Röder, *ÄZ*, 61, 57f.; Clère, *Kêmi*, 11 (1950), 24f.
[3] Spiegelberg, *Hieratische Ostraca*, pls. 19–34.

king at Piramesse, not in Memphis, and his vizir To had to
invite the Upper Egyptian local deities as guests and convey
them there in their barques. He then conferred his own name
on the endowments made by his great namesake; they were
now called 'the domains of Ramesses III, great in victories',
and they received supplementary gifts of 7,872 slaves. Moreover,
a foundation by him for the temple of Seth in Piramesse was
endowed with 106 slaves.[1] He also brought Kaenkeme under
his own endowment for Amun and the temple at Thebes: 'I
gave him Kaenkeme that is overflowing . . . with great stretches
of olives, heavy with fruit, enclosed with a wall miles long,
planted with great trees along all its roads; where the oil jars
are more numerous than the sands of the sea.'[2] Its produce,
chiefly oil, now found its way into the cellars of the temple of
Medinet Habu instead of into those of the Ramesseum.

The point has often been made that the estates, mostly composed presumably of *sharaki*-land, determined the economy of
the Delta. On the other hand herds of cattle, especially of oxen,
must have grazed the inundated areas as soon as the water re-
ceded. What resulted was an economy of a semi-nomadic kind,
for there was not sufficient land, inundated for only a short
period, to allow the creation of a predominantly arable system
of farming. Such conditions could only be changed by progressive schemes of drainage and irrigation.

After the suppression of the rebellion in Thebes that saw the
downfall of the family of the Amenhotpes which had given many
high priests to Thebes, the Commander-in-chief of the Army
Herihor assumed the robes of the High Priest of Amun and
established a theocracy about 1085 B.C. At about the same time
a Lower Egyptian counterpart was established at Tanis; power
there was seized by a family under the leadership of Smendes
son of Menkheperrē', which based their rights on the dignity of
Amen-rē' King of the Gods (known later as Amonrasonther).
We do not know whence they came but we can see how, by
their choice of name, they proclaimed themselves as related to
the great men of Dynasty XVIII, the high-water mark of
Theban power and civilization; for the prenomen of the great
Tuthmosis III was Menkheperrē'. Their conception of the state
was incorporated in the rule and worship of Amun. Their

[1] Papyrus Harris, I, 10, 12; 62a, 3.   [2] Papyrus Harris, I, 8, 5f.

power, however, was small. In building they were obliged to restrict themselves to patching together the ruins of older constructions and even to searching out old stonework to construct their royal tombs. Such activity may cause less surprise when we remember that even Ramesses II hesitated to have granite transported all the way from Aswan. These royal tombs were no longer in sacred Thebes where, at that time, royal commissions were engaged in securing rifled royal mummies in temporary tombs.[1] The Tanite rulers were actually buried within the precinct of the temple and the city walls. For, just as Medinet Habu, the mortuary temple of Ramesses III, had become the citadel in the Western City at Thebes, so Psusennes I enclosed the central district of Tanis with a wall which, however, was by no means the equal in strength of the outer wall built by the Ramesses. The inner city thus became an enclave only about one-half the size of the whole old city. Its brick walls still dominate the scene at Tell Tanis today.

Fortified walls are particularly characteristic of Dynasty XXI. Its kings built other fortresses on the narrow eastern bank of the Nile in Middle Egypt; el-Hibah became a military camp and the residence of the crown-prince, taking the place in this respect of Memphis.[2] South of el-Hibah came Acoris (now Tihna) and Matine (or Tine) north-east of el-Minia.[3] The building of such fortresses was required both by the internal and the external situations. The campaigns waged by the warlike northern peoples on land and sea had destroyed the Hittite Empire in Asia Minor while in Syria the principal bases of Egyptian control had been lost with the exception of a narrow strip of territory around Gaza. Already Ramesses III had been compelled to defend the mouths of the Nile in fierce battles with the invading sea-peoples. The enemy that now stood at Egypt's eastern door was the Philistine in the plain of Palestine. The family of Smendes certainly maintained a connection with the Phoenician coast but the vassalage of the Princes of Byblos had changed into a relationship between two equal partners. This change can be seen very clearly in the account of the adventures of Wenamun, the Theban ambassador, who was sent with an introduction from Smendes to Byblos to bring back timber

---

[1] See below, p. 278.   [2] See below, p. 282.
[3] Von Bissing and Kees, *Sb. bayr. Akad.* (1928), 8.

for the sacred barque of Amun.[1] Egyptian supremacy of the sea
was a thing of the past. Buccaneering ships of the sea-peoples
were able to hold up without fear of punishment Egyptian merchants and envoys and extort ransom from them. Property had
become insecure on the sea routes of the Eastern Mediterranean.
As for the Prince of Byblos, he acted like a man of business: 'He
sent for the account-books of his father and had them read aloud.
It was found that a thousand measures of all sorts of silver were
entered in his books.' He had supplied the coveted timber only
after Smendes and his wife had sent from Tanis an advance
payment in kind: gold and silver ornaments, linen, papyrus,
rope, hides, lentils and fish. Nevertheless trade with Tanis was
still active: 'There are 20 ships here in my harbour that are in
trade with Smendes.' The lead, however, had now passed to the
Phoenician cities and their fleets, to Byblos, Sidon and Tyre.

The fortresses in Middle Egypt meant security against the
threat offered by the Libyan tribes to the nerve centre of Egypt
ever since they had secured Heracleopolis as a stronghold in the
valley of the Nile. Neither these two fortresses, which were intended to keep open communications with the Thebaid, nor
the family ties connecting the Tanites with the house of Herihor
in Thebes sufficed permanently to serve this purpose. One hundred and forty years after Smendes Libyan commanders sat in
Tanis and Thebes and ruled as Dynasty XXII in Egypt.
The buildings at Tanis that commemorate these rulers are even
more a patchwork than those of Dynasty XXI. It is sufficient
to look at the gate of Sheshonk in front of the temple of Amun
to see this,[2] while the royal tombs found in 1939 beside those of
the Tanite rulers near the temple are even shoddier. They even
contain borrowed equipment; for example, one sarcophagus
had belonged to a chief treasurer of the Middle Kingdom and
came from the Fayum, possibly from Hawara; another had
been carved out of a hard-stone colossus carried off by one of the
Ramesses. The ornaments found with the mummies still reveal
something of the artistic tradition of the New Kingdom but
were in character far inferior to the products of that great age
such as were found in the golden splendour of the Tomb of

[1] Papyrus Golenischeff; Gardiner, *Late Egyptian Stories*, 61f.; Erman,
Literatur der Ägypter, 255f.
[2] Montet, *Tanis*, 48f.

Tutankhamun. Inner coffins of silver were all that could now be afforded; the gold that once represented the proverbial wealth of Egypt had become conspicuous by its rare appearance in the royal treasury.

Public building in Tanis decreased more and more during the Late Period although the city continued to act as the seat of administration for the Eastern nome in succession to its role as royal residence. The connection between the harbour and the defence of the eastern frontier continued to demonstrate its utility in spite of the fact that the key position in the defensive system had been advanced to Pelusium about 20 miles north-east of Sile, almost at the mouth of the most easterly branch of the Nile, the Bubastite.[1] In view of this interplay of function it is possible to observe a certain cohesion in the eastern nomes of Egypt in spite of the tendency characteristic of the feudalism of the Late Period towards the break-up of the land into small and often quite tiny nome and town governments. These petty governments based themselves on support from the nomes of Mendes (the 16th) and Sebennytus (the 12th) from which came the last soldier kings of Egypt, and which were included among the four 'heavy' nomes of Lower Egypt according to the demotic novel of Petubastis. A coffin in Berlin dating from the last years of Egyptian independence gives the name of a grand-nephew of King Nectanebos I of the 10th Sebennytic Dynasty who was nomarch not only of the Sebennytic nome but also of the 14th and the 19th Lower Egyptian nomes, that is, the whole stretch of country from Tanis to Sile.[2] This noble, as Count of Sile, bore the arrogant title 'Ruler of the Foreign Lands' as if he were the successor of the Hyksos kings. Yet he must have lived to see the end of the Egyptian empire at the time of the Persian invasion of 341 B.C. We do know by chance, however, that in the fifteenth year of the last Egyptian king, Nectanebes II (344 B.C.) that the Egyptian commander of the fortress of Sile was a certain Horakhbit.[3] In accordance with the contemporary custom he bore innumerable local priestly titles.

Under the Ptolemies the eastern frontier was still a scene of unrest. Then, however, Paraetonium (Mersa Matruh) in the west and Pelusium in the east were the corner stones of the

---

[1] Kees' article 'Pelusion' in Pauly-Wissowa, *Real-Encyclopädie.*
[2] *Urk.*, II, 24–6. [3] Spiegelberg, *ÄZ*, 64, 76.

country's defence — the Romans graphically called them *cornua*. At these points Greek commanders kept watch over the frontiers. At the same time *strategi* sat in Tanis with high-sounding military titles; but these men, who came from high-born Egyptian families and set up their honorific statues in Tanis,[1] in reality only had civilian tasks to perform such as the regulation of the waters of the inundation by the construction of reservoirs[2] and the provisioning of the temples in Tanis and Sile.

The order of precedence for these two cities is shown by the fact that the *strategos* was 'First Prophet of Amun of Ramesses' in Tanis and 'Prophet of Horus, Lord of Harpooning' in Sile. The holders of this office acted as if they were the real successors of the feudal lords of the Middle Kingdom and as the latter had so did they also call themselves viceroys of the king — although he was now a Macedonian — and bore the ancient titles of the nomarchs of the nomes of the 'Nearer East'. Similarly, like their predecessors, they occupied the highest priestly offices serving the local divinities. At this time the cult of Khons 'the child', one of the Theban triad, made its appearance among the local cults, following a development in Thebes itself. The new town of Heracleopolis[3] which appears in late classical sources such as the geographer Ptolemy, in the district between Tanis and Pelusium, owes its name to this divinity, for Khons was equated with the classical Heracles.

In spite of their high-sounding titles these men appear to have done very little. Ptolemy Soter embellished the temple temenos wall with an east gate; Ptolemy Philopator restored the temple of Anat in the southern part of the town outside the citadel. It is true that in the stoneless Delta most building materials had to be brought from elsewhere but we might have expected to find more considerable remains from this period at Tanis which classical writers always describe as a large city.

We shall now briefly look at Naucratis to illuminate the results of late Egyptian trade policy.[4] Here was played, as it were, the last act in the history of that policy when the Saite king

---

[1] Cairo Statues 687, 689, 700; Montet, *Kêmi*, 7, 123f.

[2] See above, p. 53.

[3] According to the *Itinerarium Antonini* 22 Roman miles from Tanis.

[4] See Kees' article 'Naucratis' in Pauly-Wissowa, *Real-Encyclopädie*; the literature is given there.

The Delta: Fortresses and Harbours

Amasis (569–525 B.C.) made the town a concession port for Greek trade. It evolved out of a Milesian settlement on the Bolbitine mouth of the Nile in the neighbourhood of Rosetta (for the 'Milesian wall' see Strabo, Book XVII, 801) and it is clear that Amasis aimed at eliminating this potential danger-spot where a foreign power under the cover of trade might obtain a base on the coast of Egypt. From time immemorial Egypt had been suspicious of such attempts. The decree of Amasis did, however, recognize a development that had begun early in the Saite Period and could no longer be halted. Strabo placed the beginnings, though not the foundation, of Naucratis in the reign of Psammetichus I (663–609 B.C.) but from the finds on the site, particularly the scarabs, such a date is too early. Its foundation, consequently, should be dated somewhere at the beginning of the succeeding century, possibly in the reign of Psammetichus II (594–589 B.C.).[1]

With Naucratis, for the first time in history, and remarkably late also, a port in the west Delta came into operation. It was quite unintentional. Quite apart from the presence of the Milesians on the Rosetta branch of the Nile, the Egyptians wanted to keep the Greeks out of the ports in the east Delta that handled traffic with Asia. Naucratis (now Kôm Gaif, near en-Neberah) was sited close to the west bank of the Canopic branch of the Nile on territory that had belonged to the Saite nome from ancient times and was the family property of the reigning dynasty. Here, where the dynasty was on its home-ground, it could better then elsewhere ward off disturbing influences. The administrative system would in the first place have made it impossible to attract the Greek market to Memphis, for example, in the centre of Egyptian economic life, quite apart from the fact that any such attempt would have been foiled by the resistance of the Egyptians. Nevertheless Amasis removed the camp of Greek and Carian mercenaries to whose military superiority his dynasty owed its supremacy, from Tahpanhes or Daphnae (modern Tell Defennah) east of Tanis to Memphis.[2] Greek trade was, however, exposed to sufficient hostility at Naucratis. Xenophobia had increased in Egypt since the period of Assyrian domination and those detachments of the

[1] Von Bissing, *Forsch. und Fortschr.* 25 (1949), nrs. 1–2.
[2] Herodotus, II, 154.

Egyptian army composed mostly of Nubians and Libyans envied the Greeks for the preference shown to them.

Unfortunately we know about the decree establishing Naucratis only from Greek writers and then not very accurately.[1] The act was not, however, an isolated privilege extended to the Greeks alone. It bears fully the character of concessions granted to trading bases on the Nubian frontier — the state-controlled market burdened with high dues and therefore bringing the state splendid gains. All the other mouths of the Nile were closed to Greek shipping so that Greek ships were obliged to sail up the Canopic branch and discharge their cargoes at Naucratis. This system was similar to that established by Sesostris III when he directed all water-borne goods to Acina near Wadi Halfa on the southern frontier.[2] If the Greeks regarded this restriction as an honour for Naucratis it meant for the Egyptians a practical measure to control trade and to supervise the resident alien population.

Some conclusion about the way in which the provisions of the foundation decree were carried out can be drawn from the Naucratis stela of King Nectanebos I (378–361 B.C.).[3] When he ascended the throne Nectanebos ceded the 10 per cent import tax on all goods coming from the Aegean, together with the revenue from the Naucratis monopoly to the temple of Neith in Sais just as Ramesses III (about 1170 B.C.) had conferred on the temple of Khnum at Elephantine the 10 per cent transit dues on all goods passing the area known later as the Dodecaschoenus.[4] Both these kings were surrendering ancient royal prerogatives or, to put it according to the Egyptian way of thinking, they were returning something to the gods from whom they had received their sovereignty. Industries and businesses in the Greek city were no less subject to taxation than were Egyptian concerns. Naucratis paid a 10 per cent tax on trading and industrial profits and these too the king donated to the temple of Neith at Sais to pay for a daily sacrifice of one ox, one goose and five jars of wine. In this transaction we are witnessing an act in the continual swing between on the one hand the dispensing of property to temples from taxation and its increase by donation and, on the other hand, the utilization of temple property for

[1] Herodotus, II, 179.   [2] See below, p. 317.
[3] Erman, *ÄZ*, 38, 130f.   [4] See below, p. 321.

the payment of state expenses. The monuments only mention the positive side of this process and the pious times in which endowments multiplied as a result partly of religious scruples and partly of increasing wealth, for example the endowments created in Dynasty V for the state religion and particularly for the sun-sanctuaries, the gifts made by Tuthmosis III after victorious campaigns, the endowments of Ramesses III, the small gifts of land by private people mentioned in innumerable stelae of the Late Period and the very lavish gifts of the Saite kings and their courtiers to the temples. In the intervals, however, without considering the catastrophe that overtook all temple property as a result of Akhenaten's reforms, there must have been times when the king in preparing for war laid hands on temple property in one way or another, by confiscation or taxation. The same was true of temple privileges, the freedom of crafts and trades from taxation and, particularly in later times, certain monopolies. We only learn of such sacrilegious acts from Greek sources or when the behaviour of foreigners like Cambyses was concerned, for in such cases there was no need to spare the memories. The writer known as the Pseudo-Aristotle informs us that King Tachos or Teos on the advice of the Greek Chabrias introduced a 10 per cent tax on shipping and a similar tax on crafts of all kinds to help him prepare armaments for use against the Persians.[1] Neither did he hesitate to abrogate previously granted exceptions.

We also know that even in the Ramesside Period the agricultural property of the temples was not completely exempt from taxation and that certain areas of land capable of cultivation had in fact to be placed at the disposal of the king.[2] In return royal officials carried out the extensive administrative tasks associated with the temples' maintenance and were responsible for the receipt of their revenues. Legally this system was very flexible but in practice it yielded very varying results. As a result of his study of the lists of the endowments of Ramesses III Schädel is of the opinion that to a certain extent these benefactions were intended to recompense the temples for contributions in wartime of slaves, cattle and natural produce during the years when Ramesses III waged his campaigns against the

---

[1] Wilcken, *ÄZ*, 38, 133, cf. Kees, *Kulturgeschichte*, 255.
[2] On the *khato*-land of Pharaoh, see above, p. 72.

Libyans and the sea-peoples.[1] Certain proof of this theory is wanting but it is highly probable.

The Ptolemies showed themselves to be apt pupils, therefore, of the financial teaching of the Pharaohs. The mercantile policy of Ptolemy Philadelphus would have been inconceivable but for the initial steps taken in that direction by the Egyptians. In the Ptolemaic Period, however, the State resumed the position that had been occupied during the Late Period by the privileged temples that had through concessions and monopolies steadily become the decisive factor in the Egyptian economy, especially in regard to trade. Monopolies now returned to state control and they were increased and extended. At the same time protective tariffs were raised at the frontiers. In the Zenon archive of correspondence we possess some figures for Pelusium as a customs-house for the Asiatic trade in which the Seleucid kings were the rivals.[2] From these figures we learn that the rates varied from 20 per cent on wool to 50 per cent on oil and Syrian wine, the chief imports since time immemorial. As far as Egyptian monopolies were concerned such taxes, especially in the case of oil, amounted at this figure to an absolutely prohibitive tariff. Although the Ptolemies, particularly Philadelphus, beautified Naucratis with new buildings such as the Hellenion, the economic importance of that city ended with the founding of Alexandria. This latter city, protected by the rocky island of Pharos, was the first sea-port constructed on the open coast of Egypt. Naucratis thus became superfluous as a harbour for imports and internal traffic descending the Nile came as far as Shedia, nearer Alexandria.

Architecturally very little remains at Naucratis to give us an idea of its character; and this fate it shares with other Delta towns. It is scarcely possible to determine the situation of the principal shrines from the few remaining foundations.[3] Naucratis like Alexandria was a Greek city built on the site of an older Egyptian settlement which it, however, soon surpassed both culturally and economically. The Greek towns were

[1] *Die Listen des grossen Papyrus Harris*, 70.

[2] Papyrus Edgar, 73, 75 (of 259 B.C.); *Annales du Service*, 23, 73f.; Wilcken, *Archiv für Papyrusforschung*, 7, 253.

[3] Plans in Petrie, *Naucratis*, I, pls. 40–2; II, pl. 4; better in Prinz, *Funde aus Naukratis*, pl. 1.

naturally swept high on the wave of prosperity that during the Late Period raised the Lower Egyptian towns and their temples above those of Upper Egypt in the extent of their possessions. Upper Egypt became markedly a hinterland. During the New Kingdom the estates of the Temple of Amun dominated the picture; but in the Saite Period their place was taken by those of the famous temples of the Delta towns. Thus in the reign of Apries (584 B.C.) the temple of the Ram of Mendes received 1,600 *aroura* of land in the Thebaid.[1] In time therefore the situation had been completely reversed. The land available for colonization that had been underdeveloped in earlier times had become the economic backbone of the State in the Late Period.

[1] See above, p. 69.

VIII

Heracleopolis and the Fayum

Almost exactly opposite the spot where on the east bank of the Nile the plain of Amarna ends and the precipitous walls of the Gebel Abu Feda begin to close in, the Bahr Yusuf turns away from the west bank of the river. The Gebel Abu Feda extends southwards as far as Asyut and its northern end marked the ancient frontier between the Thebaid and Middle Egypt. This frontier was still of importance economically and politically in Roman days as is shown by Strabo's mention of Theban and Hermopolitan customs posts here.[1] In times when Egypt was disunited this internal frontier formed a political division between Hermopolis in the north (the 15th Upper Egyptian nome) and Cusae (the 14th Upper Egyptian nome) or Asyut (the 13th) in the south. This was the position at the close of the Hyksos Period when the Theban king Kamose about 1570 B.C. summoned the country to a war of liberation; it was so again at the beginning of the Bubastite Period when a Libyan princely family established its rule at Heracleopolis about 1000 B.C. and founded a princedom with a priestly guise. The possession of the Middle Egyptian nomes from Asyut up to the entrance to the Fayum — the Egyptian Lake District — nomes which, for Egypt, were relatively rich in agricultural land, could mean supremacy over the whole Nile valley.

The Bahr Yusuf or Joseph's arm of the Nile is the only true side branch of the river in Upper Egypt. In ancient times it may have diverged from the Nile in the neighbourhood of Asyut, but today it leaves the main river at Deirut. It flows northwards not far from the escarpment of the Libyan desert frequently twisting and turning, passing ancient Hermopolis (Eshmunein), the

---

[1] See above, p. 105.

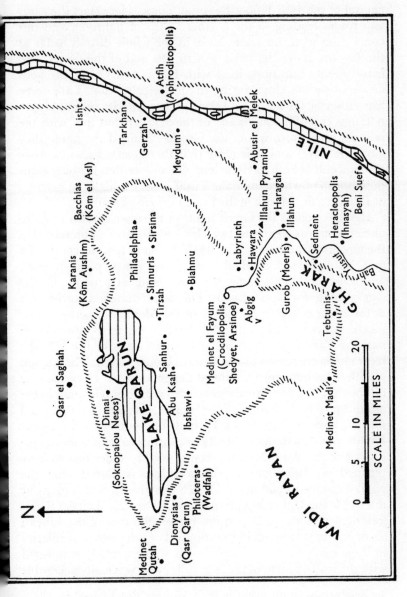

6. The Fayum and Heracleopolis

capital of the 19th Upper Egyptian nome. Here start the caravan routes leading to the northern oasis of Bahriyah and this
connection with the desert brought the whole district as far as
the Fayum under the aegis of Seth, the god of the desert, and
consequently into opposition with Horus and Osiris, the gods
favoured by the kings during the historical period. Late nome
lists proscribe the temple of Oxyrhynchus with its ancient hippopotamus cult of Thoueris and of the oxyrhynchus fish 'with the
pointed nose' from whom the Greeks obtained the name they
gave the city;[1] and it is clear that there existed also to some
extent a cult of Seth in Heracleopolis, a place that lies only eight
miles south of where the Bahr Yusuf turns through the narrows
at Illahun ('the Mouth of the Lake') into the Fayum.

Heracleopolis is the Greek name of the town known in more
ancient times as Neni-nesu, which name is obscurely preserved in
the modern Arabic name Ihnasyah. It was at first the centre of a
great nome the sign of which was the tree *n'aret*, 'pomegranate',
which eventually became the 20th and 21st nome in the
canonical list for Upper Egypt. This nome stretched northwards
as far as the southern boundary of the Memphite nome, somewhere between Lisht and Dahshur; it extended northwards
past the Fayum and formed for the west bank of the Nile the
most northerly region of the historic Upper Egypt. The Fayum
was thus brought into a natural dependence on Heracleopolis
although it was not directly associated with Heracleopolis in the
administrative ordering of the nomes, at least in the more
ancient periods. The 'Lake District' or 'southern lake' as the
Fayum was called, undoubtedly in contrast to the northern lake
district of the Wadi Natrun, seems from the older lists to have
pursued an autonomous existence. It was placed after the
20/21st nome or 22nd nome (if such was given), that is to say at
the end of the Upper Egyptian nomes.[2] The Lake District therefore occupied a special position rather like that of the Libyan
oases and in its physical formation it bore the closest similarity
to these oases excepting only that it was intimately connected
with the water system of the Nile valley and was easily accessible

---

[1] Kees' article 'Oxyrhynchus' in Pauly-Wissowa, *Real-Encyclopädie*.

[2] *Annales du Service*, 3, 76 (Tehne of Dynasty IV–V); *Urk.*, I, 3, in tomb of
Metjen who was the administrator of domains there (beginning of Dynasty
IV), cf. Gardiner, *Ancient Egyptian Onomastica*, II, 120*.

therefrom. Hence there existed an area of common ground between them that in the religious sphere was expressed in the powerful influences exercised by the cult of Seth over the frontier districts. The local deity of Heracleopolis was a ram Herishef, 'he who is upon his lake', known to the Greeks as Arsaphes; he supposedly lived in a grove by the lake and to his worship had been added that of Osiris as early as the end of the Old Kingdom, as too in the case of the ram of Mendes. The legend runs[1] that Osiris had seated himself on the throne of Rēʿ in Heracleopolis and ruled in his stead (an usurpation like that of the Heracleopolitan kings of Dynasty IX–X); all the gods did homage to him including his ancient enemy Seth who struck his nose so hard against the ground in bowing down before Osiris that it bled. (The Seth animal certainly had a very long trunk-like nose.) Osiris himself fell ill owing to the glow of Rēʿ's crown that could be dangerous to its wearer inasmuch as it was the essence of divine power. This, according to the mythical interpretation which had lost sight of its original meaning, accounted for his local name, Arsaphes, which was taken to mean 'swollen (i.e. commanding respect) face'. Thus Osiris was in Heracleopolis the 'soul of Rēʿ in his own body', as the theologians expressed it.[2]

The town itself was called '(Town of) the King's child' and its sanctuary was a pool within the temple precincts which represented the primeval place of life, an allusion here to water as the source of all life, a notion that Heracleopolis shared with Hermopolis and the Fayum. The name of the latter actually incorporates the Coptic word *phiom*, 'the sea'. Like many Egyptian cities Heracleopolis naturally claimed for itself the grave of Osiris that was supposedly to be found at a place called Naref where his soul lived in a grove.

The myth of Edfu in its later form, which is preserved on the walls of the Ptolemaic temple of Edfu, tells of the battle between Horus and Seth in this neighbourhood and of the parts of Osiris' body that they held.[3] After the temporary division of sovereignty between Horus and Seth as a result of which Seth took up residence at Shash-hotpe in the 11th Upper Egyptian nome (the

---

[1] *Book of the Dead*, chapter 175; Kees, *ÄZ*, 65, 65f.
[2] Louvre stela, C.286, l. 2.
[3] Naville, *Mythe d'Horus*, pl. 24, ll. 99–110; Chassinat, *Edfou*, VI, 221–3.

nome of Seth) and Horus at Memphis, fighting broke out anew in the course of which Horus drove Seth out of Egypt. 'Horus returned to Egypt because he was Lord of Upper Egypt and of Lower Egypt . . . because he sat upon the throne of his father Osiris and all gods and goddesses served him . . . on this day. (For) Horus on the throne of his father Osiris was more powerful than they were. Horus said: "Those who come . . . blessed Onnophris." The explanation of this speech is: When Horus departed to look for the lost member of Osiris (the phallus?), it was said to him: "It has been found in front of the Hierogrammata of the Horologion at Oxyrhynchus." And Horus went to Oxyrhynchus and he found that (. . . in the hand of Seth). And when Seth saw Horus afar off he took on the shape of a red hippopotamus.[1] And Horus took on the form of a (vigorous youth). Afterwards they fought and Horus felled him and cut off his leg . . . and he took it to Heracleopolis and gave it to the scribe that is appointed to the Horologion;[2] (it) was called . . . of that (enemy). And Horus took the lost (member) of Osiris that had been found before him and it was buried in its place in Heracleopolis. It is called 'that which cannot be bound' (*naref*) at its place to this day. The 3rd month of summer (Epiphi), the 7th day, that is the day on which Isis became pregnant of her son Horus.'[3]

Accordingly the right leg of Osiris was generally regarded as a relic preserved at Heracleopolis while the left was said to be buried in the Abaton at Philae.[4] Other texts mention the head (in Abydos) the two sides and both legs (chapter 18 of the *Book of the Dead* in the New Kingdom). To the north of Heracleopolis is a district containing cemeteries with tombs characteristic of the Naqada II Period of Predynastic civilization, also called Gerzean. Such cemeteries are found at Abusir el-Melek which lies on an isolated ridge confronting the entrance to the Fayum and at el-Gerzah itself, the point where the most frequented cross-country route from the northern Fayum over the inter-

[1] Allusion to the cult of the hippopotamus in Oxyrhynchus.

[2] Leg = the figure of the stars of the Great Bear (the stars of Seth) from which the Egyptians established the direction of North.

[3] The birthday of Horus, son of Isis, was celebrated on the 28th day of the 4th month of winter (Pharmuthi); Brugsch, *Thesaurus*, 370, 14; 609, 72.

[4] See below, p. 328.

vening desert plateau reaches the Nile valley between Lisht and the Pyramid of Meydum — the Darb Gerzah. This district undoubtedly experienced an economic drive during the closing stages of the Predynastic Period. On ethnological grounds its civilization is still to be derived from Upper Egypt and for its handicrafts the eastern desert supplied important raw materials in the form of coloured hard stones.[1] Even the pottery of this culture attempted to imitate stone vases in shape and decoration. The development of navigation and internal traffic enlarged the possible living areas in a period that at its end led to the unification of the two kingdoms.

Twice in its history Heracleopolis was given the chance of achieving leadership in Egypt. The first time was after the collapse of the Old Kingdom based on Memphis when the attempt of the House of Akhtoy to reconstruct a single kingdom in Egypt from Heracleopolis seemed likely to be crowned with success until about 2040 B.C. when it met with defeat in the final struggle with Thebes. This was the period of Dynasties IX and X. A second chance offered itself when a Libyan princely family secured political power in Heracleopolis and then, about 950 B.C. under Sheshonk I gained sovereignty over Egypt, establishing Dynasty XXII. After their victory, however, the military leaders of this family moved northwards to Memphis and Tanis and southwards by way of Hermopolis to Thebes. Heracleopolis itself was left as a patrimony to a junior member of the family who, after the fashion of the time, wore the priestly robes of the High Priest of Arsaphes. As a seat of a feudal principality favourably situated for trade and communications Heracleopolis certainly enlarged its territory at the cost of neighbouring nomes, but it never became the capital of all Egypt.

This characteristic rise in fortunes is shown most clearly by the family of Petiese and Somtutefnakhte who established in Heracleopolis a dynasty of shipmasters at the beginning of the Saite Period (about 660 B.C.) and on whom Psammetichus I conferred the privilege of controlling the traffic from Elephantine as far as the southern customs post in Memphis.[2] It was not by chance that people at this time preferred to estimate amounts in their business agreements in terms of 'silver from the House of Arsaphes' (that is according to the weights and scales used in

[1] See above, p. 35.   [2] See above, p. 105.

Heracleopolis), even in Theban territory, up to the thirtieth and in some cases the forty-fifth year of Psammetichus I's reign.[1] Heracleopolis therefore determined the value of the currency. Growing centralization, however, caused such feudal institutions to disappear apparently during the reign of Psammetichus I. Heracleopolis returned to its former position of a provincial capital.

The town of Ihnasyah with its temples is today a deserted place covered with ruins. All that is historically valuable is found in the cemeteries that take their name from the town Sedment el-Gebel that lies on the Bahr Yusuf about four miles to the north-west. Here a limestone ridge only about three miles wide separates the Nile valley from the southern part of the Fayum, known as Gharak. The cemeteries continue northwards as far as Tell Gurob immediately to the south of the entrance to the Fayum. Here is a place that took its name from the Miwer canal (in Greek *Μοῖρις*)[2] and to which from the time of the Middle Kingdom a certain importance was attached as the seat of the royal harîm. Nearby lay a favourite hunting ground of the Court. The tombs from Sedment to Medinet Gurob were built for all sorts of important people especially from the days of the New Kingdom; here are the tombs of Sennufer, High Priest of Memphis and Heliopolis in the XVIII Dynasty, of the Crown-Prince Piramessu of the family of the Ramesses (at Gurob) and of the viziers Parahotpe and Rahotpe who held office in Memphis and Piramesse under Ramesses II.[3] The presence of a garrison in this strategically important area reveals itself in the increased number of tombs of military officers especially in the Ramesside Period. Thus we find the tomb of the general Sety who was royal ambassador to all foreign countries under Ramesses II and who later became Overseer of the Treasury, of Nebenkeme, the Captain of bowmen and Fan-bearer of the royal boat, of Pahont, Deputy master of horse of his Majesty and Spokesman for the mounted and chariot troops, and of many others. Iuni, the well-known viceroy of Kush and Captain of the Medjay in the reigns of Sethos I and Ramesses II also came from Heracleopolis.

[1] G. Möller, *Sb. bayr. Akad.* (1921), XV.
[2] Gardiner and Bell, *JEA*, 29, 37f.
[3] Petrie, *Sedment*, II; Brunton and Englebach, *Gurob*.

Heracleopolis and the Fayum

Between Medinet Gurob and Illahun the Bahr Yusuf turns westwards into the pass that leads into the Lake District. Here there are two pyramids with their mortuary temples dating from the Middle Kingdom. First is that of Sesostris II at Illahun with its neighbouring Pyramid city excavated by Petrie which has become famous as Kahun; it affords an excellent example of the lay-out of a Pyramid city with its regularly divided quarters. Next there is the Pyramid of Ammenemes III (1842–1797 B.C.) about four miles to the west at Hawara (Pl. 5. a) close to the end of the pass. Ammenemes III was the king known in classical times as Lamarres who was famed throughout the whole Lake District. He was also known as Pramarres or Poremanres and as the Pharaoh Marres he was honoured with a statue placed beside those of the local divinities in the temples of the Ptolemaic Period. The classical world regarded his mortuary temple at Hawara with astonishment as a second Labyrinth.[1] He was famed for having been the first to make the Fayum accessible to mankind.

Strabo (Book XVII, 809) laid stress on the horticultural richness of this region, particularly mentioning the olive groves, which were undoubtedly the creation of the Greek colonists, as well as the vineyards, grain crops and leguminous plants (Pl. 7. b). It is its horticulture that still today gives the Fayum its individual charm. Its principal canals into which the Bahr Yusuf divides at Medinet el-Fayum spread like a network across the region, carrying running and often swiftly running water to the Birket Qarun, Egypt's only large inland lake (Pl. 10. a). In 1947 the Fayum province consisted of 413,000 *feddan* (about 435,000 acres) with 671,000 inhabitants, which gives a density of about 987 to the square mile which for Egyptian conditions and in view of the fertility of the central district is remarkably low. It is to be explained by the considerable area under water (about one-seventh of the whole) and by the existence of thinly populated frontier districts. Such districts presented the ancient world with problems of colonization which led to large-scale attempts at settlement in the reign of Ptolemy Philadelphus.

Lake Qarun (Map 6) today covers an area of about 90 square miles with a maximum depth of about 17 feet, its surface being

[1] See article 'Labyrinthos', nr. 2 in Pauly-Wissowa, *Real-Encyclopädie*.

about 147 feet below the level of the Mediterranean. The south-eastern bank touches on arable land while along the entire north-western bank runs the steep escarpment of the Libyan desert. There, cut off from the rest of the province, lie the ruins of Dimai (in Greek Soknopaiou Nesos). From Illahun where the Bahr Yusuf turns into the Fayum the ground sinks from 92 feet above sea-level to 76 feet in the neighbourhood of the provincial capital Medinet el-Fayum which the Ancient Egyptians called Shedyet and the Greeks first Crocodilopolis and later Arsinoe. The land further sinks in clearly marked stages towards the west and northwards to the Birket Qarun. The entire north of the province beyond the villages of Sinnuris (Greek Psenyris) and Sirsina is noticeably low-lying and for the greater part below sea-level.

Since the time when Herodotus wrote his description of lake Moeris (in Book II, 129) the problems of its origin and its utilization for irrigation have been subjects of much thought. According to Herodotus, whose account formed the classical tradition on this subject, subsequently handed down by Diodorus, Pliny and others, the lake is an artificial construction. He offers as proof the fact that in its midst stand two Pyramids with colossal seated figures which were the work of the King Moeris. The lake itself served as a reservoir for the Nile: 'For six months the water runs into the lake and for six months out again into the Nile.' That observant geographer Strabo further stresses (Book XVII, 810) that by means of a system of artificial locks at the entrance to the canal (at Illahun therefore) the lake was able to receive surplus flood-water and to return it as the level of the river sank. Such a fact could, however, only be conceivable in the case of a reservoir in the eastern part of the Fayum at the point where the land reaches its greatest height. Linant de Bellefonds actually accepted the classical explanation of the origin of the lake and the older school of Egyptologists in the days of Lepsius and Brugsch took it into their calculations until in 1892 an hydraulic engineer named Brown proved the impossibility of any such construction.[1] For him the ancient Lake Moeris was much more the greater predecessor of the

[1] R. H. Brown, *The Fayum and Lake Moeris* (London, 1892), cf. Baedeker, *Ägypten*,[8] (1928), 195; Kees' article 'Moeris' in Pauly-Wissowa, *Real-Encyclopädie*.

modern Birket Qarun. Subsequently further investigations especially on the northern shores of the Birket Qarun have revealed[1] that Brown's immense Lake Moeris with a circumference of 137 miles and a probable surface area of 770 square miles would have had to have a surface level 72 feet above sea-level and that it could not have existed at the time of the earliest identifiable culture of fishing folk, not even in the Neolithic Period. They showed also that from the close of the Neolithic Age the lake could only have attained a height of 7 feet below sea-level (i.e. 140 feet above the present level of the Birket Qarun) which means that it then covered land which today is dotted with an outer ring of villages from west to east — Ibshawi, Abu Ksah, Sanhur (on an ancient city-mound) Tirsa and Sinnuris (Psenyris).

These later assertions have, however, been contradicted by an Egyptian hydraulic engineer[2] who considers that the decrease in the size of the surface area proceeded so slowly that in the Old Kingdom it nearly equalled Brown's Lake Moeris with a level about 66 feet above sea-level and that in the Middle Kingdom it still stood at 49 feet above sea-level.

Petrie, however, thought that two quartzite colossi of Ammenemes III at modern Biahmu about four miles north of Crocodilopolis, which must originally have reached a height of about 40 feet and which stood on high pedestals on the southern embankment of an ancient lakeside harbour were to be linked with Herodotus' statement and were to be explained as the marks of an ancient landing place.[3] They stand at a point 53 feet above sea-level and therefore, if the theory of Brown and its most recent Egyptian supporter is accepted, Lake Moeris could at the most have reached to their foot or pedestal. On the other hand, according to the British archaeologists Miss Caton Thompson and Miss Gardner, this lake border was that of the Neolithic lake, being 206 feet above the level of the modern Birket Qarun. As is so often the case Herodotus' report can be

---

[1] Caton-Thompson and Gardner, *The Desert Fayum*, cf. Pasarge, *Fajum und Moeris-See* in *Geogr. Zeitschrift*, 46 (1940), 353f.

[2] Ali Shafei Bey, *Fayum Irrigation* in *Bulletin de la Société géographique royale de l'Egypte*, 20 (1940).

[3] Petrie, *Hawara, Biahmu and Arsinoe*, cf. L. D., I, 51, 33; Labib Habachi, *Annales du Service*, 40, 721f., with pls. 83–6.

shown to be founded on a misunderstanding of Egyptian dragomans' tales. They had told him something about two pyramids on the Moeris lake (meaning the canal) — the Pyramids at Illahun and Hawara — and in addition something about the two colossi at Biahmu of Ammenemes III, the builder of the pyramid at Hawara. He then confused the reports. We are unable to tell what purpose was served by the two colossi (their pedestals are called *kursi Fara'un* by local people); standing as they do with no adjacent buildings with the exception of an enclosure wall that may once have surrounded a court, they constitute virtually the only group of statuary in the whole of Egypt rising in isolation from the countryside. Even the colossal sphinx at Giza is not quite so isolated. There is certainly no trace of a temple in the neighbourhood. Consequently they appear to be distant outposts of the temple of Suchos which lay in the northern part of Crocodilopolis.

The figures given by ancient writers for the storage capacity of Lake Moeris are also misleading. It was impossible for it to act as a reservoir for the Nile itself in the Middle Kingdom for its level was just below sea-level or, if one accepts the highest estimate, 49 feet above sea-level, while the land-level at Illahun at the entrance to the Fayum is about 92 feet above sea-level. At the most it could have acted as a storage tank for superfluous flood-water. If the level of the Nile dropped it was possible in ancient times, as it is today, at Illahun to shut off the flow of water into the Fayum by means of sluices and to direct the waters of the Bahr Yusuf north-eastwards. In ancient times this canal ran between the desert plateau and Gebel Abusir to the Nile; today the regulating channel is the Giza canal which irrigated Giza Province. A careless observer might certainly assume that this water came from the Fayum. The ancient Lake Moeris accordingly fulfilled only one of the functions ascribed to it. In this sense therefore, neglecting the statements about the artificial construction of the lake which are only to be applied to the regulating canal at Illahun, the account given by Diodorus seems to be the most accurate: 'Through this canal he (Moeris) directed the water of the river at times into the lake at other times he shut it off ... by opening the inlet and again closing it by an artificial and costly device.' The alleged King Moeris is an understandable confusion of the name Miwer given to the canalized Bahr Yusuf and the name of King Ammenemes III, Marres or, more correctly, Lamarres.

History must give credit to the kings of Dynasty XII who lived in Lisht nearby for using the flood-water of the Nile for irrigating the Lake District, for building dykes and for bringing large areas of country around the capital Shedyet into cultivation. In this connection Ammenemes III deserves special mention. Many ruins testify to the building activity of these kings. The list opens with the remains of a group of statues depicting Ammenemes I with the goddess Bastet, which certainly came from the temple of Suchos at Shedyet. The strange monument at Abgig about three miles south-west of Shedyet which was already noted by Napoleon's expedition to Egypt and by Lepsius, dates from the reign of Sesostris I and stands like a boundary stone in open country like the colossi at Biahmu. Apart from these colossi at Biahmu there exist considerable remains of temples dating from the reign of Ammenemes III, in particular a hall with papyrus-cluster columns on the Kiman Fares where, not far from the modern Medinet el-Fayum, stood the principal temple of Suchos, the deity of the province.[1] The Italians have also uncovered a well-preserved temple of the same reign (by stripping it of its surrounding Ptolemaic additions) at Medinet Madi on the southern frontier of the province.[2] Among other ancient monuments there is the temple with no inscriptions at Qasr el-Saghah across the Birket Qarun, discovered in 1884 by Schweinfurth, about five miles north of Dimai (Soknopaiou Nesos), a broad hall with seven statue chambers — an extraordinary building that has recently been said to date even from the time of the Old Kingdom.[3] Today it lies far in the desert but in ancient times an inlet of the Lake Moeris reached almost to the eastern side of the temple. It may perhaps have had some connection with the dolerite quarries of the nearby Gebel el-Katrani from which place there still runs a recognizable road for the conveying of stone to the edge of the lake at Qasr el-Saghah.[4]

The crocodile Suchos of whose feeding in the lake of the

[1] Labib Habachi, *Annales du Service*, 37, 85f.
[2] Vogliano, *Secondo rapporto ... di Madînet Mâdi* (Milan, 1937).
[3] Menghin and Bittel, *Mitt. Dt. Inst. Kairo*, 5, 1f.
[4] Caton-Thompson and Gardner, *op. cit.*, 132f.

temple at Crocodilopolis Strabo gives a description, dominated all cults in the Lake District under widely differing local names; in some cases it is a question of whole families of crocodiles which are designated 'brothers' or something similar. As a province the Fayum was divided into a 'northern lake', also called Lake Suchos and a 'southern lake'.[1] (We here must distinguish this division from that by which the Fayum itself was the 'Southern Lake' in contrast to the northern lake of the Wadi Natrun.) A Ptolemaic boundary stone that marked the most westerly point of the frontier between the southern and northern lakes Suchos was found at Medinet Qutah about five miles from the present western end of the Birket Qarun.[2] According to the inscription the frontier divided the lake into two very unequal parts. In the New Kingdom they were also accustomed occasionally to speak of the 'central island' of the Fayum, as was the case also with the Delta; the term probably referred to the isolated water-free central districts lying around the capital.

Religious dogma took advantage of the peculiar position of the Fayum.[3] The lake was looked upon as the mythical primeval ocean (*Nun*) and the place of origin of all forms of being. At the same time it was the source of fertility and in this connection the dangerous crocodile god became the benefactor of the whole land like the Nile or like Osiris who was drowned in the flood-waters. Myth also taught that the body of Osiris rested in the Lake District. Furthermore, Shedyet was the place where life first came into existence at the creation of the world; here was the mythical primeval hill. At the time of the arrival of the flood-water on the Nile in summer when 'the Nile flows in from Elephantine to flood the Lake District' the chief festivals were celebrated. It was then that the 'limbs of the god', the different parts of the dismembered Osiris, scattered over the whole country, were assembled at the lake and thus the 42 nomes into which the country was divided along with their gods were symbolically brought together in the Fayum. Ancient tradition reported similar happenings at the Labyrinth, the mortuary temple of Ammenemes III at Hawara.

[1] Spiegelberg, *ÄZ*, 63, 108f.
[2] A. Fakhry, *Annales du Service*, 40, 897f.; cf. the same, vol. 1, 46.
[3] Kees' article 'Suchos' in Pauly-Wissowa, *Real-Encyclopädie*, after Lanzone, *Les Papyrus du Lac Moeris* (Turin, 1896).

Heracleopolis and the Fayum

The temple of Suchos at Shedyet was the true centre of the pantheon. When after twelve months came the rejuvenation of the body of the aged sun-god Rē' who at the beginning of all things first rose from out the primeval flood (the lake of the Fayum) on the back of the cow Methyer, and when on the 23rd day of the month Thoth the entry of the flood-waters of the Nile into the Great Lake was celebrated, it signified the victory of Rē' over his enemies. It also signified, in the struggle between Horus (=Suchos) and Seth over the 'things' (the limbs) of Horus' father Osiris whom Seth had murdered and dismembered, the symbolic triumph and resurrection of Osiris. Since, however, the lake lay on the western frontier of Egypt where the sun goes down and to which the dead go, it is 'the place of the Ogdoad (the eight primeval gods), where Rē' lives and Osiris rests, where the Westerners lie buried.'

Suchos worship in the Fayum displays especially close connections with King worship, not only in the customary Egyptian manner in which as the provincial deity he is regarded as the equal of the royal deity Horus and glorified with royal hymns, as is revealed in a book of hymns for Suchos of Shedyet;[1] but also far more in the sense in which the king is looked upon as the particular benefactor of the country. The king appears as the 'Horus who is a guest in Shedyet, Lord of the Upper Egyptian crown, with twisted horns, guest in the great palace, Lord of the great chair' in the temple as a co-deity beside Suchos, undoubtedly because of the exemplary benefactions of the rulers of Dynasty XII of whom two deliberately placed their monuments on the borders of the Lake District. Moreover, Osiris was especially revered in the Fayum as in Heracleopolis as 'King of the Lake Land'. A third deity that was readily associated with them as in Medinet Madi was the suckling snake-goddess Termuthis who later became an equal of Isis; she was the protectress of the harvest and the granary, a deity typical therefore of a peasant civilization.[2]

We have to thank the architects of Ramesses II for the fact that nothing is left of the grandiose buildings of the Middle Kingdom. They plundered the temples of the Fayum, particu-

---

[1] Erman, 'Hymnen an das Diadem des Pharaonen' in *Abh. Berl. Akad.* (1911), (Papyrus Golenischeff).

[2] See above, p. 59.

larly the Pyramid temples at Illahun and Hawara, just as they had plundered those in Memphis and Heliopolis. Works of art such as the unusual figure of the king represented as the Nile-god bearing sacrificial offerings of birds and fish (though the latter were ritually abhorrent to the Egyptians) which was found at Tanis perhaps once stood in a temple in the Fayum. The halls of the Labyrinth at Hawara certainly suffered severely at that time although visitors in the Classical Period saw in them many more lovely things than the fragments of monumental sculpture which subsequent excavators have picked out from buildings that had been destroyed almost beyond recognition.[1] In antiquity, as in modern times, fishing was a profitable occupation. Fishermen formed a considerable part of the population of the Fayum from the Neolithic Period, when we find fishermen of nomadic Libyan origin on the shores of the lake, down to the Ptolemaic Period. It is quite understandable therefore that in the Fayum, in place of the ritual abhorrence for fish felt by the orthodox Egyptian, there existed a religious awe towards certain kinds of fish that it was not permissible to catch, such as the oxyrhynchus-fish and the lepidotus-fish.[2]

In all other respects the Fayum was the finest hunting ground in Upper Egypt with its lakes, marshes and pools. It was specially famous for the relatively simple hunting of birds with the throw-stick which women could watch and which was in consequence particularly popular in court circles. At the time of bird migrations the Fayum must have been a paradise of birds of which the wild life of the Birket Qarun today gives only a faint idea. Sebekhotpe, an adjutant of Tuthmosis III, who came of a family of Counts of the Lake District, was particularly well appointed to be the chief huntsman there with the titles 'Companion of His Majesty in the middle island of the lake country' and 'Overseer of the bird pond of pleasure'.[3] So too was the well-known official Ti at the Dynasty V court of Memphis. The placing of a royal harîm near the entrance to the Fayum of which there is evidence from the Middle Kingdom, was also probably connected with these amusements. In the New Kingdom this privilege was enjoyed by Medinet Gurob,

[1] Petrie, *Kahun, Gurob and Hawara* and *The Labyrinth Gerzeh and Mazguneh*.
[2] Kees, *Götterglaube*, 446, on *PSI*, VIII, 901 (of A.D. 46).
[3] Spiegelberg, *ÄZ*, 63, 108f., in Theban Tomb, nr. 63.

then known as Miwer. Tuthmosis III founded the temple there
and probably completed the construction of the town where
Akhenaten's mother Tiy lived, especially after the death of her
husband Amenophis III. It is from there that came among other
precious things the unusual ebony head of the queen now in the
Berlin Museum.[1] In the same place apparently, far from the
capital and politics of state, Ramesses II housed his Hittite wife,
the daughter of the great king Hattusil, whom he married in the
thirty-fourth year of his reign. Tuthmosis III appears as a co-
deity in the temple at Gurob; yet the fame of this most able of
all the Pharaohs of the New Kingdom did not prevent Ramesses
II's masons, avid for building material, from carrying off his
building ruthlessly. We learn from tax lists, however, that the
royal harîm possessed property in land in this district in the
reign of Ramesses V.[2] Otherwise the Lake District lapsed into
great quiet with the decline of the Ramesside Period. A con-
tributory cause for this state of affairs was probably the series of
virtually continuous struggles with Libyan raiders from the time
of Merenptah. These raids were prompted largely by hunger
and they had made the Fayum a danger zone. The establishment of the families of the Libyan chiefs Nemrut and Sheshonk
as rulers in Heracleopolis about 1000 B.C. certainly stressed the
importance of the Fayum as a way of entry into Egypt from the
Libyan oases. Nevertheless Osorkon I sited his principal garrison in a new fortress that stood at the entrance to the lake
near Illahun, probably on the Gebel Abusir just to the north of
Haragah, chiefly intended to defend the entrance to the Fayum
against an attack from the north.[3] We still hear of this fortress at
the time of the Ethiopian king Piankhi's campaign about 730
B.C. In spite of the fact that it awaited the approach of the
Ethiopians 'with its wall raised' and that it held a garrison
commanded by the son of Tefnakhte of Sais, Piankhi's principal
Lower Egyptian opponent, it finally surrendered without a
fight like Heracleopolis with its Libyan commander Peftjaudi-
bastet.[4]

The Ptolemaic Period brought renewed prosperity to the
Fayum when Ptolemy Philadelphus initiated large scale schemes

[1] Borchardt, *Der Porträtkopf der Königin Teje.*
[2] Gardiner, *Wilbour Papyrus*, II, on A § 39, 111, 112, 278, 279.
[3] For the existing remains, see Petrie, *Harageh.*   [4] *Urk.*, III, 23–4.

of colonization for Greek mercenaries.[1] The surface level of Lake Moeris had by that time been lowered from about sea-level to about 33 feet below sea-level and large stretches of land that formerly had formed part of the lake's bed now lay exposed and dry, especially in the northern half of the province. At the same time efforts were made to develop the fringe areas by the construction of canals. The best-known achievements of colonization in the Ptolemaic Period were to be found in the north and north-east and the south and south-west of the province on land that today is barren. This is true of places like Karanis (Kôm Aushîm) in the north, Dionysias (Qasr Qarun) and Philoteras (Wadfa) in the west, which owed their advanced positions to their roles as points of departure for caravan traffic and as stations for the desert police. It is also true of typical agricultural settlements like Philadelphia on the Darb Gerzah, Bacchias (Kôm el-Asl) on the northern border or Tebtunis in the extreme south-east, the area known today as Gharak, which was well known for its papyrus-thickets and was perhaps an older town than the others. Apparently, however, no attempt was made from the neighbouring Gharak to develop the Wadi Rayan, a district of about 154 square miles lying to the south-west of the Fayum which in its centre sinks to about 130 feet below sea-level.[2]

The archaeological investigations on the northern edge of the Fayum that have already been mentioned have revealed among other things that attempts were made to irrigate a vineyard in the country to the north and north-west of Karanis by filling dried up depressions that had been under water in Neolithic times with water brought by canals.[3] In order to reach the high level of these gardens the canals had to bring their water from a great distance along a channel that branched off the Bahr Yusuf near Hawara on the threshold of the Fayum, passed along the eastern edge of the Fayum to Philadelphia then turned along the northern edge below Bacchias — a course closely corresponding to that of the modern Bahr Wardan. The superintendent Zenon who is famed for his reports to the Finance

---

[1] Schubart, *Ägypten von Alexander der Grosse bis Mohammed*, 185f.

[2] A. Fakhry, *Annales du Service*, 46 (1947) p. 1f. Good authorities consider the trifling remains of buildings to be the work probably of Christian hermits.

[3] Caton-Thompson and Gardner, *op. cit.*, 140f., pl. 87f.

Heracleopolis and the Fayum

Minister Apollonius in the time of Ptolemy Philadelphus, played a great part in the execution of many of these bold schemes; and yet many of them seem to have ended in failure. About this time the *sakiyah* was first used; it is a wheel with buckets that draws up water from a deep well, worked by an animal, a characteristic sight in the modern Egyptian countryside. Times of economic decline in the Third Century A.D. led to the abandonment of the greater part of the laboriously reclaimed land; even today these losses have not been made good.

In the ruins of the Greek cities of Egypt the searcher looks chiefly for the papyri from which it is possible to obtain an insight into the economic and social structure of the land to an extent not possible for any other historical period. The facial appearance of the Greek colonists, especially of the citizens of Arsinoe (Crocodilopolis), during the early centuries of the Christian era is preserved for us on the so-called mummy portraits from Hawara which in function were the successors of the ancient Egyptian anthropoid coffins.[1] Although the Greek type was predominant in the population, yet the whole colonist element, which was numerically large, became in time absorbed by the native population. Yet foreign strains can still be detected in the racial type in the Fayum today. So far the recording of town buildings with the exception of the stone-built temples has not received sufficient attention apart from a few isolated cases such as the work of the Germans at Philadelphia and the Americans at Karanis.[2] Many ancient mounds have now been completely destroyed by the diggers for *sebbakh* and are today only shapeless rubbish heaps. When Lepsius visited Kôm Fares in 1843 the mound there rose to a height of 82 feet, towering over Crocodilopolis; it was at one time the most extensive ruin of a town in Egypt, covering an area of about 558 acres.[3]

At the time when Egypt turned inwards away from the Greek rule in Alexandria nationalist circles entertained hopes that Heracleopolis would once again witness a revival of former splendours. 'It is a man from Ihnasyah who will rule as far as

---

[1] Petrie, *Roman Portraits and Memphis IV*, pls. 1–26; *Hawara Portfolio* (1913).
[2] Viereck, *Philadelphia*; Boak, *Karanis* (*University of Michigan Studies, Humanistic Series* Vol. 25, 30).
[3] Schweinfurth and Wilcken, *Ztschr. Ges. f. allg. Erdkunde*, 22, 1f., with plan.

the foreign lands (the Persians) and as far as the Ionians.'[1] Such was the promise that perhaps originated at the time of the rebellion in the reign of Ptolemy Euergetes. It was not destined to be fulfilled. The Ptolemaic heritage passed to Rome.

[1] Spiegelberg, *Demotische Chronik*, p. 6, on II, 25.

IX

Abydos, a Sacred City

The ordinary traveller journeys about six miles from the station of Balliana through fertile country to Abydos so as to admire the temple of Sethos I with its magnificent reliefs, the best preserved of all such reliefs in the pre-Ptolemaic temples of Egypt. A few only will know that Abydos derived its fame from being a sacred place of the dead. Ancient Abydos belonged to the Thinite nome, the eighth of the canonical list, but it was not itself the nome capital. The capital was This and its god was Onuris, the huntsman hero whom Egyptian theologians equated with Shu of Heliopolis, the son of Rēʿ. The exact situation of This is unknown but it certainly lay to the north of Abydos in the region of Girga. One suggestion is that it was on the site of the village of el-Birba, west of Girga, but there are no visible signs of ruins there and only the name of a temple points to it. On the east bank of the river the suggested site is a place to the south-east of Girga called Nagʿ el-Meshayikh, the ancient Lepidontopolis, where Ramesses II built a sanctuary for the Thinite lion-goddess Mehyt who was the companion of Onuris.[1]

In very ancient times Abydos lay in the heart of the area where the predynastic Naqada cultures flourished. The cemetery at el-Amrah, about eight miles south-east of Abydos which Maciver excavated in 1900,[2] is the *locus classicus* for the earlier Naqada culture which was in consequence called Amratian. The graves there were mostly humped in the shape of their superstructures and in them the corpse was usually placed on its right side with the head pointing south, looking to the east

---

[1] See Kees' article 'Lepidotonpolis' in Pauly-Wissowa, *Real-Encyclopädie* and *ÄZ*, 73, 77; 75, 85f.; Gardiner, *Ancient Egyptian Onomastica*, II, nr. 353.
[2] MacIver, *El Amrah and Abydos*.

(towards the cultivated land). In this respect they differ from the majority of Naqada culture graves. These early graves contained a remarkable number of objects: cosmetic palettes made in strongly stylized animal shapes out of green schist that was in preference obtained from the Wadi Hammamat, flint knives, mace-heads, weapons and a noticeably large number of animal figures in clay which show that their owners were not only hunters but also cattle-breeders. Even a model of a house or a boat might be included in the useful belongings of a dead man. Ornaments, combs and needles are found, often carved with artistry out of hippopotamus ivory and decorated with figures. The most usual pots are brownish-red with black tops or single coloured hand-shaped vessels in the form of bottle-shaped gourds or parts of such gourds painted all over with a chalky white paint on a dark background. The motifs added by way of decoration, in addition to that which simulated a wickerwork were mostly animal — the hippopotamus and crocodile from the river, game and hunting-dogs from among land animals.

In its later stages the Naqada culture shows a transition to that culture which is peculiar to Middle Egypt and takes its name Gerzean from the town of Gerzah, the characteristic products of which have been described elsewhere; its pottery shapes are derived from those of stone vessels and the ware has red painting on a light-buff ground. At this time the corpse in the mound-grave lies on its left side with its face usually looking to the west, as was also the case in Upper Egypt. Finds belonging to the Naqada cultures have been found in places scattered throughout the necropolis areas in the neighbourhood of Abydos, as far as el-Mahasnah in the north.

Historically, however, Abydos possessed still more important things. At the very time that Flinders Petrie the real discoverer of the Naqada cultures was digging at Naqada and at Hu (Diospolis Parva) to the north, between 1895 and 1898 the French archaeologist E. Amélineau with his assistants using the bad old excavation methods of Mariette was rummaging through the cemeteries around Abydos. In the course of his rummaging he came across the site, to the west of the temple of Sethos, which was called Umm el-Ga'ab, 'Mother of Pots', because of the great deposits of potsherds there. Here he found

SCALE IN MILES

0   ¼   ½   1

Cemeteries ▬ Middle Fort
Shunet ez Zebib ▬ Monastery
Umm el Ga'ab (Poker)
Royal Tombs of the
Early Dynasties
Temple of
Ramesses II
Kôm el Sultan
Osiris
Temple Enclosure
El Kherbah
Osireion
Temple of
Sethos I
To Balliana

El Arabah
el Madfunah

N

Shrine of Tetisheri
Terraced Temple of Ahmose
Cenotaph of Sesostris III
Cenotaph of Ahmose
Temple of Sesostris III
Pyramid ⌧

Limit of Cultivation

7. Abydos

233

huge subterranean tombs the central parts of which were burial chambers constructed of beams and planks.[1] These chambers had, however, been burnt by fire and their roofs had collapsed so that the superstructures of the tombs were destroyed beyond recognition. One of these tombs had become known to visitors as the Grave of Osiris because it contained a granite bier with a figure of Osiris and a royal name scratched on it — an undoubted work of the Late Period. Unexpectedly therefore the holy of holies of Abydos, the Grave of Osiris, had been stumbled upon, at a place which the spells of the dead designated as the district of Poker; there the soul of the god is said to live on in a grove, as is represented in reliefs and as is described of a similar grave of Osiris in the texts on the Abaton at Philae.[2] The masses of potsherds witness to the offerings presented to the dead god by innumerable generations of visitors. The excavators published a description of the tomb, but it was Sethe in 1897 who read the name Usaphais the fifth king of Dynasty I and of his successor Miebis in the inscriptions on the offerings from the tombs and proved that the tombs were royal and dated from the oldest historical period, the time of Manetho's Thinite kings. The rulers of the Thinite Period who until then had been virtually legendary figures, were thus brought into the light of history. Representations on the offerings in tombs and in particular the little tablets with the numeration of regnal years by reference to historical events or festivals, together with very archaic written notes yielded information about events which it was now important to connect with the newly discovered Naqada cultures. The Grave of Osiris then revealed itself to be the tomb of a Horus-King named Djer, apparently the earliest king of this group and perhaps the one called Athothis by Manetho, the successor of Menes.

The tombs of the kings were surrounded by close rows of smaller tombs belonging to members of the Court and to servants, men and women, dwarf attendants and hounds. Simple stone stelae indicated the burial places and carried the names of the buried in rudely inscribed hieroglyphs. In front of the flat superstructures of the royal tombs which represented the primitive grave mounds, stood pairs of stelae that in some cases are first-class examples of the stone-mason's craft. They bear the

---

[1] On the wood, see above, p. 135.   [2] See below, p. 328.

Horus-name of the kings placed in the so-called palace façade or *serekh* surmounted by the Horus falcon; the most famous is that of the King 'Serpent' Wadji who was apparently the successor of Djer (Athothis).[1] Subsequent excavations in the same place by Flinders Petrie in 1901 and 1902 resulted not only in more exact records of the construction of the tombs but also in new and important finds of funerary gifts. Fragments of rare stone vessels from among these gifts bear representations of the ancient local deity of Abydos, the predecessor, as it were, of Osiris. This deity was represented as a member of the dog family who, like Anubis, was shown in a recumbent attitude and set as a sacred animal on a standard. In later depictions when he was coloured, black was used and this colour indicated unusualness or rarity. The inhabitants of Abydos called him Khentamenty, 'the One at the head of the West', which indicated that he was the Lord of the Dead.

His was the most ancient temple at Abydos and Petrie found some remains of its decorations. It was situated significantly at the point where the road to the royal tombs left the cultivated land. In the Old Kingdom he was joined by Osiris the God of the Dead who came from Busiris by way of Memphis. Only from the time of Sesostris I do the inscriptions of the temple accord Osiris the rights of a native of Abydos in the form of Osiris-Khentamenty;[2] but this syncretism had already been prepared and built up in the royal funerary texts of the Old Kingdom. In funeral litanies Osiris was praised there 'in his name of "Great Land" (i.e. the ancient name for This)' (*Pyramid Texts* 627b); the dead king as the equal of Osiris was called 'power in the nome of This' (*Pyramid Texts* 754c) and he would sit in the other world 'invested with the form of Osiris on the throne of Khentamenty' (*Pyramid Texts* 759). From the beginning of Dynasty VI, therefore, Osiris was called, in the tomb inscriptions of the courtiers of Memphis, 'Lord of Abydos', as well as his original title 'at the head of Busiris' and he was set level with Khentamenty in his native land. This achieving of a new home by Osiris was the result of the adoption of the

[1] Stela in Louvre, see Schäfer-Andrae[3], 190; further, see Petrie, *Royal Tombs*, I and II.

[2] Petrie, *Abydos*, II, pl. 26; otherwise under Dynasty XI, see *op. cit.*, pls. 24–5 and even from the foundation deposits of Sesostris I, pl. 23.

Osiris myth in the Memphite Kingdom and of its being connected with the worship of Sokar.

Following Busiris and Memphis, Abydos now became the first place of worship of Osiris in Upper Egypt. The reason for this advancement is easy to see. At Abydos were the tombs of the Thinite kings, the divine forefathers, and since the rulers of the united Egypt professed the belief that the king in death was identified with Osiris, it followed that the prototype of the transformed kings should be included with them in their necropolis. Accordingly the place that Abydos offered him was a genuine royal tomb, deliberately, perhaps, the oldest known tomb of its kind; for his myth presupposes a royal tomb 'on the shores of Nedit'.[1]

It was not difficult to establish the Osiris myth firmly in Abydos and to call in suitable secondary deities. For this purpose there was the primeval sign of the Thinite nome that looked like a bee-hive on a pole; the name of the nome *Ta-wer* 'great (or old) land' contained a reference to the common myth of the primeval hill. If the object represented in this sign was regarded as a relic of Osiris (and theology claimed that it contained the head of the god) then the Osiris myth became bound up with the legend of the primeval hill. So, in the tomb of Osiris Abydos acquired the oldest place in the world; it was 'the first primeval place of the ruler over all'[2] — a claim put forward also by Memphis and Heliopolis — 'the blessed place since the time of Osiris, that Horus founded for the fathers whom the stars in heaven serve, the Mistress of the subject people to whom the great ones in Busiris come, *the second Heliopolis in holiness* wherein the ruler of all is pleased'.[3]

From Asyut came Wepwawet, the champion and messenger of the kings; from Cynopolis came Anubis, the burial master of Osiris, to join his fellow canine god; from Akhmîm, Horus, the son of Osiris, made contact with the person of Min. In this way a local circle of deities came to surround Osiris.[4] Furthermore Abydos took its place as a holy city beside the ancient Lower Egyptian places of pilgrimage of the Memphite Period, where the blessed dead hoped to linger, beside Buto and Sais, the royal

---

[1] Kees, *Totenglauben*, 191.   [2] De Buck, *Coffin Texts*, I, 225.
[3] British Museum stela, 581 (time of Sesostris I).
[4] Kees, *Götterglaube*, 329f.

cities of Lower Egypt, Busiris, the home of Osiris, the city of Isis and, by no means the last, Heliopolis.

The journey of the dead to Abydos was the aspiration in the future but at first it played its part in the general dualism of the country side by side with that to Busiris. You sailed upstream to Abydos but rowed downstream to Busiris. Already in the Pyramid Texts the following wish is expressed for the Memphite king: 'You go down to the canal along which you travel upstream to the Thinite nome and wander through Abydos in this your transfigured form which the gods enjoined on you.'[1]

In spite of the abundance of the remains of the Thinite Period at Abydos it is not easy to draw a distinguishing line between Memphis and Abydos. Thus, was there in fact an historical unifier of the Kingdoms called Menes? Or was the Horus king Aha, 'the Fighter', the first king of the Thinite Dynasty I? Emery, the excavator of the Early Dynastic Cemetery at Saqqara claims to have found the tomb of Aha there,[2] while in the royal cemetery at Abydos many objects bearing his name have been found, but no identifiable tomb. Did therefore the Thinite kings build tombs at Memphis and Abydos in conformity with the prevailing official dualism of Egypt? Or did the seat of government and the cemetery alternate between the two places as early as Dynasty I? This alternation certainly happened under the Thinite Dynasty II: only two of its kings were buried at Abydos, Peribsen, the Seth-worshipper who succeeded Ninetjer (Binothris) who was buried at Memphis, and Khasekhemwy who preceeded Nebka of Memphis, the last king of the dynasty.[3] Why then did the Thinites choose Abydos as a burying-place although their kings allegedly came from Hieraconpolis in the south and wore the white crown of its twin city Nekheb (el-Kab)? Sethe sought to explain this anomaly by the presence of Osiris' tomb;[4] but Osiris did not make his appearance at Abydos until long after the Thinite Period. Or did the Thinite kings in fact come from the 8th (Thinite) nome and from there gained control of Hieraconpolis that lies not far from the Nubian frontier? To all these questions the monuments offer no answers.

Nevertheless there are at Abydos the remains of Thinite

[1] *Pyr.* 1716–17, cf. 798. [2] See above, p. 152.
[3] Petrie, *Royal Tombs*, II. [4] *Urgeschichte und älteste Religion*, § 101.

Residences, the fort-like structure now known as Shunet ez-Zebib and the Middle Fort near the temple of Khentamenty.[1] They are buildings very like the 'fort' at Hieraconpolis, rectangular structures surrounded with double walls of mud brick of which the stronger inner walls are decorated with pilasters (Pl. 20. *b*). The walls of the Shunet ez-Zebib were originally about 40 feet high and covered with white plaster like the 'White Walls' of Memphis. The inner wall of the Shunet ez-Zebib enclosed an area 360 feet by 75 feet which seems only partly to have been occupied by small dwellings. The two structures at Abydos can be dated by sealings to the reigns of Peribsen and Khasekhemwy.

The Court finally left Abydos in the reign of Zoser. Two immense brick mastabas on the edge of the desert at Bêt Khallaf to the west of This are dated to this time by seal impressions of Zoser and of the Horus Sanakhte (possibly the same king as Nebka). The Step Pyramid and other buildings constructed at Saqqara for Zoser by Imhotep, the 'Greatest of Seers', introduced a new era. It could indeed be said that the Memphite Old Kingdom annexed Abydos as a holy place just as it annexed Busiris and other towns in the Delta. While Abydos and its god Khentamenty began to be discussed in Memphis the cemeteries around Abydos and This fell into disuse. This fact is clearly demonstrated at Nag' ed-Deir on the east bank of the Nile in the Thinite nome where the necropolis was carefully excavated by Reisner. At the very time when Cheops and Chephren were building their colossal pyramids at Giza (Pl. 14. *b*) the greatest poverty existed at Nag' ed-Deir.[2] A wooden coffin was there a luxury and burial in simple mound graves was again practised as an economy.

The tombs of the early Old Kingdom (Dynasty III–IV) at Abydos and also at Reqaqna to the west of This were undecorated brick constructions containing one or two cult niches in the east wall in front of which in the better tombs was built a narrow transverse chamber to serve as a place of worship or chapel.[3] These tombs are built side by side in irregular streets.

At its zenith the Old Kingdom experienced a new vital im-

---

[1] Ayrton, *Abydos*, III, pls. 5f.

[2] G. Reisner, *A Provincial Cemetery of the Pyramid Age* (*Naga-ed-Dêr*, III).

[3] Peet, *Cemeteries of Abydos*, III, 8f., pl. 15, cf. Garstang, *Tombs of the Third Egyptian Dynasty at Reqâqnah and Bêt Khallâf.*

pulse. The feudal age approached. Already King Neferirkarē'
of Dynasty V had freed the priests of the temple of Khentamenty from the control of local officials and reserved them for
services in the temple. At the beginning of Dynasty VI Teti
granted further favours.[1] After his successor Pepi I had elevated
two daughters of Thinite noblemen to be queens a few minor
additions were made to the temple of Khentamenty. Now highly
placed personages sought especially to be buried in the holy
places of Osiris. One of the first was Weni who was born in the
reign of Unas from whom he derived his full name Unas-ankh
'Unas lives'. After an exemplary career under Merenrē' as
count and overseer of Upper Egypt, in which capacity he was
head of the Upper Egyptian provincial administration, he was
buried at Abydos where his tomb was found to contain the most
circumstantial private biographical text of the Old Kingdom.
Pepi II had to extend the exemptions to cover regular sacrificial
offerings such as parts of a cow or a gift of milk brought for the
service of the statue of the King, of those of the two Queen
Mothers and of that of his uncle, the vizir Djau, which were
allotted to certain beneficiaries.[2]

After the break-down of the Old Kingdom a state of feudalism
descended on the country and during this time the Thinite
nome, the official seat of the last overseer of Upper Egypt —
that institution set up by the central government — found itself
in the thick of the struggle between the rising princely house of
Antefs and Menthuhotpes at Thebes and the house of the
Akhtoys who resided at Heracleopolis. A certain Neferukait, a
true king's daughter and the royal wife of an unnamed prince,
found herself about 2140–2090 B.C. in the harîm of one of the
Antef kings, possibly Wahankh, and became his favourite. She
maintained that she had inherited from her mother the claim to
the territory from the Elephantine nome to that of Antaeopolis
(the 1st to the 10th)[3] and as a result Antef went to war with the
Middle Egyptian Heracleopolitans over the most northerly
nomes of this region. Amid the alternating fortunes of battle and
almost at the end of a reign of fifty years Antef boasted: 'I seized
the whole Thinite nome.' He destroyed the fortresses in the 10th

---

[1] *Urk.*, I, 170–2; 207–8.　　　　　　　　[2] *Urk.*, I, 278–80.
[3] Cairo 20543 (from Denderah), cf. E. Meyer, *Geschichte des Altertums*, I,
2³ § 276; H. Stock, *Die erste Zwischenzeit Ägyptens*, 46f.

nome, that is in the district of Qau el-Kebir and made this area
into the northern gateway to his dominion.[1] His overseer of
dragomans and expert in foreign trade, Djari also mentions the
'war with the house of Akhtoy in the west of This'.[2] On the other
hand the Heracleopolitan king Akhtoy II declares in his political
testament for his son Merikarē', that he captured This 'like a
whirlwind'; he obviously won it back from the Thebans from
time to time.[3] These struggles furnished the occasions for the
sacking of the holy places of Abydos which the king describes in
warning vein to his son: 'Youth will fight with youth as our
forefathers proclaimed: Egyptians fight in the City of the Dead,
breaking open the graves.' Perhaps it was at this time that the
old royal tombs were plundered and destroyed. The victory of
the Heracleopolitans in which Tefyeb, the nomarch of Asyut,
played a decisive part 'at the beginning of the fighting . . . with
the southern nomes who joined together and came south to
Elephantine and north to This (?)' did not prove lasting.[4] The
stela of a Theban vassal who served from the time of Antef
Wahankh to that of the king who preceded the Menthuhotpe
who unified the land (perhaps even to the time of that king
himself) is dated in a 14th regnal year, which is described as the
'year of the revolt of This'.[5] The year might be 2055 B.C. and it
is likely that this revolt marked the beginning of the final
struggle.

The victory of the Thebans opened a great age for Abydos.
King Antef Wahankh and the last Menthuhotpe did indeed add
to the temple of Khentamenty. The decisive factor, however,
was that with Egypt's restored unity Abydos became the chief of
Egypt's sacred places before which the fame of the ancient
Delta towns became faint. Everybody wanted to be buried at
Abydos or at least to build there a dummy tomb with a com-
memorative inscription and an offering table. Not only were

[1] Cairo 20512.
[2] Clère and Vandier, *Stèles de la première Periode intermédiaire*, nr. 18 (in
Cairo).
[3] Papyrus Petersburg, 1116A, 11. 73–4.
[4] Griffith, *The Inscriptions of Siut*, III, l. 16.
[5] British Museum stela 1203 = Clère and Vandier, *op. cit.*, nr. 23; according to the conjecture of Stock, *op. cit.*, 77, it could refer to the Menthuhotpe
who unified the Kingdoms, for he took another Horus-name in the early
years of his reign.

the highly placed to be found there, but the middle classes also. The wish of the dead was to receive offerings on the feast days of the necropolis, to be in the company of the god on his crossing to his grave in Poker, or even to be taken into the sacred *neshmet*-barque and to be allowed to hold the rudder; that the great ones of Abydos, that is the blessed dead, would greet him with 'welcome in peace' and that he would hear the cries of joy from the mouths of the inhabitants of the nome at the passing of the procession of the god.[1] In Ramesside times a prayer for the dead that was very much favoured in Thebes ran: 'Bread will be given to you — 4 (loaves) in Busiris, 8 in Abydos, 12 in the district of Poker.'

So that he could participate in the festival offerings the Egyptian placed a stela on 'the steps of the Great God', or the *dromos*, as was later said, where the god left the temple to go to the holy tomb on Umm el-Ga'ab. Every dead person who was buried in accordance with the Osiris ritual was intended symbolically to undertake the pilgrimage to Abydos and for that purpose a model of a barque was placed in his tomb or a picture of such a journey by the dead man's soul was painted on the wall of the tomb.

It would be fascinating to reconstruct the processional way of the god through the City of the Dead. The excavation methods of today are the first that could adequately have dealt with the uncovering of the necropolis where throughout the centuries the tombs and cenotaphs were built in utter confusion. The very heart of the Middle Kingdom necropolis was, however, rummaged through by Mariette a century ago and hundreds of stelae brought to light without any attempt being made to determine the circumstances in which they were found or to draw plans. The vast majority of all the commemorative tablets that are to be found in the museums of the world came from Abydos. The cenotaphs were undoubtedly for the most part simple constructions of mud brick, at first resembling mastabas and then in the Middle Kingdom at times small pyramids. In every case the most important things were the stone stela with the offering table in front of it. The brick constructions were, however, left without attention with the result that they have collapsed and perished.

[1] Kees, *Totenglauben*, 340–1.

The stelae tell us about the festivals. These were in part holidays already included in the Old Kingdom calendar of festivals, such as the *wag*-festival and the Thoth-festival on the day after in the first month of the year (the 18th and 19th days of the month Thoth). Then there were the special Osiris festivals which came to a climax in Khoiak, the fourth month of the inundation season. They were associated with performances of episodes from the Osiris myth and were therefore called 'mysteries' although that term does not exactly convey the peculiar Egyptian dramatical form. We learn some details of these mysteries from the statements of important men who were commissioned by the king to execute various tasks in Abydos, such as the restoration of the temple, repairs to the barques of the gods or to statues. One of these men in the reign of Sesostris III was the chief treasurer Ikhernofret.[1] The conqueror of Nubia had clearly intended to present a large share of the booty, especially of the Nubian gold, to Osiris-Khentamenty. After completing his task Ikhernofret as the king's representative was allowed to direct the mystery plays of Osiris and for that purpose he received the special priestly office of 'Beloved Son'; as such he had to play in the ritual the kingly role of Horus as the son of Osiris.

He also organized one of the chief festivals of Abydos, 'the Great Going-forth', which was also apparently celebrated in the month Thoth[2] and was intended to portray the search for, discovery of and mourning for the dead Osiris. He then led the god amid the cheers of the festival crowds along the processional way to the tomb in Poker (Umm el-Ga'ab) and, as Horus, had to cast down the enemies of Osiris who opposed the passage of the sacred *neshmet*-barque. He also organized the 'Coming forth of Wepwawet' which was also called 'the First Coming forth'. At this festival Wepwawet, like a bloodhound, followed the scent round the 'circle of This' in order (like Horus) to avenge his father Osiris (the old king) on his murderer and to seize the sovereignty. Neferhotpe I, a king of Dynasty XIII, who was himself present at the festival at Abydos and personally directed the performance of the mysteries, gave a similar

---

[1] Schäfer, *Die Mysterien des Osiris in Abydos unter König Sesostris III.*

[2] Dated to the 22nd day of the month Thoth in the Theban calendar of the New Kingdom (so in the Tomb of Neferhotpe).

account of them. Further, his presence was also connected with the completion of restorations to the statue of the god.[1] On this occasion the king had his name added to the stela of one of his predecessors[2] and the inscription tells us that four boundary stones were to set out the limits of a holy place reserved for the god Wepwawet in the necropolis west of the temple of Khentamenty. Anyone who trespassed on this holy ground to build a tomb or to establish himself there without authorization as a priest of the dead was to be burnt, so incurring the loss of his future life: 'Every notable who builds his tomb within the holy place will be indicted and come under the law that applies to the Necropolis up to the present time.' A sort of cemetery law therefore existed for the City of the Dead. It may be recalled in this connection that one of the most ancient epithets of Anubis as god of the dead was 'Lord of the Holy Land'. These ordinances regulated claims to burial places and the division of offerings that were placed at the cenotaphs and that ultimately became the portion of the priests of the dead charged with the supervision of the endowments. This arrangement was necessary because even kings built dummy tombs for themselves at Abydos. We know that this was true of Sesostris III of Dynasty XII, of Ahmose, the conqueror of the Hyksos, and of Tetisheri, his greatly revered grandmother, both of Dynasty XVIII.[3] Sesostris III and Ahmose had rock-tombs similar to that of Menthuhotpe at Deir el-Bahari; Tetisheri's cenotaph was a brick shrine of which the most enduring part was a chapel containing a large stela. It is possible that the identified ruins of a brick pyramid lying to the east of this building also belonged to it. The whole group of buildings is to be found in the southern part of the necropolis, about a mile to the south of Umm el-Ga'ab. On the stela King Ahmose tells the queen about his endowment: 'Your grave and your cenotaph are now on ground belonging to the Theban and Thinite nomes respectively. I tell you this because My Majesty desires to have a pyramid and a chapel built for you on holy land near the monument of My Majesty, (i.e. his own mortuary temple) so that its pool can be dug out, its trees planted and the amount of its sacrificial bread fixed, (so that it can be) colonized with people,

[1] A stela in Cairo, cf. Pieper, *Mitt. vorderasiat.-ägypt. Ges.*, 32, 2.
[2] MacIver, *El Amrah and Abydos*, pl. 29.   [3] Ayrton, *Abydos*, III.

furnished with arable land, endowed with herds and tended by *ka*-priests and priests of the dead bound (to its service).'[1] A garden also formed part of the plan of the complex. Although the building intended for Ahmose was possibly never completed, his funerary service continued still in the Ramesside Period and had therefore survived the disturbances of the Amarna Period. A singular attachment was always shown for the house of Ahmose, far more so than for the Tuthmosides who came after; and this fact was true of Thebes as well as of Abydos.[2]

A stela dating from the fourteenth year of Ramesses II records that 2 *web*-priests laid rival claims to a contested piece of arable land before a god, as was then customary; it was, it seems, before a statue of King Ahmose which is shown in the relief carved on the stela, being borne on high by four *web*-priests and accompanied by his prophet in procession on a great festival day.[3] As we know from the statue of Amun in Thebes, the god delivered his judgement by certain movements of the portable statue that indicated assent or refusal. Clearly, therefore, Ahmose was regarded in Abydos as possessing peculiar sanctity just as his wife Ahmes-Nefertari and her son Amenophis I were regarded at the same time in the West City at Thebes.

The great kings of Dynasty XVIII naturally added to the temple of Osiris-Khentamenty. There are the remains of beautiful limestone reliefs from the time of Amenophis I, in part originating jointly from himself and his father Ahmose. Tuthmosis III enlarged the revenues of the temple.[4] In return the Thinite nome gave many tried and trusted servants to the growing Empire. Thus, from the reign of Hatshepsut, we can name Sitepihu, the Count of This, who directed the transport from Aswan of her two obelisks intended for Karnak.[5] Then there was Min, the tutor and Master of arms of Amenophis II, who was called Count of This and Count of the Oasis (el-Khargah),[6] a conjunction of titles which shows that at that time the southern

---

[1] *Op. cit.*, pl. 52 = *Urk.*, IV, 26.   [2] See below, p. 274.

[3] Cairo J.43649, see Legrain, *Annales du Service*, 16, 162, with plate.

[4] Petrie, *Abydos*, I, pls. 62–3; II, pl. 34.

[5] *Urk.*, IV, 517 (cf. below, p. 260); MacIver, *El Amrah and Abydos*, pls. 32–34, Dg.

[6] *Urk.*, IV, 976–82; Theban Tomb, nr. 109.

oases of el-Khargah and el-Dakhlah were united from an administrative point of view with the Thinite nome. Such men, the successors of the nomarchs of earlier times, occupied in This the honorific offices of curator of the principal local temple as 'Count and Overseer of prophets of Onuris' and often at the same time that of overseer of prophets of Osiris in Abydos. Such did Min who also called himself 'Director of festivals of Osiris' and in this capacity, like Ikhernofret in the Middle Kingdom, he could direct the 'mysteries' of Osiris and act as king's representative at them. This association of a military career with office at court and office in the service of the gods was typical of the time. 'May you take in your hand the guide-rope of the barge of the gods when it passes through the canal of This on its voyage to the district of Poker. May you then rejoice with the followers of Horus when he has struck down the rebel (Seth)'; such is the wish found in the tombs of dead officials at Thebes.[1]

The third great age of Abydos, the one that marked its zenith, came in the Ramesside Period when Sethos I built anew the temple of Osiris and provided it with very rich endowments. For the glorification of the dynasty he built not far from the temple a mortuary chapel for his father Ramesses I, the former viceroy of Horemheb of which the fine reliefs are now in New York. Sethos, however, was a man of large ideas. He began to construct a completely new group of temple buildings about three-quarters of a mile to the south of the ancient temple of Khentamenty; its ground-plan alone shows that on this site a great central shrine was to be erected. It was named 'The House of Millions of Years of King Menma'atrē', joyful in heart in Abydos.' Seven chapels, to each of which a processional way led through the length of the temple, lay side by side in a row, dedicated to two triads, the imperial triad of the Ramesside kings, Amun, the Theban King of the Gods to whom, as *primus inter pares*, the central chapel belonged, Rē'-Harakhte of Heliopolis and Ptah of Memphis, and the Osirian family triad, Osiris, Isis and Horus. The seventh chapel belonged to the king. Various subsidiary rooms were reserved for the worship of the Osiris cycle and the gods of Memphis, especially Soker and Nefertum. Lists of gods and the well-known list of kings

[1] Theban tomb of Paser, nr. 106 (of Dynasty XIX).

245

assured for the numerous local deities and the royal ancestors as far back as the Thinite kings a formal share in the offerings in the temple after the principal recipients 'had satisfied themselves', as the Egyptians put it.

The limestone reliefs in the temple of Sethos are justly famous for the fineness of the carving and the surprisingly well-preserved colouring.[1] At first sight the delicate profiles and the soft roundness of the figures seem to suggest a direct connection with the style of Amarna figures. On closer inspection, however, a certain coldness and hardness are discerned in comparison with the winning charm of the late Amarna art. The relationship is similar to that between the magnificent seated figure of Ramesses II in Turin and the early statues of Amenophis III. It seems that the style of the Ramesside Period is classical and that the fiery passion of the Amarna Age had burnt itself out. A sober age had begun that renounced many ideals.

Sethos richly endowed his temple, assigning to it in particular the revenues from the southern gold mines,[2] the most productive source of Egyptian wealth, and also the dues from those provinces in which Sethos had firmly established Egyptian rule by force of arms. A long decree carved on a rock a little to the north of the Third Cataract in Upper Nubia gives us a glimpse into the organization of temple economy with the widely scattered undertakings of the temples, from the possession of cargo vessels in Nubia and on the Mediterranean to the humble tasks made necessary by the requirements of the beneficiaries, employees and slaves of the temples.[3] All administrative departments and all officials from the King's Son of Kush (the viceroy of Nubia) and the military scribes (so feared for their requisitionings) to the royal administrators were forbidden to demand any form of forced labour for agricultural purposes from temple servants throughout the country, to detain any temple ship and impose dues on its cargoes, to confiscate oxen, asses, pigs and goats or to demand them as dues and similarly to leave unmolested temple fishermen and bird-catchers everywhere in the marshes. The same protection was extended to the tradesmen of temple industries, to all beekeepers, tenant farmers, gardeners and vine-tenders, even to ship-merchants,

---

[1] Calverley and Gardiner, *The Temple of King Sethos I*, vols. I–III.
[2] See above, p. 124.   [3] Griffith, *JEA*, 13, 193f.

and tradesmen engaged in the export trade (in respect of the latter two classes even the ancient royal prerogatives over trade were violated for the benefit of the temples) and in particular to the gold-washers in the mountains whom the king expressly reserved for the temple. 'Gold is the body of the God; it is not our affair.' The king himself had declared that it could not be numbered among human possessions. Having regard to the characteristic arbitrariness of the State officials, the punishments for transgressing these laws were very severe: 100 blows with 5 bloody wounds was the average punishment together with the restoration of the confiscated goods — in exceptionally bad cases with restitution in the ratio of one hundred to one — forced labour for the benefit of the temple or on the frontier and this often after the cutting off of the nose and ears. So ran the law.

Behind the rear wall of the temple of Sethos was found an unusual subterranean building that was thought at the time of finding to be a grave of Osiris. The descent is by a corridor that leads to a platform surrounding a walled ditch on all four sides of which are rows of empty niches. On the stone platform stood ten heavy granite pillars. This central part of the whole, constructed entirely of sandstone and granite, has an archaic character, particularly as there are no inscriptions or plastic decorations. Reliefs and inscriptions are found only in side rooms, like closets, that were first decorated in part by Merenptah with parts of the Books of Heaven and Hell, like the royal tombs at Thebes. The whole building was intended to serve as a cenotaph for the cult-chapel of Sethos I in the temple in front of it.[1] Nevertheless it sought to resemble the mythical grave of Osiris. On the raised platform, in which one can see today only two depressions, the tomb of the god can be imagined, rising out of the water like the primeval hill; for there can be no doubt that the surrounding ditch could be filled with water to the surface of which a descent could be made by means of two flights of steps. At the Osiris festivals offerings were brought there to the Osiris Sethos as if below in the underworld; possibly rites symbolizing resurrection were also celebrated before his statue. In the publication of the Cenotaph of Sethos (which so far is uncompleted like that of the temple) it is rightly pointed out that this building is incidentally mentioned by Strabo (Book

[1] Frankfort, *The Cenotaph of Seti I at Abydos*.

XVII, 813) in his description of the 'memnonium' at Abydos: 'At that place there is a spring lying in a hollow to which one descends through an arch cut in a monolith notable for its size and form of construction. There is also a canal that leads from the river to this place and on this canal there is a grove of Egyptian thorny acacias sacred to Apollo.' As was prescribed for the grave of Osiris and as was described in the case of the cenotaph of Tetisheri, there was here also a garden so that the soul of the dead could sojourn in the branches of the trees round the pond. Deep holes for plants have in fact been found in the stony desert soil round the cenotaph of Sethos and these were apparently occupied by tamarisks. The central part of the cenotaph with the tomb-like gallery surrounded by rows of niches is reproduced in the immense Late Period tombs at Thebes of the Governor Menthuemhat and the Chief Lector-priest Pediamenopet. Certain details of these latter constructions remain to be clarified, but it is clear that in them too we are to recognize the imitating of divine tombs.[1]

When Sethos I died his temple was only partly completed; the chapels were finished but the hypostyle hall only just begun. Ramesses II visited Abydos on his return to Lower Egypt from his first visit to the Opet Festival at Thebes — he could at that time go by boat to Abydos — and he described what he found there and what remained for him to do. Even if he did exaggerate many things in order to underline his conduct as a good son, his report is yet sufficiently informative to reveal to what extent all endowments and vested rights depended on the good will of the successor to the throne and how quickly a foundation melted away and was abandoned by priests and slaves as soon as the protective hand was removed. Ramesses II reported: 'He found the chapels of the Holy Land of former kings and their cenotaphs in Abydos falling into desolation, the buildings half finished . . . the walls fallen on to the road and not one brick adhering to another. Everything on the foundation was reduced to rubble, no other building had replaced it such as should have been done in accordance with his plan for further building, since their Lord had flown to Heaven (i.e. was dead), without there being a son there who would have restored his father's monuments in the necropolis.

[1] Von Bissing, *ÄZ*, 74, 16f.

'So was the temple of Sethos, its façade and rear part still in the course of construction when he went to Heaven, its monuments unfinished, its columns not standing on its terrace (forecourt); his statue lying on the ground, it was still not fashioned after the knowledge for it of the Gold House (Treasury). Its divine offerings had ceased (revenues) and those bound to the hourly service in the house of the god had stopped working. The produce of its arable land, the boundaries of which were not fixed, was taken and carried away. . . .'

Then followed a reorganization of the temple administration and all its associated industries: 'I instructed a man of my own choice to oversee the building of it.' Labour gangs and stonemasons were ordered there, so were painters and draughtsmen; priestly novices (*web*-priests) were named and a prophet for the statue of the god to direct its services. The granaries were provided with revenues and placed under a royal bailiff and a written register of landed property drawn up, since formerly it had apparently only existed 'verbally'. Tenant-farmers and peasants were placed on the land, herds of cattle replenished and all the temple industries which had been listed in Sethos' decree were reorganized, from the control of ocean-going ships that brought goods for the temple estates to the activities of the birdcatchers in the marshes and weaving by the wives of the slaves. So that all these tasks could be carried out the ranks of the priests responsible for the hourly services were brought up to their full complement, undoubtedly by means of fresh drafts from the villages.

The great inscription of Ramesses II on the subject of this work of restoration runs to 116 lines;[1] it is on the wall of the second forecourt of the temple of Sethos. It deals therefore with this latter building and not with the temple Ramesses II built for himself beside that of his father. This temple of Ramesses II is remarkable for the workmanship with which it was executed; its colours are in part splendidly preserved; but unhappily only the lower parts of the walls remain. In the inner parts, which were built first, use was made of the same finely modelled relief as that of the temple of Sethos. Neither the additions carried out by Ramesses II in the temple of Sethos, nor the works executed

[1] Gauthier, *ÄZ*, 48, 53f. = *Institut français d'archéologie orientale, Bibliothèque d'étude*, 4 (1912).

by him on Theban soil, such as in the hypostyle hall at Karnak or the Ramesseum, approach this high standard.

The great age of temple building at Abydos came to an end with Ramesses II. Ramesses III a century later certainly states that he established new endowments for a 'House of Ramesses III in the House of Osiris, Lord of Abydos' and that he donated two groups of 682 and 162 slaves, but from a building point of view this can only have involved, at the most, unpretentious alterations.[1] His son Ramesses IV after the violent death of his father, proclaimed on a commemorative tablet his particular devotion to Osiris whose manifold being as Lord of the Dead, Moon-god and the fertilizing Nile in time of flood, he knew how to praise in eloquent terms. As a reward for the asseveration of his pious principles he asked of the god a reign of twice as many years as was granted to the great Ramesses II — twice sixty-seven years. His importunity was of little avail for he was destined to be a short-lived epigone in a dying age.

We know the names of many men from Dynasty XIX who were of importance in This and Abydos, in particular the names of high priests of Onuris-Shu in This and of Osiris in Abydos. They were related by marriage to the leading families of high-ranking officers of state many of whom were viziers in Memphis and Thebes. Priestly families arose, the endeavours of which were directed towards ensuring that the father's high office descended to his son. This end was accomplished more easily in the non-political atmosphere of the provincial towns than in the capitals. Of their tombs for the most part only fragments remain — parts of walls, stelae, statues, offering tables, such as were retrieved by excavators in the time of Mariette from the chaos of cemeteries constantly built over. Many of these objects had undoubtedly served their purposes in other places. As far as could be discovered by later excavations, the tombs of the New Kingdom were mainly constructed of brick.[2] The subterranean burial chamber was usually covered by a vaulted roof over which rose a superstructure that at first apparently retained the form of the ancient mastaba with its built-in chapel. In later tombs the superstructure was extended by the addition of further buildings until the whole came to resemble a small

[1] Papyrus Harris, I, 61a, 5–6; cf. Petrie, *Abydos*, II, 19 and pl. 58.
[2] MacIver, *El Amrah and Abydos*, pl. 25f.; Peet, *Cemeteries of Abydos*, II, 84f.

mortuary temple, a modest imitation of that possessed by the revered Amenhotpe, son of Hapu, in the City of the Dead of Amenophis III. This tomb had a forecourt, an entrance hall and a chapel. The Ramesside Age favoured a three-roomed building topped perhaps by a pyramidal superstructure of the kind known at Thebes at the same time.

The next important historical fact that we learn is that Sheshonk, the first Libyan king, at the time when he was the local ruler in Heracleopolis, created an endowment and built a chapel in Abydos for the statue of his father Nemrut, which was under the protection of the last Tanite king; 100 *aroura* of arable land, one garden and 25 slaves were donated for its upkeep.[1] The Late Period also left behind very stately tombs in the Holy Land at Abydos. Finally Abydos was overtaken by the destiny that had befallen Busiris centuries earlier; it was overshadowed by Philae and the grave of Osiris on the Abaton (at Bigah) which became the principal holy places of Osiris.[2] Osiris once more departed south to the Nubian nome and the mythical sources of the Nile.

Religious worship ended in Abydos as in Thebes with the adoration of minor popular divinities. One of the last testimonies we possess to the religious life at Abydos praises an oracle of the dwarf-god Bes (formerly a humble protective spirit of the camp of Osiris) who still had worshippers under the Emperor Constantine;[3] and within the ancient walls of the Thinite fort Shunet ez-Zebib, sacred ibises were buried from the time of Dynasty XXII.

---

[1] Blackman, *JEA*, 27, 83f. (stela in Cairo).   [2] See below, p. 328.
[3] Ammianus Marcellinus, XIX, 12, 3.

X

Thebes, Capital of the Empire

At Qena, 460 miles upstream from Cairo the Nile turns south
again out of its great bend to the east; southwards a broad
fertile stretch of land opens up on the east of the river. This is
the Theban plain. Not too far away in the south, however, an
advance peak of the desert mountains that shimmer violet-
yellow in the morning haze, heralds the approach of new
narrows. Still nearer in the west stands out the broad, rocky,
pyramidal el-Qurn, almost 1,650 feet high, the 'western mountain peak' of the ancients. Like the Dolomites its flank descends
in a precipitous wall into which the rains of thousands of years
have cut ravines devoid of vegetation; in the plain beneath they
meet the magnificent golden-hued desert that is the Land of the
Dead. El-Qurn watches over the City of the Dead at Thebes. Fertile land is rare on that side of the river in that harsh landscape.

Thebes was the capital of the Egyptian Empire. Memphis
was dominated by the pyramids and their mortuary temples and
by the mastabas; it possessed a landscape that stretched into the
far distance. Thebes is a city of temples, the great temples of the
gods on the eastern bank of the river at Karnak and Luxor
(Pls. 17. *a* and *b*) and the royal mortuary temples on the west
bank running from Qurnah in the north to Medinet Habu in
the south where the land begins to rise in the direction of
Armant (the ancient Hermonthis). Even in the outlying temples
like that of Monthu at Medamud, far in the east across the
fields, and that of el-Tôd, south of Luxor, where the desert hills
again come close to the river, there is more still standing than in
the whole municipal areas of Memphis and Heliopolis.

Theban history first reveals itself to us clearly in the bay of
Deir el-Bahari where the rocky cliffs below the western peak are

most precipitous. There Nebhepetrē' Menthuhotpe, the second unifier of the two kingdoms who came from the princely family of nomarchs of Hermonthis, built his mortuary temple about 2040 B.C. It was a building that sought to combine a pyramid as a memorial and a temple built on a terrace partly cut out of the cliff face beneath which at the end of a long passage cut through the rock lay the actual burial chamber far down below the cliffs. The pyramid itself stood in front of the cliff on a terrace surrounded by colonnades, its base being set in the middle of a square pillared hall. The effect produced by this unusual siting of the pyramid was that of a façade to the cliff itself rather than that of a centrally sited superstructure as was the case with the pyramids on the desert plateau near Memphis.

In the sides of the magnificent semi-circle of rocky cliffs which surround the mortuary temple lie the tombs of the courtiers and officials of Nebhepetrē'; they are cave-like chambers deeply cut into the rock face and now approached by ruined causeways like ramps to which arches, long since disappeared, gave access. All these tombs were robbed a number of times in antiquity and many of them were used again as burial places by later generations. One of them, however, still witnesses in a remarkable way to the harshness of the age of the unification of the kingdoms. In it were buried sixty soldiers who, to judge by their wounds, inflicted by arrows or mace-blows, must have been killed in an attack on a fortress. All the tombs dating from this time contained weapons in great numbers, especially bows and quivers full of arrows; they were indispensable for the dead.

Close to the temple of Nebhepetrē' Menthuhotpe another age, the age of the Empire 500 years later, has left a memorial in the mortuary temple of Queen Hatshepsut. It was built for her by her favourite, the architect Senenmut, the guardian of the heiress to the throne, the Princess Neferurē'. He also claimed to have constructed buildings in Karnak, Luxor and Hermonthis, as well as the temple of Mut.[1] At Deir el-Bahari Senenmut built his temple in the form of a terrace with projecting columned halls, but with no pyramid and no burial chamber. Instead he introduced guest-cults in particular those of Amun, King of the Gods, and of Rē' to whom, in accordance with the

---

[1] *Urk.*, IV, 409; the reference to 'the Upper Egyptian Heliopolis' probably applies to activity in Medinet Habu.

Heliopolitan rite, it was customary to offer sacrifices on an altar in the open air at the time of his rising (as the sun) in the east. He also introduced the cults of Anubis, the god of the dead, and of Hathor in the form of a cow, the Queen of the West, who in one place was represented as coming forth from a papyrus thicket and in another as coming from a cave in peculiar conformity with her actual surroundings at Deir el-Bahari. By this time pyramids were no longer built because it had been found that no matter what cunning devices were employed they were no good in protecting the burial chambers from robbers.

Now the royal tomb was concealed in the mountains. This practice was introduced by Enene, the architect of Amenophis I and Tuthmosis I: 'I witnessed the hewing out of the rock-tomb of His Majesty in the solitary place where nobody could look on and where nobody could listen.'[1] A cleft in the rocky heights behind Dira' Abu'n Naga was chosen as the site of the tomb of Amenophis I, while for Tuthmosis I Enene opened up the longest and deepest of rocky gorges which starts at the northern end of the City of the Dead and runs in broad curves with many subsidiary valleys in its upper reaches to a point behind the rocky ridge that forms the bay of Deir el-Bahari (Pl. 20. *a*). This gorge has come to be known as Biban el-Moluk (Gates of the Kings). Up to the time of the last Ramesside kings this remained the royal necropolis. Enene could hardly have known, however, that his careful deliberations were to be fruitless and that the tombs that were concealed with such elaborate caution would be shown to distinguished Greek and Roman visitors as noteworthy sights, 1,500 years later. Today we call the place the Valley of the Kings.

With Enene begins the line of great architects of Dynasty XVIII who could await the judgment of posterity on their achievements with far greater confidence than the architects of the Old Kingdom. The divine royalty of Egypt learned to tolerate personalities and to record their works in so far as they contributed to the royal fame and justified royal confidence. Enene himself reports that His Majesty chose him as architect because he was a man 'of true uprightness, contented heart, ingenious lips and a discreet mouth in speaking of the affairs of the king's house'.[2]

[1] *Urk.*, IV, 57.   [2] *Urk.*, IV, 63.

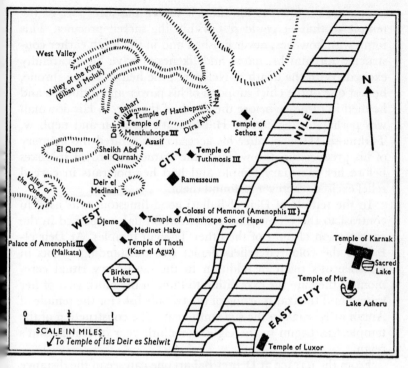

8. The Theban area

Senenmut, the builder of Deir el-Bahari, was one of those men of whose fortune and end we can learn from their tombs. Although of humble origin — this fact can be surmised from the form of the tomb he built his parents — and apparently owing his success to his abilities as an army scribe, he gained the favour of the autocratic Queen Hatshepsut, the daughter of Tuthmosis I and she made him the guardian of the heiress to the throne. At Deir el-Bahari Senenmut perpetuated his memory in the reliefs of the historic crown council which decided on the expedition to Punt; there he is the only named representative of the court with the exception of the leader of the expedition, the chief treasurer, Nehsi.[1] He even dared to have figures of himself carved behind the outer doors of the chapel-shrines, such as the rock-shrine of Hathor, and to have

[1] *Urk.*, IV, 355, 1 = Naville, *Deir el Bahari*, III, pl. 86.

a new rock-tomb cut for himself under the forecourt of the temple so that he could rest within the sacred precinct. This tomb was, however, never finished and in the tomb earlier constructed for him his name and likenesses have been carefully excised. With the death of Neferurē', the heiress to the throne, he lost one of the chief supports of his power and influence and he died in disgrace before the death of the queen. His downfall was perhaps instigated by Hatshepsut's step-son and nephew, Tuthmosis III who, after his accession, execrated the memory of his predecessor, threw down the statues and royal sphinxes before her mortuary temple and had her portraits in carved relief excised wherever he found them.

In the temple of Deir el-Bahari good limestone was used in contrast to the yellow sandstone from Silsilah employed in the construction of most of the other Theban temples. At Deir el-Bahari the coloured reliefs depict two outstanding events in Hatshepsut's reign in addition to the customary ritual ceremonies; they are the expedition to Punt in the ninth year of her reign,[1] and the transporting of the two obelisks for the temple of Amun at Karnak in the sixteenth year. The construction of the temple was begun in the eighth or ninth year of Hatshepsut's reign.

From the terrace at Deir el-Bahari one can see in the distance across the Nile the mighty pylon of the temple of Amun thrusting itself up from among the palm groves of the village of Karnak. Amun was not a local Theban deity in origin, the lord of the nome and its capital was, on the contrary, the god Monthu of Hermonthis who is represented in the guise of a falcon. Consequently the newly built temples of Amun in Karnak were ringed by shrines of Monthu at Hermonthis, at el-Tôd in the other direction, at Medamud and in Karnak itself. Yet Monthu was subordinated to Amun. The name Amun and that of his female counterpart Amunet appear at Thebes at the time of the first Antef kings who fought the Heracleopolitans.[2] He belonged to the circle of eight primeval divinities in Hermopolis who according to Hermopolitan doctrine incorporated the void of chaos before the creation of the world. The name Amun meant 'that which is concealed'. It is clear that by the adoption of this Hermopolitan conception what was being

[1] See above, p. 112.   [2] Sethe, *Amun und die acht Urgötter von Hermopolis.*

17. *a*. Columns and shadows in the Temple of Luxor, 1952.

17. *b*. Air photograph of the Temple of Karnak, 1933.

18. *a*. The West Bank at Thebes during the inundation with the Colossi of Memnon in the distance.

18. *b*. Avenue of sphinxes in front of the Temple of Amen-rē‘ at Karnak.

sought was a Theban counterpart for the ancient doctrines of Memphis and Heliopolis. The attempt made in Hermopolis to identify Monthu as Monthu-Rē' with the sun-god of Heliopolis was not held to be sufficient. As Amen-Rē', however, Amun did indeed make use of this theological bridge and in consequence Heliopolitan beliefs dominated Theban dogma and the Theban festival calendar; thus in the latter the old Heliopolitan division of the festival year into lunar months played a part. Nevertheless Thebes as THE CITY of Egypt had, like Heliopolis and Memphis, to lay claim to primeval origins and produce a primeval god akin to Atum of Heliopolis and Ptah-Tjenen of Memphis. Therefore as Amun in Karnak identified himself with Rē'-Harakhte as Amonrasonther, the King of the Gods, so also Amun in Luxor (Amenappa) identified himself with Tatjenen in Memphis who created the ogdoad of primeval deities, and also with his northern neighbour, the ithyphallic fertility god Min of Coptos. In this way Amun became 'the most primeval of the Two Lands', a 'wondrous god with a many-sided being', into whose teaching all the afore-mentioned deities were received with syncretistic generosity. This teaching was needed as an imperial state religion by the royal family of Dynasty XII, the kings called Ammenemes and Sesostris. They therefore promoted it seemingly in opposition to the policy of the conservative Menthuhotpes of the ancient princely nomarch family who were not prepared to make such a sacrifice for a new imperial concept of the state. Sesostris I, in spite of the fact that like his father he had his Residence at Lisht, was apparently the real inspirer and creator of the temple of Karnak which as a sort of central shrine for the whole country received the expressive name 'counter of the places' (*Ipet-sut*). Perhaps it was Sesostris I or even his father Ammenemes I, with whose name the inscription on a votive altar in the temple ends, who brought as a guest to Karnak Ptah 'south-of-his-wall', the god of the royal residence in the Old Kingdom. Certainly Sesostris I is represented on a polygonal pillar at Karnak as meeting that god. Tuthmosis III subsequently used the wealth derived from his first Syrian campaign to rebuild in stone the special sanctuary of Ptah that lay in the 'district' of Amun and which had been a brick building with wooden pillars.[1] His building still stands to

[1] *Urk.*, IV, 765, 878–9.

the north of the temple of Amun near the great outer wall, but enlarged by late Ptolemaic additions to its front.

Karnak, the temple of the god-king, embodies the history of the Empire (Pl. 17. *b*). The fortunes of its holy of holies, which housed the divine barque and the divine statue, would alone fill a whole volume, for every king was determined that the god should rest in a chapel bearing his name. Any king who was able to do it cleared away his predecessor's building and replaced it with his own, if possible, more beautiful building. This practice was followed especially by the kings of Dynasty XVIII — Amenophis I and Tuthmosis I together, Hatshepsut with Tuthmosis III, Amenophis II and Tuthmosis IV, some of whose unfinished work remains. Today there stands a granite chapel erected by Philip Arrhidaeus (323–317 B.C.) built after the design of a Dynasty XVIII original and probably replacing one such destroyed in the Assyrian or Persian Period.

A happy chance has brought it about that one of the earliest works of the architect Enene known to us has recently become visible. It is a building he erected for Amenophis I for his jubilee, which was completed in the name of Tuthmosis I — a shrine built of alabaster from the famous quarry of Hatnub near Amarna. It has been extracted block by block from the foundations of the Third Pylon of the Karnak temple where in all probability it has lain since it was pulled down to make room for Tuthmosis III's new buildings. Today at Karnak we can admire the low reliefs on this reconstructed monument on which the dedicatory inscription boldly declares: 'Never since the first primeval time of the earth has the like of this been made in the land.'[1] Enene may also have erected the two obelisks of Aswan granite in front of the pylon of Tuthmosis I (the fourth pylon of the western series) of which the one to the south, rising to a height of 65 feet and weighing about 140 tons, still stands as a land-mark in the development of monumental architecture.

It must be remembered that great parts of the buildings of those times were still constructed of wood, as was quite usual in secular buildings. Such was the case with the pillars and ceiling of the narrow pillared hall between the fourth and fifth pylons, both of which were built by Tuthmosis I. Here Hatshepsut had two obelisks erected to mark her jubilee which was celebrated

[1] *Annales du Service*, 24, 57, cf. *Urk.*, IV, 53, 14.

in the fifteenth year of her reign. The whole operation was a
supreme technical achievement; the obelisks were completed in
the quarry near Aswan after seven months' work and were, so
it is said, ready on the 30th day of the month *Khoiak*, the day
before that prescribed by tradition for the celebration of the
sed-festival, in the year 16.[1] The northern obelisk is 97 feet high
and weighs about 323 tons; it still stands as a witness to an
achievement that excelled all such previous achievements. The
southern obelisk, however, is overthrown and broken. When
Tuthmosis III had the whole of the inside of the temple altered
he caused the two tall monuments of his hated predecessor to be
covered in to the height of the roof, thus to be rendered invisible
from within the temple. It is, nevertheless, a remarkable fact
that of all the obelisks that he set up — and with the exception
of Ramesses II he set up more than anyone else — not one still
stands in its original position. The pedestals of two that stood in
front of the two erected by Tuthmosis I can still be seen; two
more were set up after the campaign in the thirty-third year of
his reign in front of his southern pylon (the seventh); a single
obelisk that was perhaps much higher stood midway along the
eastern axis in the rear part of the temple.[2] Four of these witnesses of past glory were carried away in ancient or modern
times to be set up anew in the capitals of the world, from Heliopolis to London and New York and from Karnak to Rome and
Constantinople. Today only two granite pillars decorated
heraldically with the plant emblems of Upper and Lower
Egypt, which probably carried a kiosk-like entablature, still
watch in the name of Tuthmosis III over the entrance to the
holy of holies. Nevertheless the annals inscribed at length on
the walls of the rooms in front of it and beside the granite
sanctuary, the many lists of offerings and the whole rear portion
of the temple (which is called the Festival Temple) bear
sufficient witness to Tuthmosis III and his deeds.

This architecturally remarkable building lies on the other
side of what now seems like an inner court, where the Middle
Kingdom temple stood to which belonged a granite naos of
Sesostris I which was later removed and which was not a
sanctuary for the sacred barque.[3] The central part of the Festival

---

[1] *Urk.*, IV, 367 (obelisk inscription).   [2] See below, p. 325.
[3] Pillet, *Annales du Service*, 23, 143f.

Temple is an hypostyle hall running across the main axis of the temple of Amun, and this the Egyptians called the 'middle building'. Like a basilica it has a central aisle with higher columns, the unique capitals of which imitate the knobs of the old buildings made of wood and reeds. This Festival Hall was a unique architectural construction resembling in the nature of its conception the building which Imhotep had built in stone at Saqqara 1,000 years earlier. The building at Thebes, however, was a ceremonial hall intended to endure for ever, designed to serve the earthly cult of the god Amun, whereas that at Saqqara was a false building designed for the other world. We do not definitely know the purpose of the Festival Hall, but its modern name is justified by many reliefs depicting ceremonies such as the king's *sed*-festival; many of the royal ancestors are also included, either in the form of statues or by name in a list of kings. Here, in adjacent rooms, are commemorated Tuthmosis III's campaigns; there are representations of supposedly Syrian animals and plants which were part of the booty he brought back; they are shown with such artistic fantasy that botanists and zoologists despair of identifying them.[1] A separate shrine with an altar for the worship of Rē'-Harakhte, which resembles that on the upper terrace at Deir el-Bahari,[2] stands on a raised platform in the north-east corner of the temple complex and is reached from the Festival Hall by a flight of steps. In the rear temple, built in Dynasty XVIII, which lies to the east of the main group of buildings, there once stood two obelisks erected by Hatshepsut of which only the pedestals remain.

Already at that time the buildings of the temple of Amun had begun to spread out towards the south in the direction of the sacred lake Asheru with the sanctuary of Mut, the ancient vulture goddess, who was revered as the wife of Amun, and still further south to the second principal Theban sanctuary of Amun a mile and a half away at Luxor. This latter was known as the 'southern harîm' and it was there that the king annually celebrated his union with the divine mother at the great festival of Opet in the second month of the season of inundation which in consequence became known as the month Pa-opet or Paophi, 'the one of Opet'. The procession of the magnificent river-barque of Amun together with those of Mut and the divine child

[1] See above, p. 85.　　　　[2] Kees, *Orientalia*, 18 (1949), 427f.

Khonsu to Luxor for the festival of Opet afforded the chief opportunity for the King of the Gods to proclaim his wishes by miraculous signs. On such an occasion the hostile relatives of Hatshepsut, with her step-son and nephew Tuthmosis who was still a youth,[1] called on the god for signs as to who should be established in the king's place; but the step-mother was the actual ruler and she interpreted similar miraculous signs of the god in her favour. She, as the young widow of Tuthmosis II, while serving as the God's-wife of Amun, had taken the place of the king at the festival of Opet and allowed herself to be crowned before all the people. In this matter one legend confronts another legend or, more precisely, one court faction confronts another court faction. The festival of Opet was therefore a time of great tension and it is easy to understand why in later times when the king no longer resided at Thebes he did his utmost to appear there during the festival.[2]

The high priest directed or interpreted the miraculous signs. He and the king alone could put questions to the god. If a matter of personal policy was at stake the high priest's role became a delicate one that required agreement between himself and the king. The Festival of Opet lasted for many days and was the great festival of the eastern city. Even today the local saint of Luxor, Abu el-Haggag, leaves his mosque in the enclosure of the temple and, seated on a festival barque, goes in procession through the streets as the successor of Amun.

The four southern pylons of the temple of Karnak of which the first two date from the reigns of Hatshepsut and Tuthmosis III (Nos. 7 and 8) mark the ceremonial way leading to the temple of Mut and on to Luxor. Along this processional way there must have been many shrines and little peripteral temples, each surrounded by an ambulatory and with a room for the sacred barque, built out of specially chosen materials. Hatshepsut and Tuthmosis III built a large number of them of which one with an alabaster room for the barque still stands in a ruined condition close to the sacred lake. Others, especially those built close to the west front of the temple in the Tuthmoside Period, were in the way when the temple was enlarged. They

---

[1] *Urk.*, IV, 157.

[2] So expressly by Horemheb, see above, p. 104; for Ramesses II, see above, p. 248.

were dismantled and used to form the foundations of Amenophis III's pylon (No. 3) by which chance their remains have been preserved for posterity.

Amenophis III built in many places. He had additions made to the temple of Mut and erected buildings in the enclosure of Monthu, north of the temple of Amun, where he built a small temple in honour of the goddess Ma'at who embodied the idea of right in the universal order and was often invoked in the Amarna Age.[1] Amenophis III was the first to lay out rows of ram-headed sphinxes along the processional ways in Karnak (Pl. 18. *b*) and he erected many statues of the lion-goddess Sekhmet, the syncretic counterpart of Mut, in the enclosure of the latter. In Karnak and Luxor, however, a new and bolder architectural conception was to find its realization. At Karnak it did not in fact come to its full fruition and the form in which it was subsequently realized by the Ramesside kings is not at first easily understood. At Luxor, however, it can quite clearly be recognized in that most homogeneous of all the Theban temples. There is a large court each side of which has a double row of papyrus cluster columns (Pl. 17. *a*), the front side not being closed by a pylon but provided with a ceremonial doorway. In front of this doorway is a row of seven pairs of papyrus columns with open capitals which, when properly covered by some light roofing materials, formed a superb processional way for god and king alike. This plan nevertheless also fell short of complete realization although the building of the temple must have been carried out in the early years of Amenophis III's reign; for he had the legend of his own divine birth as the son of Amun by Queen Mutemuia represented on its walls just as Hatshepsut had done at Deir el-Bahari. The despotic king subsequently denied such legitimist behaviour. The temple at Luxor is perhaps the work of Amenhotpe son of Hapu, a native of Athribis in the Delta, who, as a scribe of recruits directed public works. He died shortly after the king's *sed*-festival in the thirtieth year of his reign.[2] Nevertheless, the hypostyle halls of the temple of Luxor mark the ultimate achievement of the feeling for symmetry shown by the builders of Dynasty XVIII. It can still be sensed today in spite of the fact that the coloured brilliance of the original decoration has

[1] Varille, *Karnak*, I.   [2] H. W. Helck, *Militärführer*, 3f.

now given way to the monotonous basic colour of the sandstone from Gebel el-Silsilah.

Under Amenophis III the tendency to build on a colossal scale emerged. It already showed itself in the decoration of the new west pylon at Karnak (No. 3) which had eight flag-poles compared with the four that stood before the pylon of Tuthmosis I; it was also seen in the pillars of the temple of Luxor which were 50 feet high. In the Hypostyle Hall at Karnak the 75 feet high central pillars correspond even more closely with this conception of largeness. The plan of the latter may even have been engineered by Amenophis III; but the names of later kings testify that the task was not completed by him. The mortuary temple of the king in western Thebes, which was to exceed all earlier temples in size, also remained unfinished, for the last years of the king's reign were overshadowed by illness and by political crises abroad in Syria. All that now remains to testify to his architectural achievement in western Thebes are a few ruins and the two royal figures known as the Colossi of Memnon (Pl. 18. *a*), which can be numbered among the wonders of the world without taking into consideration the natural marvel of the northernmost of the pair which used to emit a sound at sunrise.[1] They were originally about 68 feet high and were carved out of that famous quartz from the quarry in the Red Mountain near Heliopolis, the stone that was known to the Egyptians as the 'magic stone' and which was chosen in preference by the kings of Dynasty XVIII for their sarcophagi. The transport of the colossi, which far exceeded in weight the 323 tons of Hatshepsut's obelisks, for more than 435 miles upstream, and their erection were carried out by the same scribe of recruits of the labour gangs, Amenhotpe, son of Hapu.[2] It is these two colossi and two others which stand before the tenth pylon at Karnak reaching a height of 78 feet, that clearly reveal the character of this monarch. Obelisks of Aswan granite were the supreme achievement of the preceding age. Amenophis III, instead of erecting obelisks, placed statues of his own divinity before the temple, and in Nubia had temples dedicated to himself and his queen.

[1] Kees' articles 'Memnon' and 'Memnoneia' in Pauly-Wissowa, *Real-Encyclopädie.*
[2] Varille, *Annales du Service*, 33, 85f., cf. above, p. 168.

We can probably distinguish the person who directed the making of the colossi in a certain chief craftsman Men, who was apparently a Heliopolitan and had himself described on a memorial stela at Aswan in front of a seated statue of Amenophis III as 'Chief Sculptor of the Great Monument of the King in that Red Mountain'.[1] Next to the mortuary temple in the West City the king also had a new quarter laid out which was to contain the royal palace and the government buildings. The palace was situated to the south of Medinet Habu in the direction of Armant at a place known today as Malkata and close to it was the ornamental lake (known today as Birket Habu) which he had constructed for Queen Tiy. This palace, in the cellars of which were found wine-jar sealings from the thirtieth and thirty-fourth years of his reign, must have exhibited many modern features about which we learn more in the domestic buildings of Amarna. Most noteworthy is the introduction of painted floors after the manner of those characteristic of Mycenean civilization. The painted figure of a bound Asiatic which certainly came from the throne-room or audience-hall, where the king could thus tread on his defeated enemy, displays a rather clumsy, not exactly naturalistic, but yet quite realistic style of painting in bright colours.

The forecourts of the Theban temples at this time were already filled with innumerable honorific statues which trusted courtiers and officials were permitted to set up as marks of the royal pleasure; those of Senenmut are some of the best known early examples. Such statues often represent these officials wearing the gold of honour or other special marks of distinction such as the double heart which Sennufer, the Mayor of Thebes under Amenophis II, wears on his breast to signify that he was in possession of the king's heart.[2] Statues of Amenhotpe, son of Hapu, were also set up at Karnak, apparently near the pylon of Amenophis III, at the feet of the colossal statue of his sovereign. In his case is revealed an unusual feature of an age which had a tendency to excess: the inscriptions on his statue offer to visitors to the temple his mediation and advocacy as though he were a saint in the forecourt of the god.[3] Moreover the

[1] Von Bissing, Sb. bayr. Akad., 1914, 3, pl. I, 1 =de Morgan, Catalogue des Monuments, I, 140, nr. 174.   [2] Cairo 42126.
[3] Helck, op. cit., 12, on the statues published Annales du Service, 14, 17f.

honours rendered to Amenhotpe on his death, which occurred apparently shortly after his sovereign's *sed*-festival in the thirtieth year of his reign, exceeded the bounds of all previous funeral celebrations. The king had a mortuary temple erected for him close to his own mortuary temple[1] and thus elevated him to divine honours in the company of the kings. And in fact the wise Amenhotpe, son of Hapu, did take his place among the heroes and his name perhaps lives on unrecognized and distorted in the name of the neighbouring temple of Medinet Habu.

The life of Minmose, the Royal Scribe and Chief Architect in the temples of Upper and Lower Egypt in the reigns of Tuthmosis III and Amenophis II, may serve as a typical example of a successful career suitably honoured with royal rewards. We possess honorific statues of him from the temples of Karnak, Medamud and Imet in the north-eastern Delta and a commemorative inscription in the limestone quarries at Masara, south of Cairo.[2] He erected buildings throughout the whole land but especially in Lower Egypt from Memphis to Buto and the 'Island of Amun' (Punamun) in the northern Delta; and even too in the sanctuary of Hathor at Byblos. He gives us a typical example of the Egyptian method of giving rewards: 'I was given in the temples in which I worked the offices of prophet and *web*-priest.' He explicitly mentions some of these temples, such as the temple of Letopolis and that of Bastet, Mistress of Ankhtawy, in Memphis, in which he was actually the high priest. Moreover, because of his title Count and Overseer of prophets of Monthu, Lord of Thebes, he was certainly curator of the temples at Medamud where one of his statues stands and where today one can still see door pillars bearing the name of Amenophis II. When one realizes that Minmose was one of the military scribes who achieved greatness through their participation in the Syrian campaigns of Tuthmosis III, his investment with priestly offices must appear to be singularly lacking in religious feeling. The Egyptians, however, unlike the Christians, did not regard secular and religious actions as being necessarily opposed to

---

[1] Robichon and Varille, *Le Temple du scribe royal Amenhotep.*

[2] *Fouilles de Medamoud* (1926), Drioton, *Les Inscriptions*, p. 52f.; Cairo 638; fragment in the Ashmolean Museum, Oxford; L. D., Text, I, 20 = *Annales du Service*, 11, 258.

each other. On the contrary they looked on both as being divinely inspired and performed in the service of the gods; they were in fact complementary. The architects and sculptors who built chapels and carved statues of the gods ('caused them to live', as the Egyptians said) were far more important than the priests who attended to the daily services and in that duty 'opened the mouths' of the statues to receive the offerings of the worshippers. Architects, sculptors and priests were all servants of the gods. Transfers from service to the king to service for a temple were quite regular happenings often brought about in practice by considerations of old age and maintenance. In the long run it proved advantageous that the great temples, especially the state temple at Karnak, inasmuch as they were the greatest employers of labour and were in consequence vast administrative organizations, should constitute themselves the training places for civil servants; and this arrangement worked provided that no opposition developed between royal service and service for the gods, as did in fact develop at Thebes from the reign of Tuthmosis IV onwards. It could not, however, have been easy for an individual to avoid hurt to himself and his career because of this twofold idea of service. A look at the tombs of the royal favourites sufficiently demonstrates the truth of this supposition. Alongside a few fortunate individuals like Amenhotpe, son of Hapu, there is to be found a multitude of men who, like Senenmut, fell into disgrace. Particularly numerous among them are administrative officials of all kinds, and the closer we advance towards the reform effected by Akhenaten the more obvious this symptom of crisis becomes. Of all the highly placed men at the Court of Amenophis III during the last decade of his reign hardly a single one seems to have come to a peaceful end. Even the tomb of his brother-in-law, Ineni who, as Second Prophet of Amun, officiated in the inner sanctuary of Rē'-Harakhte at Karnak with the title of High Priest of Heliopolis, is so badly destroyed that it proved hardly possible to identify it.[1] Religious tension in this case played a part no less considerable than the personal malice of an ailing monarch who became more and more self-willed with the passage of years.

Another noteworthy feature in the general picture of

[1] Theban Tomb, nr. 120 (after Davies).

Dynasty XVIII and its times is the small number of decorated rock-tombs dating from the reigns of Ahmose, Amenophis I, Tuthmosis I and Hatshepsut, all of whom reigned at the beginning of the Dynasty.[1] Although many of the tombs in the most immediately favoured areas, particularly to the west of the Ramesseum, were certainly destroyed to make way for later buildings, the number seems to have begun to increase to a significant degree only under Tuthmosis III when the rocky heights of Sheik Abd' el-Qurnah in the centre of the City of the Dead was so tunnelled with tombs that it resembled a honeycomb. This sudden increase had certain parallels in the Old Kingdom. Up to the reigns of Chephren and Myccrinus the number of private persons buried in the royal cemeteries was likewise very small; it was only under Dynasty V that for the first time it rose above that of members of the royal family; under Dynasty VI it reached its greatest height. There was, nevertheless, a profound difference between the two periods. In the Old Kingdom the claims of a middle class centred on the Court could only be satisfied at the expense of the royal power. Yet the royal power, when exercised in accordance with the idea of the delegation of the royal prerogative, forfeited more and more of its authority along with the broadening of the classes participating in its exercise; for the means at the king's disposal in later times were scarcely greater than those that had been available to Cheops and Chephren.

The case was otherwise under Dynasty XVIII. Then the civil service and the corps of temple-employees visibly expanded in response to an age of great achievements in foreign policy as a result of which Egypt had expanded to become an imperial power with an empire extending from the Euphrates to Napata in Nubia. Tribute from foreign peoples was beginning to flow into its coffers. Those who had participated by work or fighting in these conquests participated also in the wealth that resulted from them. The immense public works made possible by the new wealth called for an enlargement of the administrative machinery for state and temple affairs alike. This expansion was particularly necessary in financial administration, the control of taxation and the direction of public works. It is particularly noticeable in the reign of Amenophis II to what a

[1] Cf. the chronological list in Steindorff and Wolf, *Thebanische Gräberwelt*.

great extent the men who enjoyed the king's personal confidence even when they were of lowly origin and not in all cases
the sons of distinguished men, played a dominant role in the
circle of royal favourites.[1] The royal favourites came from the
ranks of the children of the harîm who grew up with the royal
children, from the sons of the royal nurses, from the husbands
of these nurses or of former inmates of the harîm and from the
children of such people. The determining factor in their choice
was not social background or hereditary rights but a relationship of personal confidence. Former wartime comrades of the
king's youthful days, often recognizable through the title royal
steward, headed the list for appointments to high offices of
state, especially to the responsible posts of the administration of
estates. In this respect they were the successors of Senenmut of
the time of Hatshepsut, who had risen from a similar stratum of
life.

Under Tuthmosis IV the military scribes who were civil servants rather than officers in the modern sense of the term,
gained the upper hand in spite of the fact that political activity
in Asia had died away to give place to a diplomatic game of
tortuous negotiations for alliances and treaties. The personal
rule of a temperamental oriental despot naturally favoured
surprising careers, promotions and equally abrupt falls from
favour; at the same time it came into conflict with forces press-
ing for an ordered system of government based on tradition and
the right of succession which was more in accord with the
Egyptian character. There can therefore be little cause for
wonder that the pasha-like temperament, devoid of all sense of
proportion, of a king like Amenophis III, provoked a crisis. His
visionary son Akhenaten by means of his self-willed policy in
religious matters gave a revolutionary character to this conflict
over tradition, personal rule and the principle of the hereditability of office, instead of confining it within reasonable bounds.

Let us remain for a while in the Theban City of the Dead.
The greater part of the population of Thebes probably always
resided on the west bank of the river. The East City, surrounding
the great temples of Karnak and Luxor, was really a city of official
buildings and civil servants, including those people employed

[1] Examples in Helck, *Militärführer*.

in the harbour on the Nile which then, as now, was situated at Luxor. The West City belonged to the domain of Amun. All the mortuary temples, therefore, lay within the 'House of Amun' and Amun was Lord there beside the king. Amun of Karnak annually visited these places in the second month of summer at the time of the Festival of the Valley, named after the rocky bay of Deir el-Bahari where the ancient mortuary temple of Menthuhotpe was situated. Consequently the name given to this month in the Theban calendar was Payni which means 'that of the Valley'. This festival was the great annual event for the Necropolis-workmen and the tomb-diggers who, having organized themselves into religious guilds, possessed the right to take part in the accompanying religious services, walking in the procession, sprinkling water and furnishing singers for the choirs. Apart from these secondary cults that steadily increased in number in the royal mortuary temples, Amun had another peculiarly holy place on the west bank, 'his really sacred place of the beginning of things'.[1] In the southern part of the West City, in the place where Amenophis III later built his palace-quarter, was the shrine of Medinet Habu. It had been begun by Hatshepsut and Tuthmosis III enlarged it.[2] It was the place where Amun's divine ancestors were said to rest. Amun of Luxor who, according to doctrinal teaching, was the very image of Tatjenen, the primeval god of Memphis, visited the shrine every ten years and brought funerary gifts for his previous forms, in particular for a primeval snake known to antiquity under the name Kneph, who rested in a sort of tomb 'in the underworld of Djeme'. During these visits the barque of Amun was laid down in a special room surrounded by a colonnade in the forepart of the temple. Amun thus united the East and the West Cities. In Thebes he was indeed so greatly revered as the Lord of the Dead that in contrast to other places there was no room for Osiris up to the time of the Late Period. Medinet Habu or Djeme, as it was called, perhaps harboured the incorporeal symbol of Amun which, like the *omphalos*, represented the primeval hill. Here the miraculous god of multifarious nature, displayed his most mysterious aspect.

[1] *Urk.*, IV, 881, 11.
[2] Hölscher, *Excavations at Medinet Habu*, II (*The Temples of the Eighteenth Dynasty*).

Cities and Districts

The pylon of Amenophis III in Karnak which today acts as the rear wall of the great hypostyle hall, has most unusually revealed itself as the preserver of even more ancient monuments. Included in its core as filling was a *peripteros* of the time of Sesostris I which is not exactly a sanctuary but rather a shrine for a processional way like those built by Hatshepsut and Tuthmosis III. It witnesses to the vigorous art of the Middle Kingdom. It was erected for the celebration of the king's *sed*-festival in the thirtieth year of his reign. On the surrounding walls and on the pillars the king had inscribed lists of the Egyptian nomes with important details of their capital cities, cults, areas and the varying high water levels for the Nile. After the disastrous collapse of some of the pillars of the hypostyle hall in October 1899, extensive work was undertaken to strengthen the hall and the pylon, in the course of which several important dismantled buildings have been removed from the pylon, including this shrine, the alabaster shrine of Enene to which reference has already been made and Hatshepsut's magnificent red chapel with its inscriptions that report the miraculous judgments of the god, and also the remains of various processional shrines and rooms for sacred barques.

The Amarna Period left in Thebes only traces of its destructiveness, such as when, in the name of the true religion, fine reliefs were damaged and statuary destroyed. The erasures of names which mark Tuthmosis III's vengeful pursuit of the memory of Hatshepsut were supplemented by the far more savage devastations of the fanatical worshippers of the Aten whose beliefs, apart from their un-Egyptian intolerance, did not contain much that was new. Long ago Hatshepsut had said of herself in Karnak: 'I am the Aten who created all being, who shaped the earth, who completed its creation.' Nothing, moreover, remains standing of the sanctuary named 'Horizon of Aten' which Akhenaten had built to the east of the temple of Amun at the time of his premature *sed*-festival. The reliefs were taken away, broken up as rubble for the new buildings of the period of restoration, in particular for the pylon of Horemheb; some went to Luxor. Among these fragments are Osiris pillars with the king's figure in grotesque caricature — a distorted 'truth' that had degenerated to abnormality.[1]

[1] *Annales du Service*, 27, 31; Schäfer-Andrae[3], 346.

Thebes, Capital of the Empire

When Akhenaten left Thebes for Amarna he bid farewell to the necropolis by perpetrating the barbarous mutilation of reliefs which were fine examples of the supreme artistic elegance of the preceding age. Attempts to introduce the current religious beliefs into the new artistic style as exemplified in the tomb of the vizir Ramose, remained rare and they too ended with the break-down of the old Theban society. Tutankhamun, the young son-in-law of the heretic Akhenaten, returned undoubtedly to Thebes fourteen years later under the protection of Ay, the Inspector of Chariot-troops. His first Opet Festival was in effect the signal for the return to tradition and it was perpetuated in a long series of reliefs in the entrance hall in the temple of Luxor which had been provisionally made ready for the festival.[1] Nevertheless, in spite of the re-establishing of the statues of the gods and the public condemnation of Akhenaten as the 'Criminal of Akhetaten', old Thebes did not return. The Regent and Commander-in-chief Horemheb undoubtedly came to Thebes from Memphis after the death of Ay to have himself publicly recognized by Amun as king and to be crowned; but the seat of government was no longer Thebes because reasons of foreign policy demanded that it should be situated in the north of the country. The king came to the Opet Festival — Horemheb expressly states that he did so every year — and stayed in the new-style palaces which, since Ay's time, were built near the king's mortuary temple; but it was as a corpse only that the king ultimately came home. For another three hundred years the kings were still buried in Biban el-Moluk.

The vizir at Thebes was the king's representative in his absence and in such circumstances the high priests of Amun became increasingly independent. Furthermore Amun was no longer the state deity *par excellence*, as he had been under Dynasty XVIII. He now shared that position with Rē'-Harakhte of Heliopolis and Ptah of Memphis, together forming a triad of deities which was established to prevent a recurrence of the Amun-crisis. Horemheb ordered that a long edict that he had dictated to his scribe should be carved on the west side of the extreme south pylon of Karnak (No. 10) as a perpetual reminder of the sins of the past and in order that 'cases of robbing in this land' should be punished with severe penalties. His principal

[1] W. Wolf, *Das schöne Fest von Opet.*

271

aim was the defence of the citizens against oppression, extortion and excessive requisitioning.[1] It is quite clear what were the results of the removal of the governing-classes and their replacement by upstarts of doubtful character.

Horemheb took up the work on the temple of Amun that had previously been abandoned. He completed two pylons (Nos. 9 and 10) on the processional way to the temple of Mut and on the western axis he raised another (No. 2) in front of the pylon of Amenophis III which produces an architectural effect quite different from that achieved in the Luxor temple, discussed earlier. At Karnak the processional way which passes through two rows of tall papyrus-capital columns, is framed for the whole width of the pylon by lateral hypostyle halls. This architectural innovation, however, resulted in the space involved being rendered useless to contain the crowds which at times of festival had access to the forecourt of the temple, and it necessitated, therefore, the construction of a new forecourt in front of the outermost pylon (No. 2). It is impossible to determine to what extent Amenophis III's architects had previously worked on the plans for the hypostyle hall. Its actual construction was the work of Sethos I and Ramesses II. The lateral halls accordingly do not have the beautifully formed papyrus-cluster columns of Dynasty XVIII (Pl. 17. *a*) but only schematic truncated columns with simplified capitals in which the original plant models are hardly recognizable. They carry many kinds of non-natural decoration in the form of inscriptions and representations. This forest of columns at Karnak with its 134 shafts is a wonder of the world; but its oppressive confined character, which blocks every side vista with a mass of stone, denies it the airier beauty of the forecourt of the temple of Luxor with its four rows of columns.

The royal architects now began to place large battle-scenes on the outer walls of temple buildings. Sethos I started with the north wall of the hypostyle hall, depicting chariot fights, skirmishes, storming of towns, endless lines of captives following behind the chariot of the victorious homecoming monarch, all scenes which in their principal details were evolved out of the older hunting scenes. A new form of annals in the shape of great scenes devised for outward effect now takes the place of and

[1] See above, pp. 78, 90, 104.

19. *a.* Shattered colossus of Ramesses II in the Ramesseum.

19. *b.* Necropolis workers' village in Western Thebes at Deir el Medinah, 1937.

contrasts with the sober chronological inscriptions and endowment lists of Tuthmosis III. These scenes were intended not
merely to record historical events but also, inasmuch as they
recorded the typical actions of the victorious theocratic kingdom, to exercise an apotropaic influence, to ward off disaster
from gods and king alike. The position of the scenes was chosen
to accord with this principle.

Ramesses II inherited Amenophis III's love of the colossal
and of the effect of mass. In his case, however, it degenerated
into a sacrifice of quality and taste. In spite of the innumerable
sculptures set up by this most ardent of all Egyptian temple
restorers, whose name is known to every donkey-boy, there are
few among them that can rank with masterpieces like the seated
statue in the Turin Museum; those that may be so ranked can
certainly be dated to the early years of his reign. Mass production subsequently led to a lowering of the standard of
artistic achievement; and no king before or since Ramesses II
has shown himself so unscrupulous in clearing away older
buildings and in appropriating statues by placing his own name
on them. The colossus is, nevertheless, a true creation of his
mind. Remains of such lie at Memphis and Tanis, four such
giants are hewn out of the living rock on the façade of the Nubian
rock-temple at Abu Simbel; and in the first court of the Ramesseum at Thebes he set up a statue of Aswan granite 56 feet high
which is only a little smaller than the colossi of Memnon. Its
original weight has been estimated at about 1,000 tons which is
three times the weight of one of Hatshepsut's obelisks at Karnak.
Today it is overturned and broken in pieces like most of the
colossi (Pl. 19. *a*). These colossi were certainly outstanding technical achievements and their transport and erection called for
great organizational skill. The custom of obscuring façades with
colossi reaching as high as the house-tops was, however, from
an artistic point of view, a misuse of the human figure which
would have been completely disapproved of and avoided by the
ancient master craftsmen who undoubtedly took into their calculation the effect of size.

The tendency to megalomania found expression in the vain-
glorious boasting about the battle of Qadesh against the Hittites in the fifth year of Ramesses II's reign, a victory of a very
dubious nature; in countless battle-scenes and inscriptions on

temple walls and pylons the story is told and retold. Yet some recognition must, from a human standpoint, be accorded the personal bravery shown by the young king who hurled himself into the midst of the battle that had been lost from the outset by tactical mistakes. Furthermore the deification of the king's person, which was mainly current in military circles and the foreign provinces, especially Nubia, was copied by Ramesses II from the example of Amenophis III.[1] Again, the proliferation of public enterprises must have resulted in an overworked and greatly inflated administration. Royal scribes became the governing class which very soon became vastly increased in numbers. Yet fewer men of outstanding character and ability came to the fore than had been the case in Dynasty XVIII. The powerful rule of the few was replaced by a levelled-down civilization which was accompanied by a far-reaching division of power.

When the Court left Thebes the West City there rose to prominence over the East City. The mortuary temples of the kings, extending in a line from that of Sethos I at Qurnah by way of the Ramesseum to that of Ramesses III at Medinet Habu, grew into centres of economic activity which received the largest shares of the royal donations and particularly of prisoners who were sent to work on the temple estates. The wealth of Amun benefited them accordingly, but only indirectly. It was at this time that the first 'God's Wife' known to history, Ahmes-Nefertari, together with her son Amenophis I, achieved importance as the patron saints of the City of the Dead. Their cult spread out from their funerary temple beneath the rocky heights of Dira' Abu'n Naga, at the northern end of the necropolis. The guilds of the state-craftsmen who dwelt in a settlement in a valley behind Deir el-Medinah, right beneath the western spur of the Qurn mountain, were particularly devoted to this cult. Mountain paths led from their settlement directly over the mountain to the Valley of the Kings where the labour corps worked on the royal tombs. The god of the western peak was said to live in a cavern on the height in the form of a snake. The workmen's settlement, which resembled a camp in the regularity of its plan, contained seventy small houses (Pl. 19. *b*) and in style was a descendant of the Pyramid Cities of the Old

---

[1] See above, p. 201.

and Middle Kingdoms (as at Kahun) and, of more recent date,
of the workers' suburb in the eastern quarter of Amarna.[1] We
know the names of the stone-masons and painters, their squad
commanders and foremen, from the nearby graves and the
numerous commemorative stelae on which are inscribed prayers
inspired by a naïve piety to the minor local deities — the snake
on the mountain, the western peak itself; in cases of illness or
personal distress, a cat or a swallow might be invoked; and
there also occur expressions of gratitude for deliverance from
such misfortunes.[2]

Life was undoubtedly rough in this labour corps. Squad commanders abused their powers and leased out the labour under
their command to make money for themselves. They also
employed the men on tasks for their own private benefit such as
the construction of their own tombs.[3] Such happenings are not
unknown in the East where only the most outrageous cases
attract attention and result in criminal proceedings. An exact
record was indeed kept of the work itself whereas the obligation
to work was interpreted very loosely. Idleness was widespread
and found its justification in very obvious excuses.

The administration was housed in offices in the mortuary
temples. Ramesses III's temple in particular developed into an
administrative centre for the West City and here were to be
found the offices of many central authorities including the
Courts of Justice and sometimes the bureau of the Vizir of Upper
Egypt. The West City had its own mayor and its own police
force mainly recruited from foreign mercenaries under the
command of the Chief of the Medjay. This force had been in
existence as early as Dynasty XVIII. 'The House of Millions
of Years' of Ramesses III, next to the ancient sanctuary of Amun
at Medinet Habu, was the largest of all the mortuary temples.
Architecturally it is a model temple in the uniformity of its lay-
out, like the very stately building in front of the Ramesside west
pylon at Karnak (Pl. 17. *b*),[4] which was intended to serve as a
wayside shrine for the barque of Amun. It lacks originality,

---

[1] Bruyère, *Fouilles de l'Institut français*, vol. 16.

[2] Erman, *Sb. Berl. Akad.*, 1911, nr. 49.

[3] Kees, *Kulturgeschichte*, 169, and the literature quoted there.

[4] Complete survey in the Oriental Institute of Chicago Publications,
Vols. 25, 35.

however; in its heavy Osiride pillars and the truncated shafts of its columns, as at Karnak (where the defect is emphasized by badly shaped capitals), it reveals a grave lack of proportion. Original architectural features are to be found in the residential palace at the side of the first court at Medinet Habu where the king gave audience at the ceremonial window and rewarded favourites.[1] The 'Walls of Djeme' were also unusual; these were strong walls of sun-dried brick which surrounded the whole temple area. They were pierced on the east and west sides by lofty fortified gateways built of stone. At a little distance beyond this wall was another lower defensive wall which protected the temple precinct from surprise attacks; it gave the whole ensemble the appearance of a citadel.[2] These walls of Djeme which are frequently mentioned in contemporary documents, gave their name to the whole West City and an echo of it was preserved by the Greeks in their name 'Thebes'. In documents concerning the West City the temple itself is simply called 'The House'. The lists of offerings which fill the greater part of the south wall of the temple[3] together with the statements in the Great Harris Papyrus, reveal that Medinet Habu surpassed all older temples in the receipt of donations. Of 86,486 slaves which Ramesses III donated to all Theban temples, Medinet Habu alone received 62,626; its share in landed possessions and natural produce was correspondingly great. It was the older temples, particularly the mortuary temples of earlier kings which were placed at a disadvantage inasmuch as it was they that bore directly or indirectly the burden of the new endowments.[4] For, since Ramesses II in his twenty-first year (1269 B.C.) had concluded a treaty of perpetual peace and friendship with the Hittite king by which it was finally recognized that the State of Amurru in northern Syria belonged to the Hittite sphere of influence, no Egyptian victory was ever again to be achieved on Syrian soil. Moreover, Egypt's direct possessions were restricted to a few island-like zones by the appearance of the seafaring peoples who included the Philistines. Consequently Ramesses III in the Twelfth Century B.C. had hardly any newly

[1] U. Hölscher, *The Excavations at Medinet Habu*, III, 37f., pls. 3–4; and *ÄZ*, 67, 43f.

[2] Hölscher, *op. cit.*, vol. I.

[3] H. H. Nelson, *Medinet Habu*, III.   [4] See above, p. 66.

won possession to give away apart from prisoners of war who were mostly Libyan in origin. The walling-in of the granaries and administrative buildings of this new foundation at Medinet Habu shows, however, that they were not regarded as safe, despite the sanctity of the place. The danger lay in the breakdown or depletion of the state economy. Documents tells us that in the twenty-ninth year of Ramesses III (about 1169 B.C.) the state labour corps often received its rations only after great delay and that this led to demonstrations of protest.[1] On the 10th day of the month Mechir the disgruntled workers crossed the five walls of the Valley of the Kings and declared: 'We have been hungry for 18 days in this month.' They took up a position of protest at the rear of the temple of Tuthmosis III to the north of the Ramesseum; but when nothing happened they advanced as far as the door of the Ramesseum and thus came dangerously near the citadel of Medinet Habu. Yet the tone of their complaints seems remarkably humble: 'We have come here by reason of hunger and thirst; we have no clothes, we have no ointment, we have no fish, we have no vegetables. Send (word) to Pharaoh, our good lord, and write to the vizir, our superior, in order that the means of living be provided for us.' Only then did they receive their monthly rations. Still we witness similar demonstrations in the following months and again they are given advance supplies against the rations due to them. The vizir and the mayor of the East City eventually had to come to the rescue. Nevertheless no lasting settlement was reached and the threat was produced that they would lay their complaints before the High Priest of Amun. Undoubtedly the cumbersome system of requisitioning and distribution broke down by reason of unprofitable economic undertakings combined with favouritism and oriental carelessness; too many profiteers and falling production prevented better results.

Barely three years after these events the king fell victim to a harîm conspiracy. Less than half a century later we become aware of more menacing signs of an approaching storm. In the sixteenth year of the reign of Ramesses IX (about 1122 B.C.), investigations were set on foot into the plundering of the tombs of the kings, following an accusation made to the vizir by the

[1] Gardiner, *Ramesside Administrative Documents*, p. 48f. = Papyrus Turin, 42–48; Edgerton, *JNES*, 10.

mayor of the East City against his inefficient colleague in the West City.[1] Although this incident formally closed with a farcical verdict which openly acquitted the principal defendants, the enquiry was never abandoned because the deplorable state of affairs in the City of the Dead could no longer be kept a secret. Now began the removal of the royal mummies from the plundered tombs and finally in Dynasty XXI the rulers, who combined the offices of king and high priest, found it no longer possible to assure their safety in the Valley of the Kings. Some, it is true, were deposited in the tomb of Amenophis II, but a larger number found a resting place in the ancient tomb of Queen Inhapi in a side-valley south of Deir el-Bahari.[2] A supervisory commission had in the meanwhile taken measures to ensure that the mummies should be superficially restored and wrapped in fresh bandages. The mummies then remained undisturbed in this tomb until 1870 when the modern descendants of the ancient tomb-robbers discovered the famous hiding place. In 1881 after years of joint plundering, mutual quarrels led to the betraying of the existence of this hiding place. In the years when the royal tombs had been plundered in antiquity nobody had bothered about the robbery of ordinary tombs. Want and greed had transformed the labour corps which built and made safe the royal tombs into their most skilful plunderers.

Another source of danger revealed itself in the existence of 'foreigners' in the country. Under the Ramesside kings men of various racial origins found themselves holding high offices of trust at court, often with no clearly defined sphere of activity, with the title of Royal Steward. They were in effect the equivalent of Roman freedmen and they were employed in preference by the king for special tasks, by no means to the pleasure of the Egyptian civil servants. Furthermore, the State was clearly no longer able to maintain order among the numerous foreigners scattered throughout the country, partly in garrisons like the Libyans in the fortress of Gebelein, south of Thebes, partly in prisoner settlements on temple estates or domains. We infer this state of affairs from the cautious testimony of records and from entries in the journals of the labour corps during the reigns of Ramesses IX to Ramesses XI (about 1138 to 1081

[1] Peet, *The Great Tomb Robberies.*
[2] Winlock, *JEA*, 17, 107.

B.C.).[1] A little evidence is enough: the foreigners who were occasionally called more explicitly Libyans or Meshwesh, were the terror of the West City and especially so of the humble people. If foreigners were about the labour corps stopped working 'on account of the foreigners' (it happened thus in the third year of the reign of Ramesses X). Everyone stayed at home waiting for acts of terrorism and there were in fact many public complaints about plundering, spoliation of temples and other similar acts, sometimes even involving murder. In some cases these acts were certainly committed in the course of regular troop movements; sometimes they were undoubtedly committed by riot squads sent to intimidate rebellious elements in the West City which were beyond the control of the local police. The regular troops exercised their rights of requisitioning in the manner so strongly condemned by Horemheb and it is probable that the riot squads exercised them even more severely.

Want threatened from both sides. We learn about it from the rapidly rising grain prices in the Theban market in the last years of the Ramesside Period.[2] Years afterwards at the time called the 'Rebirth' people recalled the miseries of the famine 'in the years of the hyenas when famine reigned';[3] they were the conditions that had already existed at a time of political disunity at the beginning of Dynasty XI.

The high priest of Amun stood out as the only firm figure in a time of disintegration. When Ramesses II had first attended the Festival of Opet at Karnak he had appointed Nebunenef, a former high priest at Denderah, to the vacant office of high priest of Amun, as the direct choice of the god himself. Since that time there had evolved in respect of the person of the highest-ranking ecclesiastical official in Egypt a certain continuity which favoured the preservation of the office within the same circle and even in the same family.[4] This tendency can be clearly observed in the reigns of Ramesses II and his successors in the persons of the high priests Bekenkhons and Rome. The high priest's successor was always one who had risen gradually to the

---

[1] Botti and Peet, *Il giornale della necropoli di Tebe* (Turin, 1928); cf. Kees, 'Herihor und die Aufrichtung des thebanischen Gottesstaates' in *Gött. Nachr.* (1936), p. 6 for details.

[2] See above, p. 76.   [3] Peet, *JEA*, 12, 258 (Turin fragment).

[4] Lefebvre, *Histoire des Grands Prêtres d'Amon* (1928).

highest office from the lower priestly ranks in the same temple. This tradition was probably lost in the anarchy that prevailed at the close of Dynasty XIX; but only about forty or fifty years later, after the deaths of Ramesses III and his successors had followed in swift succession, there arose in Karnak a new dynastic family which held, in addition to the high priest's office, the subordinate offices of the prophets and of the chief steward of Amun; it thus secured firmly within its grasp the administration of the temple property. This family derived from the circle that in the Ramesside Period had produced a line of royal scribes. Meribastet, the father of Ramessesnakhte, the first high priest from this family, was, during the reign of Ramesses III, the chief steward in Hermopolis in Middle Egypt; a son of Ramessesnakhte served Ramesses V as chief steward and chief tax officer.[1] We also meet people of this senior official class as the principal usufructuaries of the state. When we remember that the high priest and his chief steward commanded an army of slaves (from the beginning of Dynasty XIX the high priest also bore the title General of Amun) and that this force was at their disposal not only for public works but also as a militia in times of need, it is not difficult to understand how this power in the Theban area eventually stood on an equal footing with that of the weak sovereign in Tanis. It is also understandable that with the increase of poverty in the country and the irregular issue of rations to the labour corps and mercenaries, discontent and anger eventually vented themselves upon the temples with their overflowing storehouses. The most significant act of the time, however, happened under Ramesses XI when Amenhotpe, the second son of Ramessesnakhte was high priest; then the disturbances developed into open revolt against the formerly sacred person of the high priest. It was probably at this time that the west door of the temple-fortress of Medinet Habu was destroyed. It signified an insurrection against the highest local authority in Thebes and, as in the Amarna Period, nothing remained except to call in the last regular force in the country, the army, commanded then by Panehsi, the Viceroy of Kush. His troops were composed for the most part of Nubian and Libyan mercenaries — the foreigners so much dreaded in Thebes. We hear in these years of a 'rebel-

[1] See above, p. 68.

lion in the northern part (of the country)', that is, outside the Thebaid, which he was compelled to put down. Hartai (modern es-Sheikh Fadl), the capital of the 17th nome in Middle Egypt, was captured and plundered in the course of this operation,[1] in which many Thebans, and among them no less than 15 of those involved in the investigations into the plundering of the royal tombs, lost their lives.[2] They had probably been forced into the service. At the end of nine months Panehsi's foreign troops had also apparently suppressed the rising in Thebes.[3] During the restoration of order the high priest Amenhotpe and his relatives disappeared and, about 1085 B.C., a *novus homo*, Herihor, appeared as the new high priest, coming probably from the entourage of the viceroy. As high priest he became a new supreme ruler, but his power derived from his position as commander-in-chief of the army in Upper Egypt. In the future no other form of government could be contemplated for the 'Divine State' of Thebes. During the lifetime of the last of the Ramesses, and probably in the nineteenth year of his reign (for there is proof that his tomb in the Valley of the Kings was still being constructed in his seventeenth and eighteenth years), Herihor proclaimed the age of 'Rebirth', a renaissance of the divine order. Once again the god had to cover up for the legitimacy that was lacking and once again a 'miracle' happened at the Opet Festival. In a solemn oracular utterance the god assented to and confirmed the proposals of the high-priestly autocrat who had in the meanwhile assumed the secular office of vizir and also, probably after the death of Panehsi, that of Viceroy of Kush which assured for him valuable military support.

Herihor commemorated this event on the walls of the temple of Khonsu whose cult as a god of healing and a worker of miracles had steadily increased during the Ramesside Period. In his form, known as 'Khonsu-in-Thebes-Neferhotpe' he had become more popular than Amun, the King of the Gods. From the time of Ramesses III virtually all building activity had been lavished on the temple of Khonsu which was situated close to

---

[1] British Museum Papyrus, 10052, 10, 18f., in Peet, *Great Tomb Robberies*, pl. 31.

[2] Mayer Papyrus A, 13; B, 3 (edited, Peet); cf. Kees, *Herihor*, 8.

[3] Mayer Papyrus A, 6, 6f.

the *temenos* of the Amun Temple on the processional way leading
to Luxor (Pl. 17. *b*). Herihor allowed it to be completed in the
name of Ramesses XI but hereafter this shadowy king disappeared from the pages of history, his tomb in the Valley of
the Kings remained unfinished and Herihor became king in his
stead. He was the first monarch to unite in one person the
secular and religious dignities and thereby he solved the ancient
problem of the influence exercised by the kings upon the high
priests by means of a return, as it were, to the state of affairs that
had existed in the far off early days of Egyptian history. King
and priest were once more the same person and thus the former
unity was re-established.

Nevertheless the real significance of this union had changed.
The office of high priest of Amun now became in practice that
held by the heir to the throne. By the same manner of thinking
the highest offices of state such as those of vizir and overseer of
the Treasury were from now on concealed under the guise of
priestly offices in the temple administration and behind priestly
titles. State property and temple property again appear to be
united and it seems that this unusual mixed form of political
development had proved to be the only solution possible. Yet
violent shocks still occurred in spite of the fact that the House of
Smendes in Tanis had established for the Lower Egyptian half
of the realm a similar theocracy of Amun and soon allied itself
by marriage with the House of Herihor.[1] Time and again the
god was called upon to act as the ultimate authority. Scarcely
fifty years after Herihor's death, when the high priest at Karnak
was Masaharta (who, to judge by his mummy, was a little stout
man), son of King Pinodjem and grandson of Herihor, there
arose a struggle for mastery at Karnak between two parties.
Supporters of the opposition were relieved of their offices and
banished to the Oasis of Khargah. Still the god had formally to
approve the judgment. Subsequent serious disturbances forced
the crown-prince Menkheperrē' who bore the same compelling
name as the great Tuthmosis III, to go from his headquarters at
el-Hibah in Middle Egypt to Thebes where, as the new high
priest, he had to arrange for the offending measures to be formally withdrawn by an utterance of the god expressly to that end.[2]

[1] See above, p. 203.

[2] Louvre stela, C.256; Brugsch, *Reise nach der grossen Oasen El Chargeh*, pl. 22.

The god, therefore, was not infallible. Yet, these very internal disorders of the kind that had originally brought Herihor to the leadership of the Theban theocracy, supported with the help of the arms of foreign troops, now brought about a new change of government a century after his death. Libyan chiefs ruling in Heracleopolis secured the mastery over the whole of Egypt and once again when Amun announced his wishes by means of miraculous signs the army was there, outwardly as spectators, but in fact the impressive background to the event, showing where the power actually lay. From this time, in Egyptian popular speech, the word for 'crowd', even when referring to the people at a festival, was the same as the word for 'army'. The Libyans still continued to make use of the theocratic form of government for ruling the country, but they inclined quite openly to a feudal rather than to a centralized system.

Thebes was never again a city of royal residence. The Libyan kings even had themselves buried at Tanis. Thebes, however, remained an ecclesiastical principality outwardly enjoying all the privileges of a free state, but in fact existing as the domain of the younger son of the Libyan rulers and the headquarters of the commander-in-chief of Upper Egypt. This age saw few new buildings though the courts of the temples were populated anew with the honorific statues of members of successful Theban families. Such men as 'Eyes of the King' carried out simultaneously the duties of ecclesiastical and royal offices and all were clad, in accordance with the ideas of the period, in the robes of the priests of Amun. At their head stood the high priest who was usually the son of the Libyan ruler. The higher offices were confined to a few families by heredity and these families married into each other and into the royal family. Not a few members of such families were honoured by marriage with Libyan princesses. Thus there developed a feudal system of government in the country in which the Thebaid formed the largest individual unit. Once again political use was made of the office of 'God's wife of Amun' which, during Dynasty XVIII, had been held by future queens, among them women like Ahmes Nefertari and Hatshepsut, so that the heir to the throne should be born the legitimate son of Amun.[1] Now it be-

---

[1] Sander-Hansen, *Das Gottesweib des Amun*.

came a feudal institution which shaped the appearance of the theocratic state more powerfully than the holder of the office of high priest at any given moment, in so far as its holder was the local representative and protector of the interests of the ruling dynasty. On the stelae of the god's wives appear the names of members of the ruling dynasty, first of Libyan, then of Ethiopian princesses and finally of the daughters of the Saite kings from Lower Egypt. Marriage with the king, however, once the key-factor in the institution, was discontinued after the assumption of power by the Ethiopian kings. Their orthodoxy abhorred the idea of the god's wife becoming the actual physical possession of the god.

Sumptuous tombs now once again made their appearance in the City of the Dead which rival in size the royal tombs, or even surpass them as is the case with the relatively late tomb of the Chief Lector Priest Pedamenopet of which the subterranean part covers some 2,435 square feet. These tombs are huge underground buildings with hypostyle halls and passages adorned with inscriptions while above ground strong brick pylons give entry into broad courts. They lie in the hollow of the valley below Deir el-Bahari, called the Asasîf, and they belong chiefly to members of the households of the god's wives — chamberlains, chief-stewards of the major-domo category who recall the feudal age of the Middle Kingdom with their resounding titles such as 'Overseer of Upper Egypt, Count and Ruler of the Deserts, Overseer of the Door of the Foreign Lands'. It says much that their tombs far excel the smaller and architecturally unimportant mortuary chapels of the contemporary god's wives which are situated in the temple area of Medinet Habu.

The Theban 'Renaissance' which began with the arrival of the Ethiopians in the Eighth Century B.C. can be studied in the tombs of these men such as Pebes and Aba, and also in the statues of the Governor of Thebes, Menthuemhet, who served the Ethiopian kings and survived the Assyrian invasion and the assumption of power by the Saite kings in 663 B.C. This renaissance was prompted by the attitude of the Ethiopians who held themselves the orthodox revivers of the theocratic state. They looked on the period of Dynasty XVIII as the ideal age in Theban history and they modelled their own memorials on those of that age. The reliefs in the tomb of Pebes could almost be taken as being of the same period as those in the tomb of Khaemhet which were executed in the reign of Amenophis III. The people of the later age certainly studied the reliefs of Dynasty XVIII and in the tomb of Aba they copied the inscriptions in the temple of Deir el-Bahari. The statues of Menthuemhet, however, which were placed in the temples of Amun and Mut in Karnak, derived their artistic inspiration from those representing old people dating from the Middle Kingdom. The style of the Ramesside period which finds an echo in the sculptures of Bubastis was abandoned; it was an abandonment based consciously on the rejection of the policy of imperialism that had in the final result proved itself to be a failure. Moreover, Menthuemhet, whose statues represent a new peak of achievement in plastic art, was also the last great lord from a Theban family, an Egyptian too, not foreign-born as he has unjustly been described because he and his ancestors were supporters of the Ethiopians. Nevertheless his last wife was an Ethiopian princess.

The kings of the Saite Dynasty that followed looked on the theocratic state of Thebes as nothing more than a province in their realm, and with them comes to an end the history told by the buildings of Thebes. It is impossible to tell who ordered the vast work of clearing away the hundreds of statues from the forecourts and from before the pylons of Karnak and the throwing of them into a vast pit in the north-east corner of the court to the north of the seventh pylon of Tuthmosis III, where they were covered with earth. It contained, nevertheless, statues, including those of kings, down to the end of the Late Period (Dynasty XXX); their being deposited there may have been a work of rescue in a time of desperation. To it, at all events, we owe the greatest find of statuary in the whole history of Egyptian excavation; it was made in 1903 by G. Legrain whose name will for ever be associated with it.

In the Ptolemaic Period the first task to be undertaken was the restoration of the sanctuaries that had been destroyed, doubtlessly in the Persian Period. Thus the room of the barque of Amun at Karnak was restored in the time of Philip Arrhidaeus, while that in the temple of Luxor was restored by Alexander the Great. New buildings, however, were restricted to a few monumental doorways as in the temple of Amun and in the temples of Monthu and Khonsu, to some additions to the front of the ancient temple at Medinet Habu and to small shrines for popular cults such as the small and tasteful temple at Deir el-Medinah in West Thebes which Ptolemy Philopator dedicated to Hathor and Ma'at and the sanctuary of Opet who, in the guise of a pregnant hippopotamus was the protectress of women, built near the temple of Khonsu in Karnak. The new west pylon at Karnak (No. 1), however, on which a start had been made, remained unfinished and political disturbances which had found support in Thebes constantly from the Second Century B.C., caused the later Ptolemies to favour Armant at the expense of Thebes, its neighbour. Large parts of the West City were included in the administrative jurisdiction of Armant, in particular the central area of the Memnoneia from the walls of Djeme to the Ramesseum.[1] The last Theban temples were thus erected on the soil of Armant — the small unfinished sanctuary of Thoth at Kasr el-Aguz, south of Medinet Habu, that dates from Ptolemaic times and the temple of Isis at Deir es-Shelwit, built under Hadrian and the Antonines.

At the beginning of the Roman Period Thebes had become the ancient city to which the sights attracted famous visitors including emperors and proconsuls. Among the sights were the 'Tomb of Osymandias' (the Ramesseum), the singing statues of Memnon and the *syringes* (pipes or corridors) which was the name by which the royal tombs, plundered and lying open, were known. Otherwise the Upper Thebaid served as a place of banishment for exiles or proscribed persons such as Juvenal; it consequently came into the same category as the Libyan oases and other frontier districts. Thus far had the capital of the Empire sunk. Whatever remained of official life collected round the ancient temple of Luxor near the harbour on the east bank of the Nile (Pl. 17. *a*).

In the Holy of Holies at Deir el-Bahari in the West City there continued to exist up to late antiquity a cult of the deified Imhotep and of Amenhotpe as healing deities. The upper terrace of the ancient mortuary temple became a 'sanatorium' for miraculous cures.[2] The walled district of Djeme, the Castron

---

[1] Kees' articles 'Memnon', 'Memnoneia' in Pauly-Wissowa, *Real-Encyclopädie*.

[2] Milne, *JEA.* 1, 96f.

as it was called, later became the centre of a Christian settlement and Christian basilicas were set up in the courts and halls of Medinet Habu, as happened also at Luxor. The buildings of the last surviving native cults were occupied by monasteries, the existence of which is indicated by ruined brick walls standing here and there. The numerous place-names beginning with Deir (monastery) especially testify to their former existences; there are Deir el-Bahari (the Northern Monastery), Deir el-Medinah, Deir el-Bakhit on the hill above Dira' Abu'n Naga and many others less well known.

XI

El-Amarna — the Horizon of Aten

The steep slope of the Arabian desert that marches close to the east bank of the Nile throughout Middle Egypt (Pl. 1. *a*) leaves the river in a curve south of the hilly necropolis of Sheikh Sa'id in the slopes of which the nomarchs of the 15th Upper Egyptian nome (Hermopolite) found their resting places in the time of the Old Kingdom. Here an open area is left between the desert and the river extending about seven miles to the south where it is closed by the rocky barrier of the Gebel Abu Feda. This stretch of land has become famous under the incorrect name of Tell el-Amarna, as the home of the sun-worshipping King Akhenaten. Vegetation grows only on a strip of land along the river bank averaging about one-half a mile in width, while the broad semi-circle behind rises up in stony undulating slopes to meet the even stonier downward slope of the desert. A few *wadis* run down from the desert into this bay and their courses extend to the land on the river's edge.[1] The ancient architects built without a thought on this land much threatened by waters in spate rushing down the *wadis*; storms have since washed away all remains of their buildings.

The river affords the only easy way of reaching this area and on the other side there lies a stretch of cultivated land extending to a depth of twelve miles through which the Bahr Yusuf canal flows. The less fertile land on the east bank was settled in the early Eighteenth Century by Arabs of the Beni Amran tribe who built four villages, el-Till in the north and el-Hag Qandil, el-Amariah and el-Hawata in the south — an excellent example of the infiltration into the Nile valley from primeval times by nomadic peoples who then eventually became peasants. The

[1] Timme, *Tell el-Amarna vor der deutschen Ausgrabung.*

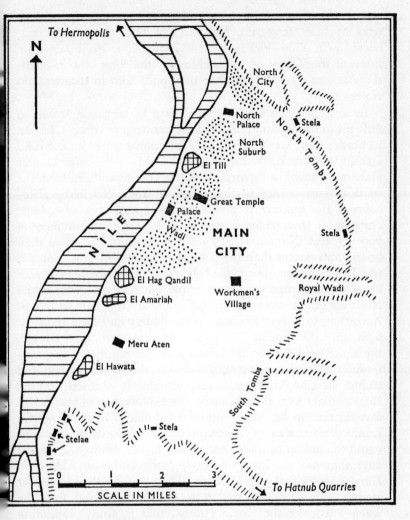

9. Akhetaten, the City of Akhenaten

local *fellaheen* instinctively feared this immigrant population because of its origin. Tribal feuds were secretly carried on until very recent times. Blood feuds between the neighbouring villages of el-Till and el-Hag Qandil even interfered with the modern excavations and endangered the finds. It seems almost as if the ominous fate that overshadowed the beginning and the end of the City of the Aten still brings disaster upon those who lay bare its secrets. The name of Amarna is closely connected with discoveries more astonishing than any apart from those of the Tomb of Tutankhamun, the king who brought the Amarna Period to a close unhappily also in disaster and violence.

In ancient times this restricted area of land which was so difficult to reach, could hardly have known any villages, but on its border there was a supply base for quarry workers. The road leading to Hatnub — 'the House of Gold' — the most famous alabaster quarry in Egypt, started into the mountains from the south-eastern corner of the plain. In 1891 Newberry rediscovered the quarry. It presented the appearance of a huge crater more than 98 feet deep and with a cross measurement of 200–325 feet. Numerous tiny stone huts, more like caves than houses and poorer than the poorest herdsman's hut in Europe, standing by the road or on the heights, witnessed to the miserable lot of the workmen who were employed there and who in the New Kingdom were mostly prisoners of war and convicts. According to inscriptions there,[1] the quarry had been in use at least since the time of Cheops and from it came, for example, the stone used for the splendid statues set up in the funerary temple of Mycerinus and also, probably, the alabaster floors and facings in Chephren's mortuary temple. In the feudal First Intermediate Period the quarry, the exploitation of which was a royal monopoly, came within the domains of the powerful princely nomarchs of Hermopolis whose wordy inscriptions vaunt the philanthropic deeds of their family during the critical days that saw the struggle between the House of Akhtoy in Heracleopolis and the Thebans. They praised themselves for having preserved their city 'on the day of plundering, from the worst terrors of the Royal House', that is, from plundering troops. A gigantic alabaster statue, 13 cubits high, was carved for the lower funerary chapel of Djehutihotpe, a nomarch of Hermopolis who was buried in the reign of Sesostris III in a rock-tomb at el-Bershah, five miles to the north of the plain of Amarna. It was transported the very considerable distance from the quarry across the plain on a sledge dragged by men, a noteworthy achievement for the Middle Kingdom. The in-

[1] Anthes, *Die Felseninschriften von Hatnub.*

scription in his tomb can be believed when it says: 'The way along which they went was hard beyond all belief.'[1]

We can also believe the words of Akhenaten on the boundary stela when he says that he built his new capital on virgin land and had ascertained that this place 'belonged to no god and to no goddess, also not to any lord or any mistress, and no other person has the right to tread upon it as the owner'.

As early as the time of Lepsius who had drawings made in the tombs near Amarna, Egyptologists realized that the flat-topped hill between el-Till and el-Hag Qandil concealed the royal city 'Horizon of Aten'. Unmistakable testimony to this fact was provided by the inscriptions in the numerous tombs on the edge of the plain to the north and the south, and in particular the king's boundary stelae placed around the site. At that time, however, ruins of brick houses with no visible remains of stone buildings, exercised little attraction. The brick remains were therefore abandoned to the *sebbakheen* who used the dried mud from the ruins as valuable fertilizing material which they scattered over their fields. Yet, as so often happens, a chance discovery drew the attention of the world to the place and made the name of Amarna synonymous with a period in the history of the world. *Sebbakh*-diggers unexpectedly came upon a palace quarter south of el-Till where they found in a building hundreds of clay tablets covered with cuneiform writing which they then proceeded to dispose of to the dealers in antiquities who, from the autumn of 1887 onwards placed them on the market. The majority was acquired by the Berlin Museum for the reason that the importance of these tablets had been recognized by German Egyptologists at a time when the rest of the learned world questioned their authenticity. How did these cuneiform texts come to be in Egypt?

What had in fact been found was part of the correspondence between the Egyptian king and powerful Asiatic princes and Syrian vassals. When the documents had been translated a lively picture full of dramatic events was revealed of the international situation in the last decades of the reign of Amenophis III, during the chaotic period of Akhenaten's reign and down to the reigns of his sons-in-law Smenkhkarē' and Tutankhamun. Before the discovery of these documents the events of those years

[1] Newberry, *El Bersheh*, I, pl. 15.

had been only imperfectly understood; now it became possible to watch the diplomatic game in all its intricacies and so to understand what really happened in the years that witnessed the threat to the Asiatic possessions of Egypt from the advance of the Hittites in the north and the migrations of peoples from Transjordan in the south. It was the very isolation of Amarna that enabled Egyptologists to get this unexpected glimpse into a lost world. The immediate consequence of the discovery was that in the winter of 1891–2 Flinders Petrie excavated the site of the find without, however, finding more tablets. The principal result of his labours was the uncovering of a number of painted floors.[1]

Petrie's methods of excavation were, nevertheless, unsuitable for the peculiarly difficult conditions of the site and, as no sensational results were forthcoming, further exploration was not encouraged there. In the years that followed, apart from a few sporadic attempts at excavation, the only substantial work at Amarna was the copying in full of the inscriptions in the tombs and on the boundary stelae by N. de Garis Davies. Then in 1907 the German Oriental Society decided, on the suggestion of Ludwig Borchardt, to begin a large-scale excavation of the area covered by the city. It was now realized that there was a possibility that by a singular chance the city had not been built over and that it might therefore be possible to obtain a picture of a capital city and seat of government in the Fourteenth Century B.C. in all its details. Akhetaten might turn out to be the Egyptian Pompeii.

The excavations were started in 1907 and they resulted not only in the clearing of a large area of the ancient city but also, in the years 1912 and 1913, in the discovery of several sculptors' workshops, in particular the storeroom of models belonging to a certain Djehutmose and, above all, of the greatest find of sculpture made on Egyptian soil. This was the painted bust of the beautiful Queen Nefertiti which has become the most discussed piece of Egyptian portraiture. Even the golden glory of the Tomb of Tutankhamun which was discovered in 1922 only occasionally has rivalled it in fascination.[2]

Unhappily disaster overshadowed success. At the beginning

---

[1] Petrie, *Tell el Amarna.*
[2] L. Borchardt, *Porträts der Königin Nofretete.*

of 1912 men from el-Hag Qandil, out to revenge themselves on the men of el-Till who had been appointed watchmen on the site, hacked to pieces the best preserved of the floors found by Petrie which had perhaps decorated a pillared hall in the royal harîm.[1] The political consequence of the first Great War deprived German Egyptologists of their concession at Amarna and ruined the possibility of the systematic completion of their excavations. The German excavation plan therefore remained uncompleted. In 1920 the Egypt Exploration Society secured the concession and worked at Amarna until 1936, partly continuing the German excavations in the 'Main City' and partly working in other districts especially in the palace quarter near the principal temple and in the area to the north of the city. The excavations were careful but had very varied results.[2] The great destruction in the administrative quarter of the city presented even the most modern excavation methods with an extremely difficult and thankless task. Yet, notwithstanding these difficulties so much material was collected that the period between 1400 B.C. and 1350 B.C. is today one of the best known of Egyptian history, not only in respect of the historical events but also for domestic architecture, religious thought, general culture and pictorial art. The more exactly we are able to visualize the period, however, the more complicated become its human problems.

The stelae with which the king marked out the city's boundaries on all sides give the official version of the founding of the new capital, Akhetaten (which means 'Horizon of Aten') in the sixth year of the king's reign.[3] The king desired to build a town for his father Aten on the east bank of the Nile in 'the place that he shut in for himself with mountains and in its midst set a plain that I might there make offerings to him'. He rejected the advice given to him to abandon the building of the city there and to build it at another place. On the contrary, he would build there a sanctuary for the Aten and other places for his worship; the king's palace should also stand there and the palace of the queen; the tombs for his family should be constructed in the mountains to the east of the city and also those for the priests of the Aten

---

[1] Cf. the plan in Pendlebury, *The City of Akhenaten*, III, pl. 13a.

[2] Peet, Frankfort and others, *The City of Akhenaten*, I–III.

[3] Text in Davies, *The Rock Tombs of el Amarna*, V, and Maj Sandman, *Texts from the time of Akhenaten*.

and for the officers of the king's household. Akhenaten indicated in a part of the inscription that is unhappily irretrievably damaged, the reason why he abandoned the former capital. It was something terrible that he had been forced to listen to in past years, something even more terrible than that which his father Amenophis III and even his grandfather Tuthmosis IV had been forced to listen to. We can attempt to reconstruct the true circumstances only from events in Thebes.

Akhenaten, the son of Amenophis III and Tiy, was known as Amenophis IV in the first years of his reign when he was co-regent with his sick father. He continued, as had been surmised by many scholars, to carry out his father's policy on broad lines, but at the time of his coronation he had himself proclaimed High Priest of Rē'-Harakhte, thereby basing his spiritual authority on a peculiarly Theban cult and disregarding the claims of Amun as King of the Gods. In the fifth, or at the beginning of the sixth, year of his reign Amenophis IV celebrated his jubilee or *sed*-festival, prematurely, erecting in his own name a sun sanctuary on the Heliopolitan model for Rē'-Harakhte to the east of the temple of Amun at Karnak. It must have been at this time that his religious policy led to an open break with the priests of Amun and with the Theban tradition. The sculptures in the sanctuary, especially the statues of the king, reveal a sudden change to a mannered style which the king desired in the name of 'truth'.[1] The name of Aten and a new representation of the god as the sun-disc whose rays shine down beneficently, took the place of the old Heliopolitan form of the falcon-headed Rē'-Harakhte. With equal suddenness the king changed his name from Amenophis to the symbolical Akhenaten which means 'It pleases the Aten'. Similarly the old names were quickly altered in the new Aten temple at Karnak, as in the reliefs commemorating the king's *sed*-festival. Hitherto Karnak could have been spoken of as the Upper Egyptian Heliopolis and, in accordance with the Heliopolitan tradition, the holy of holies of the new sanctuary of the sun as the 'Obelisk House'. Leading men of the old regime like the vizir Ramose sought to accommodate themselves to the new style in art; Anen, the brother of Queen Tiy, still possibly officiated as Second Prophet of Amun and simultaneously as a special priest in the sanctuary of the rising sun-god

[1] Preliminary account in *Annales du Service*, 26, 121f.; 27, 143f.

in Karnak. Such was, however, a feature of times of transition and it could not heal the breach.

Already on the fourth or thirteenth day of the fourth month of the winter season in the sixth year of his reign, the king as Akhenaten had issued a proclamation from Amarna in which he announced the founding of the city of Akhetaten as a residence for his god, the Aten, the creator of all things 'who decides the destiny (of all persons and all things)' and for the Aten's son Akhenaten who alone knew the Aten's intentions. In the eighth year of his reign he repeated on the city's boundary stelae the solemn oath that he would never cross the established boundaries. From an oath made to establish the irrevocable nature of his decision to build a new capital a solemn vow now had been made that he would never again leave the city, not even as a corpse. It was clearly a revolt against the Theban tradition that the king now led with an all-consuming ruthlessness that did not stop at the closing of temples, the confiscation of their vast estates, particularly those of the temples of Amun. It was at the same time a retreat into splendid isolation.

The isolation of the town was in fact complete. From the reliefs in the Amarna tombs we see that the whole municipal area was guarded by strong detachments of mercenaries among whom were strikingly large numbers of foreigners, Nubians and Asiatics; barriers were erected and when members of the royal family went out driving in chariots they were invariably accompanied by running military escorts.[1] The whole countryside around Amarna as far as the top of the desert slopes was crossed by patrol tracks still distinguishable today, from which it was possible to observe any approach to the area. A large tract of the deep belt of fertile land on the west bank of the river was included in the metropolitan area; thus the northern boundary stela stands not far from Tunah el-Gebel, the necropolis of Hermopolis in Ptolemaic times. The inclusion of such a large area was an economic necessity; it was required for the provisioning of the capital, and we shall see shortly that the aristocratic country houses built there were like farms and, as such, were self-supporting.

The new city was quickly built and the terrain determined its lay-out with several principal streets running parallel to the

[1] Davies, *op. cit.*, IV, pl. 22.

bank of the Nile. The mounds with remains therefore lie mostly along the edge of the cultivated district. The area containing the temple and the palace occupied a space about half a mile square near the village of el-Till and the royal palace itself was mainly situated in what today is fertile land close to the river-bank. The main residential district of the town ran southwards for about one and a half miles, almost as far as the village of el-Hag Qandil. The villas of the officials and the priests here stood about in widely separated groups while the side-streets were filled with the small houses of the middle class, of servants in the houses of the rich, of business men and tradesmen. Its character in general was more that of a sprawling provincial town in-habited by prosperous gentleman-farmers than of an ancient oriental city in which houses were crowded together for mutual protection. Here nature had taken over the protection of the town and the few ways leading to it were easy to guard. Summer palaces and country houses for members of the royal family sprang up outside the central quarter of the city while to the east and the north of el-Till quite large suburbs were developed in the last years of building activity. The settlements for the working-classes, especially the camp-like villages for the stone-masons and other workers in the necropolis in the eastern part of the plain, were sited away from the city. The sculptors' studios, of which something more will be said later on, were, on the other hand, situated in the main streets of the residential quarter. The greater part of the main street, which runs east-wards across what is today desert, was cleared by the German and English excavators working between 1911 and 1922.[1] The Germans called it the Street of the High Priest because they found on it the house of the high priest of the Aten. It was possible to ascertain the names of the owners of many of the elegant houses from the inscriptions on the stone door-frames which were fashionable at Akhetaten. Most of them lie in the centre of the city. To the south we find the villa of Nakhte (numbered K.50.1, according to the grid system used by the excavators) who was the new vizir and as such the most im-portant official in the capital. Then there is the house of Pawah (O.49.1), the high priest already mentioned, whose title was 'Greatest of Seers of the Aten in the House of Rē"", and that of

[1] H. Ricke, *Der Grundriss des Amarna-Wohnhauses*, pls. 1–2.

an overseer of cattle of the temple of Aten (Q.46.1). The overseer of cattle was always a rich man because the herds of cattle
formed a large part of the temple wealth. This fact is confirmed
by a very well-equipped house close to the south-east corner of
the great temple of the Aten (T.41), which belonged to Panehsi,
the First Servant of the Aten in the Domain of the Aten in
Akhetaten, and, at the same time, Overseer of Storehouses and
Overseer of the Cattle of the Aten. Among military men we
meet the Enroller of recruits, Ramose, whose pretentious villa
is also in the centre of the city (P.47.19) and whose tomb is also
known; and also Ranufer, the Chief Charioteer of His Majesty
and Overseer of the Horses in all the stables, who belonged to
the inner circle of the king and whose house is now numbered
N.49.18. Architects were also appropriately represented by
Manakhtef, the Overseer of Bricklayers in Akhetaten, an 'assistant who was taught by His Majesty (himself)', whose house is
M.47.3; and by Hatiay, the Chief Architect, whose house is in
the northern suburb (T.34.1). Yet among them we can find
scarcely a single member of an old Theban family or any supporter of the old regime surviving from the time of Amenophis
III and Tiy. Even the vizir Ramose who in Thebes had
associated himself at once with the revolution, is missing. Perhaps Ipy, the royal steward in Memphis whose father had
certainly been Chief Steward of the King in Memphis under
Amenophis III, also held an office at Akhetaten and had a
tomb constructed for himself there.[1]

We meet for the most part a new class of courtier who hoped
to gain advancement and riches in return for obedience to the
king's personal teaching; this is quite frankly admitted in their
tombs. What is remarkable for the entourage of a religious re-
former is that in its ranks was scarcely a single ecclesiastic; there
were, however, many soldiers both retired and in active service,
stewards, chamberlains, royal scribes and architects. Foreigners
too found a place there, such as Tutu, the Syrian chamberlain,
who as First Prophet of the Divine King and 'Mouth of the
Whole Land' exercised apparently a pernicious influence over
the king;[2] he consequently plays an equivocal part in the cunei-

---

[1] Door lintel, Berlin 21597; Davies, *op. cit.*, IV, 19f. On the person, see
Helck, *Militärführer*, 47f.

[2] Ranke, *ÄZ*, 56, 69; for the tomb, Davies, *op. cit.*, VI.

form correspondence with the Asiatic vassal princes. These courtiers often prided themselves on their humble origins, for such was then the fashion, whereas formerly it had been customary to draw attention to the offices and families of one's father and mother. Now he who paraded his aristocratic genealogy in the bustle of the tradition-free court of Amarna was certainly looked on as a suspicious reactionary. Such people therefore most certainly remained silent about their antecedents.

The fashionable house was so arranged that in its ordering and appointments it would have satisfied even modern requirements (Pl. 22. *b*). The front part of the house was occupied by a transverse hall with a roof carried on wooden pillars and, when possible, facing north.[1] Here visitors and petitioners gathered. As is customary in the east it was not entered from the front but in a discreet fashion from the side, usually through an anteroom which was reached by a short, open flight of stairs. There were adjacent rooms for the servants and the doorkeeper. In the centre of the house behind the front hall was the owner's reception room which was often of noble proportions. It was loftier than the adjacent rooms and received both air and light through windows placed high up directly under the ceiling level, the ceiling being carried, according to the owner's wealth, on from one to four pillars. The height of the ordinary rooms was normally 9 feet and of the central reception room 13 feet, which for southern conditions seems rather low. In the rear wall of the reception room was a blind niche artistically set, and in front of it was a raised step for the chairs of the owner and his wife, provided at the side with a stone basin for ablutions before meals. In these rooms in houses occupied by officials a family altar approached by steps and holding a representation of the royal family that could be shut from view by wooden shutters completed the furnishing. Custom of the time required the recognition of the omnipresence of the king to whom the owner owed his office and wealth. 'One lives, one is in health, when one sees him', say the fanatical texts, when his subjects kiss the earth at his feet in fawning humility. The divine grace directly manifested itself in the daily life of the royal family.

[1] L. Borchardt, *Zeitschrift füt Bauwesen*, 66 (1916), pts. 10–11; Ricke, *op. cit*. The house here reconstructed, numbered T.36, 11, from the northern district of Amarna, is after *JEA*, 19, pl. 4.

Behind the reception room was the bedroom, recognized as such by the raised alcove for the bed, and, adjoining it a bathroom with basins and running water and a lavatory. No house, no matter how humble, was without these hygienic arrangements. The rear part of the house was occupied by the women's rooms with similar appointments. Many houses of well-to-do people had upper stories with loggias facing north where the household could enjoy the cool breeze of the north wind and where they could also sleep in the open as is the custom in the south during the hot season. The square reception room was frequently decorated with murals painted on stucco in the manner of the period consisting mostly of brightly coloured garlands of flowers, occasionally with figures executed in the lively style that had been introduced into Egypt and the Near East from Crete. The wooden pillars in the form of plants, especially of palm-trunks, were sometimes overlaid with coloured plaster and, in the royal palace, even with gilded plaster.[1]

Each house also had its kitchen and other offices set apart from the living quarters, with storage bins for grain, bakers' ovens, poultry houses and stalls for cattle which were stall-fed. Above all there was a garden (Pl. 22. b). Gardening had always been the diversion of the cultured classes from very ancient times. In an age which eagerly studied Nature's creative activities no trouble was spared to make fruitful the desert soil on which most of the houses were built. Holes were dug and filled with earth from the inundated areas and plants were grown in them, wells were sunk deep and spiral stairs led down to the water. There were also ornamental ponds the surfaces of which were made gay with nymph-like maidens and nearby would stand a frivolous kiosk which probably housed a statue of the king, which thus was placed in the midst of natural surroundings; for the creative life of the Aten revealed itself in his divine son and the holy family.

The royal family's love of nature has left its mark on the palace and its environs. The so-called Northern Palace had an aviary and a zoo and its walls were decorated with hastily executed but lively paintings of bird-life in a papyrus swamp.[2] The summer-house of Meru-Aten to the south near el-Hawata

[1] Petrie, *Tell el Amarna*, pl. 6; Peet, *City of Akhenaten*, I, pl. 40.
[2] Frankfort, *Mural Paintings of el 'Amarneh*.

had halls with decorative pools and painted floors on which animals and plant life in the bush was again vividly depicted by the use of a rhythmic gouache technique which was really in no sense naturalistic.[1] These natural motifs, placed as they are beside the representations of rows of bound prisoners in the centre of the floor on which the king trod, produce an effect derived from two different worlds. On the one hand there was the delicate rococo of a world of make-believe and on the other the quite opposite scene to which belonged the agitated cries of the Asiatic vassals hard pressed by enemies, calling for soldiers and fighting chariots, and the reminder of the discord arising from the persecution of the ancient gods of the country.

When the houses of high officials had offices attached in which servants and scribes could work, these were set apart from the actual dwelling of the lord, although part of the same block.[2] The oriental knows how to guard his personal privacy in his home. It is not surprising, when we consider how quickly the city was built, that sculptors and architects were numbered among its most important inhabitants. Sculptors were kept busily employed because of the need of the citizen to show proof of his allegiance to the teachings of the solar king by setting up statues of the royal family in the reception rooms of his house and even in his garden. The taste and self-assurance of the artists were severely tested also by the commissions for the decorations of the temple that poured in to an extent hitherto unprecedented.

In the years 1911–13 the German excavators came, by a happy chance, upon a number of sculptors' studios which yielded finds that have been most instructive for the study of the artistic outlook and studio methods of that age. The chief sculptor Djehutmose stands out as a personality among the Amarna sculptors who have become known to us. His villa with its modelling room and studio was discovered in the winter of 1912;[3] it is a dignified corner building at the northern end of High Priest Street (numbered P.47.2 by the excavators), and

[1] Von Bissing, *Der Fussboden aus dem Palast des Königs Amenophis IV zu el Hawata.*

[2] A good example is the 'Tax-collector's group' (V, 36, 7), in the northern district, *City of Akhenaten*, II, pl. 13.

[3] Borchardt, *Mitt. Dt. Orientsges*, nr. 52; cf. *Porträts des Königin Nofretete*, 30f.

therefore situated in the most fashionable quarter. The modelling room was established in a room leading off the usual entrance hall so that fashionable visitors could easily visit it. Many models were left behind when the town was evacuated; they were no longer saleable in the changed circumstances. The model head of Akhenaten was quite clearly deliberately broken but that of Queen Nefertiti remained standing on a shelf attached to the wall. When this shelf collapsed the queen's bust luckily fell on a pile of mud rubble that had fallen from the ceiling and the walls. This fact explains its remarkably fine state of preservation. The queen's bust and others too have shown us how artists reconciled their skill with the wishes of the king for a new 'true' approach. It is easy to see that Djehutmose avoided the mannered unnatural style of the sculpture dating from the last years in Thebes, best exemplified in the statues of Akhenaten from the temple of the Aten at Karnak, which are revoltingly ugly. Furthermore, in the studios of Djehutmose and other sculptors were found model heads made of gypsum plaster of the king and the queen, of an aged king (certainly not Akhenaten — see Pl. 24. *a*) and a representation of the unmistakably plump face of Akhenaten's father with its turned-up nose. There were also model heads of men and women of the most varied types (Pl. 24. *b*) many of which are so individually treated that they may be taken as studies from life. They are, however, certainly casts from clay models from which the artist could decide to what extent he would reproduce personal characteristics in a statue and what he should smooth out or even blot out.[1] There are heads among them that closely resemble a finished likeness in stone; others create so realistic an impression that the Egyptian sculptor would certainly not have dared to reproduce them in stone. He was evidently interested in the heads of his sitters and the formation of the faces; the body was less studied; at most the hands and arms of a few sitters were modelled.

The heads of the private people reveal much more impressively the real appearance of the ruling classes in Amarna than do the stereotyped formulas of the texts and reliefs in the tombs. In looking at them one often has the feeling that one is concerned not with an 'intelligent upper class' as Roeder described them, but with men of the lowest origins with dangerous

[1] G. Röder, *Jahrbuch preussisches Kunstsammlungen*, 62 (1941), 145f.

brutality and cunning.[1] It was the sociological result of the method of selection based on negative principles practised by Akhenaten the hater of tradition. This impression is in no way contradicted by the official accounts of the careers and origins of such favourites.

Another noticeable thing is that the statues of the portable altars set up in family shrines exhibit the mannered style far more than the works of the leading sculptors.[2] This fact is also true of the deeply sunk reliefs in the rock tombs. Here theories of evolution in style do not apply; what is involved is a fundamentally different artistic outlook. These reliefs were for the most part mass produced and in them the manual worker showed his devotion to the modern artistic tendencies while the knowledgeable craftsman wisely kept himself in the background. Djehutmose's head of Nefertiti reveals discreetly by the slenderness of the throat, its bent position under the weight of the crown, the bitter character of the mouth and a certain weariness in the whole expression, the signs of the age in which she lived. He did not debase his art into the decadence shown in the morbid distortions characteristic of the deep-cut reliefs and in certain fashionable works composed of pieces of brightly coloured stones.

A small house stood near but apart from Djehutmose's villa; it resembled the office of an official and was perhaps the home of his chief assistant. The gypsum-plaster workshop was built directly on to Djehutmose's house. His technical equipment is exemplified by remains of all sorts of colour tests, abandoned tools, chisels, drills, etc.; his daily activities are illuminated by other remains — wine-stoppers, house keys, fishing hooks, etc. The villa is surrounded by modest habitations doubtlessly intended for journeymen and stone-masons. We also know the name of at least one of the artists who worked on the building of the temple of the Aten. He was the head sculptor, Bak, the son of that head sculptor, Men, who has already been mentioned as the sculptor of the great quartzite colossi of Amenophis III.[3]

A working-class district lay apart from the city itself, near the eastern edge of the plain, so that the work-people were close to their work on the rock tombs. Their 'village' was a square

[1] R. Hamann, *Ägyptische Kunst* (1944), 238.
[2] Borchardt, *Porträts des Königin Nofretete*, 3f.   [3] See above, p. 263.

302

compound with sides of about 230 feet long with 74 houses built on 5 parallel streets, according to a regular lay-out singularly unoriental in appearance.[1] It belongs, however, to a class of similar 'villages' to which belong the Pyramid City of Sesostris III at Illahun or Kahun, of the time of Dynasty XII–XIII, and the Ramesside settlement for the guilds of the necropolis-workmen at Deir el-Medinah in West Thebes (Pl. 19. b). The settlement at Amarna differed from that at Kahun in the uniformity of its houses. The latter settlement, which was five centuries older, was far more extensive, being contained within a rectangle 985 feet by 1,310 feet. At Kahun more commodious houses lay in the large eastern quarter while the western quarter held 200–250 tiny houses. This difference points to important social distinctions between the different sections of the population, which accords well with what we know of the ancient Pyramid City. In the Amarna workers' village, however, only the corner house at the entrance beside the parade ground, exceeded the others in size; it was no doubt the house occupied by the camp commandant. Nevertheless, in spite of its small size, the average house was more comfortable than the hut occupied by the *fellah* in an Egyptian village today. These houses were not intended for the use of the conscripted manual worker but of the regularly employed stone-masons, painters and builders, who socially formed a class similar to that composed of the inhabitants of the artisans' village at Deir el-Medinah. They were also mentally their equals. We have found the graves of this humble middle class and their obligatory memorial stelae and amulets. In the texts on these objects they declare themselves to be the adherents of the ancient popular deities such as Isis and the 'Deliverer' who warded off scorpions, Thoueris, the Theban hippopotamus goddess who assisted women at birth and Bes, the dwarf-god.[2] We even find the scribe putting his trust in the baboon of Thoth, his old patron god.[3] These people were clearly not supporters of the king's religion of the Aten. Moreover, it is interesting to note that the period of restoration that followed was precisely the time when people turned openly to the benevolent household gods instead of to the great gods of the official system who had lost their influence through the crisis.[4] The

[1] Peet, *City of Akhenaten*, I, pl. 16.   [2] Peet, *op. cit.*, pls. 12, 28.
[3] *JEA*, 19, pl. 17.   [4] See above, p. 274.

religious reform carried out by Akhenaten had certainly swept away all the old governing families, particularly those of Thebes, but it in no way derived its support from a broad wave of emotion coming from a host of believers. It based its strength on a numerically small class of upstarts whose characteristics have already been described here.

The rock tombs which these workers constructed for the great men of the city are only in a few cases finished and most of them were never even used. This is also true of the tombs of the royal family which Akhenaten boasted of having built in the eastern mountains. In one rock tomb which, to judge by the few completed scenes, was intended initially for the king and the queen, the youthful and prematurely deceased princess Maketaten was buried, and for that purpose a side part of the tomb was hastily decorated with a few reliefs and inscriptions. The collapse of the regime which threatened even before the death of the king, prevented any further work on it. The crisis brought about by the failure of the king's foreign policy was heightened by opposition within the royal family; and this opposition increased with the advent of sons-in-law who aspired to the succession since Akhenaten's only legitimate children were daughters. The seeking out and erasure of names on buildings dating from the last years of Akhenaten's reign, particularly in the summer palace of Meru-Aten, reveal a rivalry between Queen Nefertiti and the heir to the throne, Smenkhkareʿ, who had married the eldest princess Meritaten and was co-regent with Akhenaten during the last two years of his reign.

The women of the royal family had been of stronger character than the men ever since Amenophis III had taken a clever girl of inferior rank named Tiy from his harîm and made her his queen. R. Hamman has recently described her as a 'decadent, ugly, half-breed type' from her celebrated ebony head from Medinet Gurob. Nefertiti's daughters were likewise of strong character. Palace intrigues and internal struggles certainly played a part in the attempt to reach a compromise with Thebes and the Priests of Amun by the abandonment of the king's self-chosen doctrine of the Aten. These attempts were already to be observed in the last year of Smenkhkareʿ's co-regency, that is about the seventeenth and last year of Akhenaten's reign. The Egyptian queen after the death of her husband, to protect her-

21. *a*. On the banks of the Nile at El Kab in Upper Egypt.

21. *b*. Rock-tombs of the nomarchs of Elephantine, 1952.

22. *a.* Gebel Barkal with the Temple of Napata.

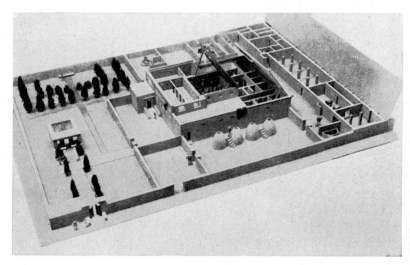

22. *b.* Model of a house at Amarna.

self from these intrigues and to maintain her own position, turned to the victorious Hittite king who then stood before Carchemish on the Euphrates, and offered him her hand in marriage and the Egyptian crown for one of his sons. The Hittite prince was, however, assassinated by noble Egyptians on his way to Egypt. The king named Bibkhururia in the Hittite report is no longer thought to be Akhenaten, as Eduard Meyer maintained, but Tutankhamun.[1] The prenomen of Akhenaten, Neferkheperurē' becomes Napkhururia in cuneiform; that of Tutankhamun, Nebkheperurē', would be Nibkhururia. The queen responsible for making the proposal should then be identified not as Nefertiti but Ankhesenpa-aten, the third daughter of Akhenaten, who must have been about twenty-one years of age at the time of the death of her husband Tutankhamun. She based her offer on the ground that she refused to marry her 'slave' Ay, who was the husband of the nurse of Nefertiti, her mother, and who was in consequence called 'Father of the God'. Yet this marriage became her fate.[2] No matter how this business was finally decided, the pride of the royal house had indeed fallen far since the time of Amenophis III when a daughter of the king rejected even the king of Babylon with the words: 'From time immemorial a daughter of the king of Egypt has been given never to no-one.'

When, however, voices, particularly army voices, made themselves increasingly heard, more distinctly on the subject of the troubles in Syria, and when it was no longer possible to avoid throwing the pick of the army into the struggle, the court moved the residence back to Thebes. This move possibly took place during the last year of Smenkhkarē''s regency, for the second year of his rule is the last definitely found on objects from Amarna; it certainly happened or had happened when Tutankhaten became king and changed his name to Tutankhamun. The guardian of the royal couple who were still only children was Ay the 'Father of the God' and 'Inspector of the Chariot Troops'. The City of Akhetaten was deserted by the same generation that had built it. Its existence barely covered a span of fifteen years.

Akhenaten himself was degraded from being 'Son of the God'

---

[1] So, most recently, Edel, *JNES*, 7 (1948), 14f.
[2] Newberry, *JEA*, 18, 50f.

'who came from the sun' to the 'Blasphemer of Akhetaten'. No trace is left to tell what happened to his body and to that of the queen. The body of Smenkhkarē' was placed in a coffin intended by Akhenaten to receive the body of a female member of his family, such as his daughter Maketaten. He was then buried hastily in the Valley of the Kings in a tomb presented to him by Akhenaten, but from which the hated names had been scratched or cut out.[1] When the tomb was discovered in 1907, the corpse and the coffin were thought to be those of Akhenaten. Furthermore, a part of the furnishings originally intended for the tomb of Smenkhkarē', including one of the golden shrines enclosing the sarcophagus was subsequently used for Tutankhamun after the cartouches had been altered. All these unusual events indicate that it was a period of unrest. The golden splendour of the tomb of Tutankhamun invests the name of this king, the last of the legitimate line of Dynasty XVIII, with undeserved brilliance (Pl. 25. *b*). He was, after all, only a pawn in a game played by much stronger principals; for when Ay became king for a few years in Tutankhamun's stead, with the youthful Ankhesenpa-aten at his side, Egypt was already waiting to hear the footsteps of Horemheb, the commander-in-chief and governor-general in Memphis, the autocrat who was to bring order out of chaos.

Everything of value was removed from Akhetaten; the stone door-frames were left, but not the wooden pillars of the houses — a fact that testifies to the shortage of wood in the country. The doorways of the houses were walled up except where poorer people stayed behind and established themselves. Blocks of stone from the destroyed temple of the Aten were used, as at Karnak, for the reconstruction of temples in the surrounding country which had been desecrated during Akhenaten's reign. The last German expedition excavating before the Second World War found whole rows of broken Amarna reliefs in the foundations (of Ramesside date) of the temple in neighbouring Hermopolis.[2] The temples and palaces of Amarna were in fact so completely destroyed that scarcely more than a few doubtful ground-plans have been recovered even by modern excavation methods. What are known with certainty are the streets through which the

---

[1] Engelbach, *Annales du Service*, 31, 98f.; 40, pls. 23–4.

[2] *Mitt. Dt. Inst. Kairo*, 9, 59f., pls. 6–8; *Annales du Service*, 39, pls. 137–41.

king's chariot raced from the palace, the site of the magnificent window in the palace at which the king appeared to reward his trusty followers with the gold of honour;[1] even the 'writing room of the king' in which he attended to correspondence is known. In this connection we remember the Amarna tablets which were found in this part of the palace, and the place called the 'House of Life' (Q.42 on the excavators' grid) where books and learned scholars were to be found.

Nevertheless the principal gain from the excavations at Amarna was the uncovering of the dwelling houses, for the city was never lived in again and therefore presents us with the evidence for a homogeneous secular civilization. The place never became a Tell or mound of occupation like other seats of government in Egypt where for century after century houses were built in layers one above the other.

[1] Pendlbeury, *City of Akhenaten*, III, 2, 14.

XII

The Frontier Region — Aswan, Elephantine and Philae[1]

Aswan exists under frontier conditions. The frontier can be sensed in the strange dark granite ridges that rise like streams of lava from the water and the sand, taking the place of the soft shapes of the dark yellow Nubian sandstone (Pl. 2.a). The frontier character is demonstrated in the dark-skinned Nubian population and in the peculiar shape of their houses. Here too the desert makes itself felt. In the *wadis* round Shellal the nomadic Bisharin set up their tents and trade camels. Their territory, which is separated from that of their tribal relatives, the Ababdah, at the latitude of Aswan, extends about twenty-four miles northwards. At the northern limit, near Daraw, just south of Kôm Ombo, caravan routes open out into the south-eastern desert at the place where in early days the chief market of the nomadic Bedja, the descendants of the ancient Medjay, was held. At Daraw lies the linguistic frontier between Arabic speakers and Nubian speakers. Here, if one looks up at the starry sky one realizes that the Tropic of Cancer has been crossed; the magnificent Southern Cross sheds its light over the late night sky of Nubia.

Two ancient names indicate the special character of the frontier zone: Abu or Elephantine, the name of the most northerly island of the First Cataract, opposite Aswan, and Sunu or Syene, 'The Market', a settlement on the eastern bank. Elephantine was not so called by the Egyptians in memory of the elephants who inhabited the area in predynastic times, but because it was an emporium for ivory, the most sought after com-

[1] Articles 'Syene' and 'Philae' in Pauly-Wissowa, *Real-Encyclopädie*.

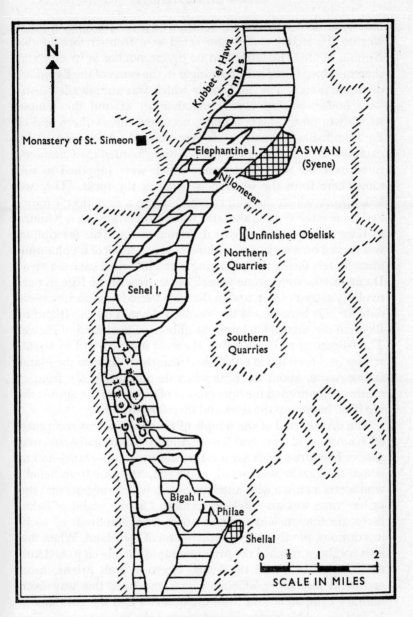

10. The Elephantine region

modity in the trade with the south. The principal ancient town was on the island and it also acted as a frontier fort for the Nubian nome. The latter had no divine symbol as its sign and therein showed itself to be a stranger in the ranks of the Egyptian domestic nomes. The old fortress which was an unwalled town with houses packed closely together all around the temple which was on the highest point, occupied the southern end of the island. Black granite reefs here mark the beginning of the cataract (Pl. 2. a). The ram-god Khnum, 'Lord of the Cataract', ruled over the new flood-waters which were supposed to rise somewhere from the whirlpools between the rocks. 'The two holes (from which the water comes) are in a cave that is mine, and mine is the right to allow the water to overflow', says Khnum to King Zoser on the so-called Famine Stela. This inscription was carved on a rock on the Island of Sehel, south of Elephantine immediately facing the beginning of the principal cataract area. Divine myths were prone to seek the sources of the Nile in particularly sacred places, and in the Late Period a favourite candidate for this honour was the so-called Abaton on the Island of Bigah in the cataract, a larger neighbour of the island of Philae. The Nilometer at Elephantine, the most southern in Egypt, still retains its fame;[1] it was established near the temple on the island facing Aswan about the time when the pushing of the frontier southwards afforded the opportunity of observing the approaching flood higher up the river and therefore earlier.

The divine triad of the temple of Elephantine was composed of Khnum and two goddesses, Anukis whose gaily-coloured feather headdress gives her a rather barbaric appearance and to whom the gazelle was sacred, and Satet, 'the One from Sehel', who wears a crown with antelope horns, which suggests that she at one time was an antelope goddess. On the island of Sehel there are few ancient remains apart from hundreds of rock-inscriptions, mostly at the southern end of the island. When this part had been reached the principal rapids had been passed and the inscriptions recall the kings, viceroys, high priests, head architects and other officials who came back this way from military campaigns and from the quarries and the gold mines. In fact the whole region in and around the cataract, extending well into the desert, is full of inscriptions left by visitors; it is, as

---

[1] See above, p. 49.

it were, a visitors' book in which adventurous men recorded their names. Among these we find the names of many whom we met in the turquoise mines in Sinai or in the stone quarries of the Wadi Hammamat, members of the families of those ancient explorers who left their mark upon the frontier regions. We also find the names of kings, for at all periods they won their first and easiest trophies of victory in the negro lands to the south of the kingdom. The history of the cataract and of the surrounding country is written in these inscriptions and in the texts in the tombs of the nomarchs of Elephantine who, from Dynasty VI onwards, had themselves buried in the cliffs by the riverside at Kubbet el-Hawa with its wonderful outlook across the river (Pl. 21. *b*).

These great men regarded themselves as natives of the frontier zone although they had passed their youthful years in the capital and had held their first offices at court there. The men of whom we read in the rock-inscriptions were very different in type from the early nomarchs, such as Isi who, in the reign of Teti, was sent to be nomarch in the neighbouring nome of Edfu as a provision for his old age. He was a great lord who bore the title of vizir and he was regarded with such astonishment by the local people at Edfu that he was revered after his death at his tomb as a 'living god', like a modern local sheikh.[1] He was very different in character from his son Kar whom King Merenrē' also sent as nomarch to Edfu 'as the representative of My Lord at the head of all the chief men in the whole of Upper Egypt'.[2] This man, who had grown great in the service of the court, called himself 'Master of the secrets of all secret words that come out from the narrow doors at Elephantine', as if he himself exercised control over them. At the time when he went to Edfu and when the well-known Weni, another successful courtier who is buried at Abydos, received towards the end of his career the title, 'Count and Overseer of Upper Egypt' with supervisory powers over all the nomes from Elephantine northwards, men came to power at Elephantine who bore the honorific title 'Overseer of Dragomans'. They were responsible for all the problems of the southern countries in respect both of the river and of the land. They equipped the caravans and were responsible also for the fitting out and commanding the ships that

[1] Alliot, *BIFAO*, 37, 93f.   [2] *Urk.*, I, 251f.

sailed down the Red Sea to Punt, the Land of the God.[1] King Merenrē' himself had inspected the frontier, as the inscriptions in the cataract area inform us; he 'stood on the back of the mountain' while the beduin Medjay and the chiefs of Lower Nubia from the lands of Irtjet and Wawat paid homage to him.[2] Under him and his successor Pepi II a certain Harkhuf held office in Elephantine. He too styled himself 'Overseer of Upper Egypt' and also 'Overseer of all Deserts in the Head of Upper Egypt who set the terror of Horus in the foreign lands'.[3] The operations he engaged in were not truly military campaigns since his object was to avoid engagements and to induce the chiefs to supply willingly the coveted raw materials he sought. He did not achieve this without force and his expeditions often had to change direction and objective when the tribes combined to oppose the extortion of tribute. Such an action was regarded by them as an ancient right and it was similar to the law of the desert. In Africa it is called *tonga*.

The limits reached by these expeditions can only approximately be determined since the ancient Nubian tribal- and place-names are not definitely identified with known geographical areas. From his inscription we know that Harkhuf was away from Egypt for seven months on his first expedition to the land of Iam 'in order to open the way into this land'. For him it was clearly an exploratory expedition into an unknown land. A second expedition 'along the Elephantine way' (certainly the customary way for ivory traders) kept him away for eight months. A third expedition over the desert route (perhaps by way of Khargah) certainly did not start from Elephantine but from a base further north (possibly Hu in the 6th nome of Upper Egypt).[4] We have already mentioned this last expedition in the account of the oases; in its course the Egyptians encountered the Prince of Iam on a foray against the Libyan tribes.

Expeditions did not, however, always pass off so peacefully. It is known of Sabni, one of the last Counts of Elephantine, that he had to retrieve the body of his father Mekhu who was slain on one such expedition and that in doing so he 'pacified' these lands, which means that he conducted a punitive expedition against them.[5] To die in a foreign country was for the Egyptian

---

[1] See above, p. 110.   [2] *Urk.*, I, 110–11.   [3] *Urk.*, I, 120, 14; 124, 2–3.
[4] *Urk.*, I, 125, 14; see above, p. 129.   [5] *Urk.*, I, 136.

a horrible idea. It was not for nothing therefore that in the Story of Sinuhe of the time of Dynasty XII reference is made to a burial in a foreign country with barbaric customs as being one of the strongest arguments that led the hero to return to Egypt from Asia. In the New Kingdom, those who lived on earth were still assured 'as truly as you praise your city gods you will not taste the fear of another land but will be buried in your own tombs'.[1]

The goods that were acquired by trade in the south were in demand throughout the ages: ivory, animal skins, spices, ostrich feathers and minerals, and, from the nomads, cattle and goats. In exchange the Egyptians offered unguents, honey, textiles, gay glazed composition beads and similar articles. Harkhuf recorded as a great achievement that he was able to acquire a real dwarf, a 'dancer of the gods', from the 'land of the dwellers of the horizon', like the one that Bawerdede, the Treasurer of the God, had brought back from Punt in the reign of King Asosi, many years before. The young king Pepi II was so excited by this news that he issued a special decree ordering that exceptional precautionary measures be taken to ensure the safety of this rare booty; he even suspended all privileges throughout the country during the dwarf's journey to the Residence.

The goods were carried on donkey trains. Harkhuf claims that he brought back 300 laden donkeys from his third expedition.[2] It is unlikely that permanent trading posts were set up in the more distant places as early as the Old Kingdom, such as we know existed in the Middle Kingdom at places like Kerma, south of the Third Cataract.[3] If it was necessary to travel into the district around the Second Cataract it was absolutely essential in the Old Kingdom to engage the services of the native tribes, particularly the Medjay whose nomadic habits had made them peculiarly familiar with the desert. They would help in the search for and the transport of the mineral wealth to be found in the desert — gold and semi-precious stones and the rare hard stones used by sculptors in their work in the royal mortuary temples. What the ancient prospector could accomplish is demonstrated in the modern rediscovery of the place from which

[1] *Urk.*, IV, 965.   [2] *Urk.*, I, 126–7.
[3] Säve-Söderbergh, *Ägypten und Nubien*, 106f.

in Dynasty IV came the diorite used for the statues of Chephren in his mortuary temple and probably also the paving blocks in the mortuary temple of Cheops.[1] The labour corps euphemistically called this place the 'Place of snaring of Cheops' as if it were a fertile oasis. It lies in the desolate Libyan desert at latitude 22° 46' N., about forty miles north-west of Abu Simbel and not very far from the caravan route which led from Aswan by way of the Oasis of Dunkul to Nakhle and the Darb el-Arba'in. The place was marked by cairns (called *'alamat* in Arabic). Stelae found there bearing the names of Cheops and Djedefrē' prove that it was already being exploited at a time when tradition is silent in Elephantine.[2] Nearby lay an amethyst mine. The transport route that can still be distinguished reached the Nile in the neighbourhood of Toshka, a little to the north of Abu Simbel. From there by river to Giza was a distance of more than 750 miles.

Native labour was needed for the transport of these minerals and it seems that the local population was only too glad to serve the wealthy foreigners. From the inscription of Weni we know that during Dynasty VI contingents were furnished by the Medjay and other Lower Nubian tribes for Egyptian military expeditions and that they were already employed in Egypt as policemen.[3]

In the time of Cheops and Chephren the leaders of the expeditions did not dare to commemorate their own names in inscriptions even in the most distant parts of the desert, out of respect for the king's majesty. Such men are to be found in the ranks of the royal sons and royal descendants who, in the days of the patriarchal monarchy, served as treasurers of the god and captains of the royal ships, being at the same time often overseers of all the buildings of the king or commanders of the labour corps with the title General.[4] They were the direct representatives of His Majesty, for the discovery and exploitation of raw materials was a royal monopoly. For the most part they served as leaders of expeditions when they were young and

---

[1] *Annales du Service*, 38, 369f.

[2] Whether the district of Ibhat is the place where Weni obtained the block of stone for the sarcophagus of Merenrē' can only be decided by an examination of the sarcophagus in that King's pyramid at Saqqara.

[3] See above, p. 142.   [4] See above, p. 163.

with the approach of old age they were transferred to administrative or priestly offices. As a result of the social revolution in the country from the time of Dynasty V onwards the ranks of treasurer of the god were extended to include men from outside the royal family. From the rather more informative inscriptions of these newcomers we learn, among other things, something about their expeditions. One of the oldest biographical inscriptions of this kind was composed by Kaemtjenet, a son of King Asosi; it is preserved in his tomb at Saqqara but unhappily only in a very incomplete state. In the fashion of the later counts of Elephantine he describes himself as 'he who set the fear of Horus in the foreign lands'.[1] Tjetji and Khui, the two treasurers of the god with the rank of count who have already been mentioned in connection with expeditions to Punt, carried out many expeditions to Byblos and Punt in Dynasty VI and they are buried at Aswan.[2]

Since the discovery of the diorite quarry of Cheops a little to the north-west of Abu Simbel, it is possible to assume without doubt that the furthest point reached by the expeditions led by the counts of Elephantine was the territory to the south of the Second Cataract. It can also be surmised that the Land of Iam lay in the neighbourhood of Amarah, north of the Island of Sai.[3] In this area contact was sought with the trade coming from the interior of the Sudan. The 'knots' of Irtjet that Harkhuf had to overcome on his way home from Iam could then be the rocks of the Second Cataract which the Arabs graphically call 'Belly of Stone' (Pl. 2. *b*). The diorite hill of Cheops may well have been a chance find, for what was sought as a rule was quartz with its gold-bearing veins. The uses of different stones and of semi-precious stones varied from period to period, governed in part by fashion. Thus diorite was used for stone vessels in Dynasty II whereas mottled breccia was characteristic of the vessels of the predynastic Gerzean period. From the time of Snofru the liking for diorite and for coloured stones in general diminished and alabaster began its triumphant rise to popularity. The use of semi-precious stones in jewellery and trinkets

---

[1] *Urk.*, I, 180–6 = Mariette, *Mastabas*, D.7.
[2] *Urk.*, I, 140–1; de Morgan, *Catalogue des Monuments*, I, 157, 199–200, cf. above, p. 111.
[3] Säve-Söderbergh, *op. cit.*, 14f.

also varied in different periods, the changes being due in part undoubtedly to chance discoveries of new materials and the exhaustion of old sources of supply.

Towards the end of the Old Kingdom the participation of the Nubian tribes in Egyptian undertakings declined in face of increasing opposition. The ill-starred expedition of Mekhu mentioned above was perhaps a sign of the times. A part in this development was also played by racial movements in the Sudan which brought to Nubia the Kushites, a tribe with a strong love of independence. Now the ethnographical term Kush makes its appearance in Egyptian records, usually in the form of the contemptuous phrase 'vile Kush'. The highwater mark of the racial migration coincided with the downfall of the Old Kingdom. The migratory wave broke over the frontier at Elephantine and only subsided at the ethnic frontier at Daraw — an ethnic frontier that still exists today.

The Menthuhotpes of Thebes embarked on the re-subjugation of Lower Nubia about 2100 B.C. and once more overseers of dragomans were appointed. This time, however, serious resistance was encountered and the Egyptian advance proceeded in a very different manner from that in the time of the Old Kingdom. The war progressed as a series of punitive expeditions against rebels; as Sesostris III says: 'I took their wives by force, I gathered in their dependants, I descended to their watering-places, killed their cattle, scattered their corn on the ground after it had been set on fire.' Ultimately it was Nubian gold that attracted the Egyptians to the south. Sesostris I and Sesostris III conquered Nubia as far as the Second Cataract and secured it with a closely organized system of forts of which Bigah and Elephantine formed the last line.

The building of the forts at Quban on the east bank of the Nile and of Ikkur on the west bank dates back earlier than that of the others to the reign of Sesostris I. These two forts were intended to guard the entrance to the Wadi Alaki in which lay the most productive gold mines worked in the Middle Kingdom. They were situated at a place called Umm el-Garajat about sixty miles from the Nile at 22° 40′ north and 30° 18′ east (according to Schweinfurth). Here there are many traces of the ancient settlement, particularly of hundreds of tiny stone huts for the workmen. Under Sesostris I, Ameni, the nomarch of

Beni Hasan in Middle Egypt, went as the companion of the king's son, Ameni (later Ammenemes II) to these mines with four hundred picked militia-men who had no doubt fought in the Nubian campaign and he was able to bring back gold from there.[1] They probably made use of the local people for the laborious tasks of extracting the gold-bearing quartz and the subsequent crushing and washing, just as English prospectors sought to employ Ababdah beduin as workmen when they reworked the ancient gold mines in the Wadi Alaki.

About 1870 B.C. Sesostris III closed the frontier at the Second Cataract by building forts at Semnah and Kummah on opposite banks of the Nile, with a chain of block-houses, partly on islands and partly on the banks of the river, to ensure that the fortified zone was not outflanked.[2] The frontier regulations furnish us with a picture of the state of affairs that must similarly have existed in more ancient times at Elephantine and the 'Market' of Aswan.[3] The Nubians (Kushites) who lived south of the frontier were forbidden to travel by ship or by land through the restricted area and the only trading-point allowed them was a place called Iqen (possibly the same as another place called Ikina) which was perhaps on the west bank of the Nile opposite Wadi Halfa. Here they were allowed to engage in the barter of cattle and goods, for the forts were not intended to stop trade with the south but to direct it to a controlled market within the Egyptian zone, an obligatory staple market such as was subsequently imposed on imports from the Aegean at the privileged port of Naucratis.[4] The market of Aswan was certainly the model for that at the Second Cataract. From reports written in the form of a journal dating from the close of the Middle Kingdom we learn how carefully the entry of each smallest body of natives was reported by way of information: 'as one fort communicates to another'.[5] At one time it is the Nubians who call for special consideration, at another it is the Medjay. Patrols were sent out to watch over the ways of approach and, like trackers, to follow up suspicious new trails.

On the other hand, the fort, which in fact was only an un-

[1] Newberry, *Beni Hasan*, I, pl. 8 = *Urk.*, VII, 15.
[2] Review in Säve-Söderbergh, *op. cit.*, p. 89f., with map.
[3] Berlin, 14753 = Sethe, *Lesestücke*, 83–5.
[4] See above, p. 208.   [5] Smither, *JEA*, 31, 3f.

walled settlement, attracted the frontier trade. An advance trading post was therefore set up at the same time far over the frontier in the country south of the Third Cataract close to the modern Kerma. Its ruins, which consist of an enormous pile of mud bricks looking like the stump of a pyramid and appearing to be a mountain fort in miniature, was examined by Reisner.[1] It was clearly the residence of a Nubian chieftain just as Aniba was in the time of the New Kingdom. The tomb of a prince discovered there contained among other things statues of Hepdjefi, the well-known nomarch of Asyut in the reign of Sesostris I and his wife; they had probably been presented to the native chiefs as marks of honour. Similar statues found their way as far as Crete at this time and, through Syria, to Cilicia, for the same purpose. Similarly alabaster vases bearing the names of kings of Dynasty VI found a home in Kerma. The trading post there continued to exist until the Middle Kingdom began to decline.

After the frontier had been advanced to the Second Cataract Elephantine became the base and final control-point for the traffic from Nubia. Again nomarchs of the Middle Kingdom lie buried in finely cut rock-tombs at Kubbet el-Hawa, in company with their predecessors of the Old Kingdom. They no longer call themselves overseers of dragomans, but they governed in the king's name with markedly feudal autocracy. Among them we know Sirenput who must have taken part in the conquest of Nubia under Sesostris I (1971–1926 B.C.), but he does not mention a word about it in his biographical inscription.[2] Only indirectly do we discover his powerful and independent position. In the representations in his tomb is one in which he is shown in the customary inspection of the herds of cattle. Nomarchs of the same period in Middle Egypt respectfully record that such inspections were carried out for the royal cattle-levy; but Sirenput in his role as overseer of the prophets of Khnum, Lord of the Cataract, lets it be understood that in his case it was done 'in order to direct the festival of all the gods of Elephantine'.[3] He therefore regarded himself as responsible for the dues of the local temple. Recent finds in the heaps of debris on the island of Elephantine have still further underlined the nomarch's

[1] Reisner, 'Excavations at Kerma' in *Harvard African Studies*, 5–6, and *ÄZ*, 52, 34f.; cf. Säve-Söderbergh, *op. cit.*, 103f.   [2] Gardiner, *ÄZ*, 45, 123f.
[3] H. W. Müller, *Die Felsengräber der Fürsten von Elephantine*, 33.

powerful position. Sirenput built a mortuary chapel for his statue — the Egyptians called such a *ka*-house — near the temple of Khnum which at that time had just acquired fine limestone reliefs. At the same time he renovated a similar chapel belonging to one of his predecessors who bore the name Heqa-ib, a favourite name at Elephantine from the time of the late Old Kingdom (Sirenput himself had three sons so named). He also donated an offering table in the memory of Heqa-ib. Undoubtedly he regarded himself as the legitimate successor of the powerful ruling family of the Old Kingdom although there can hardly have been any blood relationship between him and them. A large number of offering tables, stelae and statues shows that the mortuary cult of the men who had held the reins of government in their hands here was cared for in a fashion that recalls the deification of the former vizir Isi at Edfu. It went to even greater lengths. The frontier was ready to give recognition to the energy of its defenders. Consequently these rulers were ranged among the local gods just as Sesostris III in Nubia and Snofru in Sinai were regarded as tutelary deities and were ranked among the deities of those countries. We know nothing of the origins of the Lords of Elephantine. Sesostris I probably selected Sirenput from among his most trusted captains of the Nubian campaigns. The old soldier seems to speak in his honorific title 'He who fills the heart of the king as Commander of patrols at the gateway of the southern lands'. He records his distinction in high-flown words: 'His Majesty distinguished me from all the land in that I was raised before the nomarchs — I was elevated to heaven in a moment.' The words do not suggest that he came from one of the old feudal families of Egypt but rather from the circle of courtiers, like Sinuhe of the well-known contemporary story. His family seems to have continued in power until the reign of Sesostris III when a more rigorous form of government was set up in Nubia.[1] Then there was no longer any room for independent power at Elephantine.

A rigid organization of trade and the requisitioning of all raw materials were only possible when the administration and controlling authority were directly exercised in the king's name and when semi-independent authorities were unable to intervene for their own profit. It is precisely in Nubia that we can observe how,

[1] On the family, see Labib Habachi, *JEA*, 39, 54f.

in the course of time, a system so rigid at the outset was relaxed by the king's cession of royal prerogatives chiefly for the benefit of the temples. This situation seems to have developed mainly as a result of changed economic conditions in the New Kingdom.

We have already heard how about 1310 B.C. Sethos I assigned the revenues from the gold mines, particularly from those in the neighbourhood of Barramiyah, to the newly built temple of Osiris at Abydos.[1] This concession had far-reaching consequences. In a decree carved on an isolated rock at Nauri about 20 miles below the Third Cataract, the king glorifies his endowment with eloquent words and stresses its far-reaching privileges.[2] The 'holding up of ships on the river' and their inspection are expressly mentioned, all requisitionings from the endowment are forbidden and all employees of the endowment anywhere on the soil of Nubia, including the charterers of ships, foreign traders, gold washers and others are guaranteed freedom from taxes. It is furthermore specifically stated that no commandant of the fort actually built by Sethos near Nauri should take gold or other goods from 'the fleet of the tribute of Kush' which belonged to the temple of Sethos at Abydos. These provisions show on the one hand that the trading privileges of the temple at that time extended far into the Sudan and that the temple possessed its own trading establishments and prove on the other hand that transit dues were customary. This latter fact recalls the primitive *tonga* rights of the native chieftains. To whose benefit, however, were the dues levied if the whole trade was legally the king's? Certainly to the benefit of the institutions and persons who exercised the prerogatives ceded to them by the king. Voices can be heard in Nubia claiming these privileges. In the Famine Stela at Sehel, mentioned above, there is a claim, based on an ancient legend, that the temple of Khnum at Elephantine had a claim over the district later known as the Dodecaschoenus which extended from the cataract at Aswan to Hierasykaminos. On the advice of the wise Imhotep, Zoser made a present of this land after seven years of famine to Khnum of Elephantine in order to secure better floods from him.[3] All mining rights in minerals and stone were given to him and a list was made of the taxes and imports with which the estate was

---

[1] See above, pp. 124, 246. [2] Griffith, *JEA*, 13, 193f.
[3] Translation by Röder, *Urkunden zur Religion des alten Ägypten*, 177f.

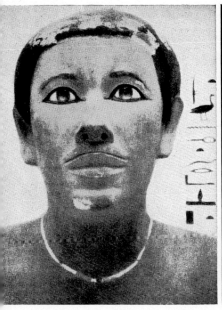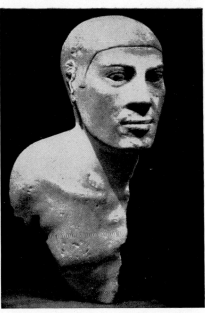

23. *a*. Prince Rahotpe, the son of   23. *b*. Old Man (Cairo 72221).
     Snofru.

Expressive faces of the Old Kingdom.

24. *a*. Elderly Man.   24. *b*. Man.

Model heads from a sculptor's studio in Amarna.

25. *a*. Festal boat with girls (alabaster composition from the Tomb of Tutankhamun, in the Cairo Museum).

25. *b*. The King of Gold (the coffin of Tutankhamun, now in his tomb in the Valley of the Kings).

burdened as feudal dues. These latter constituted the real value of the donation; they were dues levied on the harvest yield in addition to what had already been delivered, 10 per cent of the yield from the fisheries and the snaring of birds and also from the game slain in the desert, 10 per cent of young cattle — the increment of the herds, 10 per cent of all valuable stone worked on the east bank of the river of which a complete list is given (including many unidentified items) and finally, 10 per cent levied on all gold, ivory, timber of all kinds and all goods imported into Egypt from the southern countries and on all the people who came with them. It is clear that transit dues, like those of the Suez Canal, were known even in those distant times. The only articles exempted from dues were those intended for the 'House of Gold' of the temple, that is, for the statues of the god.

We find here a ten-per-cent transit duty on imports like that found in the statute of Naucratis[1] and also the recognition of the temple monopoly — a relatively recent idea. The inscription at Sehel seems to have been carved on the rock in the Ptolemaic Period, doubtlessly by the priests of Khnum of Elephantine who sought thereby to defend their more ancient rights against the pretensions of Isis of Philae who had become the new patron of the Dodecaschoenus. There are in existence parts of protective decrees apparently dating from the reign of Ramesses III in favour of the temple of Khnum at Elephantine, freeing its commercial activities from taxation.[2]

Sethos forbade dues of this kind to be imposed on his new foundation at Abydos and its business concerns; and it is certain that other temples could point to similar royal benefactions. It is unlikely therefore that any official in the frontier region could have known what was in fact the law. These privileges in consequence experienced the same fate as those in Germany in the Middle Ages; they became open to question on every change of ruler. The results were universal uncertainty, continual infringements and, on the other hand, monstrous punishments. It is symptomatic of the period that in the New Kingdom the temple monopolies arose out of royal privileges; in the Ptolemaic Period the fiscal administration was forced to come to terms with these.

[1] See above, p. 208. [2] Griffith, *JEA*, 13, 207f.

The successful results obtained from gold mines, particularly in the province of Lower Nubia (Wawat) during the New Kingdom, can be read in the annals of Tuthmosis III. At that time Lower Nubia yielded a tribute of between 475 and 510 lbs. of gold, while Kush produced far less.[1] Nubian gold played a decisive part in the economy, especially in comparison with gold from the Fuakhir district of the desert of Coptos. An inscription of Ramesses II near Kuban at the entrance to the Wadi Alaki throws light upon new arrangements for the increase of production.[2] Whereas his father Sethos had devoted particular attention to the enlargement of the Barramiyah mine, Ramesses II turned his attention to that of the Wadi Alaki. It is clear that unfavourable reports had reached him from there, because he openly voiced his criticism of the intolerable losses in the waterless desert — a thing that rarely happened in self-congratulatory Egypt. It happened at a crown council at Memphis in his third year, when he said: 'Much gold is in the desert of Akita but the way (into) there is miserable beyond measure by reason of the (lack of) water. Whenever some of the workmen go there to wash gold, only half their number reach it, for they die of thirst on the way, together with their asses. They cannot find water to drink on the way there or back out of the waterskins. One therefore gets no gold in this desert because of the lack of water.' The young king's criticisms applied to many workings; old wells everywhere had dried up and water had to be brought from a distance on donkey back. A good example is furnished by the old gold mine in the Gebel el-Hudi about sixteen miles southeast of Aswan, recently described by a German desert explorer.[3] There it is still possible to see the worn tracks made by the convoys of donkeys bringing water from the valley of the Nile. The workings are of very considerable antiquity because not far away lies a deposit of amethysts carefully marked by stone cairns (in Arabic, 'alamat) which, according to the inscriptions left by visitors, was worked from the end of Dynasty XI into Dynasty XII.[4] At that time it was probably the principal

---

[1] Säve-Söderbergh, op. cit., 210–11.
[2] Sander-Hansen, Historische Inschriften der 19. Dynastie, 30f.
[3] Von der Esch, Weenak — die Karawane ruft, 122f.
[4] A. Rowe, Annales du Service, 39, 187f.; Fakhry, The Inscriptions of Wadi el Hudi (Cairo 1952).

source of these semi-precious stones that were so much used in the jewellery of Dynasty XII. The Egyptians regarded the cataract region as the place in particular from which amethysts came and also a red stone, possibly carnelian; Sinai on the other hand supplied better red granite than Aswan.[1]

Furthermore the ancient methods of extracting gold involved the laborious washing of the crushed quartz and for this large quantities of water were required which had to be brought from somewhere. Ramesses II had that vivid picture perpetuated in order to emphasize that it was he (which actually means that it was the viceroy of Kush of the time, under whose jurisdiction the Nubian desert lay) who had succeeded in finding underground water in a well at a depth of 12 cubits in which the water rose to 4 cubits in depth, while Sethos I had failed to reach water in the same place by boring to an alleged depth of 120 cubits. The new well is supposed to have been situated by the rocky hill known as Huqab el-Askar, thirty-three miles up the Wadi Alaki where the Nubian sandstone changes to metamorphic rock and where numerous inscriptions have been left by visitors.[2] It is nevertheless remarkable to observe how completely the gold-bearing veins of quartz have everywhere been detached from the primeval rock and with what thoroughness every deposit of gold was tracked down and exploited even in the most remote coastal valleys, so that modern attempts to start gold-mining again always end in disappointment.[3]

The acquisition of Nubian gold gave an impetus to the craft of the Egyptian jeweller from the beginning of Dynasty XII and the results are revealed to us in the wonderful jewellery found at Dahshur and Illahun. This jewellery belonged to members of the royal house, chiefly princesses to whom the king had given such treasures as presents; but temples and friendly foreign princes also had their share. Nubian gold made possible the mission undertaken by the chief treasurer Ikhernofret on behalf of the temple of Khentamenty at Abydos in the reign of Sesostris III; it also provided the material for the gifts found in the princely tombs at Byblos. We have also seen in the survey of

[1] Lucas, *Ancient Egyptian Materials*[3], 445, 448; cf. above, p. 126.
[2] Černý, *JEA*, 33, 54.
[3] Schweinfurth, *Auf unbetretenen Wegen in Ägypten*, 303f.

raw materials to what a great extent Egypt's policy in Asia was furthered by gold.[1]

If gold formed an unseen background to the fort and market at Elephantine, the quarrying of stone left unmistakably clear traces at Aswan and in its neighbourhood. The quarrying of granite was of ancient origin. The procuring of granite did not at first involve actual quarrying as was needed for limestone at Turah; it was a question of working individual rocks lying on the surface of the ground which first had to be trimmed of the destructive surface decomposition characteristic of granite. The convenient situation of the workings, not far from the banks of the Nile, and the excellent transport facilities, were offset by the hardness of the stone which was mastered by the use of mauls of harder stone and laborious chipping in the absence of suitable metal tools. Yet the predynastic Egyptians in fashioning stone vessels quite mastered the hardest materials, using a drill worked with an abrasive. In one royal tomb of the Thinite Period at Abydos there is a floor of Aswan granite. Plastic art in the Old Kingdom was obstinately set on the use of granite and huge quantities of Aswan granite were used in the royal mortuary temples of the Pyramid Age. At the end of Dynasty V King Unas had the transport of granite palm-trunk columns depicted in his mortuary temple along with the wooden doors of the temple.

The greatest achievements in the working of stone were the monolithic obelisks erected by the kings of Dynasty XVIII. Nevertheless, Sesostris I, the conqueror of Nubia, with his obelisk nearly 67 feet in height at Heliopolis, achieved a record that Tuthmosis I was unable to better four centuries later with his two obelisks at Karnak. Yet the greatest of the obelisks lies unfinished in the quarry. From it we can understand the wearisome task of liberating such a mass of stone from its bed.[2] The completion of the external surfaces was effected by hammers of dolerite with blows from which the outer surface of the granite was gradually ground down. The final step was to free the block from the surrounding mass. This gigantic unfinished obelisk was originally planned to reach a height of 137 feet with an

[1] See above, p. 137.
[2] Engelbach, *The Aswan Obelisk*; Somers Clark and Engelbach, *Ancient Egyptian Masonry*, 27f.

estimated weight of 1,168 tons; it was subsequently modified in
height to 105 feet which yet would have been considerably
higher than the 96 feet of Hatshepsut's obelisk at Karnak. It
probably dates from the last year of Tuthmosis III, remaining
unfinished at his death. Amenophis II gave up the dedication of
obelisks, but Tuthmosis IV reported that he had had another
obelisk completed (about 1420 B.C.) which had been prepared
by Tuthmosis III but had lain ready for erection at Karnak for
thirty-five years.[1] This obelisk also measured 105 feet and was
probably intended as the partner of the one left unfinished in
the Aswan quarry. In the dedicatory inscription on the one set
up at Karnak, Tuthmosis III says that he had resolved to set it
up on its own in Karnak; but this statement perhaps conceals a
solution forced on him because the other was not finished in
time for a particular festival, possibly the *sed*-festival. Nevertheless the other found its place on the eastern axis of the great
temple of Amun, in that rear part of the temple that opened out
towards the east.[2]

In the New Kingdom Aswan lost its character as a frontier
town. The viceroy of Kush and his two deputies for the two
Nubian provinces resided further upstream; he himself apparently at Aniba and one of the deputies at Amarah, south of
the Second Cataract. Both places were the seats of local princes.
The age of empire also saw the erection of costly temples on the
Island of Elephantine in place of the humble earlier brick
buildings. In this activity Tuthmosis III set the lead. Amenophis III has to receive the credit for two particularly charming
peripteral temples standing on raised platforms which were undoubtedly intended as wayside shrines for the festival of the local
god like those at Karnak. The scholars of Napoleon's expedition
were able to make drawings of the one that was still in a good
state of preservation. Under Mohammed Ali they were torn
down and used as material for the construction of the wall of the
new quay. Only a few poor fragments were left on Elephantine.

From the reign of Amenophis III the activity of the Viceroys
was particularly devoted to the building of towns and temples
in the newly developed Upper Nubian territories. The far less

---

[1] *Urk.*, IV, 584–5. In A.D. 357 Constantine the Great set it up in the Circus
Maximus in Rome; today it stands in front of the church of St. John Lateran.
[2] *Annales du Service*, 50, 257f.; cf. above, p. 259.

civilized populations of these areas could more directly believe in the cult of the reigning Pharaoh in 'his living form on earth', as being one of the great gods of the country, than the indigenous population in Egypt.[1] Furthermore, on the west bank of the Nile opposite the New Kingdom temple buildings on Elephantine there is only one important tomb of the late XVIIIth or early XIXth Dynasty in the ancient burial ground at Kubbet el-Hawa. The individual Nubian way of life at the same time disappeared beneath the surface of an Egyptian upper-class society. Yet history sought to repeat itself after an interval of centuries. In the Eighth Century B.C. Ethiopian kings of Hamitic ancestry invaded Egypt from Napata and fought on Egyptian soil in the name of Amun with the petty Libyan kings. At all times the warlike Kushite tribes and the Medjay of the southeastern desert had lent their support to Thebes and furnished Egypt with soldiers. It seemed as if the extremely ancient relations between Egypt and Nubia which are to be seen so clearly in the earliest phases of civilization in the Thebaid, were working to create a situation that existed at the time of the unification of the Two Lands. The initial success achieved was, however, rendered nugatory in the Seventh Century B.C. by Asiatics, in this case Assyrians.

Under the Saite kings more peaceful and prosperous times returned and once again we hear of donations to the temple at Elephantine. Neshor, a general of Apries, who was governor of Upper Egypt, reports: 'I built for (the temple) nesting-houses in this town; I gave very good wine from the southern oasis (Khargah), emmer and honey in these magazines that I built anew in the great name of His Majesty. I gave castor oil for lighting the lamps in the temple of this town.'[2]

Again the time changed. In the New Kingdom Kushite contingents had defended Egyptian claims in Asia and the camp in the extreme north-east of the Delta to which Psammetichus had sent Ionian and Carian mercenaries, still retained its name Tahpanhes (Tell Defennah or Daphnae) which means 'Fort of the Negro' (*Jeremiah* 2, 16; 43, 5–7).[3] Now, in the Persian Period, Asiatic detachments came to Elephantine. Once again the Fort of Abu was talked of and there was stationed a Jewish garrison

---

[1] See below, p. 338f.   [2] Louvre stela, A.90.
[3] N. Aimé-Giron, *Annales du Service*, 40, 444.

serving as a Persian defence force against Nubia. Security on the frontier was a thing of the past. New waves from the south dashed themselves time and again against and into the frontier district. In 25 B.C. an Ethiopian force burst across the frontier and into the camp of the Roman legionaries at Syene; as a result the Proconsul of Egypt, Petronius, was compelled to conduct a punitive expedition to Napata to ensure peace and order for the future. At the close of antiquity new racial migrations threatened to overwhelm Lower Nubia which was defended only with great difficulty. Now the tribe of the Blemmyes makes its appearance to become the terror of Upper Egypt. The emperor Diocletian summoned the Nobadae tribe to defend Lower Nubia against the Blemmyes and in so doing made use of an ancient tribal feud for his own ends. Aswan, then known as Syene, once more became a frontier town. We know that for a time these warlike Nobadae swept the Blemmyes tribesmen from the whole of Lower Nubia northwards as far as Shellal at the beginning of the Aswan Cataract.[1] Yet this did not bring peace; the contrary was in fact the case. In the Fifth Century A.D. Shenute of Atripe complained of incursions by 'Nubians' who plundered monasteries in the Thebaid and in doing so apparently made common cause with the Blemmyes (or Bega).[2] Possibly tradition has in this case confused the names Blemmyes (Bega) and Nubians (Nobadae). Furthermore, tradition has it that both tribes were involved in the disaster that overcame them when Marcianus in A.D. 451 compelled them both to keep the peace for an hundred years. From this period of frontier warfare probably dates the series of walls that guard the district from Aswan along the east bank of the Nile as far as Shellal from attacks from the desert.

The sacred Island of Philae at the southern end of the Cataract alone presents a peaceful picture amid all the uproar of the frontier district. From the time of Nectanebos I, the last native King of Egypt in the middle of the Fourth Century B.C., magnificent temple buildings rose on the island to form that unique city of temples which a materialistic age eventually drowned beneath the waters of the reservoir south of Aswan. The chief

---

[1] Inscription of the king Silko in the temple of Kalabsha in the Dodecaschoenus.

[2] *Leipoldt, ÄZ,* 40, 126.

temple was dedicated to Isis, who in classical times was the Mistress of the Dodecaschoenus, a region that had previously owed allegiance to Khnum of Elephantine. The cult of Osiris may have reached Philae by way of Elephantine where it had become associated with that of the fruitful ram Khnum — a process that had occurred centuries earlier in Mendes and in Heracleopolis.[1] It now made Philae and Bigah, a neighbouring island in the Cataract (which in the Middle Kingdom had formed part of the line of fortresses) places that outrivalled Abydos itself in sanctity. The Abaton, the mythical grave of Osiris on the bank of the river, overshadowed by a tree called *Menta* . . . was said to be on Bigah.[2] The sacred soul of Osiris came there in the form of a bird and perched in the trees of the grove; the theologians said it came from the Obelisk House at Heliopolis and in saying so clearly had the phoenix in mind. They also taught that at Bigah the Nile with its fertilizing flood-waters came out of a cavity in which lay a relic of Osiris in the form of his left leg. 'Thy thigh is in the Thinite nome, thy leg is in the Nubian nome', says a Pyramid Text (No. 1867a), by which it means parts of the slaughtered sacrificial animal that in the ritual was regarded as the enemy of the god. Later dogma, on the contrary, regarded it as a relic of Osiris. At the time of the inundation Osiris came into his own again: 'The ringed snake conceals him in the tomb, his handsome form is (indeed) in the realm of the Dead, but he causes the fields to flourish with golden corn.'

Strict laws were enforced for the Abaton. No human dare enter there, no word should be spoken aloud on the sacred day, fishing and the netting of birds were forbidden, no music should be heard there. Only Isis and the priest in his monthly service, who from time to time took milk to place on the 365 offering tables, crossed to the island from Philae. Osiris had now become Lord of the Inundation and relegated Khnum of Elephantine to the background, just as Isis of Philae had succeeded in achieving her acceptance as Mistress of the Dodecaschoenus.

Other mythical associations met with on Philae held warnings of nearby foreign territory and the proximity of the desert. A

[1] In a Ramesside tomb Elephantine is numbered among the places with Osiris cults; Griffith, *The Inscriptions of Siut*, pl. 17, l, 42.

[2] Junker, *Das Götterdekret über das Abaton.*

particularly vital element of the cult on Philae was the legend of the angry goddess Hathor-Tefnut, the lioness of the desert whom her companion tamed and led home. There were special shrines there for her and for her 'good companion'. On Philae too, as Strabo reports (XVII, 818) was kept a falcon, distinguished from other Egyptian falcons by its size and gay colouring. It was said to have come from Ethiopia and to be the image of the soul of the Divine King Horus (whom the legend called the son of Isis) as well as of that of the sun-god Rē'.[1] The place where he showed himself as a ruler was situated above the great main door of the temple of Isis; and if he was asked whence he came his reply was the same as that of the lioness — from the distant south-east, the 'land of the gods'. Both these cults preserved the association with the eastern desert and its inhabitants. It is therefore not surprising that Strabo calls Philae a dwelling place common to Ethiopians and Egyptians. At Philae in Roman times there was also a shrine of the Nubian god Mandilis, the local divinity of Kalabsha.

The racial conflicts that raged on the frontier did not penetrate to the island. Even the wild hordes of the Blemmyes worshipped Isis of Philae and their priests shared the right of entry there with the Egyptian priests. The worship of Isis continued until the time of Justinian; but already in the Fourth Century A.D. Christian fanatics had broken the truce of the God on the island and slain the last sacred falcon.[2]

Subsequently Nubia remained under the rule of the Christian princes until the Middle Ages when Saladin conquered the country in the Twelfth Century and Nubia's individual existence was submerged in Islam. The monastery of St Simeon on the west bank of the Nile at Aswan, one of the greatest Coptic monasteries in Egypt, was also apparently abandoned in the course of the Thirteenth Century. Near the present frontier with the Sudan, just within modern Egypt, are important princely tombs, the remains of one of those Nubian princedoms of late antiquity which rose quickly to power and disappeared again often no less rapidly, engaging in constant internecine warfare during their short existences.[3] The huge burial mounds

---

[1] Junker, *Wiener Zeitschrift für der Kunde des Morgenlandes*, 26, 42f.
[2] Wilcken, *Archiv für Papyrusforschung*, I, 396; Spiegelberg, *op. cit.*, vol. 8, 186f.
[3] Emery and Kirwan, *Royal Tombs of Ballana and Qustul*.

contain sacrificed camels, sheep and men, just like the princely tombs at Kerma dating from the Twentieth Century B.C. Their most striking contents were horses with silver-mounted trappings similar to those placed in the tombs of the Ethiopian kings of Napata,[1] and also much valuable booty in the form of finely wrought objects of the late antique period. The presence of Christian emblems suggests plundered monasteries rather than the Christian beliefs of their last possessors. The tombs can, with reasonable certainty, be ascribed to the princes of the Nobadae who ruled about A.D. 400.[2] They indicate the last individual contribution made by Nubia to the centuries-long communal association with the superior culture of the Egyptian part of the Nile valley.

[1] See below, p. 340.
[2] Von Bissing, *Archäologischer Anzeiger* (1939), 570f.

XIII

Napata, the Most Southerly Town of the Empire

In the Thebaid the Nile runs to within a hundred miles of the Red Sea coast; in Lower Nubia, however, it turns increasingly to the south-west while the coast runs to the south-east, so that the desert zone between becomes increasingly great. Modern through traffic on its way south leaves the valley of the Nile just before the Second Cataract at Wadi Halfa on lat. 21° 55′ N., the first Sudanese town of size to be reached. The modern railway from Wadi Halfa to Khartum was built in 1896–7 when the Anglo-Egyptian army advanced to free the Sudan from the Mahdi's rule; it runs 217 miles across the desert south-eastwards to Abu Hamed, thus cutting off the great westerly curve of the Nile.

The country lying between the Second and Fourth Cataract is one of the districts on the Nile furthest removed from traffic and at all ages it has been difficult to develop because of the natural barriers. The cataracts rendered through-navigation impossible and the transit trade therefore, inasmuch as it had draught-beasts (particularly camels) capable of crossing the desert, by-passed the entire zone by undertaking long desert marches. To the west of the Nile ran the infamous slave traders' route, the Darb el-Arba'in, which ran from Asyut by way of the Oasis of Khargah and various uninhabited oases and wells to el-Fasher in Darfur. To the east of the river ran an old trade-route, the precursor of the railway; it left the Nile valley at Korosko in Lower Nubia and did not return to the river until it reached the neighbourhood of Abu Hamed. Other routes starting from the Aswan area avoided the whole Cataract district by passing through the territory of the Bisharin tribe. Today there is a branch railway 150 miles in length connecting Abu Hamed with Kareima below the Fourth Cataract and from there a steamer runs a shuttle-service as far as Kerma at the southern end of the Third Cataract, a distance of about 210 miles.

The district between the Second and Third Cataract is a dead land; it exists only as a link in the line of communications between Egypt and Upper Nubia. In 1897 at the time of the advance into the Sudan, a railway for supplies and reinforcements was built from Wadi Halfa to Kerma, but it was subsequently abandoned as uneconomic and it was ultimately dismantled. This district, which comprises the former province of Halfa, is that least capable of development on the Nile and it is only when the neighbouring province of Dongola is reached, south of the Third Cataract, that the country takes on a more fertile appearance. At all times this area has served as a transit zone and a gathering place for people migrating from the Sudan, and as such it has endured many hard knocks of fate. It was from here that once the Kushites pushed forward into Lower Nubia; the Danagla (Barabra) in Dongola are held to be the most genuine descendants of the slave-traders, just as the Kushites in ancient times furnished Egypt with its most efficient police and soldiers. At the beginning of the Nineteenth Century when Mohammed Ali conquered the Sudan, these Barabra occupied the land as far as the Fourth Cataract, sharing the land with and dominated by the Shaikiyah Arabs, a related but younger tribe.

At Old Dongola the Nile abandons its south–north direction and, for one travelling upstream, it bends to the east and then to the north-east and the Fourth Cataract. From Old Dongola and Dabba caravan routes run westwards to Darfur and Kordofan (along the Wadi Milk) through a district in which the desert gradually changes to barren steppe, until the pastures of the Kababish beduin begin to appear. Other routes leave the valley of the Nile further upstream to the east at Merowe or Abu Dom, about eighty miles from Dabba. Merowe is today the capital of the district; it lies on lat. 18° 29' N. and long. 31° 49' E., which makes it further east than Wadi Halfa, the longitude of which is 31° 19' E. The routes from here run south-eastwards through the Bajuda plains to the neighbourhood of

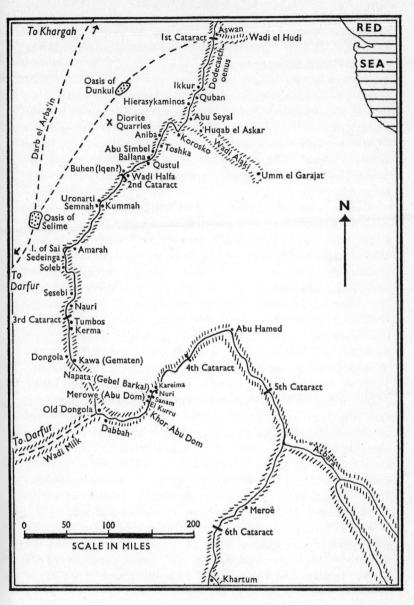

11. Nubia and the Upper Nile

the mouth of the Atbara and to Meroë, the capital of the old Ethiopian Empire. Here it is not surprising to find that the primitive conflict between nomads and peasants has continued to result in bloody clashes for existence down to the most recent times. The Mahdist rule in the Sudan from 1885, in its last years under the so-called Kalifa, was supported largely by the Bakkara tribes from Darfur, who were cattle-breeding nomads similar to those who left the prehistoric rock-drawings on the Gebel Uwenat. These were the tribes at whose hands the peasant population of the northern provinces suffered the worst outrages.

A short way downstream to the south-east of the railway station of Kareima, the isolated flat-topped hill of Gebel Barkal rises out of the pebbly desert plain; it has precipitous sides and on its southern flank there projects a cone-shaped pillar of rock (Pl. 22. *a*). At the foot where the ground is littered with fallen boulders, are the remains of an ancient temple, a few pillars with rather ill-formed Egyptian capitals and parts of walls bearing representations of Egyptian gods and kings wearing Egyptian crowns. Egyptian hieroglyphics can also be seen, and yet the whole effect is peculiarly contorted and barbaric. This is the temple of Napata, the first capital of the Ethiopian Empire, founded by the 'pure mountain' on which the Ethiopians' principal deity, Amun, sat enthroned. The abode of the god who bore an Egyptian name, was in the first place undoubtedly the pillar of rock below which his temple stood. On this side of the river a small strip of cultivated land runs along the river, but on the broader eastern bank the land is carefully cultivated; there, in contrast to the stark desolation around Gebel Barkal, are tidy villages in the shelter of palms whose inhabitants are industrious and physically well-developed.

The administrative centre of the district is Merowe, not to be confused with the ancient town of Meroë. It lies between the villages of Abu Dom and Sanam and was the creation of Sir H. W. Jackson, the Governor of Dongola Province for many years. Its centre consists of the barracks and the fort built by Kitchener at this strategically important point to serve as a base for his advance on Khartum. It stands on the top of a flat-topped, sandy hill from which one can look to the east to the far distance beyond the river and on the foundations built by the

334

Ethiopian king Taharqa who ruled over Egypt until his defeat at the hands of the Assyrians in the Seventh Century B.C. To the west of Gebel Barkal can be seen slender Ethiopian Pyramids; but the largest of such pyramids are at Nuri on the east bank of the river where the beginning of the Fourth Cataract is marked by rapids running between islands. A still older royal necropolis lies downstream at el-Kurru.

The first person to bring back definite information and useful copies of scenes and texts from Napata was Cailliaud who in 1822 accompanied the Egyptian army, commanded by Ismail Pasha, the son of Mohammed Ali. In 1844 Lepsius took copies of the most important remains. Shortly before the First World War Griffith excavated at Sanam and from 1916 onwards Reisner investigated all the temples of Napata and firmly established the history of the royal cemeteries at el-Kurru and Nuri. The principal periods of Ethiopian history have since then taken their place among the better known important periods of ancient history.

Nevertheless the funerary inscriptions and other monuments are silent about the first appearance of the Egyptians in this area. We spoke earlier of the ancient Egyptian trading-post at Kerma at the southern end of the Third Cataract.[1] It was there that the Egyptian traders discovered for themselves the products of the fertile land of the province of Dongola and the access to the trade routes leading further south. The Egyptians did not forget these things even in the worst days of the Hyksos rule when a foreign tyrant ruled in the Delta and an independent prince in Nubia. It was just at that time that the war-tested Medjay, the beduin tribes of the eastern desert, poured into the Thebaid as soldiers. Their presence in Egypt is marked by their own special cemeteries that continue as far north as Asyut, but no further. Their tombs are shallow pits now known as 'pan-graves' and their burial customs are quite un-Egyptian, but characteristically African. In the days of the Theban kings these mercenaries had their own settlements on Egyptian soil.[2]

The kings who created the Egyptian Empire, as a result of their fight to expel the Asiatic Hyksos, were in the habit of beginning their reigns with military campaigns in the south in order to win military glory at little cost. Stage by stage the

[1] See above, p. 318.   [2] See above, p. 142.

frontier was advanced.[1] About 1545 B.C. Amenophis I regained the frontier established by Sesostris III at the Second Cataract. His son Tuthmosis I, who was the first Pharaoh to reach the Euphrates, broke through the line of natural defences of the southern tribes at the Third Cataract and reached the Plain of Dongola. He also fortified Kerma where in the Middle Kingdom had been established the advanced factory for the Egyptian southern trade. Kerma was also an important tribal centre for the Kushites, the people of the culture called C-group in Nubian archaeology.

Tuthmosis I mounted this campaign in his second year. Rock inscriptions on the Island of Sai in the Tangur rapids record that His Majesty travelled southwards to subdue vile Kush and that the boats were dragged through the whirlpools of both cataracts with great labour. At Tombos a little north of Kerma the king called himself 'he who opens the valleys which his predecessors did not know and which the wearers of the double crown had not seen. His southern frontier (now) reaches to the beginning of this land. . . .'[2] The king here suppresses the fact that the country lay open as far as the Fourth Cataract.

Tuthmosis I certainly did not reach Napata. It was first reached by Tuthmosis III who also completed in Asia the work begun by his grandfather. Nevertheless the sole memorial of Tuthmosis III at Napata is a large granite stela dated in his forty-seventh year, which Reisner found.[3] At this time the Syrian wars had in fact finished and the Egyptian system of vassal states in Asia Minor was functioning well. It may well have been at this time that the great king decided to make the final frontier of his realm at the most southerly province. Can this stela be the one mentioned by the extremely busy chief architect, Minmose, in an inscription in the limestone quarry at Masara near Memphis? He praises himself for erecting such 'in the land of Kari' and also one in the land of Naharin, probably the victory stela to commemorate the crossing of the Euphrates.[4] It is easy to understand why the Egyptian armies did not advance

---

[1] Säve-Söderbergh, *Ägypten und Nubien*, 145f.

[2] *Urk.*, IV, 85, cf. Säve-Söderbergh, *op. cit.*, 148, 154.

[3] Reisner, *AZ*, 69, 24f.

[4] L. D., Text, I, 20 = Breasted, *Ancient Records*, II, § 800 (from the 4th year of Amenophis II). On the person, see above, p. 265.

any further, for here the course of the Nile, going upstream, turns eastwards into the fresh desolation of the Fourth Cataract and away from the main direction of the caravan trade that pushed directly southwards.

Later, under Amenophis III, the district of Kari is again referred to as the southern boundary of Egyptian rule. The name is perhaps echoed in the modern el-Kurru, a place about eight miles south-west of Napata with a royal necropolis of the later Ethiopian kingdom. No architectural remains of the first Egyptian period are left in Napata; but Tuthmosis III speaks of Amen-Rē', Lord of the Holy Mountain, as 'He who was called by men "Throne of the Two Lands" when he (otherwise) was not known'. In this matter Napata with its temple of Amun, as the primeval home of the god of the Egyptian Empire, was accorded greater fame than Karnak itself, which was called with the holy name 'Throne of the Two Lands'. Here we see in course of formation the legend on the basis of which the Ethiopian kings, eight centuries later, legitimized their conquest of Egypt as executors of the will of Amun. From it too came the tradition in antiquity that the Ethiopians were the most ancient people on earth, as Diodorus Siculus claims (Book III, 3). The temple of Amun at Gebel Barkal was probably protected by fortified walls just as was the case with all the Upper Nubian towns founded by the kings of Dynasty XVIII. Napata was called '(Tuthmosis III) who slays the foreigners'. In this way the name of Tuthmosis III, so feared in the south, was kept as much alive as it was in Syria, as the Amarna correspondence of centuries later shows. Furthermore, the powerful Amenophis II, son of Tuthmosis III, had one of seven rebellious princes of Takhsi (Takhash) in Northern Syria whom he had slain with his own hand, brought to Napata and hung head downwards from the wall of the fort 'in order to cause the might of His Majesty to be seen for all eternity'.[1]

The Egyptian military governor of Nubia during the New Kingdom, who was known as the 'King's Son of Kush', was responsible for everything, for Egypt maintained a more rigorous administration in Nubia than in the tributary city-states of Syria. The Empire and its buildings called for great revenues, while the army demanded more and more recruits for the

[1] On the Amada and Elephantine stelae see Säve-Söderbergh, *op. cit.*, 156.

foreign garrisons. These latter were obtained from the reservoir of black man-power in the south. Mohammed Ali's troops were likewise sent south to bring back 'Gold and Slaves'. In this 'colonial' territory the power of the Pharaohs was exercised in a more immediate manner; tribal chieftains rarely make an appearance and when they are depicted in Egyptian tombs they are at the most shown as the humble leaders of the tribute bearers. Their slaves, however, were sent as soldiers to fight for the Egyptian possessions in Asia.

Egyptian gods entered the newly developed countries south of the Second Cataract in company with Egyptian officials and military scribes. It must be admitted that the age of Amenophis III, a period of great wealth, in which the reins of government in Syria were allowed to slip dangerously from the hands of the central administration, yet showed itself full of energy in the frontier districts to the south. In about 1408 B.C., the fifth year of his reign, the king undertook his one great campaign. It was probably directed against revolts in Upper Nubia and also perhaps in answer to threats from nomadic Libyan tribes. The desire to eliminate these sources of rebellion can be seen in the intensified programme of building fortified towns south of the Second Cataract in which temples to the Egyptian gods were always erected. This series of fortified towns comprised Amarah (West), Sedeinga, Soleb, which contained a temple dedicated to the thirtieth anniversary of Amenophis III's accession, Sesebi, and, in particular, Kawa, the only town built south of the Third Cataract. The ancient name of Kawa was Gematen, first given to it probably during the reign of Akhenaten. It means 'The Aten is found' and was given to the place probably as a reformist proclamation of faith with the introduction of the new teaching in the far south. Under the Ethiopian kings of Napata Kawa remained an important place of worship which was honoured with state visits by many of them including Harsiotef and Nastasen.[1]

The credit for this building activity must go to the viceroys in Nubia. In the newly founded temples they set up statues of the reigning Pharaoh and at Sedeinga even one of Queen Tiy also, to serve as local gods for their subjects. In this they followed the example of Sesostris III who had established the frontier at the

[1] *Urk.*, III, 120, 149.

Napata, the Most Southerly Town of the Empire

Second Cataract by his campaigns. In Napata, however, the monuments still remain silent. The foundation deposits of the oldest temple of Amun belong in type to the time of Tuthmosis IV,[1] while the next stage in the construction of the building clearly belongs to the time of Tutankhamun and Horemheb, when the viceroy was the able Huy whose tomb at Thebes we know. Only of the time of Ramesses II can we speak of affairs there with certainty.

For the understanding of the over-all picture, however, there is one not unimportant fact: in the southern provinces, in contrast to the Asiatic provinces, the authority of Egypt remained unimpaired throughout the Amarna Period. There soldiers stood on guard, like Horemheb in Memphis. Moreover, they were not threatened by a redoubtable enemy. Yet Ramesses II had himself portrayed in scenes of battle as victor over the southern peoples in all the Nubian temples, including that at Amarah where in the Ramesside Period the King's Son of Kush had his residence as head of the administration of the province.[2] It may be questioned, however, whether these scenes of battle depict actual historical events or were only the indispensable pictorial epithets akin in character to the exuberantly phrased inscriptions. As a monumental architect Ramesses II, strangely, has not left anything like the mark on Napata as he did upon Abu Simbel and the other Nubian towns. Nevertheless the power of the viceroys of Kush remained unbroken and, in the period of the general decay of authority from the time of Ramesses III, it seems as if the southern provinces actually gained in importance with the support of the viceroy's Nubian army. Historical testimony confirms that Egyptian officials were in continuous residence at Napata up to the time of Ramesses IX, and at Aniba, Amarah and other places up to the time of Ramesses XI, the last of that name. Furthermore, it is not by chance that we find Panehsi, the viceroy of Kush, not only appearing as the restorer of order in Thebes after the rebellion against the high priest Amenhotpe, but also engaging in Middle Egypt in local warfare with, perhaps, invading Libyans.[3] Again, the royal high

[1] On the dating, see Reisner, *JEA*, 4, 213f.; 6, 247f.
[2] Fairman, *JEA*, 34, 11.
[3] Kees, *Herihor und die Aufrichtung des thebanischen Gottesstaates*; see above, p. 281.

priest Herihor, as commander-in-chief in Egypt, kept the very important post of viceroy of Kush in his own hands.

With Herihor's son Piankhi the curtain descends on Nubian history (about 1050 B.C.) and when it rises again in the middle of the Eighth Century B.C. Ethiopian kings named Kashta and Piankhi are ruling in the Holy Mountain at Napata and they in their turn advance into Egypt to restore order in the name of Amun. We do not know the origin of their family but they certainly preached the orthodox faith of Amun which had merely been outwardly observed in theocratic Thebes since the time of Herihor. In Thebes there ruled high priests of Amun who were the descendants of the families of Libyan chieftains. Their authority was supported by the army and by a small number of local families who invested their high offices of state with priestly titles. In Napata, however, a real priestly caste held power and it, by means of oracular pronouncements by the god Amun, influenced state policy and frequently even the choice of the royal pretenders.[1] They recorded the royal annals in Egyptian hieroglyphs in the good Egyptian manner of olden times. They buried their dead, particularly their royal dead, with all the offerings associated with Egyptian funerary customs: scarabs, statuettes of the gods and all kinds of amulets in accordance with the ritual of Osiris. In this way the families of Kashta, Piankhi and their successors were buried at el-Kurru.[2] It is not quite certain whether the much damaged superstructures of their tombs were in fact real pyramids like those of their successors at Nuri.

Piankhi, who, about 730 B.C., had made a victorious advance into the Delta, had his personal chargers buried beside his tomb, as did his successors Shabaka, Shabataka and Tanutamun (who was the immediate successor of Taharqa), usually four horses in each case. This practice was like that followed centuries later by the princes of the Nobadae buried south of Abu Simbel.[3] The Ethiopians were fine horsemen and lovers of horses, like the Shaikiyah Arabs from Dongola in the days of Mohammed Ali. This characteristic is wholly un-Egyptian and probably part of the beduin heritage, like their great political ability. After cap-

[1] Stela of King Aspelta from Napata (VIth Century, B.C.), *Urk.*, III, 81f.; buried in Pyramid nr. 8 at Nuri.

[2] Dows Dunham, *El Kurru, The Royal Cemeteries of Kush*, I.

[3] Reisner, *Bulletin of the Museum of Fine Arts, Boston*, 19, nrs. 112–13.

turing Hermopolis in Middle Egypt, Piankhi first of all visited the stables of Namlot the Bubastite prince who ruled there and he severely rebuked him for not having his horses better looked after.[1] The great cemetery of commoners that Griffith excavated at Sanam (Napata East), near the temple of Taharqa, was, both in the offerings found there and in the lay-out of the tombs, purely Egyptian despite the fact that it was not the cemetery of an Egyptian colony.[2] There was no trace there of the characteristically Ethiopian civilization such as we find flourishing at Kerma before the New Kingdom.

The arrival in Egypt of these believers in Amun yet did not arouse wholehearted sympathy. A 'rebirth' of the old regime had been hoped for under Herihor; now, under the leadership of 'vile Kush' which had formerly been the most distant province from Thebes, what was dreamed of was a renaissance in religion, language and art modelled on the example of that established by the founder of the Empire.[3] From a military point of view the new movement fell victim to the superior military strength and organization of the Assyrians; but it also seems as if the more brutal habits of the Ethiopians were less welcome to the Egyptian governing class than the rule of Libyan chieftains inclined towards feudalism, who had their residences in the capital cities of the Egyptian nomes and who kept the highest priestly offices in their own hands.

It is true that Menthuemhat, a contemporary of Taharqa, who lived through the Assyrian invasion, was, as Governor of the Thebaid, a supporter of the Ethiopian kings. His forefathers had held the highest office, the vizirship, in Thebes;[4] but his and other similar leading families formed obviously a small group. Soon afterwards Psammetichus of Sais, a descendant of one of those Lower Egyptian Libyan chieftain families, liberated himself from Assyrian rule about 663 B.C. and, in 655 B.C. Tanutamun, the successor of Taharqa, abandoned Thebes and withdrew to Napata. Nubia then became the buffer between the two alien and hostile states of Egypt and Ethiopia.

---

[1] *Urk.*, III, 21–2.

[2] Griffith, *Liverpool Annals of Archaeology and Anthropology*, 10, 73f.

[3] E. Meyer, 'Gottesstaat, Militärherrschaft und Ständewesen inÄgypten' in *Sb. Berl. Akad. phil.-hist. Kl.* (1928), nr. 28.

[4] See above, p. 285.

Cities and Districts

The Kingdom of Napata was by this time forced to rely on its own strength and the time had come also to test whether Egyptian civilization had really taken roots in this former Egyptian colony. The historical scene unfortunately once again becomes veiled in mists, but we are able to learn the succession of kings and queens from their tombs in the cemetery at Nuri.[1] Egyptian culture and a false archaism continue on the surface but barbaric elements appear. Thus the faces of the royal statues have thick lips and the crowns worn are too ornate, suggesting that primitive desire for display which led eventually to the extravagances of the crowns of the Nobadae princes found in their tombs at Qustul, dating to about A.D. 400. When ultimately they sought to replace the Egyptian tradition with something else, they had inevitably to seize upon as a replacement the Hellenistic-Alexandrian style. This renouncing of the Egyptian tradition, which was certainly accompanied by a retreat from priestly rule, has been ascribed to the influence of the Greek-educated Ergasthenes, about 220 B.C.; and the effects are to be observed principally in Meroë, the later capital of the Ethiopian Empire.

Nuri, to the north-east of Napata, was chosen by Taharqa, who died towards the end of 664 B.C., as the site on which to build the largest pyramid built until then in Ethiopia. The pyramids of a succession of about twenty kings there proves the continued existence of the Egyptian tradition up to the reign of Nastasen about 300 B.C. He had grown up and been chosen king in Meroë, but he was crowned at Napata and lies buried in its cemetery at Nuri in pyramid 15. These Ethiopian pyramids have the steep sides of the brick pyramids that it was fashionable to erect over the façades of tombs in Ramesside Thebes, particularly at Dira' Abu'n Naga and Deir el-Medinah. The angle is much steeper than the 52° used generally for the royal pyramids of the Old and Middle Kingdom. In this matter the Ethiopian kings had been inspired well but the realization of their inspiration was unthinkable without Egyptian craftsmen and knowledge, just as the setting up of statues and the erection of inscriptions in their underground burial chambers failed likewise. In spite of his defeat in Egypt, Taharqa is strangely the

[1] Reisner, op. cit., vol. 16, nr. 97; Dunham and Macadam, JEA, 35, 139f., with genealogical tree.

one ancient Ethiopian king who is most strongly in evidence architecturally in the temple of Amun below Gebel Barkal and at Sanam (Napata East). The temple at Sanam, moreover, was decorated with historical reliefs in which Ethiopians are depicted with their four- and six-wheeled chariots and also as riders, apparently mounted on mules.[1]

The wealth and importance of Napata was founded on its situation at the head of the caravan routes leading to the interior of the Sudan. It was probably due to the stagnation of the cultural, political and economic relations with Egypt that resulted in the transference of leadership from Napata to Meroë. This city lay to the south of the junction of the Atbara with the Nile in the area where the savanna country begins and it looked to the south-east. The political death-blow suffered by Napata was its destruction by Petronius in 23 B.C. during his punitive campaign against the Ethiopian ruler or Kandake, in reprisal for the attack on Syene. This destruction brought about its end as a capital city. On the Island of Argo there lies a colossus of an Ethiopian king of this period, represented wearing an Egyptian double crown and on it a laurel wreath, the symbol of another civilization, and a sign, perhaps, of a victory over Roman legions. The erection of this statue at Meroë was possibly prevented by the defeat inflicted by Petronius.[2] The golden age of the Kingdom of Meroë left at Napata not one memorial comparable with those in the new capital and when Nero's ambassadors passed through Napata they found it only a small town.

The Christian Period alone left traces in Napata in the darkness that now enveloped it for hundreds of years. In spite of what Nubia had to suffer in late antiquity from migrations and wars, Christianity showed there a strong individual life in opposition to Islam up to the Thirteenth Century. Then it was rooted out far more radically than in Egypt and with the brutality that at all times has characterized Nubian tribal and religious struggles. Riding from Napata East (Sanam) over the Khor Abu Dom for about eight miles up the Wadi Ghazzali one comes across the ruins of a monastery with a stately church built partly of white

[1] Griffith, *op. cit.*, vol. 9, pls. 24, 31f.

[2] Dunham, *JEA*, 33, pl. 14, 7 who thinks King Natakamani's dates were about 15 B.C.–A.D. 15 (the high-water mark of the Meroitic Empire).

sandstone and partly of brick in a desert region of a few thorn bushes and water-holes, surrounded by the tracks of giraffes and jackals.[1] In 1844 Lepsius rescued from the cemetery of the monastery a number of Coptic and Greek gravestones which he sent to Berlin.

Napata lay far away from the native soil of Egypt, but all that we find there it owed to Egypt, from Amun on the Holy Mountain and Egyptian hieroglyphics to the Christianity that came to the Sudan from Alexandria, like many other things that enriched Meroitic civilization. For that reason may Napata fittingly close this album of the Egyptian countryside.

[1] Plan in L. *D.*, I, 131, cf. Text, V, 291f.

Summary Outline of Egyptian History

c. 4000 B.C. In upper Egypt the cultures of Der Tasa and Badari. In Lower Egypt the culture of Merimdah in the West Delta.

c. 3700 B.C. Naqada I or Amratian culture in the Thebaid.

c. 3300 B.C. Naqada II or Gerzean culture in Middle and Upper Egypt. The peasant culture of Ma'adi, showing Asiatic influences flourishes in the Cairo area.

EARLY DYNASTIC OR THINITE PERIOD

c. 2980 B.C. Unification of Upper and Lower Egypt by the Upper Egyptian Kings of Hieraconpolis (Menes). Subjection of the North-western Delta (formerly Libyan) — Kingdom of Sais and Buto. Reign of Horus 'the Fighter' (Aha).

c. 2950–2677 B.C. Dynasty I: Royal tombs at Abydos from the reign of Djer (Athothis). Foundation of Memphis. Dynasty II: Royal tombs at Abydos and Memphis. Growing strength of the North. Occurrence of the first royal names with Rē' included (Nebrē'). Other kings: Ninetjer (Binothris), Peribsen (Tlas), Sethenes, Khasekhemui, Nebka (?).

OLD KINGDOM

c. 2676 B.C. Dynasty III: Zoser and the transfer of the royal Residence from This to Memphis. Imhotep, the

345

Summary

High Priest of Heliopolis, introduces the use of stone in building in the Step Pyramid complex at Saqqara.

c. 2627–2513 B.C. Dynasty IV: The great Pyramid builders — Snofru, Cheops, Chephren, Mycerinus.

c. 2512–2376 B.C. Dynasty V: Kings for the first time call themselves 'Sons of Rē' — Userkaf, Sahurē', Neferirkarē'. Under Isesi occurs the emergence of the cult of Rē' as the state religion. From the time of Unas the Pyramid Texts are inscribed in Pyramids.

c. 2375–2194 B.C. Dynasties VI–VIII: Kings of the VIth Dynasty: Teti, Pepi I, Merenrē', Pepi II. Development of feudalism especially in Upper Egypt where the nomarchs increase in power. Towards the end of the period an influx of Asiatics into the Delta and simultaneously social unrest leads to the downfall of the Old Kingdom.

First Intermediate Period

In Memphis, the ephemeral descendants of the Old Kingdom, the so-called Coptos Dynasty from Upper Egypt (about 2130 B.C.).

c. 2160–2040 B.C. Dynasties IX, X in Heracleopolis — 'the House of Akhtoy'.

c. 2140–2000 B.C. Dynasty XI in Thebes; Antefs and Menthuhotpes from Hermonthis originally.

Nebhepetrē' Menthuhotpe (*c.* 2070–2019 B.C.) reunified Upper and Lower Egypt.

Middle Kingdom

1991–1786 B.C. Dynasty XII from Thebes. Residence at Lisht. Kings mostly named Ammenemes and Sesostris. Dissolution of the feudal system. Conquest of Nubia.

1785–*c.* 1670 B.C. Dynasty XIII. Gradual decay of the central authority. Residence at Memphis or Thebes. Kings mostly called Sebekhotpe or Neferhotpe.

Summary

SECOND INTERMEDIATE PERIOD

c. 1700–1570 B.C. Suzerainty of the Asiatic Hyksos in the Delta with Avaris as the capital.

c. 1570 B.C. Liberation of Egypt, starting from Thebes, by the Kings of the XVIIth Dynasty, the last of whom was Kamose.

NEW KINGDOM — THE EMPIRE

Dynasty XVIII:

c. 1568–1545 B.C. Ahmose the final conqueror of the Hyksos; his wife, Ahmes-Nefertari.

c. 1545–1524 Amenophis I.

c. 1524–1507 Tuthmosis I — advanced as far as the Euphrates.

c. 1507–1504 Tuthmosis II.

c. 1503–1483 Hatshepsut.

c. 1503–1449 Tuthmosis III, the real founder of the Empire which stretched from Napata to the Euphrates.

c. 1449–1422 Amenophis II.

c. 1422–1413 Tuthmosis IV.

c. 1413–1377 Amenophis III.

c. 1377–1360 Amenophis IV, later called Akhenaten; he removed the Residence to el-Amarna (Akhetaten).

c. 1362–1318 Return of the old order under Smenkhkareʿ, Tutankhamun, Ay and Horemheb.

c. 1317–1085 Dynasties XIX and XX:
The Ramessides from the Delta: Ramesses I, Sethos I, Ramesses II (rules 67 years), Merenptah.
Foundation of Tanis (Piramesse), revival of Memphis.
Syrian wars.
Ramesses III (*c.* 1198–1166 B.C.), the last great temple builder in Thebes — Medinet Habu. Wars against the Libyans and the Peoples of the Sea.
Under the last Ramesside Kings (Ramesses IV–XI) a general decline.

Summary

TRANSITION TO LATE PERIOD OR
THIRD INTERMEDIATE PERIOD

c. 1085–945 B.C. Dynasty XXI: Herihor in Thebes, Smendes in
Tanis. Establishment of the divine state of Amun
at Thebes.

c. 945–718 B.C. Dynasties XXII and XXIII: Kings of Libyan
origin, mostly named Sheshonk and Osorkon;
from the feudal régime established in Heracleopolis. Tombs of these Kings in Tanis.

LATE PERIOD

c. 750–663 B.C. Dynasty XXV: Ethiopian Kings from Napata
— struggle with Assyrians for the lordship of
Egypt. Kings named Piankhi, Shabaka, Shabataka, Taharqa, Tanutamun. Contemporary
petty princes in the Delta, e.g. Tefnakhte in
Sais. Beginning of a cultural renaissance.

c. 663–525 B.C. Dynasty XXVI: Saite Kings: Psammetichus I,
Necho, Psammetichus II, Apries, Amasis,
Psammetichus III.
Flowering of the cities of the Delta.

PERSIAN PERIOD

525–404 B.C. Dynasty XXVII. Cambyses conquers Egypt.

404–341 B.C. Dynasties XXVIII–XXX: Warring Kings in
Lower Egypt; Egypt from time to time freed
from Persian suzerainty.
Nekhthorheb (Nectanebos II), the last native
ruler of Egypt, overcome by Artaxerxes Ochus.

332 B.C. Alexander the Great conquers Egypt.

N.B. For the Early Dynastic Period and the Old Kingdom the
lowest possible dates are given; they could scarcely be reduced
further.

Short Bibliography of Books in English for further reading

Baedeker, K. *Egypt and the Sudan*. 8th edition (ed. G. Steindorff), Leipzig, 1929.

Baikie, J. *Egyptian Antiquities in the Nile Valley*. London, 1932.

Ball, J. *Description of the First or Aswan Cataract of the Nile*. Cairo, 1907.
> *Contributions to the Geography of Egypt*. Cairo, 1939.
> *Egypt in the Classical Geographers*. Cairo, 1942.

Breasted, J. H. *Ancient Records of Egypt*. 5 vols. Chicago, 1906–7.
> *A History of Egypt from the Earliest Times to the Persian Conquest*. 2nd Edition, London, 1927.

Englebach, R. *Introduction to Egyptian Archaeology with special reference to the Egyptian Museum, Cairo*. Cairo, 1946.

Erman, A. *The Literature of the Ancient Egyptians*. London, 1927.

Cerny, J. *Ancient Egyptian Religion*. London, 1952.

Gardiner, A. H. *Ancient Egyptian Onomastica*. 3 vols. Oxford, 1947.

Glanville, S. R. K. (ed.). *The Legacy of Egypt*. Oxford, 1942.

Hayes, W. C. *The Scepter of Egypt*. 2 vols. New York, 1953, 1959.

Hume, W. F. *The Geology of Egypt*. 2 vols. Cairo, 1925, 1935.

Lucas, A. *Ancient Egyptian Materials and Industries*. 3rd Edition, London, 1948.

Montet, P. *Everyday Life in Egypt*. London, 1958.

Moret, A. *The Nile and Egyptian Civilisation*. London, 1927.

Smith, W. S. *The Art and Architecture of Ancient Egypt*. Harmondsworth, 1958.

Weigall, A. E. P. *Guide to the Antiquities of Upper Egypt from Abydos to the Sudan Frontier*. London, 1910.

List of Abbreviations

Abh. Berl. Akad.	*Abhandlungen der preussischen Akademie der Wissenschaften.* Berlin.
Amenemope	The Wisdom of Amenemope contained in British Museum Papyrus 10474; for convenient text see H. O. Lange, *Das Weisheitsbuch des Amenemope.* Copenhagen, 1925.
Annales du Service	*Annales du Service des Antiquités de l'Égypte.* Cairo.
Anz. Wien. Akad.	*Anzeiger der philosophisch-historische Klasse der wiener Akademie der Wissenschaften.* Vienna.
Archiv. f. Pap.	*Archiv für Papyrusforschung und verwandte Gebiete.* Leipzig.
ÄZ	*Zeitschrift für ägyptische Sprache und Altertumskunde. Leipzig and Berlin.*
BIFAO	*Bulletin de l'Institut français d'archéologie orientale.* Cairo.
Forsch. und Fortschr.	*Forschungen und Fortschritte, Korrespondenzblatt der deutschen Wissenschaft und Technik.* Berlin.
Gött. gel. Anz.	*Göttingische gelehrte Anzeigen.* Göttingen.
Gött. Nachr.	*Nachrichten der Akademie der Wissenschaften in Göttingen.* Göttingen.
JEA	*Journal of Egyptian Archaeology.* London.
JNES	*Journal of Near Eastern Studies.* Chicago.
Knudzton	J. A. Knudzton, *Die el-Amarna Tafeln.* Leipzig, 1915.
L.D.	R. Lepsius, *Denkmäler aus Ägypten und Äthiopien,* 6 vols. Berlin, 1849–58.
Mém. Inst. fr. or.	*Mémoires publiés par les Membres de l'Institut français d'archéologie orientale du Caire.* Cairo.
Mitt. dt. Inst. Kairo	*Mitteilungen des deutschen Instituts für ägyptische Altertumskunde in Kairo.* Cairo.

List of Abbreviations

Mitt. dt. Orientsges.	*Mitteilungen der deutschen Orientsgesellschaft zu Berlin.* Berlin.
Mitt. vörder-asiat.-ägypt. Ges.	*Mitteilungen der vörderasiatisch-ägyptischen Gesellschaft.* Leipzig.
OLZ	*Orientalistische Litteraturzeitung.* Berlin and Leipzig.
PSI	*Papiri della Società italiana per la ricerca dei papiri greci e latini in Egitto.* Florence.
Rec. de Trav.	*Receuil de travaux relatifs à la philologie et à l'archéologie égyptienne et assyrienne.* Paris, 1870–1923.
Sb. bayer Akad.	*Sitzungsberichte der bayerischen Akademie der Wissenschaften.* Munich.
Sb. berl. Akad.	*Sitzungsberichte der königlich-preussischen Akademie der Wissenschaften.* Berlin.
Schäfer-Andrae[3]	H. Schäfer and W. Andrae, *Die Kunst des alten Orients.* 3rd edition. Berlin.
Syria	*Révue d'Art et d'Archéologie publiée par l'Institut français d'archéologie de Beyrouth.* Paris.
Untersuchungen	*Untersuchungen zur Geschicht und Altertumskunde Ägyptens.* Leipzig.
Urk.	G. Steindorff (editor), *Urkunden des ägyptischen Altertums.*
	I. *Urkunden des alten Reiches* (K. Sethe).
	II. *Hieroglyphische Urkunden der griechisch-römischen Zeit* (K. Sethe).
	III. *Urkunden der älteren Äthiopenkönige* (H. Schäfer).
	IV. *Urkunden der 18. Dynastie* (K. Sethe and W. Helck).
	V. *Religiöse Urkunden* (H. Grapow).
	VI. *Urkunden mythologischen Inhalts* (S. Schott).
	VII. *Urkunden des mittlere Reiches* (K. Sethe).
Wreszinski, Atlas	W. Wreszinski, *Atlas zur altägyptischen Kulturgeschichte*, I–III. Leipzig, 1923–38.
Ztschr. Ges. f. allg. Erdkunde	*Zeitschrift der Gesellschaft für allgemeine Erdkunde.* Berlin.

Index

Note: The letter m indicates a map reference. Place names should be sought both with and without the 'El', 'Gebel', etc. prefixed.

Index

Acacia groves, significance of, 78; acacia wood for barques, 108, 109

Achoris, Siwa recognises Egypt's sovereignty in person of, 132–3

Acina (near Wadi Halfa) in Greek trade, 208

Acoris (now Tihna), 99 m, 203

Aegean art, Egypt and, 138–9

Agatharchides of Cnidos, on mine-working in 130 B.C., 125

Aghurmi, fortress temple of, 132

Agni district, near el-Kab, 71

Agriculture, see Farming

Ägyptische Wörterbuch, 108 n

Aha ('the Fighter'), Horus king, 237; tablets of, 108

Ahanakhte, nomarch of Hermopolis, 130

Ahmes-Nefertari (Queen), cult of in Thebes, 79, 274, 283; as mother of Amenophis I, 67; as wife of Ahmose, 244

Ahmose, King, 72; conqueror of Hyksos, 243; house of consistently revered in Abydos and Thebes, 244; cenotaph and terraced temple of, 233 m; dummy tomb of, Abydos, 243; small number of decorated rock tombs under (cf. Amenophis, Hatshepsut, Tuthmosis I), 266–7

Aimé-Giron, N., 326 n

Akhenaten, King, at Amarna (son of Amenophis III), 76, 137, 138, 143, 227, 288, 291; aviary of, 95; effects on Theban art of ideas of, 176, 271; 'Horizon of Aten' sanctuary of, 270; names Gematen (later Kawa), 338; reforms of as detrimental to temple property, 209; reforms of, generally, 266; statue of in Aten temple at Karnak, 301; degradation of, as 'Blasphemer of Akhetaten', 305–6; as Amenophis IV, 294 seqq.

Akhetaten ('Horizon of Aten', capital city), foundation of by Akhenaten, 293; location of, 289 m; house owners in, 296–7; isolation of, 295; lay-out of, 296–7; official titles in, 297; desolation of, 305, 306

Akhmim, 99 m, 119 m, 236

Akhtihotpe (vizir under Asosi), 70, 188; mastabas of, 166

Akhtoy II, King, Heracleopolitan, 120, 191; house of at Heracleopolis, 217; reconquest of This by, 240; Theban struggles of, 290; Akhtoy-Antef wars, 239–40

Akita, desert, for gold, 322

Alabaster, see Hatnub; festal boat of, from tomb of Tutankhamun, Pl. 25a; vases, from Kerma, 318

'Alamat defined, 314, 322

Alexander the Great, 132, 180; restores barque room to Amun temple, Luxor, 285

Alexandria, 21 m, 184, 186 m, 210, 344; absence of Minoan trading post noteworthy, 140; founding of, 210; Greek rule in, 229; olive trees of, 81

Ali Shafei Bey, on Fayum irrigation, 221, 221 n

Alliot, 170 n; BIFAO, 311 n

Almásy: Unbekannte Sahara, 20 n, 22 n, 129 n

Amada stela, 337 n

Amarah, 315, 325, 333 m, 338

Amarna (el Amarna) culture, 53 n, 67, 81, 95, 99, 104, 137, 139, 143, 147, 175–6, 196, 212, 244, 262, 275, 280, 288 seqq., 290, 298 n, 337; Pls. 23–4; art of, 246; Cretan palace culture decline of, and 141; excavations, peculiar value of, 307; garden shrines, 79 n; houses of, 298–9; impressionistic floor paintings, 84; royal palace design, 299–300; ruling-class types, as shown by sculptured head, 302; sculptures, see Sculptures; in southern provinces, 339; Thebes showing slightest traces of destruction of, 270; wine-jar stoppers, 82; workers' villages, 158

354

Index

Amasis (Saite king), 69, 71, 132, 180; makes Naucratis concession port for Greek trade, 207; stela of, Cairo, 109 n

Amélineau, E., excavations of, Abydos cemeteries, 232

Amenappa, 257

Amenemope, 98 n

Amenhotpe, high priest, son of Hapu, 193, 286; temple of, 251, 255 m; as possible builder of temple of Luxor, 262–3; Karnak statues of, 264, 265; Amenhotpe, high priest, second son of Rames-senakhte, 280, 281, 339

Ameni, son of Sesostris I and later Ammenemes II, 316–17

Amenmose, son of Tuthmosis I, 173

Amenophis I, son of Ahmes-Nefertari, 67, 244, 254, 258, 274, 336

Amenophis II, 139, 141 n, 173, 258, 265, 336 n; new 'royal favourites' policy of, 267–8; royal mummies in tomb of, 278; gives up dedica-tion of obelisks, 325

Amenophis III (father of Akhena-ten), 20, 59 n, 68–9, 81, 104, 109, 137, 138, 172, 174, 175, 193, 227, 264, 266, 285, 294, 297, 305, 325–6; Asiatic contacts of, 291–2; Aswan memorial stela of, 264; City of the Dead of, 251; crisis under, 268; fortified towns of, south of Second Cataract, 338; Horemheb's work on Karnak pylon of, 262, 270, 272; in southern development generally, 338; initiates the colossal scale in building, 263; marries Tiy from harîm, 304; Memnon colossi of, 168; Palace of, 196, 258 m; peripteral temples of, Elephantine Island, 325; quartzite colossi of, 302; ram-head sphinx of, at Karnak, 262; region of Kari under, 337

Amenophis IV (Akhenaten, q.v.), 44, 137 n; Astarte, Amun and Baal worship under, 174

Amen-Rē', King of the gods, later Amonrasonther, 202, 257, 337; chief temples of Tanis dedicated to, 199; Karnak state temple of, 65, Pl. 18b; see also Amun

Amethyst mining, 314, 322–3

Ammenemes I (XII Dynasty), 172, 200, 223, 257

Ammenemes III, 172; Biahmu quartzite colossi of, 221; Hawara Pyramid of, 168, 219; Shedyet cultivations under, 223

Ammianus Marcellinus, 251 n

Amonrasonther, see Amen-Rē'

Amratian civilization, 23, 35, 36; confined to Thebaid, 28; origin of name, 231; pre-dynastic pottery of, 78

Amsety (dill) as medicinal herb and Canopic Jars divinity, 77–8

Amun, King of the gods, 23, 26, 61, 66, 67, 68, 69, 72, 82, 86 n, 87, 88, 94, 97, 112, 129, 174, 195, 253, 283, 341; Amenappa identifica-tion of, with Tatjenen, in Memphis, 257; Amen-Rē' or Amonrasonther identification of, 257; Akhenaten, as high priest of Rē'-Harakhte, disregards, 294, 295; estates of (economic impor-tance), 201, 211; as Ethiopians' principal deity, 334; 'General' of, 280; high priests of, 271, 279, 282; 'Island' of, 33; Khonsu ousting, 281; 'Oasis' of, and as Lord of the Oases, 128, 132; 'on the Holy Mountain', 344; Puyemrē', tomb of Second Prophet of, 128; as one of triad (Amun of Thebes, Rē'-Harakhte of Heliopolis, Ptah of Memphis), 271; worship of as conception of state, 202

Abydos chapel to, as Theban King of gods, 245; Gebel Barkal temple of, 337, 343; Hibah temple of, 71; Horemheb's work on

355

Index

Karnak temple of, 272; Karnak temple of, 66, 79, 256, 258, 260, 269, 272, 285, 325; Karnak temple of adjoined by Akhenaten's temple to Rē'-Harakhte, 294, 295; Luxor temple of, 66, 260; 'of Luxor', at Theban City of the Dead, 269; Medinet Habu sanctuary of, 275; Philip Arrhidaeus' restoration to room of barque of, 285; room of barque, Karnak, 285; sacred barque of, 204, 269, 275, 285; Ptolemaic restorations, 285–6; Tanis temple of, 199, 200, 204; Thebes statue of, 244; 'House of', Thebes 'City of the Dead', 269; Thebes temple of, 189, 200, 202, 256, 269; see also Turin Papyrus

Amun-Min, festival of, 58

Amunet, associated with Amun at Thebes, 256

Amurru, state of, as Hittite sphere of influence, 276

Anat ('milch-cow of Seth'), temples of, 199, 206

Andjti, 29

Anen, brother of Queen Tiy, 294–5; dual role of, in Akhenaten's Amun to Aten transition, 294–5; see also Aten

Aniba, 318, 325, 333 m

Animals: bones of, in palaeolithic strata, 18; in rock drawings, Eastern desert wadis, 19, 20; domestic, 86–95; for cults, see named animals and deities

Ankhesenpa-aten, Queen, 305, 306; confusion of, with Nefertiti, in Bibkhururia story, 305

Ankh-tawy (Western quarter, Memphis), 160, 265

Annales du Service refs., 19 n, 28 n, 88 n, 121 n, 124 n, 171 n, 174 n, 181 n, 190 n, 210 n, 214 n, 221 n, 222 n, 223 n, 224 n, 228 n, 244 n, 258 n, 259 n, 263 n, 264 n, 265 n, 270 n, 294 n, 306 n, 314 n, 326 n;

see also Derry, Labib Habachi, Aimé-Giron, and incidental refs. in quoted works of others

Antaeopolis, 69, 99 m, 239; see Qau el-Kebir

Antef-Akhtoy struggles (Thebes-Heracleopolis rivalry) (Antefs and Menthuhotpes, princes), 239–40, 256

Anthes: *ÄZ*, 130 n; *Die Felsenschriften von Hatnub*, 290 n; *Hatnub Graffiti*, 103 n

Anthropomorphism, late Naqada period, 39

Antinoopolis, 120 n

Antonines, Deir es-Shelwit Isis temple of age of, 286

Anubieion (Memphis), untraced shrine of Anubis, 161

Anubis, from Cynopolis, 235, 236; cult of, at Thebes, 254; as 'Lord of the Holy Land', 243; Anubis-Imiut shrine, 161

Anukis, gazelle goddess, 310

Apa Jeremias monastery, Saqqara, 159, 176, 182

Aphroditopolis (Atfih), 186 m, 213 m

Aphroditopolis (in Thebaid), 99 m

Apis bull cult, 31, 62, 161, 162, 175, 181, 182; 'running forth of Apis', 150; burials of, 161, 177, 179; 'Apis-Osiris, King of Heaven', 175

Apophis, Hyksos king, 172, 198

Apollonius, finance minister to Ptolemy Philadelphus, 179, 229

Apries, King, 69, 211, 326; Ionian triremes of, 109

Aput, Queen-mother in Coptos, 103

Arabs: as conquerors, 135; as herdsmen, 22; Arab-Nubian linguistic frontier, 308; 'Arabia' as Greek name for Eastern Egypt, 190; see also Shaikiyah

Arcadius, the Emperor, and Apis cult, 182

Archery contests, 173

Architects, XVIII Dynasty, com-

Index

178 n, 181 n, 194 n, 197 n, 198 n, 200 n, 201 n, 205 n, 208 n, 209 n, 224 n, 226 n, 231 n, 248 n, 297 n, 318 n, 336 n

Baal, worship of, 174
Bab el-Mandeb, 21 m; Straits of, 112
Babylon, Egyptian gold sent to, 137
Bacchias agricultural settlement (Kôm el-Asl. q.v.), 213 m, 228
Badari, 23, 99 m; Badarian culture, 23, 24, 36; use of turquoise, steatite in, 126
Badawy, A., *Annales du Service*, 173 n
Badrashein, 149 m, 171
Baedeker, *Ägypten*, 124 n, 220 n
Bahr Bilama, 127
Bahrein, 129 n
Bahr el-Ghazal (Sudan), 18
Bahr el-Libeini, 147
Bahria, Bahriyah (el-Bahriyah) oasis, 21 m, 82, 132 n, 214; as Middle Egypt — Siwa link, 132
Bahr Wardan, 228
Bahr Yusuf, 99 m, 186 m, 212, 213 m, 212, 214, 218, 219, 222, 223, 228; canal, 288
Bajuda plains, 332
Bak (Amarna sculptor), work of in Aten temple, 302
Bakkara tribes, Darfur, 334; cattle of, 22
Balah, Lake, 117, 187 m
Balamun, 186 m
Ballas, 23, 119 m
Balliana, 119 m, 231, 233 m, 333 m
Barbed harpoon nome, 28
Barley: in agriculture, 74–5; beer from, 82
Barramiyah, 119 m, 124, 124 n, 322; gold mines of, 136, 320, 322
Basin-irrigation, *rei* and *sharaki* land under, 53–4
Bastet (cat goddess), 95, 160, 223, 265
Battle scenes, on temple walls, 272, 273, 274

Baumgartel, E., *Cultures of Prehistoric Egypt*, 23 n
Bawardede (official), 111, 313
Beans, légumes generally, 78
Beasts of prey, in royal symbolism, 24–6
Bedja nomads (*see* Medjay), 136, 142, 308
Beduin, as hereditary enemies, 28, 29, 39, 40, 118, 142, 143, 192; *see also* Goran; as mercenaries in Egyptian armies, 143
Bega, *see* Blemmyes
Behbet el-Hagar, town of Isis, 33, 184, 186 m
Behnesa, 99 m; for oasis, *see* Bahria (el Bahriyah)
Bekenkhons, high priest of Amun, 279
Bekhen-stone (schist or greywacke), 121, 124; for use of green schist, *see* Cosmetic palettes
'Belly of Stone' (rocks of Second Cataract), 315
Benben stone as cult-image (Rē' worship), 155–6
Benha (Athribis), 34–5, 183, 186 m
Beni Amran tribes (Arabs), villages built by, 288
Beni Hasan, 77n, 99 m, 123, 125, 126, 130; Khnumhotpe's tomb at, 118; lioness cult at, 125–6
Beni Suef, 99 m, 213 m
Bent Pyramid, Snofru builds, 159
Berbera, 21 m
Berenice (on Foul Bay), 21 m, 115, 119 m, 122, 124; *see also* Sikket Bender
Berg, Bengt: on disappearance of birds, 93; *Mit den Zugvögeln nach Afrika*, 93 n
Berlin: Coptic and Greek gravestones at (Lepsius find), 344; door lintel, 297 n; ebony queen's head, of Tiy, 227; Papyrus, 76 n; tablets (clay) of Amarna, 291
Bes (dwarf-god), 161, 251, 303

358

Index

Bêt Khallaf, 119 m, 238, Pl. 5b

Biahmu, Ammenemes III's Pyramids at, 222; quartzite colossi at, 221, 223; *see* 213 m

Biban el Moluk, royal kings' burials at, 255 m, 271; Tuthmosis I's tomb site at, 254

Bibkhururia, Hittite king, E. Meyer's identification of with Akhenaten, 305; and Tutankhamun, 305

Bigah, Island and fort, Aswan Cataract, 48, 113, 309 m, 310, 316, 328

Binothris, 154

Bir Aras, 119 m

Bir Beiza (Jovis), 124

Bir Fuakhir, 119 m, 120

Bir Kasaba, 21 m, 128

Bir Murr, 21 m, 128

Bir Natrun, 21 m, 128

Bir Qarûn, 55, 223, 226

Bir Seyala, 119 m, 121

Birket Habu, 255 m, 264

Birket land, 69

Birket Qarûn, 219, 221; as possibly Lake Moeris, 221

Bisharin people, 308, 332

Bitter Lakes, 114, 191, 192

Blackman, in *JEA*, 76 n, 251 n

Blemmyes tribe, attacks Lower Nubia, 327; as worshippers of Isis of Philae, 329

Blood-red sacrificial drink, 37

Blue Nile, 21 m

Boak, *Karanis*, 229 n

Bolbitine (Rosetta) Nile mouth, 186 m

Book of the Dead, 33, 57, 79, 91, 97 n 107 n, 215 n, 216

Borchardt, L., initiates large-scale Amarna excavations, 292; on Nilometers, 50, 51; on predynastic unified kingdom, 43-4; *Das Grabdenkmal des Königs Saḥure*, 35 n, 126 n, 178 n; *Mitt. Dt. Orientsges*, 300 n; *Nilmesser*, 50 n; *Porträtkopf der Königin Teje*, 227; *Porträts der Königin Nofretete*, 292 n,

300 n, 302 n; *Das Re-Heiligtum des Ne-woser-Re I*, 156 n; *Zeitschrift Dt. Architekten*, 177 n; *Zeitschrift für Bauwesen*, 298 n

Borollos, Lake, 186 m

Botti and Peet in *Il Giornale della necropoli di Tebe*, 279 n

'Bouquets of Life', 79-80

Breasted: *Ancient Records*, 132 n, 336 n; *History of Egypt*, 114 n

Breccia, mottled, vessels of, 315

Brick tombs, New Kingdom, 250

British Museum: Papyrus, 281 n; stela, 80 n, 164 n, 236 n

Bronze alloys, dating of, 137

'Brown Mediterranean race', Naqada period, 27, 28

Brown, R. H., *The Fayum and Lake Moeris*, 220, 220 n, 221

Brugsch, in Dictionnaire Géographique, 78 n, 195 n; on Lake Moeris, 220; *Reise nach der grossen Oasen El Chargel*, 282 n; *Thesaurus*, 216 n

Brunton, G., *Mostagedda and the Tasian Culture*, 24 n; and Caton-Thompson, *Badarian Civilization*, 24 n, 126 n

Bruyerè, *Fouilles de l'Institut Français*, 275 n

Bubastis (modern Zagazig), 34, 35, 172, 186 m, 189, 190, 285

'Bucolic mouth', 31 n

Buhen, 333 m

Bull, as royal animal, 24, 26; *see* Apis; Bull nomes, *see* 'Dismembered bull'

Bull Kingdom, 30

Bulletin of the Metropolitan Museum of Art, 101 n

Bukoloi risings, 30, 30 n

Burckhardt, *Travels in Nubia*, 20 n

Burraburiash, 137 n

Busiris (Abusir, home of Osiris, *djed* pillar, holy place), 29, 33, 41, 150, 151, 184, 186 m, 188, 235, 236, 237, 238, 241, 251

Buto (Pe), holy place, 32, 33, 91, 94,

Index

Index

Index

Index

Emerald, beryl etc., as inconsiderable, 127

Emerald Mountain (Gebel Zabarah), 124

Emery, W. B., excavations by of Early Dynastic cemetery, Saqqara, 237; *Hor Aha*, 152 n; *The Tomb of Hemaka*, 152 n; with Kirwan, *Royal Tombs of Ballana and Qustul*, 329 n

Emmer crop, 32, 58, 74, 169, 326; wild, 75

Enene (chief architect of Amenophis I and Tuthmosis I), 82, 88, 254, 258; alabaster of shrine of, 270; garden of, described (Thebes, XVIII Dynasty), 80–1

Engelbach: Annales du Service, 306 n; *The Aswan Obelisk*, 324 n; *see also* Somers Clark

Epagomenal days, 49 n

Ergasthenes, 342

Erman, A., 42, 66; *Ägyptische Grammatik*, 42 n; *ÄZ*, 111 n, 178 n, 181 n, 208 n; *Hymnen an das Diadem des Pharaonen (Abh. Berl. Ak.)*, 225 n; *Literatur der Ägypter*, 59, 86 n, 88, 103 n, 130 n, 204 n; *Sb. Berl. Akad.*, 275 n; 'Die Sphinxstele', 174 n; *Zur Erklärung des Papyrus Harris*, 89 n; and Ranke, *Ägypten*, 124 n

ἐρημοφύλακες (Ptolemaic desert police), 130

Eshmunein, *see* Hermopolis

Ethiopian kings, appearance of in Egypt, Eighth Century B.C., 44; effect of, on Thebes art, 181; fish-eating abhorred by, 92–3; of Napata, 338; invade Roman camp at Syene, 25 B.C., 326, 327; and Theban Renaissance generally, 180, 181, 284–5; Pyramids of, west of Gebel Barkal, 335, 342; daughters of, as 'gods' wives', 284, 285

Es-Sheikh Fadl, 281; *see* Hartai

Esna, 38, 119 m

Euphrates, 336

Evers, *Staat aus dem Stein*, 172 n

'Eyes of the King', 283

Fairman, *JEA*, 339 n

Fakhry: *Annales du Service*, 224 n, 228 n; *Bahria Oasis*, 132 n; *The Inscriptions of Wadi el Hudi*, 322 n

Fakus, 29, 117, 183, 186 m, 201

Falcon symbolism, 24, 26; falcon god of west nome, 28; of Philae, as image of soul of Horus, 329

'Famine stela' of Zoser, 50 n, 51 n, 320, 321

Farafra oasis, 21 m, 131, 132

Farming and horticulture, 74–86

Fayum, the (district of the Lakes), 19, 22, 23, 32, 35, 55, 57, 59, 65, 132, 158, 171, 186 m, 200, 204, 213 m, 214, 215, 219, Pls. 5a, 7b, 10a; basins of, two-crop farming in, 52; dependence of, on Heracleopolis, 214; in relation to Heracleopolis, 213 m; fishermen of, 226; irrigation of, 219 seqq.; modern racial type in, 229; northern edge of, investigated archaeologically, 228–9; olive trees of, 81; province divisions of, 224; in Ptolemaic period, 227–8; temples of, plundered, 225; water-birds of, 93

Festivals, agricultural background of, 56; 'of the Valley of Thebes', 269; *see* named gods, Horus, Khnum, Osiris, etc.

'Field of the Hittites', significance of name of, 179

'Field of Reeds', in paradise, 60, 61

'First coming forth', *see* Wepwawet

Firth and Gunn, *Teti Pyramid Cemeteries*, 170 n

Firth and Quibell, *The Step Pyramid*, 39 n

Fish: as ritually abhorrent, 92, 226; as sacred, 92, 226, *and see* Lepidotus, Oxyrhyncus; fish-goddess nome of Mendes, 32, 38;

Index

trampling of, at Edfu Horus festival, 92

Flax crop, 77, 185

'Flight from the land', 73-4

Flint tools, 17, 19, 24, 232

Flowers as festival feature, 82-4

Fortresses, harbours (Delta), 183 seqq.; fortified walls as XXI Dynasty characteristic, 203

Foucart, *Tombeau de Panehesy*, 61 n

Fouilles de Medamoud (1926), 265 n

Foul Bay, 21 m, 122

Fowls, domesticated, 94

Frankfort: *The Cenotaph of Seti I at Abydos*, 247 n; *Mural Paintings of el 'Amarneh*, 299 n; *Studies in the Early Pottery of the Near East*, 139 n; *see also* Peet

Fuakhir (Hammamât), 123; gold of, 322; stones quarried at, 121

Fum el-Khâlig (Nile-Heliopolis canal), 54

Funerary endowments, 63 seqq.

Fustat, 149 m, 180

Gardens: importance of, to Egyptians, 85; of Amarna houses, 299

Gardiner, A. H., 65 n, 75 n, 80 n, 85 n; *Ancient Egyptian Onomastica*, 214 n, 231 n; *ÄZ*, 318 n; in *JEA*, etc., 33 n, 57 n, 69 n, 73 n, 137 n, 191 n; *Ramesside Administrative Documents*, 277 n; *Late Egyptian Stories*, 204 n; *Wilbour Papyrus*, 54 n, 68 n, 76 n, 227 n; and Bell, *JEA*, 218 n; and Gunn, *JEA*, 124 n; and Peet and Černý, *Inscriptions of Sinai*, 117 n

Garstang, *Tombs of the Third Egyptian Dynasty at Reqâqnah and Bêt Khallâf*, 238 n

Gateways, Memphis, artistic importance of, 172

Gauthier, *ÄZ, Institut Français d'Archéologiè Orientale*, 249 n

Gaza, 21 m, 116, 203

Geb (the earth), 56, 61, 83; (the successor to throne of Atum), 151

Gebel Abu Feda, 99, 99 m, 212, 288

Gebel Abu Hammid, 119 m, 136

Gebel Abusir, 222, 227, Pl. 2b

Gebel el-Ahmar (Red Mountain) quarry (yellow quartz), 149 m, 168

Gebel el-Arak, 26, 119 m; carved knife-handle of, 36, 40

Gebel Arkenu, 20, 21 m

Gebel Atika, 187 m

Gebel Barkal, 333 m, 334, 335, 337, 343, Pl. 22a; stela, 108 n, 109 n

Gebel Dukhan (Mountain of Smoke), 22, 99 m; Roman porphyry workers' encampment near 125; as Mons Porphyrites, 122; quarrymen's village at, Pl. 12b

Gebel Fatiri (Mons Claudianus), 99 m; as grey granite source, 121

Gebel Haridi, Pl. 1a

Gebel el-Hudi, near Aswan (gold source), 136 n, 322

Gebel el-Katrani, dolerite quarries of, 223

Gebel Qattar, 122

Gebel Shayib, 22, 99 m

Gebel Silsilah (source of sandstone), 48, 49, 100, 119 m, 263; as former Nile dam, sandstone barrier, 17

Gebel el-Tarif, 100

Gebel Uwenat, 18, 20, 21 m, 22, 334; pastureland of, 128

Gebel Zabarah, 'Smaragdus Mons', source of emeralds, 119 m, 127

Gebelein, 100, 105, 111, 119 m; Libyans in fortress of, 278

Gematen, 333 m, *see* Kawa

German Oriental Society, Amarna work of, 292 seqq.

Gerzah, 213 m, 232; pottery of, 232

Gerzean civilization, 40, 42, 216, 232, 315: 'Second Naqada' background to, 28, 35-7

Gharak, 213 m, 228

Gilf Kebir, 20, 21 m, 22, 128, 129

Girga, 119 m, 231

Giza, 149 m, 152, 158, 186 m, 198, 238, 314, Pl. 15a; Pyramids

Index

goddess, and 'Mistress of the Valley Entrance', 125–6, 329
Hat-mehyt, fish-goddess, 38; *see* Mendes
Hatnub, alabaster from ('House of Gold'), 99 m, 108, 168, 258, 289 m, 290
Hatshepsut, Queen (XVIII Dynasty), 32, 67, 96, 107, 110, 113, 140, 244, 261, 268, 269, 270, 283; Deir el-Bahari (Thebes) temple of, 113, 114, 253, 255, 255 m; jubilee obelisks, at Karnak, and Karnak temple, 48 n, 258, 263, 270, 273, 325; at Thebes, *see* Deir el-Bahari, *above*
Hattusil, Hittite king, 227
Hau-nebet defined, 140
Haunch, nome of the, 185
Hawara (Fayum), 168, 186 m, 198, 204, 213 m, 219, 224, Pl. 5a; Ammenemes III's mortuary temple as 'second Labyrinth', 219; Pyramid, 222; labyrinth and pyramid temples plundered, 225–226; 'mummy' portraits from, 229
Hayes: *Glazed Tiles from a Palace of Ramesses II at Kantir*, 201 n; in *JNES*, 81 n, 196 n
'Head of Upper Egypt' defined, 125
Hebnu (Kôm el-Ahmar, q.v.), 99 m, 120, 192
Heqa-ib, 319
Helck, H. W., *Militärführer*, 193 n, 268 n, 297 n
Heliopolis, 31, 34, 35, 54, 65–6, 79, 94, 118, 149 m, 151, 164 seqq., 173, 180, 186 m, 226, 231, 237, 252, 257, 324; artists' work enriched by sun-worship of, 165; cult of sun-god at, 41; festivals of, enumerated, 155; gifts of Ramesses III to, 178–9; gods 'transplanted' to, from Memphis, 184–5; great Ennead of, 155; as holy place, 236–7; Memphis inclining to sun-worship of, 154; Obelisk House at 328; as predynastic capital, 43;

priests' duties at, 163, 164; religion of, first appearance, 154; ship canals of, 171; Theban dogma under sway of, 257; waning of, before influence of Akhetaten, 166, 294–5; *see* 'House of the Nile', *see* Memphis
Hellenion, at Naucratis, 210
Helwan, 149 m, 152, 186 m; earliest example of monumental limestone blocks for subterranean burial chamber, 165; First dynasty burials, 27
Hemaka, canal-master, 152
Henku, nomarch of 'Cerastes-mountain' nome, 71
Hepdjefi, nomarch of Asyut, 79, 318; on goat sacrifice, 91
Hephaestus (? Ptah), 163
Heracleopolis (and the Fayum), 212 seqq.; town of, 30, 38, 71 n, 89, 90, 103, 105, 131, 200, 206, 213 m, 239; in Antef-Akhtoy wars, 240; cult of Seth in, 214; as Ihnasyah, or Neni-nesu, 186 m, 214; as first Libyan foothold, 132, 204, 212; narrowly fails to secure dominant position, 217, 229; early association of Osiris with Khnum at, 328; Sheshonk as ruler in, 251; struggle of, with Thebes, 290; Heracleopolitan cattle levies, 88; *see* Herishef
Heracles and Khons, 206
Herihor: Commander-in-chief and High Priest of Amun, 202; Amenhotpe's successor, 281, 282, 283; historical importance of, 282; house of Thebes, 204; as viceroy of Kush, 340, 341
Herishef (ram, local deity of Heracleopolis, Greek 'Arsaphes'), 215, *and see* Arsaphes
Hermonthis (*see also* Armant), 19, 65, 119 m, 253, 256
Hermopolis (Eshmunein), 67, 99 m, 103, 105, 130, 184, 186 m, 196, 212, 215, 217, 280, 288, 289 m;

Index

broken Amarna reliefs used by, 306; customs posts at Gebel Abu Feda, 212; exploitation of Hatnub by, 290; Piankhi's capture of, 341

Herodotus quoted, 24, 33, 51 n, 74, 91 n, 92, 113, 147, 172, 174, 179, 184, 207 n, 208 n, 220, 221, 222

Heron, as ruler of birthplace of gods, 32

Hibah, Island of, 71

Hibis oasis, 21 m; as region for anchorites, 131

Hide-tax, 90

Hieraconpolis, 32, 36, 119 m, 148, 237, Pl. 20b; as oldest capital of Upper Egypt (modern Kôm el-Ahmar), 125; fort of, resembling 'Middle Fort' of Abydos, 238; rock tombs of, 26, 100 n; statues of Khasekhemui at, 153; *see also* Horus; falcon

Hierasykaminos, 320, 333 m

Hieroglyphic Texts, 80 n

Hikuptah (later Greek 'Aigyptos'), Memphis as, 157

Hilzheimer, ÄZ, 112 n

Hippopotamus cult and symbolism, 33, 216 n

Hippopotamus ivory carvings, 232

Hittites, 135, 143, 276; empire of, 21 m; famine among, 76; Asian cattle of, 86; invade Northern Syria, 138, 193; lose empire in Asia Minor, 203; El-Till evidence (cuneiform-written tablets) advance of, 291–2; Nefertiti and, 305

Hol, *see* Hurun

Hölscher: *Excavations at Medinet Habu* (*The temples of the Eighteenth Dynasty*), 269 n, 276 n; *Grabdenkmal des Chephren*, 158 n; *Libyer und Ägypter*, 28 n, 39 n

Horakhbit, commander of Sile fortress, 205

Horemheb, military dictator, 73, 90, 103–4, 115, 125, 194, 261 n, 279;

edict of, against garden-produce seizure, 78; against ship requisitioning, 103 n, 194; in Memphis, 306, 339; return of to Thebes, from Memphis, 271; under Tutankhamun, Ay, 176; tomb of, 176; material for pylon of, 270

'Horizon of Aten' sanctuary, Karnak, 270

Horun (Tanis falcon statue) as deity, 199; *see also* Hurun

Horus, 26, 31, 56, 61, 63, 102, 103, 150, 151, 162, 236, 242, 245, 312, 315; 'Horus (King) Aha' name ('The Fighter') on tomb offerings, 152; 'Horus Coming from Akhmin', 236; Birthday of, 216 n; as chief deity of Sile, 195; 'Divine King', 329; of Edfu, 41, 58, 66, 67, 92; falcon of Nekhen (Hieraconpolis), 32; falcon, 235; 'divine harpooner', 33; Horus Kings of Lower Egypt, claims of, 188; 'Horus from Libya', 28; Horus Sanakhte, possibly Nebka, 238; *serekh* stelae names of, 234–5; with Seth and Osiris in Fayum myth, 225 (*see* Seth, for Seth-Horus rivalry); severed hands of, crocodile recovers, 33; 'swine abhorrent to', 37

House burial, 23

'House of the Inundation' in Old Cairo, 48, 50

'House of Life' (Amarna), 307

'House of Millions of Years' (Ramesses III, Medinet Habu), 275–6

'House of the Nile', name for Heliopolis, 171

'House on the Dunes', 197

Hu (Diospolis Parva), 98, 119 m, 127, 128, 312; Petrie's excavations at, 232

Huqab el Askar, 323, 333 m

Human-form pots, late Naqada, 39

Hur, near Hermopolis, 38

Hurbet, 186 m, 201

Index

Index

Index

Index

Kiman Fares, 223

'King of gold', Pl. 25b

'King's House' and 'House of Princes' in Memphite and Heliopolitan myth, 151

'King's Son of Kush' (military governor of Nubia), 125, 337, 339

Kitchener, Lord, in Khartum, 334

Klebs, *Die Reliefs des Alten Reiches*, 77 n, 81 n

κνῆκος-oil, from saffron, 77

Kneph (primeval snake) as early Amun form, 269

Knudtzon, 137 n, 138 n

Kôm el-Ahmar, 99 m, 125, 192; *see* Hebnu

Kôm el-Asl, 213 m, 228

Kôm Aushim, 213 m, 228

Kôm el-Fakhry, recent excavations at, 161–2

Kôm el-Hisn, 186 m

Kôm el-Kala, 160, 177

Kôm el-Sultan, 233 m

Kôm Fares, ancient mounds at destroyed, 229

Kôm Gaif, near en-Neberah, 207

Kôm Ombo, 18, 100, 119 m, 124, 308

Kôm Teman (Memphis, excavated by Petrie), 148, 181

Kordofan, 332

Kornbeutel, *Der Ägyptische Sud- und Osthandel . . .*, 115 n

Korosko, old trade route from, 331

Köster, *ÄZ*, 112 n

Kuban, 322

Kubbet el-Hawa, 309 m, 311, 318, 326

Kufra oasis, 21 m, 128, 129

κυλλῆστις-bread, 74

Kummah fort, Second Cataract, 49, 317, 333 m

Kursi Faraʿun colossi pedestals, Fayum, 222

Kush, viceroys of, region of (*see also* Nubia, viceroy of), 21 m, 86 n, 134, 194, 322, 323, 325, 339, 340,

340 n; convict labour of, 125; gold of, 123; Kushites of Kerma tribal centre, 336; Kushite support for Thebes, 326; Kushite advance into Nubia through Halfa, 316, 332; in army of Kamose against Hyksos, 142, 143; restrictions on travel of, 317; 'vile Kush', origins of, 316

Labib Habachi, *JEA*, 319 n

Labyrinth, 213 m; mortuary temple of Ammenemes III, Hawara, described, 224

'Lady of Sycomore' cult, 177

Lake District, *see* Fayum

Lakeita, 112, 119 m, 120; *see* Phoenikon

Lakiza oasis, 21 m, 128

Lamarres (*or* Poremanres, *or* Pramarres, *or* Pharaoh Marres), *see* Ammenemes III

Land: ownership categories, 61 seqq.; as war veterans' reward, 72; royal possession of, 61–3

'Land of the Cow', 131, 132; *see* Farafra

'Land of the Papyrus', 184

Lanzone, *Les Papyrus du Lac Moeris*, 224 n

Lapis-lazuli, Egypt's imports of, 126

Late-period (Memphite) style, 181

Latonpolis (Esna), 'City of the latus fish', 92, 119 m

Lauer, *La Pyramide à degrés*, 155 n

Lebanon, 21 m; timber of, 108–9

Lefebvre, *Histoire des Grands Prêtres d'Amon*, 292 n; *Tombeau de Petosiris*, 196 n

Legrain, Thebes statuary finds by, 285; in *Annales du Service*, 244 n

Leipoldt, *ÄZ*, 327 n

Lelet en-nukta as Coptic date of Nile rising, 54

Leontopolis (modern Tell el-Yahudiyah), 30, 155, 186 m

Lepidontopolis (later Nagʿ el-Meshayîkh), 92, 119 m, 231

372

Index

Index

166; *Abydos*, 161 n; *Mastabas*, 163 n

Marmarika, the, 185; Ramesside Kings lose foothold in, 133

Marres, *see* Lamarres

Masaharta, high priest of Amun, Karnak, 282

Masara limestone quarries, 149 m, 164–5, 174 n, 336; commemorative inscription of Minmose at, 265

Mastabas, 152, 165, 166, 167, 238

Matariyah, 187 m

Matine (Tine), 99 m, 203

Mayer Papyrus, 281 n

Mecca (Darb el-Hagg), 118

Medamud, 119 m; honorific statue of Minmose at, 265

Medinet el-Fayum (Shedyet of Ancient Egypt, Arsinoë of Greeks; at one time, Crocodilopolis), 186 m, 213 m, 220, 223; Bahr Yusuf's division into canals at, 219

Medinet Gurob (Miwer), 218, 219, 226–7; ebony Queen Tiy head from, 304

Medinet Habu (Thebes), mortuary temple of Ramesses III, 20, 66, 73, 94, 156, 202, 203, 252, 253 n, 255 m, 264, 265, 269, 274, 275, 276, 277, 280, 284, 286; Christian basilicas set up at, 287; Ptolemaic restorations to, 286

Medinet Madi, 213 m, 223, 225

Medinet Qutah, 213 m

Medjay beduin: as allies of Thebes, 44, 326, 335; 'police force', origin of name, 142; people of (Bedju), 130, 275, 308, 312, 313, 314, 317; timber from, 107

Mehyt, lion goddess, 231

Meir (Cusae), 99 m

Mekhu, 312, 316

Meks defined, 61, 62

Memnon: Colossi of, 168, 255 m, 263, 264, 273, Pl. 18a; singing statues of, 286; Memnoneia, area of Armant, 286

Memphis, 21 m, 27, 31, 34, 35, 39, 49, 58, 62, 65, 66, 68, 76, 79, 89, 105, 114, 118, 123, 147 seqq., 149 m, 179, 186 m, 194, 217, 226, 235, 236, 252, 257; Menes as founder of, 147; as true capital of Egypt, 180; dominating, with Heliopolis, Old Kingdom, 147 seqq.; as 'balance of the Two Lands', 150; with Abydos, Heliopolis, makes 'oldest place' claim, 236; becomes political centre of gravity at end of Thinite period, 152; as administrative superior of Heliopolis, 178–9; fate of, 180; difficulties of Abydos-Memphis demarcation, 237, 238; ruins of ancient, Pls. 16a, 16b; Colossi of, 273; date palms of, 80; dualism of office in, 164; as 'granary of Egypt', 151; and the Greek market, 207; monumental stone gateways of, 172; 'Memphitic Theology' of, 151, 152; necropolis lay-out at, 165; Nile dykes at, 51; Nile rise at, 54; Ramesses II's building at, 176–8; ship canals of, 171; Sokar festival at, 56; Tanis removes granite statues, etc., from, 198; 'White Walls' of, cf. Shunet ez-Zebib Walls of Abydos, 238

Men, sculptor, 302

Menat-Khufu, royal domain, 120

Mendesian mouth of Nile, 186 m

Mendes (Tell Roba) nome, ram cult, Ram Temple, 31, 38, 51 n, 69, 98, 186 m, 190, 205, 211, 215, 328; 'First of the Fish', god of, 92

Menes, first King of I Dynasty, 24, 152, 234; as possible unifier of Kingdoms, 237

Menghin, 37 n; *see* Junker, Mustapha Amer; and Bittel, *Mitt. Dt. Inst. Cairo*, 223 n

Menkeperrē‘, Crown Prince, in Karnak rivalries, 282

Menma‘atrē‘, King, 'House of

374

Index

Index

Index

Nebenkeme, captain of bowmen, tomb of, 218

Nebeshah, 187 m

Nebet, *see* Ombos

Nebhepetrēʿ Menthuhotpe, 47, 192; as second unifier, 253; Thebes mortuary temple of, 253

Nebka, of Memphis, last Thinite king, 153, 153 n, 237, 238

Nebrēʿ, a predecessor of Binothris, 154

Nebunenef, high priest of Amun, 279

Nechesia (Mersa Mubarak, 115, 119 m, 124

Necho, King, 162; Nile to Red Sea canal of, 113–14

Nectanebos I, 'Ruler of Foreign Lands', 'Count of Sile', 205, 327; Naucratis stela of, 208

Nectanebos II, 67, 181; as last King, 344 B.C., 205

Nedit, 236

Neferhotpe I, 77 n, 242–3; Tomb of, 242

Neferirkarēʿ, King, V Dynasty, 190 n, 239

Nefer-seshem-Ptah, Saqqara tomb of, Pl. 6

Nefertiti, Queen, German excavators find painted bust of, 292; Djehutmose's head of, 301, 302; daughters of, 304; rivalry of, with Smenkhkarēʿ, 304

Nefertum, Memphis god of ointments, son of Ptah and Sekhmet, 162; as lotus primeval god, 83; at Abydos, 245

Neferukait favourite of King Wahankh, 239

Neferurēʿ, Princess, 253; Senenmut's decline after death of, 256

Negeb, 21 m, 117; Nehsi, chief treasurer of Punt expedition, 255

Neith, arrow goddess and Queen, of Sais, 28, 32, 33, 159, 162, 184; goods tax attributed to temple of, 208

Nekhbet, female vulture as tutelary deity, 25, 125

Nekheb (modern el-Kab, q.v.), 119, 125, 126

Nekheb, 119 m

Nekhen, (Hieraconpolis) 25, 32; 119 m

Nekhthorheb, 133

Nelson, H. H., *Medinet Habu*, 87 n, 91 n, 94 n, 276 n

Nemrut, father of Sheshonk, 227; Abydos chapel statue of, 251

Neni-nesu, 214

Neolithic age, 19 seq.

Neo-Memphite style, 181

Nephthys (god), 162

Nepre (corn-god), 162

Nero, ambassadors of in Napata, 343

Neshor, General (of Apries), 69, 326

Neshmet-barque, 241, 242

Nestorius, Bishop, in oasis exile, 131

Nesunefer, 164 n

Neugebauer, O., in *Acta Orientalia*, 44 n

Newberry, P. E., 30; rediscovers Hatnub, 290; *Beni Hasan*, 118 n, 317 n; *Egypt as a Field for Anthrop. Research*, 30 n; *El Bersheh*, 87 n, 105 n, 291 n; *JEA*, 305 n

Niau Tribes, 130

Nile, *see also* Bahr Bilama; banks, Pls. 3b, 7a, 18a, 21a; basins and dykes, 32–3, 51, 52; Blue and White joining, 47–8; as means of transport, 96 seqq.; seasons and, 47–52; shipbuilding and ports of, 106–15; valley of, 17–44, 21 m; valley settlement, 22–44; various mouths of, 186 m, 187 m; Bolbitine mouth, 207; Bubastite arm, 89, 183, 190, 191, 193, 205; as old Red Sea canal terminus, 113, 114; Canopic arm, 28, 81, 88, 184, 189, 207, 208; Damietta arm, 29, 31, 184, 188, 190; hippopotamuses of, 34; Joseph's arm (*see* Bahr

377

Index

Yusuf), 212; Pelusian arm, 191, 193; Phatnitic arm, 186 m, 31 n; Rosetta arm, 30, 207; Sebennitic arm of, Tanite arm, 187 m, 193, 196; control of, and state unity, 53; conquest of (Libyan) 950 B.C., 132–3; fish of, as sacred, 92; irrigation by flood-waters of, 52–7; flood-waters' desirable height, 50, 51; navigational obstacles in, 98, 100, 101; Red sea ship route to, meagre evidence for, 113; struggle for mastery of, later epochs, 143 seqq. *See also* Cataracts, place names

Nilometers, 48, 49, 50, 51, 54, 171, 309 m, 310

Nilopolis, 171

Ninetjer (Binothris), Thinite tomb at Memphis, 237

Niuserrē ',King, 166, 169 n, 189 n; sun temple of, Abusir, 32, 89, 93, 94, 156, 176, 177

No-Amun, 189, 189 n

Nobadae tribe and princes; Abu-Simbel burials, 330, 340, 342; Diocletian summons to defend Lower Nubia, 327

Nomes and nomarchs, 28 seqq. and *passim*; earliest known division of Lower Egypt into 185, 188; 'heavy', 205

North Tombs, *see* Akhetaten

Nubia, Nubians (and Hamitic civilization, Egypt's general relations with, 135 seqq.; amethyst from, 126; gold from, 123, 316, 322, 323; timber from 107, 108; *see* Frontier Region, 308 seqq.; Nubians in Egyptian employment, 142, 208; as Amarna tomb guards, 295; Christianity among, 329, 343; Saladin conquers, 329; Aswan's Nubians, 308; Assyrians and 326; Jewish garrison against (Persian period), 326–7; becomes chief buffer between Ethiopia and Egypt, 341; Lower Nubia subjugated, 101; Middle Kingdom

conquest of, 49; decline of influence of, at Old Kingdom ending, 316; deification of King's person in, 274; and Osiris, 242, 52n Upper Nubian rock-carved decree, 246; viceroys of, 125, 246, 338, *and see* (also for tombs) Amenophis III. *See* 333 m, *also* 17, 20, 24, 27, 28, 39, 73, 124, 129, 237

Nun, primordial legend of, 48; as Fayum Lake, 224

Nuri, Ethiopian burials and Pyramids at, 333 m, 335, 340, 342

Nut (sky god), 83, 151

Oases, historic rôle of, 20, 23; as places of exile and refuge, 130, 131; *see also* Libyan oases, and oases as named on maps

Obelisk myth, 156

Obelisks, Aswan granite, 263; Heliopolitan, 173; present locations of, 259; *see* named obelisks

Obsidian vessels, gold-rimmed, 138

'Offering dance', 39 n

Ogdoad (8 primeval gods) in Fayum myth, 225, 257

Oil-producing crops, 76–7; oil of lilies, or of lotus, 83–4; olive, of Libya, 81; vessels for, 139

Old Cairo, 48, 50, 150, 171, Pl. 1b

Old Dongola, 332, 333 m

Old Kingdom, 153 seqq.; typical faces of, Pls. 23–4

Old Qoseir (Leucos Limen), 111, 115, 119 m, Pl. 11a

Olive oil, *see* Oil

OLZ, 40 n

Ombos, near Ballas, 119 m, 123, 125

Omphalos, representing primitive hill, 269

Onions and leeks, growing of, 77

Onuris (god), 25–6, 26 n, 231, 245; Onuris-Shu, high priests of, in This, 250

Opet festival, 104, 248, 260, 261, 271; Opet sanctuary, Karnak (of

378

Index

379

Index

Index

381

Index

Ramesses IV, Abydos Osiris tablet of, 250

Ramesses V, 65 n, 227, 280

Ramesses IX, increased tomb plundering under, 277–8

Ramesses X, 279

Ramesses XI, 278, 281; revolt against high priests in time of, 280

Ramessesnakhte, high priest of Amun, 68, 280

Ramose, vizir under Akhenaten and predecessors, 271, 294, 297

Ränke, *ÄZ*, 297 n

Ranufer, chief charioteer, Akhetaten house of, 297

Raphia, Battle of, 217 B.C., 191

Raw materials, 135–43

Rēʿ, king of gods, in various manifestations, 37, 65, 91, 166, 167, 175, 199, 215, 231, 253–4; with cow Methyer in Fayum mythology, 225; as 'Horus of the Horizon', 155, 156, *and see* Rēʿ-Harakhte; Philae falcon as image of, 329; Rēʿ, waters of, Bubastis, 89

Rēʿ-Harakhte (falcon-head) of Heliopolis, 65, 147, 173, 174, 245, 257, 294; Abydos chapel of, 245; Amun and Ptah with, as joint state deities, 271; obelisk to, 173; Sphinx representing, 174; Aten's sun-disc replaces, 294; Karnak sanctuary, 266; Tuthmosis III's shrine and altar to, 260

Real-Encyclopädie (Pauly-Wissowa) 81 n, 128 n, 147 n, 161 n, 196 n, 205 n, 206 n, 214 n, 219 n, 220 n, 224 n, 231 n, 263 n, 286, 308

'Rebirth' concepts, 279, 284 seqq.

'Red Crown of Sais' (or Buto), 32

Redesîyah, 124; temple, 119 m

Red Mountain quartz, 263; *see* Gebel el-Ahmar

Red Sea, 116 seqq., 333 m; beryl from mountains of, 127

Rei and *sharaki*, 53–4

Reisner, Kerma, Nagʿed-Deir, Napata investigations of, 238, 318,

335; *ÄZ*, 83 n, 336 n; *Bulletin of the Museum of Fine Arts, Boston*, 340 n; *Excavations at Kerma* (Harvard African Studies), 318 n; *JEA*, 339 n; finds Tutmosis III's stela at Napata, 336; quoted on Nuri, 342; *A Provincial Cemetery of the Pyramid Age (Naga-ed-Dêr)*, 238 n

Renni (el-Kab), cattle levy report by, 87

Reqaqna, Early Kingdom tombs at, 119 m, 238

Reservoir construction, 129

Reshef, Syrian god, 174

Rhinocorura (el-Arish), 187 m, 194

Ricke, *ÄZ*, 95 n; *Bemerkungen zur ägyptische Baukunst des alter Reiches*, 155 n; *Der Grundirss des Amarna-Wohnhauses*, 296 n, 298 n

'Road of Forty Days' (Darb el-arbaʿin) from August, 128

Road of Sepa, 171

Robichon and Varille, *Le Temple du Scribe royal Amenhotep*, 265 n

Rock tombs, *see* named sites *and* Pl. 21b; rock paintings, 35, 36, Pl. 3a

Roda, Island of, 49, 54, 149 m; 'zero' at, in Nilometric readings, 51

Röder, G., *ÄZ*, 201 n; *Jahrbuch preussisches Kunstsammlungen*, 301 n; on society of Amarna, 301; *Urkunden zur Religion des alten Ägypten*, 320 n

Rome, high priest of Amun, 279

Rome, as inheritor of Ptolemaic heritage, 230

Rosetta, 186 m; *see* Nile

Rowe, A., *Annales du Service*, 322 n

Royal hunts, 33, 34

Royal spells for dead, 166–7

'Royal stewards' defined', 278

Rylands Demotic Papyrus, 80 n, 83 n

Saad, Z. Y., *Royal Excavations at Saqqara and Helwan*, 27 n, 165 n

Index

Index

385

Index

Index

the Curved Pond', 160; Sokaris, old Memphite festival, 91; as Soker of Memphis (at Abydos), 245

Soknopaiou Nesos (Dimai), 213 m

Soleb, 333 m, 338

Somaliland, 112; myrrh from, 112

Somers Clark and Engelbach, *Ancient Egyptian Masonry*, 324 n

Somtutefnakhte, *see* Patiese

Sopdu of Saft el-Hennah (god), 'Lord of the Foreign Lands', 35, 35 n, 40, 199

Sothis, the 'coming forth' of, 49, 50; Sothic calendar, 43, 44, 44 n, 49, 50, 54, 56

'Southern Lake' in reference to Fayum, 224

Speos Artemidos, 99 m

Sphinxes, *see* Karnak; 'likeness' of Chephren, 174; ram-headed, 262; sun-god association, 175; *see* 149 m

Spiegelberg, *ÄZ*, 205 n, 224 n, 226 n; *Hieratische Ostraca*, 201 n, 329 n; *Sb. bayr. Akad.*, 191 n

'Star of Horus' estate wine, 82

Steindorff: *ÄZ*, 132 n; in *Voss. Zeit.*, 135 n; and Wolf, *Thebanische Gräberwelt*, 267 n

Step Pyramid of Zoser, Saqqara, 149 m, 181, 238

Stock, H., on Eastern Delta, 41 n; *Die erste Zwischenzeit Ägyptens* 239 n, 240 n

Stones, coloured and semi-precious, 126, 217, *and see* Sinai, *also* named stones

Strabo quoted or cited, 51, 51 n, 81, 105, 113, 114, 207, 212, 220, 223, 224, 247–8, 329; on Nile flood waters, 51, 54, 55; on Philae, 329; on richness of Fayum, 219; on 'White Walls' of Memphis, 161

Strategos (Graeco-Roman), 53, 206

Suchos: crocodile of, 79, 223–4; Shedyet temple of, 222, 223, 225,

and see 213 m; Lake, 224 Fayum worship of, and book of hymns for, 225

Sudan, 18, 19, 23, 344; Egypt's advances into, 315, 332, 344; Mahdist rule in, 334; Nubian frontier's princely tombs, 329–30; racial movements in, 316; southern cattle breeders of, 29

Suez, as 'racial bridge', 28, 40, 41; canal forerunners, 113–14; and earliest Punt voyages, 110; Canal, 321. *See* 187 m

Sukari gold mine, 124

Sun-boats, 106

Sunu (Syene), 308; *see* Syene

'Sweet-fruit' tree, 80

Sycomore trees (incense), 78, 79, 107, 162

Syene, 119 m, 309 m, 327, 343

Syria, Syrian wars, 21 m, 141, 173, 194, 203, 263, 276, 305, 336; cattle of, 86 n; imports from, 210; under Amenophis III, 337, 338

'Syringes', 286

Syropersikon, Syro-Persian Memphis settlement, 179

Taba (Tana), 184

Tachos (Teos), King, 209

Tadjura, Gulf of, 21 m, 112

Taharqa, Ethiopian king, 335, 340, 341; Nuri pyramid burial of, 342

Tahpanhes (Daphnae, *or* Tell Defennah, q.v.), 326

Takhsi, Takhash, Syrian princes of, 337

Tahta, 99 m

Tangur rapids, 336

Tana, Lake, 21 m, 47

Tanis (Avaris, Piramesse), *see* 187 m, 53 n, 81, 93, 114, 183, 184, 189, 190, 193, 195–206 passim, 280, 282; colossi of, 273; figure of King as Nile-god found at, 226; as Libyan kings' burial place after fall of Thebes, 283; lack of private tombs and regular necropolis at,

Index

200–1; economic life of, 201–2; older monuments absorbed by, 177–8; as 'House of Rē'', 201; Syrian Hurun and, 174; sphinxes of, 200; strategic reasons for establishment of, 196; Late Period decline in, 205; Tell Tanis, 203

Tanitic mouth of Nile, 187 m

Tanutamun, Ethiopian king, 340, 341

Tarkhan mastabas, 152, 213 m

Tasa, Upper Egypt, 24, 27, 99 m; Tasian discoveries, 28

Tatjenen (form taken by Horus), primeval god in Memphis, 150, 257, 269

Ta-wer, 236

Taxation: considerations affecting, 53, 57, 208, 209, 210; on animals, 87–8; on date palms, 80; on ferries, 98; on leather, 89–90; on navigation, 106; on use of 'Ways of Horus', 195

Tebtunis, 213 m, 228; T. Papyri, 104 n

Tefnakhte of Sais, 227

Tefnut (god), 162

Tefyeb, nomarch of Asyut, 240

Tehne, King, 214 n

Tell Abu Sefah, 190

Tell Abu Sêfe, nr. Qantarah, 117

Tell Balamun, 33, 33 n, 50

Tell Defennah, 191, 207

Tell el-Amarna, 288; *see* Amarna

Tell el-Bakliah, 186 m, 190

Tell el-Fara'in, 184, 196

Tell el-Maskutah, 192

Tell el-Yahudiyah, 155, 186 m

Tell Fara'un, 93, 187 m

Tell Gurob, 218

Tell Nebeshah, 196

Tell Roba, 186 m, 190

Tell Tanis, inner city of Tanis, *see* Tanis

Tema el-Amdid, 184, 186 m, 189

Temple property, legal basis of, 65–6; New Kingdom increase in,

189; surroundings, 94 seqq.; servants of, protection for, 246–7; *see* cities

Termuthis, 225; festival of, 58, 59

Terra-cotta heads, Graeco-Roman, from Memphis, 179

Teti, King, 166, 239, 311; high standard of sculptures, reliefs in buildings of, 166; Pyramid of, 161, 166, 167, 170, 176

Tetisheri, Abydos dummy tomb of, 243–4; shrine, 233 m

Teudjoi (modern el-Hibah), 71, 99 m

Thebaid, Thebes, 17, 18, 21 m, 23, 24, 48, 49, 66, 67, 79, 80, 81, 94, 100, 104, 119 m, 131, 134, 142, 168, 171–2, 189 n, 192, 196, 199, 206, 239, 252, 255 m. 339, 340; Ahmose's sanctuary in, 244; Akhtoy defeat by, 217; Akhenaten breaks with tradition of, 294, 295, 297, 303–4; Amenhotpe family's decline in, 202; City of the Dead, 158 seqq.; as city of temples, 252 seqq.; forecourts of temples, 264; 'foreigners' at, 278–81; Memphis more cosmopolitan than, 174; Memphis superseding, 173–176; Merenptah royal tomb decorations, 247, 248; minor popular gods in, 251; Panehsi suppresses rising in, 280–1; pork eating in, 92; Ram Temple of Mendes acquires land from, 211; under Ramesses III, 66, 178; routes eastward from, 124; at opening of Roman period, 286; under Saite kings, 285; Tomb No. 162, 86 n; Upper Thebaid as place of exile, 286. *See* Pls. 18a, 19b

Thinite nome, kings, period, 50, 71, 81, 102, 126, 152, 184; ancient Abydos under, 231; Antef's seizure, 239–40; Apis, 'the running forth of', at, 182; art of, with beduin-slaying theme, 40; de-

388

Index

father), 136, 138, 174, 175, 266, 294, 325; at Karnak, 258; at Napata, 339; upsurge of 'military scribes' under, 268

Tutu, Syrian chamberlain, 297–8

Tylor, *Tomb of Sebeknakht*, 71 n

Tyre, Tyrians, 179, 204; camp of, Memphis, 174

Udimu, King (1 Dynasty), 152

Umm 'Ebeida valley temple, 133. *See* 21 m

Umm el-Ga'ab ('Mother of Pots', Abydos region), 232–3, 243; holy tomb of, 233 m, 241, 242

Umm el-Garajat, 333 m; gold mines (Alaki), 316

Umm Rûs gold mines, 115, 124. *See* 119 m

Unas, King, high level of sculpture and reliefs under, 166; Unas Pyramid, 160, 177, 239; great tombs and mastabas near, 167, 181

'Upland' defined, 53, 54

Upper arrow nome, 28

Upper Egypt, 119 m

Upper Thebaid, as place of exile (Ptolemaic), 131

Urk refs., 30 n, 32 n, 70 n, 71 n, 72 n, 73 n, 80 n, 81 n, 85 n, 87 n, 88 n, 90 n, 91 n, 93 n, 95 n, 98 n, 103 n, 107 n, 110 n, 111 n, 123 n, 129 n, 140 n, 141 n, 155 n, 163 n, 164 n, 169 n, 171 n, 172 n, 173 n, 185 n, 190 n, 191 n, 195 n, 196 n, 205 n, 214 n, 227 n, 239 n, 244 n, 253 n, 254 n, 255 n, 257 n, 258 n, 259 n, 261 n, 269 n, 311 n, 312 n, 313 n, 315 n, 317 n, 325 n, 336 n, 338 n, 341 n; *see also* named authors

Urontari Island (Malikarti), 101, 333 m

Usaphais, King, 33; gravel-floored tomb of, 165; Sethe ascribes 'Grave of Osiris' (Poker) to, 234

Userkaf, King, 163; Pyramid of, with tombs adjoining, 181

Ushabtis (substitute workmen for dead 'blessed'), 60

Usimare'nakhte, 68

Valley of the Kings, 254, 255 m, 274, 281, 306; royal mummies removed from, 278; Valley of the Queens, 255 m. *See* Pls. 20a, 25b

Vandier, J., *La Famine dans l'Egypte Ancienne*, 53 n; *Manuel d'Archéologie Egyptienne*, 24 n; *Syria*, 139 n

Varille (*see also* Robichon), *Annales du Service*, 263 n; *Karnak*, 262 n

Viereck, *Philadelphia*, 229 n

Vine-growing regions, 81

Vogliano, *Primo rapporto degli scavi . . . di Medinet Mädi*, 59 n; *Secondo . . . Mädi*, 223 n

Von Bissing, 248 n; *Archäologische Anzeiger*, 330 n; *Archiv für Orientforschung*, 181 n; *Forsch. und Fortschr.*, 207 n; *Der Fussboden aus der Palast des Königs Amenophis IV zu el Hawata*, 300 n; *Sb. bayr. Akad.*, 264 n; and Kees, *Rē'-Heiligtum*, 62 n, 92 n, 156 n; *Sb. bayr. Akad.*, 203 n

Von der Esch, *Weenak die Karawane ruft*, 129 n, 136 n, 322 n

Vulture as tutelary deity, 25; *see* Nekhbet

Wadfa, 213 m, 228

Wadi Ab(b)ad, 119 m, 124, Pl. 3a

Wadi Abu Shar, 122

Wadi Alaki, 136, 316, 317, 322, 323, 333 m

Wadi Atrash, 99 m, 122

Wadi Beiza, 119 m, 124

Wadi el Hudi, 119 m, 333 m

Wadi el Tih, 149 m

Wadi Gasus, 99 m, 111, 114, 119 m, 121, 122

Wadi Ghazzali, 343

Index

Index

Zenon letters, 178, 210, 228–9

Zizyphus spina Christi (nbs), and other trees, respect for, 78, 80

Zoan (Old Testament), the Field of Tanis, 196

Zoser, King (Pyramid, stela, etc.): his Heliopolitan shrine as oldest of Great Ennead, 155; Court leaves Abydos in reign of, 238; reign of, 35 n, 39 n, 50 n, 84, 102, 154, 163, 167, 170, 182, 185, 238, 320; 'Famine Stela' of, 310; limestone sculptures of, 165; Step Pyramid of, 152, 154-5, 158, 181, *See* Saqqara